Financial Services Marketing
A Reader

Financial Services Marketing:
A Reader

Edited by
Arthur Meidan, Barbara Lewis and Luiz Moutinho

The Dryden Press
Harcourt Brace & Company Limited
London   Fort Worth   New York   Orlando
Philadelphia   San Diego   Toronto   Sydney   Tokyo

The Dryden Press
24/28 Oval Road,
London NW1 7DX

Copyright © 1997 by
Harcourt Brace & Company, Limited for the collection.
Copyright for individual pages—various, see title pages.

All rights reserved

No part of this book may be reproduced in any form by photostat, microfilm or other means, without permission from the publishers.

A catalogue record for this book is available from the British Library
ISBN 0-03-099-019X

Typeset by Mackreth Media Services, Hemel Hempstead, Herts
Printed in Great Britain at WBC, Bridgend, Mid Glamorgan

Contents

Preface ix

PART I: Marketing Environment

Introduction to Part I 3

1 Bank Marketing—Myth or Reality? 6
   M. J. BAKER, *International Journal of Bank Marketing*, (1993), **11** (6), 5–11.

2 The Consumer Rules? An Examination of Rhetoric and 'Reality' of Marketing in Financial Services 16
   D. KNIGHTS, A. STURDY and G. MORGAN, *European Journal of Marketing*, (1994), **28** (3), 42–54.

3 Management of Financial Services Marketing: Issues and Perceptions 28
   C. EASINGWOOD and D. ARNOTT, *International Journal of Bank Marketing* (1991), **9** (6), 3–12.

4 Problems of Integration and Differentiation in the Management of 'Bancassurance' 45
   G. MORGAN, *The Service Industries Journal*, (1994), **14** (2), 153–169.

PART II: Consumer Behaviour

Introduction to Part II 61

5 Consumer Buying Behaviour in Financial Services: An Overview 64
   S. MCKECHNIE, *International Journal of Bank Marketing*, (1992), **10** (5), 4–12.

6 Retail Financial Services Segmentation 78
   R. SPEED and G. SMITH, *The Service Industries Journal*, (1992), **12** (3), 368–383.

7 The Youth Market for Financial Services 91
   B. R. LEWIS and G. H. BINGHAM, *International Journal of Bank Marketing*, (1992), **9** (2), 3–11.

8 Mapping Customer Segments for Personal Financial Services 106
   T. S. HARRISON, *International Journal of Bank Marketing*, (1994), **12** (8), 17–25.

PART III: Product Innovation

Introduction to Part III 121

9 Success Factors for New Consumer Financial Services 124
   C. J. EASINGWOOD and C. STOREY, *International Journal of Bank Marketing*, (1991), **9** (1), 3–10.

10 Bank Customers' Perceptions, Innovations and New Technology   136
   L. MOUTINHO and A. MEIDAN, *International Journal of Bank Marketing*, (1989), **7** (2), 22–27 (1989).
11 Insurance Product Development: Managing the Changes   147
   A. JOHNE, *International Journal of Bank Marketing*, (1993), **11** (3), 5–14.

PART IV: Customer Care and Service Quality

Introduction to Part IV   165

12 Developing an Instrument to Measure Customer Service Quality in Branch Banking   169
   N. K. AVKIRAN, *International Journal of Bank Marketing*, (1994), **12** (6), 10–18.
13 Service Quality: Relationships Between Banks and Their Small Business Clients   183
   A. M. SMITH, *International Journal of Bank Marketing*, (1989), **7** (5), 28–35.
14 Service Quality: Recent Developments in Financial Services   198
   B. R. LEWIS, *International Journal of Bank Marketing*, (1993), **11** (6), 19–25.

PART V: Communication and Pricing in Financial Services

Introduction to Part V   211

15 Promoting Financial Services with Glittering Prizes   213
   S. PEATTIE and K. PEATTIE, *International Journal of Bank Marketing*, (1994), **12** (6), 19–29.
16 Direct Marketing in the Financial Services Industry   229
   D. THWAITES and S. C. I. LEE, *Journal of Marketing Management*, (1994), **10**, 377–390.
17 Mortgage-Pricing Determinants: A Comparative Investigation of National, Regional and Local Building Societies   242
   A. MEIDAN and A. C. CHIN, *International Journal of Bank Marketing*, (1995), **13** (3), 3–11.

PART VI: Branch Management and Distribution

Introduction to Part VI   259

18 Bank Branch Managers: Their Roles and Function in a Marketing Era   262
   S. DENG, L. MOUTINHO and A. MEIDEN, *International Journal of Bank Marketing*, (1991), **9** (3), 32–38.
19 The Changing Lending Role of Managers in the Financial Services Sector   273
   M. HUGHES, *International Journal of Service Industry Management*, (1992), **3** (4), 30–43.
20 Network Management and the Branch Distribution Channel   287
   S. J. GREENLAND, *International Journal of Bank Marketing*, (1995), **13** (4), 12–18.
21 Branch Networks and Insurance Selling   299
   G. MORGAN, *International Journal of Bank Marketing*, (1993), **11** (5), 27–32.

PART VII: Marketing Strategy

Introduction to Part VII   311

22 Competition between Banks and Building Societies in the Retailing of Financial Services   313
   P. J. McGoldrick and S. J. Greenland, *British Journal of Management*, (1992), **3**, 169–179.

23 Customers' Strategy and Performance   327
   R. Speed and G. Smith, *International Journal of Bank Marketing*, (1993), **11** (5), 3–11.

24 Strategic Marketing in Financial Services: Retrospect and Prospect   340
   C. T. Ennew, M. Wright and D. Thwaites, *International Journal of Bank Marketing*, (1993), **11** (6), 12–18.

Index of Cases   351

Preface

We hope that students and instructors of marketing of financial services find this book to be a useful and valuable resource. The book has been designed to meet the needs of an increasing number of undergraduate- and masters-level students studying a course in the marketing of financial services area, as well as researchers conducting studies in this important sector of the economy. This collection of 24 selected articles has a sequential structure which is closely linked with an effective coverage of relevant topics to be included in any course on marketing of financial services. We hope that both the content and the structure of the book will prove to be a very helpful learning and researching tool.

As the title indicates, this book is intended to serve as an overview of the critical aspects of marketing of financial services as well as provide an analysis and discussion of new concepts and trends in the area through a compilation of key academic articles.

This reader has seven major sections:

Section I. Marketing Environment. This section consists of four articles that present what we believe to be the essentials of marketing management in the financial services environment. Our objective in this section is to present material that could be useful in analysing relevant concepts, consumer trends and key management issues. Pertinent research and review literature serve as the bases for the concepts and areas of discussion presented. The highlights of this section include a conceptual analysis of bank marketing, an overview of new emerging consumer roles and patterns pertaining to the marketing of financial services, a discussion of marketing management issues in the sector as well as a more focused analysis of the problems of integration and differentiation in the management of bancassurance.

Section II. Consumer Behaviour. This section presents insights into consumer buying behaviour in financial services. In addition to providing an overview of the topic, some of the selected articles focus on retail financial services segmentation and perceptual mapping issues.

Section III. Product Innovation. This section presents some important racers of product innovation in the development of new consumer financial services. The range of topics covered includes an analysis of key success factors in new financial product development, bank customers' perceptions of innovations and new technology in banking and also management of change in insurance product development.

Section IV. Customer Care and Service Quality. This section contains a focused discussion on customer service quality in the financial services industry. In keeping with the needs of intended readers, the purpose of the section is to help students and researchers develop theoretical and practical skills in the measurement and management of customer service quality. It also offers sources from which important marketing information on the topic can be found. The content of the section covers some critical areas such as the development of a research instrument to measure: customer service quality in branch banking service, quality relationships between banks and their small business customers, and recent service quality developments in financial services.

Section V. Communication and Pricing in Financial Services. This section contains three relevant articles tackling specific facets in the areas of communication and pricing in financial services, which can be used as a resource for the analysis of many types of marketing problems in these two fields. The content of the section includes discussion on the use of sales promotion tools within the context of financial services, explains the key determinant of mortgage-pricing as applied to national, regional, and local building societies, as well as introducing an analysis of the utilization of direct marketing in the financial services industry.

Section VI. Branch Management and Distribution. This section is designed to cover some of the most pressing issues related to branch management and distribution of financial services. The topics discussed include the future roles and key functions of bank branch managers, the changing lending role of managers in the financial services sector, developments in network management and the brand distribution channel, and also insurance selling through branch networks.

Section VII. Marketing Strategy. This section of the book explores some crucial aspects related to the design of marketing strategies for financial services. The discussion of these key issues evolves from the analysis of competitive postures between banks and building societies, to the interactive process between strategy and performance along with an assessment of the strategic bank marketing paradigm.

We acknowledge the authors of all the articles included in this reader and publishers of the selected source journals for giving us permission to publish. We would also like to thank Jennifer Pegg, executive director of Dryden Press for her support and skilled efforts in the editing and production of this readings book.

The currency and usefulness of this reader could not be achieved without the synergetic effect of all these contributions.

Arthur Meidan
Barbara Lewis
Luiz Moutinho

May 1996

Part I

Marketing Environment

CONTENTS

Introduction to Part I   3

1 Bank Marketing—Myth or Reality?   6
   M. J. BAKER, *International Journal of Bank Marketing* (1993), **11** (6), 5–11.
2 The Consumer Rules? An Examination of Rhetoric and 'Reality' of Marketing in Financial Services   16
   D. KNIGHTS, A. STURDY and G. MORGAN, *European Journal of Marketing* (1994), **28** (3), 42–54.
3 Management of Financial Services Marketing: Issues and Perceptions   28
   C. EASINGWOOD and D. ARNOTT, *International Journal of Bank Marketing* (1991), **9** (6), 3–12.
4 Problems of Integration and Differentiation in the Management of 'Bancassurance'   45
   G. MORGAN, *The Service Industries Journal* (1994), **14** (2), 153–169.

Introduction to Part I

Since the end of the 1970s, the financial services sector has been subjected to an unprecedented scale of deregulation. With the opening up of competition in the UK financial services sector, branch networks have become a focus of the development of business strategies for both banks and building societies.

We now think increasingly in terms of qualities rather than quantities. Consumers do not want more of the same, but different and better. Consumers have been scarred by the roller-coaster to boom and recession. Consumers are increasingly aware of the alternatives on offer and rising standards of service and so their expectations of service and quality are elevated and they are increasingly critical of the quality of service they experienced. Consumers have smaller zones of tolerance, the difference between desired and adequate expectations. The 1990s is the decade of microsegmentation and narrow niches and also mass customization. Positioning issues are also in. A much clearer positioning (no overpositioning or confused positioning) is needed. Financial services institutions need to manage the details because it is these that provide the differentiation of the product. They need also to improve the service architecture—i.e. the systems concerned with the creation and delivery of the service. Banks and other financial services providers are increasingly developing service quality initiatives and monitoring their effectiveness. Quality of service and customer care will remain key components of the marketing strategy.

The role and structure of the branch network, in the context of an ever increasingly competitive financial services industry, will be determined by the interaction of four key driving forces. These relate to the impact of: (1) technological innovations; (2) the drive for greater profitability; (3) the threat from non-bank retailers; and (4) the impact of the single European market. Technological developments are driving change in the financial services industry in several respects, particularly with regard to the facilitation of and support for cost-effective product processing, customer service and the management of information. Customers will increasingly take advantage of other forums of service delivery, such as the telephone, self-service automated teller machines, and other methods, including video and multimedia.

Banks and building societies are coming under increased pressure to improve their profitability and cost-effectiveness in order to achieve the freedom necessary to take advantage of the opportunities arising in an increasingly competitive marketplace. This will place greater attention, therefore, on the use of branch networks, particularly with regard to the generation of profits arising from fee-earning products (such as insurance services, personal equity plans, personal pension schemes, share dealing, etc.). The dividing lines between different sectors of the financial services spectrum are becoming increasingly blurred as the major financial institutions move towards the position of bancassurance and Allfinance: it remains to be seen, however, whether or not all of the existing players can survive in such a marketplace and whether or not competitive pressures will force a move back to core operations by some financial organizations.

While the traditional financial institutions compete across their own frontiers, the threat from new entrants into the financial services industry is growing—in particular the threat of entry by major non-bank retailers (e.g. Marks & Spencer). It is likely that there will be further incursions into the marketplace by a number of other major non-bank retailers, each of which will be seeking to provide services in those segments of the market where they have a particular competitive advantage. It is expected that such encroachments by retailers and many other non-banking institutions will bring about further fundamental changes in the competitive environment of the financial services sector in the future. Change within the national financial services arena will also continue to be affected by developments within the EU, stemming from the establishment of the single European market and the progress towards Economic and Monetary Union. The single market for financial services is now in place and competition has increased, encouraging further entry into member states of the wider European Economic Area by non-domestic institutions. Acquisitions, mergers, joint ventures and the extension of branches are adding to an increasingly hostile and unpredictable competitive environment.

The distribution of financial services is an extremely dynamic area that has been completely revolutionized over the past ten years. The principal motivating forces behind this stem from the ever growing need for enhanced efficiencies and the drive for accountability in bank functions: (1) greater industry competition and economic hardship have dictated that marketing activities must be more effective; (2) since deregulation banks have had to compete more directly with building societies and their friendlier image; (3) merger/acquisition activity has produced a confused corporate identity across some networks, as well as 'over banking' in certain areas; (4) many outlets dating from the 1960s/1970s are out of fashion and need renovating to satisfy present day tastes; (5) the dynamism found in many core retail areas, especially within the rash of shopping centre developments in the 1980s and early 1990s, has resulted in many branches now finding themselves in less than optimum locations; (6) financial consumers have become more sophisticated, with discerning needs that must be catered for, and frequently hold accounts with several institutions; (7) the number of financial products and services on offer has grown substantially and outlets providing specialist services have been developed; (8) technological developments and miniaturization have improved efficiencies and reduced the branch space required for duties such as administration. These have enabled processing and enquiry functions to be performed at highly efficient centralized locations. A significant proportion of cash withdrawals are via cost-effective automated teller machines (ATM) networks; (9) the role that the branch can play in achieving numerous marketing objectives has been more fully realized and, accordingly, network management has become a focus of attention. The branch is now recognized as an important contributor to competitive advantage and has resulted in complete restructuring and rationalization of network activities; and finally, (10) highly efficient telephone banking service delivery systems have been developed, refined and implemented by many financial institutions. The major industry players have continued expanding ATM networks and introduced telephone banking services helping facilitate considerable rationalization and restructuring of the branch channel. Outlet and staff numbers have been significantly reduced and the branch function re-orientated to more of a retail and selling role. Despite declining numbers, the branch has become an even more prominent element in financial services marketing mix strategies, and although its role, design and format has been completely transformed, it remains the key distribution channel.

It is widely recognized that the development of a marketing orientation in service industries has lagged behind that of other sectors. In the first article of this section, the author seeks to evaluate the degree of customer orientation and adoption of the marketing concept by establishing what role marketing might have to play in the marketing profession, reviewing what appears or is claimed to have happened in practice and assessing how effective, or otherwise, this has been. As a way of a challenge, the author concludes that currently bank marketing is more myth than reality.

In the second article, the authors examined critically the concept of need deployed in marketing and the claims of an increasingly market-led approach within UK retail financial services. They have pointed out that heightened competition has encouraged increasing managerial attention to consumer needs. But consideration of costs and profitability are also intensified by competition. Cost considerations encourage a ('profitable') product-led approach whereby segmentation techniques are used to select out, where possible, 'non-profitable' products and consumer segments almost irrespective of consumer needs. As the authors have argued, such a view neglects the way in which needs are as much a consequence as a condition of marketing and other supplier activities rather than a property of individuals which is identifiable prior to consumption. In addition, and in financial services especially, it overlooks the possibility that consumers continue to be comparatively indifferent to the product and, to a lesser extent, to the nature of service delivery. It appears that the increased marketing (and other media and consumer pressure group activity) in financial services is, somewhat paradoxically, raising the interest or 'sophistication' of some (e.g. the middle and professional classes) consumers. Such a development is reinforcing the pressure to become more market-led.

The third article in this section describes the perceptions that marketing managers in the financial services sector have of the activities they perform that are most deserving of priority attention. Marketing managers were asked to evaluate a number of areas of marketing activity on the extent to which each area offered scope for improvement, on the sensitivity of organizational performance to improvements in the areas, and on the degree to which it would be possible to improve performance in each area, given prevailing circumstances. Pricing, followed by customer interface and marketing influence, were thought by the marketing managers to be worthy of priority attention. Improvements here would be most likely to result in better company performance.

Finally, the last article in this section examines the development of 'bancassurance' operations in the UK. It considers the competitive and regulatory pressures which have contributed to these developments. It argues that there is a continuum in terms of the integration of banking and insurance. 'Putting bancassurance into operation' is a complex process as insurance selling continues to be seen as a distinctive skill needing to be differentiated from traditional deposit-taking functions. The article reviews three cases that differ markedly in terms of how they seek to balance the conflicting pressures of integration and differentiation.

1

Bank Marketing—Myth or Reality?

Michael J. Baker

Writing in the December 1992 issue of *Long Range Planning*, Kevin J. Bourke opened his article 'Implementing a Marketing Action Programme for AIB Group' with the observation that:

In the past 25 years, banks throughout the world have wrestled with the problem of creating a structure and culture that would be driven by the needs of the external marketplace rather than by the traditional, inward looking norms of a closed profession.

Given such effort one might reasonably assume that bank marketing is an established fact and that the developments in the field have kept pace with those in other areas of marketing. From the somewhat detached perspective of an academic generalist and the closely involved interest of a customer, it does not actually look like that. Indeed, over the past ten years there is much to suggest that banking's perception of marketing is antithetical to many of its basic principles and, that in seeking to apply these misperceptions, they have distanced themselves from their customer base. Sweeping generalizations cannot possibly apply to all banks in all contexts. Nevertheless, there is a sufficient groundswell of dissatisfaction with UK banks to support the view that they are not particularly customer-oriented and so cannot be seen to have adopted and implemented the marketing concept.

In this article we seek to evaluate this suggestion by establishing what role marketing might have to play in the banking profession, reviewing what appears or is claimed to have happened in practice and assessing how effective, or otherwise, this has been. To begin with, it will be helpful to go back to first principles and ascertain how the concept of bank marketing has evolved. From this we shall see how the concept has been applied in practice by reviewing the case study of AIB Group mentioned in the opening paragraph, and compare this bank's experience with the criticisms which have been directed at the UK banking system in recent years. Based on this review, we shall then seek to establish whether the banking profession has adopted the substance of the marketing concept or is merely toying with the trappings of the subject.

THE EVOLUTION OF BANK MARKETING

Fifteen years ago the Institute of Bankers in Scotland invited the author to contribute an article explaining what contribution marketing might have to offer to the banking profession. To address this question it was felt necessary first to examine what appeared to be the key or distinguishing features of marketing and their application to and effect upon business practice. Against this background it would be possible to speculate upon the potential for applying marketing thinking and practice to the banking profession (Baker, 1977).

While it is impossible to pinpoint precisely the emergence of the modern marketing concept, most commentators believe that it began to come to light in the 1950s and received widespread recognition with the publication of Ted Levitt's seminal *Marketing Myopia* in 1960. Elsewhere, however, we have argued that the essence of marketing is 'mutually satisfying exchange relationships' (Baker, 1991). If this is, in fact, the case, then the practice of marketing can be traced back to the first exchange in which two people discovered that by giving one thing and receiving another in its place one could improve one's overall standard of living. The whole of economic history and development has been concentrated on optimizing this principle. In the process task specialization, the division of labour, innovation and industrialization resulted in a physical and psychological separation between producer and consumer. For centuries each improvement in our supply capability resulted in population growth which largely absorbed the productivity gains this represented. In the twentieth century, however, in the advanced industrial economies supply capability has continued to increase exponentially but population growth has slowed and with it the demand for goods and services. To compensate for these changes in the environment we have seen major changes in business orientations—from a production orientation concentrating on volume to meet an unsatisfied demand, to a sales orientation concerned with stimulating demand to absorb excess supply, to a marketing orientation concerned with adding value and emphasizing quality rather than quantity in the production function.

Recognition of the potential for excess supply first became apparent in markets for low cost, frequently purchased consumer goods such as foodstuffs, household cleaning materials and clothing. In the absence of any means of discriminating between the output of different suppliers, it is not surprising that consumers behaved according to the tenets of economic theory and bought from the lowest cost supplier. As a result of this behaviour there was considerable concentration in manufacturing industry throughout the nineteenth century, as the economies of scale available to larger companies enabled them to acquire or put smaller firms out of business. Faced with the prospect of monopoly in many industries the governments of most countries enacted legislation to limit a firm's share of market. With the potential of further economies of scale denied them the cost structure and, therefore, prices of the major suppliers to a market became stabilized. It followed that the only way to improve profitability was to increase margins through higher prices and that, in turn, the only way of doing this was through adding value by a strategy of differentiation.

In the markets for fast-moving consumer goods the shortest route to differentiation was through the development of brands and active promotion of these to both intermediaries and final consumers. In the longer run, however, it became clear that branding, targeting and positioning would all be much more effective if the supplier had some tangible advantage to offer the intended consumer. Thus the new question was 'what is it that customers want and how can we develop new products containing these attributes which will enable them to distinguish them from other competitors' offerings'. In other words, producers needed to reduce the physical and psychological distance which had deprived them of the continuous feedback which characterized early markets in which supplier and user came into direct contact with one another.

In the opinion of marketers then, recognition of the need to establish closer contact with the consumer predicates the adoption of a marketing approach, which may be summarized as consisting of the following basic steps:

(1) Identification of a need which can be satisfied profitably within the constraints and opportunities represented by the potential supplier's portfolio of resources and which is consistent with the organization's declared objectives.
(2) Definition of a particular segment or segments of the total demand which offers the best match with the producer's supply capabilities (the target audience).
(3) Development of a specific product or service tailored to the particular requirements of the target audience.
(4) Preparation of a marketing plan specifying the strategy to be followed in bringing the new offering to the attention of the target audience in a way which will differentiate it from competitive alternatives. The main elements of such a plan will comprise policies for pricing, promotion, selling and distribution.
(5) Execution of the plan.
(6) Monitoring of the results and adjustment as necessary to achieve the predetermined objectives.

It is these steps which constitute the marketing function and translate the concept or philosophy into a practical managerial activity.

THE TRANSFERABILITY OF THE MARKETING CONCEPT

As noted earlier, the adoption and application of a marketing approach first occurred in markets for fast moving consumer goods. In turn, the approach was widely adopted for other consumer goods, so that by the 1950s the practices of market research, product development, branding, advertising and promotion were widely used throughout the consumer goods industries. It was in the 1950s that recognition of the growing imbalance between supply, and the market's ability to absorb this supply, became apparent. In turn, this resulted in recession and the impact of this was felt more keenly in firms manufacturing capital and industrial goods than in those producing consumer goods. In examining what it was that differentiated the practices of consumer goods manufacturers from those serving industrial markets, one distinctive feature which soon emerged was that consumer goods companies practised something called marketing, but this function was largely absent from industrial companies. Clearly, the critical question was 'what is marketing?' and, assuming it can be defined, 'can it be transferred into other spheres of activity?' During the 1960s many industrial firms successfully diagnosed the essence of the marketing concept and modified their practices to reflect it. Unfortunately, large numbers of other firms misconstrued the underlying implications of the marketing concept, mistakenly believing that it was all to do with advertising and promotion and failing to appreciate that it called for a fundamental evaluation of their customers' needs and the best ways of serving them.

Unsurprisingly, those firms which misinterpreted the implications of the marketing concept were vocal in their denouncement of it when they failed to achieve the improvement in results they had looked for. It was this problem which prompted B. Charles Ames to write 'Trappings vs. Substance in Industrial Marketing' (*Harvard Business Review*, 1970) the key arguments of which may be summarized as follows.

In seeking to adopt a marketing orientation many firms made changes which were reflected in the following 'trappings' of marketing:

- Declarations of support from top management—speeches, annual reports.
- Creation of a marketing organization—appointment of a marketing head and product or market managers, transfer to marketing of the product development and service functions, establishment of a market research function, salesmen reassigned around markets, advertising function strengthened.
- Adoption of new administrative mechanisms—formal marketing planning approaches, more and better sales information, reporting system restructured around markets.
- Increased marketing expenditures—staffing, training and development, advertising, research.

But, as Ames observed:

These moves . . . by themselves are no guarantee of marketing success. The kind of change that is needed is a fundamental shift in thinking and attitude throughout the company so that everyone in every function area places paramount importance on being responsive to market needs.

As a result Ames identified three sources of the apparent failure of marketing:

(1) Marketers are failing to understand the fundamental concepts.
(2) There is a lack of commitment to marketing action.
(3) Organizations are failing to implement the *substance*.

Table 1. Ten questions for identifying the substantive nature of marketing

1. Can you describe at least three feasible strategic focuses that have been evaluated and seriously considered for each of your product/market businesses?
2. Can you cite specific steps your marketing department has taken over the past three years that effectively blocked the competitive threat of international as well as domestic competitors?
3. Can you cite changes in the specifications or characteristics of your product/service package that are linked directly to the identification of changing needs in specific customer segments?
4. Is there an effective interchange of ideas among your marketing, operating and financial functions—in both the development of product/market strategy and the execution of it? Is top management actively involved in this process?
5. Do you have an organized channel of communication to ensure that the views of those men working most closely with the customers are taken into account in identifying product needs and opportunities?
6. Do you have a clear picture of the relative profit contribution from sales of individual items to all your customer channels/segments?
7. Have you within the last 12 months, evaluated—and made a conscious decision whether to drop or retain—those products that account for less than 10 per cent of sales and profits?
8. Have you made a comparison of your economics and those of your competitors, as well as a comparative value analysis of all the individual items where you compete head-to-head?
9. Are your marketing organization and your planning and control system designed around end-use market characteristics?
10. Can you honestly say that four out of every five men filling your top marketing positions are serious candidates for future general management jobs?

This led Ames to propose 10 questions for identifying the substantive nature of marketing which are summarized in Table 1.

Ames's article makes it clear that the concept and practice of marketing were and are transferable from one industrial domain to another. He also makes it clear that successful transfer requires a clear understanding of the principles or substance of marketing and that tinkering with the trappings is unlikely to have any beneficial effect.

But what has all this got to do with bank marketing? Put simply—everything. Given the constantly increasing productivity of manufacturing industry, and the growing affluence of the population, the twentieth century has seen a massive switch of employment from secondary or manufacturing industry into tertiary or service industry. Perhaps more important still, we have seen the industrialization of service and the emergence of large organizations seeking to provide standardized services on a large scale, both nationally and internationally. Thus the question has become 'How can you maintain the essence of personal service (the marketing concept) while developing a mass production and distribution system for services?' As with manufacturing industry, the answer must surely be through the adoption and application of the marketing concept. To examine the extent to which this has occurred it will be useful first to take the case of the AIB Group referred to earlier.

APPLYING THE NORMATIVE THEORY

In the article cited earlier, Bourke describes the progress of the AIB Group since 1985, towards the development of a marketing culture. AIB (formerly Allied Irish Banks) was formed by a merger between three banks, all of which shared a culture borne out of their history as clearing banks. 'This culture was focused on the dominant objective of making the clearing system work in a uniform manner throughout the organization.' To achieve this there was a rigid top management style with an emphasis upon inflexible operating procedures and little or no scope for initiative. In modern parlance the organization was production orientated. 'It was a situation in which customers came to the banks seeking services, rather than one in which the bank sought to sell its services to customers.'

As AIB responded to environmental change and opportunity new branches were opened in other countries and new functions, such as merchant banking, were added. However, these were kept separate in subsidiary companies and the core business largely retained its traditional clearing house culture. As is so often the case, it was the appointment of a new chief executive in 1984 which led to the recognition of the need for a root and branch organizational change. The two key elements in Gerald Scanlon's blueprint for change were:

(1) A regrouping of activities around customer needs.
(2) The articulation of a group mission statement emphasizing the delivery of 'high quality service on a competitive basis'.

Bourke comments: 'AIB could not hope to achieve sustainable competitive advantage through pricing or product innovation alone. The reality was that it would provide services that were broadly similar to those provided by competitors. *How* it provided them would, therefore, be the basis of any competitive advantage. This was seen as the key not only to future growth, but also to future profitability, because customers would be prepared to pay a premium for what they perceived as superior service' (my emphasis).

It was realized that to achieve this depended on effective delivery at the customer interface by all the banks' employees. 'Adopting this approach was a recognition that the change needed in AIB was deep and fundamental, rather than cosmetic. For this reason it was important that the change was fully understood and communicated internally before any attempt was made to present it to an external marketplace'.

'It was important that the change was fully understood'.

The first phase for implementing this change extended over five years from 1986 to 1991 and was based on a framework containing six key elements—strategy, information systems, leadership, professionalism, structure, and technology.

In turn, implementation recognized four phases:

(1) creating awareness,
(2) defining the change in management approach,
(3) involving staff in ideas for change,
(4) connecting change to the marketplace.

First, awareness of three things had to be created—the need for change, the direction (i.e. market-focused) in which the organization needed to move, and the need for the involvement and commitment of everyone in the organization. With 9500 employees (1200 managers) in 500 locations in eight countries this was no mean task and was achieved through a combination of videos, print material and face-to-face meetings reinforced by week-long seminars for group executives.

Phases two and three concentrated mainly on the executives and managers responsible for leading the change process but also provided opportunities for individuals to contribute their own ideas.

The fourth phase called for the new awareness and commitment to be translated into action and was addressed through a 'Marketing Effectiveness Programme' in each of the business units. Bourke describes these as comprising five elements:

- Build understanding of marketing principles and how to apply them.
- Improve customer focus by practical action on the ground.
- Focus on the specific changes that are necessary in the way we do business.
- Provide a bottom-up input into strategy development.
- Define what the new customer-focused job role should be.

Internal research into the programme in 1989 showed widespread support for the programme as well as highlighting other aspects in need of more attention. These have now been built into the programme.

A corporate identity programme was launched in 1988 with the theme 'You bring out the best in us'. All divisions were designated first as AIB with an appropriate suffix and the redesigned corporate logo.

Overall, Bourke's paper is in the nature of a progress report as the process is ongoing. He concludes that cultural change is not a one-shot activity but a continuous cycle of commitment to change in an ever-changing environment. In the process the company is becoming a learning organization which is truly adaptive.

'Marketing techniques are transferable into the banking domain'.

The AIB case history summarized above is a classic instance of the application of normative theory to practice. Its key features are the recognition of the need for radical organizational change in order to transform the company from a production to a marketing oriented organization. Allied to this was a recognition that while the organization would seek to pursue competitive advantage through pricing and product innovation, in and of themselves these would not be enough. What was required was to build upon its existing relationships with its customers and to seek to serve them better.

In turn, it was recognized that to achieve this it would be necessary to completely reorientate the internal culture of the bank and the initial phase of the programme was concentrated on communicating to employees what needed to be done, for what reasons and with what intended benefits. Against this background the redesign of the bank's corporate identity and restructuring became highly symbolic and not the cosmetic exercise which is true of so many other similar attempts elsewhere.

Only having achieved this reappraisal of values and corporate culture does management seek to introduce marketing practices through its 'marketing effectiveness programme'. Clearly, this is radically different from the acquisition of trappings as described by Ames, where the imposition of marketing practices upon employees unfamiliar and sceptical about them can be highly counterproductive.

From this case study it is clear that the marketing concept and marketing techniques are transferable into the banking domain. The question remains 'How successful have other banks been in taking up the marketing challenge?'

THE PRACTICE OF BANKING

From the foregoing discussion it is clear that there are at least two dimensions of marketing: (a) a functional dimension concerned with product planning, pricing, distribution and promotion and (b) a philosophical dimension which proposes that the needs, wants and values of consumers should be the common focus of all marketing decisions—the marketing concept. There is much evidence extending over a long period that the banking profession has largely failed in adopting the marketing concept. Writing in 1967, Brien and Stafford claimed that their research showed that 'bank marketing programmes ... are largely mismanaged' and '... there apparently is substantial misunderstanding of the marketing concept as a management philosophy'. They went on to state that 'at the functional level, banks generally are doing insufficient or misdirected marketing research; they are suffering from virtually stagnant product policies; and they are placing too much faith on advertising. At the philosophical level, banks evidently have mistaken friendliness for true customer orientation'. The authors then proceed to examine each of these charges in detail.

Specifically, Brien and Stafford say that in marketing research banks are following a superficial approach and so do not get an accurate insight into consumer motivation/behaviour. For example, customers may claim that they did not take loans from banks because they didn't know they could or they thought the interest rate was too high—responses which would predispose banks to step up factual promotions to cover these points. In reality, sophisticated behavioural research has shown that the strength of banks as places to deposit your money—authority, integrity, and financial expertise—are perceived negatively by some people when it comes to borrowing, i.e. bankers will look down on persons wanting personal loans. If the latter is, in fact, the case then clearly a different advertising strategy is required. Much the same criticisms apply to advertising which is seen as often being mistaken for marketing (as is public relations) and too much dependence placed on it. Despite the emphasis upon advertising by banks much of it is seen as ineffective and unimaginative, largely because banks lack knowledge of customer needs. Obviously the question which these comments raise is 'To what extent does this description fit the situation today?' In many instances it is clear that not a great deal has changed. This appears to be the case from the growing swell of criticism and complaints from both individual customers and small businesses. In *The Sunday Times* Business Focus (31 January 1993) banks were accused of seven deadly sins summarized as:

(1) *Cheeky charges*, i.e. imposing hefty charges and refusing to itemize them.
(2) *Fat fees*.
(3) *Clumsy calculations*, mistakes in calculating interest, etc. always seem to favour the bank.
(4) *Costly clock watching*, i.e. charging fees by the hour like solicitors and accountants.
(5) *Pushy policies*, i.e. pressing customers to buy other services like insurance.
(6) *Piling on the pressure*.
(7) *Asset assault*, e.g. getting spouses to sign over their assets as security.

These criticisms seem positively mild compared with comments contained in a report in the *Sunday Express* for 7 February 1993 by Mark Porter. In his article 'Tragic Price of Small Firms' Massacre', Porter states that 'Brighter figures from the Department of Trade and Industry suggest a slow-down in the rate of bankruptcies. But, without a rapid change in attitudes, a vast number of smaller firms will be wiped off the economic map. Last year's failure record was up 31 per cent on 1991, with 46 per cent coming from the once prosperous South-East':

- 'They are being crucified ruthlessly', claims John McQueen of the Bankruptcy Association. 'While the banks are desperately trying to appeal as sensitive listeners on the one hand, they are slitting throats with the other.'
- Leading accountants, Coopers & Lybrand, have called for a radical change in the insolvency laws.
- Existing rules amount to 'bayoneting the wounded', according to Christopher Hughes, managing partner of the firm's insolvency practice.
- Banks attract bitter criticism over increased charges. In the last three-and-a-half years the big four—NatWest, Barclays, Lloyds and the Midland—have put up charges, commissions and fees by 47 per cent—an increase of £1561m.
- The smaller four, TSB, Abbey National, Royal Bank of Scotland, and the Bank of Scotland, have also pushed their rates up.
- Between 1989 and 1991–92 overall charges by the eight banks rose by over £2.1 billion to £6.283 billion.

The report containing these quotations from reputable sources also includes a number of specific examples of banks taking ruthless action with customers experiencing cashflow problems. No doubt the examples selected are among the more extreme instances.

Whether this is the case or not there can be no doubt that many bank customers regard them as anything but customer-oriented.

'... the bank marketing profession is in decline ...'

It was as a consequence of the wave of public antipathy towards banks that the then Chancellor, Norman Lamont, initiated an inquiry into their lending practices. The findings of this inquiry, published in January 1993, were that, contrary to expectations, banks had not failed to pass on interest rate cuts to their customers and the gap between base rates and loan interest rates had only widened slightly (*Financial Times*, February 1993). While this must have given some comfort to beleaguered bankers, at least two conclusions are inescapable:

(1) Public opinion does not believe the report (the earlier quotations from *The Sunday Times* and *Sunday Express* post-dated publication) probably because other charges have increased significantly.
(2) Banks have been incompetent in understanding their customer needs and behaviour and so failed to appreciate the inherent risks in lending to small businesses.

Both conclusions point to a clear lack of marketing in both principle and practice in the UK banking system—a finding echoed in commentary on the performance of US banks. In the August 1990 issue of *Bank Marketing*, Leonard Berry opened with the statement that 'Today the bank marketing profession is in decline. Good people who have devoted their careers to bank marketing are moving from one beleaguered institution to another—or have left the field altogether'. Why? Because 'as America's banks compete with an ever-increasing array of non-traditional competitors such as AT & T it is imperative to adopt the mind-set of full-fledged service-marketers'. From Berry's analysis and prognosis it is clear that what he perceives as service marketing reflects the adoption of the marketing concept and its application to service industries with the corollary that whatever has passed for 'bank marketing' in the past does not conform essentially with his 'Ten Commandments of Services Marketing'. These may be summarized as:

(1) Focus on quality.
(2) Turn marketing into a line function.
(3) Market to existing customers, i.e. build on existing relationships.
(4) Market for employees, i.e. recruit the right people, 'the employees *are* the service'.
(5) Market to employees, i.e. internal marketing.
(6) Manage the evidence, i.e. present the tangibles in the most effective way.
(7) Tangibilize the service.
(8) Manage the details—it is these that provide the differentiation.
(9) Improve the service architecture—i.e. the systems concerned with the creation and delivery of the service.
(10) Brand the company.

MYTH OR REALITY?

It is often claimed that the appearance of learned journals marks the coming of age of a topic or discipline. As this journal (*International Journal of Bank Marketing*) celebrates its tenth anniversary it is clear that much remains to be done before Bank Marketing ceases to be the oxymoron it currently is. The AIB case history proves it can be done but it calls for the fundamental reappraisal which is based upon an understanding of the substances of marketing and not the cosmetic tinkering which is deceived by its trappings. One can only conclude that currently Bank Marketing is more myth than reality.

REFERENCES

Ames, B. C. (1970), Trappings vs. Substance in Industrial Marketing, *Harvard Business Review*, July–August.
Baker, M. J. (1977), Bank Marketing, *The Scottish Bankers Magazine*, Vol. LXIX, No. 274, August.
Baker, M. J. (1991), *Marketing: An Introductory Text*, 5th edition, Macmillan, Basingstoke.
Berry, L. (1990), Ten Commandments of Services Marketing, *Bank Marketing*, August.
Bourke, K. J. (1992), Implementing a Marketing Action Programme for AIB Group, *Long Range Planning*, December.
Brien, R. H. and Stafford, J. E. (1967), *The Myth of Marketing in Banking*.

2

The Consumer Rules?
An Examination of the Rhetoric and 'Reality' of Marketing in Financial Services

David Knights, Andrew Sturdy and Glenn Morgan

INTRODUCTION

Over recent years the financial services have been subject to considerable disruption in their traditional ways of doing business. The boundaries between banks, building societies and insurance companies have begun to disappear as government policy and economic deregulation has forced them into competition with one another. Political re-regulation, although largely self-administered, has shaken the insurance industry to its roots, resulting in regular revelations of highly respectable companies suffering the humiliation of hefty fines from the regulators for non-compliance with the Financial Services Act (FSA) [1]. Admittedly, the new regulations have not been entirely constraining. In conjunction with other stimulants, they have encouraged banks and building societies to be more strategic in their pursuit of fee income from insurance and investment products, if only to compensate for declining profits in their traditional fields of business activity.

As service organizations, the objective towards which the financial services are directed in accommodating these and various other changes, such as the growth of new information technologies [2-4], is the consumer. More precisely, they have been concerned to improve their service to the customer for purposes of promoting profitable sales. In doing so, they have begun to embrace a market- rather than product-led approach to their business [5-7]. The focus, it is claimed, is on identifying the pattern and content of consumer 'needs' and (re-)designing products and targeting their distribution so as to exploit this knowledge profitably. In short, the marketing concept combined with market segmentation is seen to be the emerging model for business activities in financial services.

The marketing concept is often cited as underpinning progressive marketing practice both in the literature and by practitioners. Recognizing that it has been the focus of some definitional debate [e.g. 8-11] our concern here is with the restricted but common usage of the marketing concept as focused on establishing and satisfying (responding to) consumer 'needs' profitably. As elsewhere in marketing theory, this assumes that consumers have identifiable 'needs' prior to consumption and that they act on them. It implies that such 'needs' should be incorporated into products and services delivery either to the extent that it is profitable to do so or because in competitive markets where 'sovereign' consumers can make informed 'choices', those companies which respond to 'needs' will necessarily be profitable as a result [12].

Within the context of the UK personal financial services market and in relation to relevant literature, we challenge some of the assumptions about consumer 'needs' and highlight the tension with the marketing concept between responding to 'need' and achieving profitability. First, it is argued that consumer 'need' is a category for ordering and making sense of behaviours which are the outcome of producer/consumer relationships (e.g. the sale) rather than a property of individuals, as is conventionally assumed. Accordingly, in the context of many financial services, but particularly life products, individuals are transformed into consumers only at the point of sale when their lives are reconstituted as a problem (need) to be resolved (satisfied) by the product on offer. Research to identify 'needs' prior to consumption is then highly artificial since it is abstracted from the circumstances in which 'needs' are created and sustained. Second, and contrary to the conventional view within financial services of an increasing competitive climate prompting a greater market/customer orientation, we highlight how competitive pressures also limit this tendency by reinforcing managerial concerns with costs and profitability. Here, high cost/low profitability consumer segments and hence their 'needs', are selected out through pricing and targeting. Relatedly, and reinforcing established critiques of the concept of consumer sovereignty [13], there is considerable consumer inertia in relation to many financial services which allows for, and even encourages, a (profitable) product-led approach to the market.

Although primarily theoretical, this article draws selectively on empirical data gathered over a number of years through links with financial services companies in academic research and practical involvement in the industry. The article is organized as follows: first, the literature documenting and often prescribing an increased market orientation in financial services and the conditions of its emergence are briefly reviewed. Our critique of this approach is then presented, first in relation to the concept of need itself and second with regard to the pre-eminence of profit in marketing practice. The article is not seeking to deny the 'sea swell' of change in the direction of marketing in financial services but merely to curtain the excessive claims regarding its success and, more importantly, its potential. We turn now therefore to an examination of the growth of marketing applications in this sector of the economy.

THE MARKETING ORIENTATION IN UK FINANCIAL SERVICES

The UK financial services sector (i.e. banks, building societies, insurance companies and their distributors) is perceived as having been highly undeveloped and reluctant to adopt the marketing concept [14–16]. It has been characterized as supply orientated—principally concerned with operational, risk and financial issues and, in marketing terms, product led. A range of well-established products would be sold, 'hard' in some areas such as life assurance, or left to be 'bought' in others [5, 6, 14, 17]. Relatedly, marketing activities, ideas and departments within companies were limited in their scope and afforded low status in relation to other business 'disciplines' such as accounting and actuarial work [18]. An early exception to this generalization was the retail banks which, according to Clarke *et al.* [16, p. 10], were by 1988 entering the 'final' evolutionary stage of marketing development—the 'marketing control' era—where the marketing concept drives the whole organization.

The new competitive climate, however, is forcing a transition in the direction of accelerating the development of marketing practices throughout the whole sector. Companies are increasingly adopting a strategic marketing orientation where the emphasis is on consumer 'needs'—their identification and the tailoring of products and services for purposes of satisfying them profitably [16, 17, 19–21]. The transition is recent and rapid, indicated by a survey of companies' self-perceptions which recorded 53 per cent as being 'market-orientated' compared with 2 per cent five years earlier [17]. Similarly, another survey found that 48 per cent of the sample companies had established their marketing departments only in the last five years [18]. Market research and segmentation techniques in product development (i.e. tailoring products to specific market segments) have also proliferated in recent years [6, 22]. For example, more companies are using information technology in the application of relatively modern forms of segmentation such as 'lifestyles' in focusing on customer needs [19, 23, 24]. Speed and Smith claim that 'market segmentation has become accepted and followed as a strategy in the financial services industry' [7, p. 376]. More specifically, banks and building societies have been expanding their product range and distribution channels by cross-selling tailored, targeted and, often, branded products and services [6, 24–26]. It is this strategy of 'farming' the customer base that is most closely associated with the increasing emphasis on consumer 'needs' and segmentation.

Despite this groundswell of activity, one needs to be cautious of the extent and quality of the changes that are deemed to be taking place, for they are reminiscent of earlier claims that the industry was subscribing to the marketing concept [15, 27]. Marketing literature, let alone practice, in this field still remains undeveloped particularly in relation to consumer behaviour [28]. Financial services continue to lag behind other sectors in the use of strategic and other marketing techniques, including segmentation [5, 17]. For example, Davison *et al.* [18], show that 72 per cent of their financial services sample had no market research function and 16 per cent, no marketing department in 1989 [29]. Although the paucity of market research may be partly a consequence of the relative ease with which competitors can imitate one another's products in financial services, such findings suggest a considerable variation in the extent of marketing development and practice.

This variation has often been the focus of literature which seeks to measure and categorize marketing developments implicitly as a 'progressive' force. Larger companies are found to be more 'advanced' [14, cf. 11] and it is possible to provide evolutionary accounts of marketing in the sector. In this context, Thwaites and Lynch [6, p. 440; see also 11] constructed three company typologies of approaches to marketing among building societies, suggesting that a developmental pattern existed from 'marketing myopics', through 'departmental promoters' and 'advanced functionalists' towards the ideal of 'guiding philosophers'. As many as 40 per cent of building societies were seen to fit the latter category where marketing informed and stimulated every activity, and not just the marketing function. In providing evidence of the character and variability of marketing practices, such research is valuable. However, the unexplicated evolutionary and prescriptive assumptions underlying the research require critical examination.

Typologies of this kind suggest a trajectory in which there is an inevitable logic of development from one stage to the next as organizations move closer to the ideal prescribed by the researcher. Any constraining or countervailing pressures are often underplayed or bypassed and the concept of marketing itself is presumed to be 'progressive' and unproblematic even though, as we seek to show, there may be some tensions in its application to this sector of industry. Before focusing on these issues, we offer a brief examination of the conditions in which the transition towards a more comprehensive use of the marketing concept is emerging.

The conditions of emergence

There are a number of accounts which outline the key factors associated with the emergence of the current form of heightened competition and of an increased marketing orientation [5, 14, 16, 19]. There is no attempt here to duplicate the detail contained therein; the aim is merely to provide a brief overview. First, a series of (de-/re-) *regulatory changes* reflected in the legislation of the early 1970s and late 1980s have transformed internal sector boundaries, intensified competition, stimulated market demand and generated a greater concern with consumer protection (e.g. selling to 'need'). Associated *ideological changes* towards neo-liberalism have raised the value of 'consumer sovereignty' in society with consequences for organizations and their relationships with 'external' customers. This has helped to raise the legitimacy of marketing as a specialism in relation to other managerial/professional groups [cf. 30]. Other changes in the *socio-economic* profile of the population have stimulated demand in some areas and generated 'new' financial services 'needs'. This includes the continued 'demassification' of society to increasingly diffuse groupings (or market segments) with different lifestyles [31, 32].

Increased personal income in the 1980s combined with market saturation of certain core products saw the development of 'new' products and increased segmentation. Indeed, in the marketing theory of product life-cycles, market saturation is a classic condition for segmentation [33, 34]. More recently, the economic recession and housing 'crisis' have focused managerial attention more acutely towards costs and profitability as well as new markets. At the same time, and partly as a consequence of increased marketing, government regulation and the attention of the media and consumer groups, it is claimed that financial services consumers are becoming more financially literate, sophisticated and discerning (i.e. 'sovereign') in their choice of product, service and company. Finally, innovations in information technology (IT) have facilitated increased and more flexible use of data in service distribution and new product development [4, 35, 36].

In addition to the largely acknowledged factors listed above, two further conditions relating to company practices help to account for the nature and growth of marketing in financial services. First, forms of segmentation are inherent to traditional banking and insurance activities. Actuarial and credit scoring techniques, like those of market segmentation, are derived from early statistical classifications of people and behaviour [37]. They are used to measure, classify and locate risks. The first forms of market segmentation used such information to target 'good' risks for motor and life insurance, for example. This tradition of 'segmentation-selection' has helped to shape contemporary market segmentation with its focus on the costs and profitability of products and segments.

Second, through targeted advertising in particular, the marketing (and production) practices of manufacturing companies since the 1960s have helped to structure the diversified market for personal consumption in ways which provide the basis for the segmentation strategies deployed by financial services companies [32, 38, 39]. Furthermore the development, dissemination and promotion of marketing techniques and approaches, combined with those associated with strategy and accounting knowledges, are conditions as well as consequences of changing marketing practice [37].

While no doubt necessary, the dissemination of new knowledges and techniques cannot be seen as a sufficient condition for their widespread adoption. According to historical accounts of the growth of marketing activity, the most crucial stimulus is intensified competition for industry, in general [33, 40] and financial services, in particular [8]. The key, if not distinctive [see 5, p. xii], characteristic of the recent changing climate of regulation and competition has been the erosion of technical product boundaries in markets which, in many senses, may be seen as oversupplied. These and other competitive factors have not only contributed to the increasing attention given to diverse consumer 'needs', but have also helped to shape the way in which market segmentation strategies are implemented [37].

LIMITATIONS IN RESPONDING TO CONSUMER NEEDS

As has been intimated, there is a general view that current competitive conditions have forced financial service companies to develop or modify their products, customer service and methods of distribution in accordance with a prior assessment of consumer 'needs' or preferences [5, 15, 41]. However, we are sceptical of claims that consumer 'needs' predominate. First, our scepticism revolves around the very concept of 'need' so readily and unproblematically adopted by marketing theorists and practitioners. We believe the concept to be problematic within marketing as a whole but especially with respect to those aspects of financial services (e.g. life insurance, pensions and other long-term savings products) where the consumer is often inert or inactive as a buyer until the actual point of sale. Second and relatedly, we argue that even if the problems surrounding the concept of 'need' were resolvable, suppliers of financial services would be heavily constrained from satisfying consumers' 'needs' by the higher priority of selling profitable products. In short, competition may also act to limit the extent to which perceived needs are addressed.

The concept of 'need'

The concept of 'need' has a long history within the field of industrial psychology where it was originally seen to fill the conceptual gap between stimulus and response in behaviourist theory. The stimulus was seen to elicit a response if the individual had a need that could be satisfied by such a response. It was particularly adopted in motivation theory when the presumed causal relationship between job satisfaction and work productivity/performance failed to be confirmed in several empirical studies [42].

While there is not space here to enter into a long philosophical debate about our epistemological and ontological misgivings with the concept of 'need' [43], it is appropriate to point to its inadmissible essentialist and individualistic nature. Largely because of a preoccupation with 'scientific' respectability, marketing is dominated by a reduction of its field (i.e. human behaviour) to a set of measurable variables, and 'need', like all marketing concepts, falls into this paradigm and is operationalized so as to remove the sense of ambiguity, uncertainty or precariousness in its meaning.

Through this process, 'need' is made really to exist as an essential feature of the individual psyche which is itself seen to have autonomous existence. But, in effect, the belief in its existence serves to influence the exercise of power (e.g. advertising, selling and marketing) by producers in such a way as to reproduce the kinds of behaviour in consumers that sustain the belief. It also reinforces an individualistic perception on the part of consumers that anxieties, frustrations and desires can be satisfactorily managed through buying products that are deemed to fulfil deeply held 'needs'. The irony in all this is that while holding assumptions which disregard the social construction of reality [44], the concept of 'need' is ultimately validated precisely because of such constructions, albeit supplemented by powerful practices on the part of producers and distributors. Marketing then claims to be satisfying a range of consumer 'needs' which it plays a large, although not exclusive, part in creating.

It may be suggested that conventionally we attribute need to individuals as a *post hoc* rationalization to account for and render rational and meaningful some recurrent behaviour we have observed. 'Need', then, is not a property of the customer so much as a category for ordering and making sense of behaviours which are a complex outcome of the producer/distributor/consumer relationship. This is the case in any consumption process but even more so with respect to insurance and associated products in financial services, where individuals are transformed into consumers only at the point of sale when their lives are reconstituted as a problem (need) to be resolved (satisfied) by the product on offer. If 'needs' are socially constructed within effective sales encounters, the process is accomplished by the sales person with particular products in mind (i.e. those available for sale); it is then somewhat exaggerated to argue that financial services now *respond* to consumer 'needs'. They do so only insofar as the 'need' that the salesperson has been active in constructing, can be apparently satisfied from within the product range on offer.

Of course, the original design of products may well have been developed by using various market research techniques to secure a better 'fit' between product and what a sample of the population anticipate people might want. But these techniques can never simulate consumer behaviour since, by definition, they are abstracted from the actual circumstances of consumption. Moreover, if consumers do not often know what they want prior to the construction of a problem or 'need' in the sales encounter, then such market research has a marginal role to play. This takes us to our second reason for being sceptical of the claims regarding the centrality of consumer 'needs' in the distribution of financial services—the concern to sell profitable products to profitable consumers.

The pre-eminence of profit

While we recognize the concept of need to be problematic as illustrated, this in itself would not preclude financial services companies from developing a stronger orientation to the consumer. But, as we have intimated, profit acts as a constraint on, as well as an incentive for, such practices. In one sense, this is an obvious point. Indeed, it is clear from the earliest discussions of a market-led approach that consideration of cost and profitability limit the possible diversity of products and services offered to the consumer [33, p. 401]. This is underplayed if not neglected in the marketing literature at a time when, owing to intensified competition, the tension surrounding the potential conflict between profit and responding to consumer 'needs' has heightened.

Selecting profitable consumers has been a concern of financial services companies in a variety of forms such as the exclusive bank account or the pricing of 'bad' risks out of the market through strict insurance underwriting. With increased competition, and, in banking, the push for cross-selling, market segmentation has simply added another technique which can make this search for the profitable consumer more precise and effective. As one bank insurance director expressed it:

We are actually encouraging—largely as a result of targeting—this search for the 'holy grail', the good customer who never makes a claim—we're giving him(sic) such competitive premiums but what's it doing at the other end of the book . . . we're seeing cases now where the choice is not which insurer, but do I insure? The premium increases are such that it is becoming beyond some people's means.

The more this increases, however, the less plausible becomes the rhetoric of responding to consumer 'needs', since the qualification has to be added that they must be low-risk or high-priced 'needs' [45–49].

The preoccupation with profitability does not merely restrict those to whom financial services companies sell their products but also what they are prepared to sell. In insurance and investment, the demands of the Financial Services Act to give 'best advice' (i.e. selling to 'need') from across the whole range of a company's products resulted in products being withdrawn from the range simply on the basis of their low profitability. Even where such questionable practices are not adopted, sales staff are often in a position to sell those products that attract higher rates of commission and policing 'best advice' has not seriously affected commission-based selling [50, 51].

The selection of 'profitable' products and consumers and the concomitant 'selecting out' of others can, in part, be attributed to managerial short-termism or the continued predominance of 'non-marketing' management groups' priorities within organizations [17] such as those of financial accountants, actuaries, underwriters and sales managers [30]. Moreover, it could be argued that profitability, in the long term at least, is more likely to result from addressing consumers' 'needs' than by neglecting them. This is particularly the case where 'repeat' business or 'cross-selling' depends on consumer satisfaction with a company's service. It is sometimes explicit in the literature when, for example, high company performance is seen to be linked with the practice of relationship marketing [21], albeit with a high net worth (i.e. more 'active' and profitable) customer base. Thus, the apparent neglect in the marketing literature of the cost constraints on a marketing orientation may well stem from the assumption that there is no tension involved. This is because it is assumed that high levels of competition in financial services will 'protect' consumers from the tendencies of companies seeking to determine or ignore their 'needs'. Only those companies which satisfy the consumers' 'needs' will survive, it is argued. But the competition argument is dubious even in areas of consumption such as consumer commodities because of the tendency of retailers not to stock comparable models of the same product [30]. In the long-term business aspects of financial services especially, it has little impact because, on the whole, the consumer is inactive and/or indifferent.

Set against the claims of increasing consumer sophistication, there is some consensus in the literature that the key factors for most consumers remain simply a confidence in the security of the organization and, in particular, convenience of purchase [25, 28, 51, 53–55]. Even in the relatively transparent and price sensitive market of motor insurance, convenience of supply is the primary consideration [56]. Through the provision of a range of packaged and branded products conveniently available in high street branch networks and numerous other channels of distribution, it might be argued that the financial services companies are responding to these consumer 'needs'.

The apparent preference for convenience and confidence is typically understood as a product of consumer ignorance resulting from the complexity and non-comparability of financial services. However, an alternative account is that it reflects not so much consumer preference or ignorance, but, a lack of interest in, or even an indifference towards, financial services—an attitude which is reinforced by the complexity of products in this field. Even in terms of service provision or delivery, there remains considerable 'inertia'— consumers do not tend to 'vote with their feet' [51, 52]. As Watkins notes, with some exceptions, such as consumers switching from bank accounts to interest bearing building society accounts in the 1980s:

There is little hard evidence of substantial shopping around by the majority of buyers in choosing financial services, nor of switching between suppliers on a large scale . . . [53, p. 48]

This is particularly evident in insurance [56]. Indeed consumers' lack of interest in insurance is given as one reason why there is little use of market research (an essential element of the marketing orientation) in this area [18, 41, p. 146]. In life assurance especially, despite years of successive educational campaigns from the industry and increased marketing activity and media attention, the adage that it is not bought but must be sold because of 'ignorance of the product and distaste for the message' (i.e. associations with death) [15] remains relevant. This 'requirement' for a sales push/product-led rather than market-led approach highlights the active role of sales and marketing in helping to construct consumer 'needs' and shape preferences across financial services. This is, once again, typically neglected or underplayed in the marketing literature for it directly contradicts the notion of an active and sovereign consumer [13, 57].

At the very least then, widespread consumer inertia reduces the incentive for companies to design products primarily on the basis of prior 'needs' analysis. Rather, for many companies there are only the mass and the more active or sophisticated high net worth markets and life stages within them. Indeed, it is claimed that the financial services market is, as yet, less differentiated than other sectors [58]. This is also acknowledged by some practitioners. For example, one bank insurance director described the packaging of standard products for convenience and presenting/selling them as if they specifically met the consumers' 'needs' as 'mass marketing to units of one (consumer)' and as an ideal to be sought. Moreover the banks' strategy to 'farm' the captive customer base by life-long cross-selling is informed more by the resulting cost savings (claimed to be as much as three to seven times cheaper than selling to new customers) than responding to diffuse needs.

This is not to argue crudely that companies simply exploit customers. Rather, it is to raise questions about the claims that competitive pressures have led companies to respond to consumer 'needs'. Competition can work on companies in at least two ways: to offer better products and services in order to increase or maintain market share, and to contain costs in order to survive or maximize profitability. In both cases needs may be conveniently bypassed as 'costly' consumers are avoided and consumer inertia provides the opportunity or rationale for adopting a profitable product-led approach. Until such time as consumers do become more sophisticated 'financially self-disciplined subjects' [44], such strategies may well be appropriate in this sector.

CONCLUSIONS

In this article we have sought to examine critically the concept of need deployed in marketing and the claims of an increasingly market-led approach within UK retail financial services. As with earlier marketing developments in the USA and particularly with respect to manufactured goods, heightened competition has encouraged increasing managerial attention to consumer needs. But consideration of costs and profitability are also intensified by competition. While it is acknowledged in the general marketing literature that such concerns place a limit on the scope for responding to needs, it is rarely the focus of academic attention. Cost considerations encourage a ('profitable') product-led approach whereby segmentation techniques are used to *select out*, where possible, 'unprofitable' products and consumer segments almost irrespective of consumer need. Moreover, such practices are made possible and reinforced not only by the dominance of 'accounting' interests within management, but also by the comparative inertia evident among financial services consumers. The marketing concept assumes consumers to be knowledgeable and interested in the products on offer—therefore, if companies respond to consumers' needs, increased market share will necessarily follow. As we have argued, such a view neglects the way in which needs are as much a consequence as a condition of marketing and other supplier activities rather than a property of individuals which is identifiable prior to consumption. In addition and in financial services especially, it overlooks the possibility that consumers continue to be comparatively indifferent to the product and, to a lesser extent to the nature of service delivery.

It appears that the increased marketing (as well as other media and consumer pressure group activity) in financial services is, somewhat paradoxically, raising the interest or 'sophistication' of some (e.g. the middle and professional classes) consumers [cf. 13]. Such a development is reinforcing the pressure to become more market-led. An example of this is the provision by some banks of independent financial advice to high net-worth customers. However, and more generally, to the extent that profit retains a primacy over attention to 'needs' and products are sold as if they have been tailored ('mass marketing to units of one'), there is a danger that increased consumer awareness combined with expectations of a 'personal service' will provoke consumer resistance and/or demands for customized products. Or it is possible that, as the regulators seem to be advocating, a 'professional' or advice-based model rather than a 'sales' approach is more appropriate to the future of financial services. In which case, marketing would have to take a 'back seat' or undergo a dramatic transformation in the direction of assisting the process of financial education rather than advancing the effective and profitable consumption of products.

ACKNOWLEDGEMENT

The authors acknowledge the special editors and anonymous reviewers for their helpful comments on an earlier version of this article. We also thank Helen Dean as secretary of the Financial Services Research Centre (FSRC). The research was supported by the TS-funded FSRC at UMIST.

NOTES AND REFERENCES

1. For example, such respectable companies as Scottish Widows, Guardian Royal Exchange, and Sun Alliance have suffered fines as a result of investigations by the Life Assurance and Unit Trust Regulatory Organization (LAUTRO).
2. Kerfoot, D. and Knights, D., Management, Manipulation and Masculinity, *Journal of Management Studies*, Vol. 31 No. 4, 1993, pp. 659–79.
3. Knights, D. and Willmott, H., 'It's a Very Foreign Discipline: Expenses Control in a Mutual Life Insurance Company', *British Journal of Management*, Vol. 4 No. 4, 1993, pp. 1–18.
4. Sturdy, A. J. (Ed.), *Managing Information Technology in Insurance*, Longman, Harlow, 1989.
5. Ennew, C. T., Watkins, T. and Wright, M. (Eds), *Marketing Financial Services*, Heinemann, Oxford, 1990.
6. Thwaites, D. and Lynch, J. E., 'Adoption of the Marketing Concept by UK Building Societies', *Service Industries Journal*, Vol. 12 No. 4, 1992, pp. 437–62.
7. Speed, R. and Smith, G., Retail Financial Services Segmentation, *Service Industries Journal*, Vol. 12 No. 3, 1992, pp. 368–83.
8. *Journal of the Academy of Marketing Science*, Special 20th Anniversary Issue, Vol. 20 No. 4, Fall 1992.
9. Hunt, S. D., Marketing Is . . . *Journal of the Academy of Marketing Science*, Vol. 20 No. 4, Fall 1992, pp. 301–12.
10. Bennett, P. D., *Dictionary of Marketing Terms*, American Marketing Association, Chicago, IL, 1988.
11. Hooley, G. J., Lynch, J. E. and Shepherd, J., The Marketing Concept—Putting Theory into Practice, *European Journal of Marketing*, Vol. 29 No. 9, 1990, pp. 7–24.
12. Kotler, P., *Marketing Management*, 5th ed., Prentice-Hall, Englewood Cliffs, NJ, 1984.
13. Smith, N. C., 'Consumer Boycotts and Consumer Sovereignty', *European Journal of Marketing*, Vol. 21 No. 5, 1987, pp. 7–19.
14. Morgan, N. and Piercy, N., 'Marketing in Financial Services Organizations: Policy and Practice', in Teare, R., Moutinho, L. and Morgan, N. (Eds.), *Managing and Marketing Services in the 1990s*, Cassel, London, 1990.
15. Newman, K., *Financial Marketing and Communications*, Holt, Rinehart and Winston, Eastbourne, 1984.
16. Clarke, P. D., Edward, P. M., Gardner, E. F., Feeney, P. and Molyneux, P., 'The Genesis of Strategic Marketing Control in British Retail Banking', *International Journal of Bank Marketing*, Vol. 6 No. 2, 1988, pp. 5–19.
17. Hooley, G. J. and Mann, S. J., 'The Adoption of Marketing by Financial Institutions in the UK', *Service Industries Journal*, Vol. 8 No. 4, 1988, pp. 488–500.
18. Davison, H., Watkins, T. and Wright, M., 'Developing New Personal Financial Products— Some Evidence of the Role of Market Research', *International Journal of Bank Marketing*, Vol. 7 No. 1, 1989, pp. 8–15.
19. Joseph, L. and Yorke, D. A., 'Know Your Game Plan: Market Segmentation in the Personal Financial Services Section', *Quarterly Review of Marketing*, Vol. 15 No. 1, 1989, pp. 8–13.
20. Within this framework, Speed and Smith [21] identify three interrelated dimensions of strategic marketing in financial services—an emphasis on customer selection, internal operations or an overall strategic orientation.
21. Speed, R. and Smith, G., 'Customers, Strategy and Performance', *International Journal of Bank Marketing*, Vol. 11 No. 5, 1993, pp. 3–11.
22. Ennew, C. T., 'Marketing Strategy and Planning', in Ennew, C. T., Watkins, T. and Wright, M. (Eds), *Marketing Financial Services*, Heinemann, Oxford, 1990, pp. 60–79.
23. Wells, W. D., 'Psychographics—A Critical Review' *Journal of Marketing Research*, Vol. 12, May

1975, pp. 196–213, reprinted in Ennis, B. M. and Cox, K. K. (Eds), *Marketing Classics*, 6th ed., Allyn & Bacon, London, 1988.
24. Lewis, B. R., 'Bank Marketing', in Ennew, C. T., Watkins, T. and Wright, M., *Marketing Financial Services*, Heinemann, Oxford, 1990, pp. 157–77.
25. McGoldrick, P. J. and Greenland, S. J., 'Competition between Banks and Building Societies in the Retailing of Financial Services', *British Journal of Management*, Vol. 3 No. 1, 1992, pp. 169–79.
26. Sturdy, A. J., 'Banks a Lot (Banks, General Insurance and the Consumer)', *Post Magazine*, 4 December 1992.
27. Watson, I., 'The Adoption of Marketing by the English Clearing Banks', *European Journal of Marketing*, Vol. 16 No. 3, 1982.
28. McKechnie, S., 'Consumer Buying Behaviour in Financial Services—An Overview', *International Journal of Bank Marketing*, Vol. 10 No. 5, 1992, pp. 4–12.
29. The absence of specific marketing departments in this case was not considered as a reflection of a highly advanced 'stage' of development involving the diffusion of marketing throughout the organizations surveyed.
30. Whittington, R. and Whipp, R., 'Professional Ideology and Marketing Implementation', *European Journal of Marketing*, Vol. 26 No. 1, 1992, pp. 52–63.
31. Baudrillard, J., *Selected Writings*, Procter, M., (Ed.), Polity Press, Oxford, 1988.
32. Featherstone, M., *Consumer Culture and Postmodernism*, Sage, London, 1991.
33. Smith, W. R., 'Product Differentiation and Market Segmentation as Alternative Strategies', *Journal of Marketing*, July 1956, pp. 3–8, reprinted in Ennis, B. M. and Cox, K. K. (Eds), *Marketing Classics*, 6th ed., Allyn & Bacon, London, 1988.
34. Zollinger, M., *Marketing Bancaire*, Dunod, Paris, 1985.
35. Dyer, N. and Watkins, T. (Eds), *Marketing Insurance—A Practical Guide*, Kluwer, London, 1988.
36. Knights, D. and Murray, F., *Divided Managers: Organisational Politics and IT Management*, Wiley, Chichester, 1994.
37. Sturdy, A. J., Knights, D. and Morgan, G., 'Marketing the Soul—The Subjectivity of Segmentation and the Segmentation of Subjectivity', paper presented at 11th European Group on Organisation Studies Colloquium, Paris, 1993.
38. Curtis, T., 'The Information Society—A Computer Generated Caste System?', in Mosco, V. and Wasko, J. (Eds), *The Political Economy of Information*, University of Wisconsin Press, Madison, WI, 1988.
39. Goldman, R., *Reading Ads Socially*, Routledge, London, 1992.
40. Engel, J. F., Fiorillo, H. F. and Cayley, M. A. (Eds), *Market Segmentation—Concepts and Applications*, Holt, Rinehart and Winston, New York, NY, 1972.
41. Watkins, T. and Wright, M., *Marketing Financial Services*, Butterworths, London, 1986.
42. Vroom, V. H., *Work and Motivation*, John Wiley & Sons, New York, NY, 1964.
43. Knights, D. and Willmott, H., 'Humanistic Social Science and the Theory of Needs', *Interpersonal Development*, Vol. 12 No. 1, 1974, pp. 213–22.
44. Knights, D., 'Risk, Financial Self-discipline and Commodity Relationships', *Advances in Public Interest Accounting*, Vol. 2, JAI Press, New York, NY, 1988, pp. 47–69.
45. It is somewhat ironic that techniques originally developed in nineteenth-century studies on the plight of the poor such as the family life-cycle [46, 47] and what is now termed 'geo-demographics' [48, 49] are effectively being used to select-out similar groups from financial services.
46. Rowntree, B. S., *Poverty: A Study of Town Life*, Macmillan, London, 1901.
47. Wells, W. D. and Gubar, G., 'The Life Cycle Concept in Marketing Research', *Journal of Marketing Research*, Vol. 4 No. 4, November 1966.
48. Booth, C. (Ed.), *The Life and Labour of the People of London*, Macmillan, London, 1889–1902.
49. Rothman, J., 'Geodemographics (Editorial)', *Journal of Market Research*, Vol. 31 No. 1, 1989, editorial and pp. 139–50.
50. Grey, C. and Knights, D., 'Investor Protection and the 'Cowboy' Stereotype: A Critical View', *Managerial Finance*, Vol. 16 No. 5, 1990, pp. 29–30.
51. Mitchell, J. and Weisner, H., 'Savings and Investments—Consumer Issues', Occasional Paper to OFT, Office of Fair Trading, London, 1992.

52. Knights, D., Morgan, G. and Sturdy, A. J., 'Quality for the Consumer in Bancassurance?', *Consumer Policy Review*, Vol. 3 No. 4, 1993, pp. 232–40.
53. Watkins, T., 'The Demand for Financial Services', in Ennew, C. T., Watkins, T. and Wright, M. (Eds), *Marketing Financial Services*, Heinemann, Oxford, 1990.
54. Carter, R. L., Chiplin, B. and Lewis, M. K., *Personal Financial Markets*, Philip Allan, Oxford, 1986.
55. Ennew, C. T., 'Consumer Attitudes to Independent Financial Advice', *International Journal of Bank Marketing*, Vol. 10 No. 5, 1992, pp. 13–18.
56. Evans, P. and Gumby, J., 'Going for Broke?' *Post Magazine*, 28 May 1992, pp. 9–12.
57. DuGay, P. and Salaman, G., 'The Cult(ure) of the Consumer', *Journal of Management Studies*, Vol. 29 No. 5, 1992, pp. 615–33.
58. Jayasinghe, S. and Yorke, D. A., 'A Technique to Evaluate Secondary Data on Personal Financial Services to Identify Potential Customer Segments', Occasional Paper, Manchester School of Management, UMIST, 1991.

FURTHER READING

Beane, J. P. and Ennis, D. M., 'Market Segmentation: A Review', *European Journal of Marketing*, Vol. 21 No. 5, 1987, pp. 20–42.
Berger, P. and Luckmann, T., *The Social Construction of Reality*, Penguin, Harmondsworth, 1967.
Stanley, T. J., Moschis, G. P. and Danko, W. D., 'Financial Service Segments—The Seven Faces of the Affluent Market', *Journal of Advertising Research*, Vol. 27 No. 4, 1987, pp. 52–67.

3

Management of Financial Services Marketing: Issues and Perceptions

Christopher Easingwood and David Arnott

It has frequently been noted that the services sector of the economy is experiencing rapid change: technological changes, changes in distribution patterns, increased numbers and types of competitors, legislative changes, deregulation, industry boundary shifts, 'free-market' economics, better informed and more demanding customers (Bitner and Zeithaml, 1987). These changes apply just as forcibly to the financial services sector as to the rest of the service sector. In the face of this complexity and the demands of a rapidly changing environment, marketing management in the financial services sector must pay particular attention to prioritising the different areas of their work. Marketing, like other areas, is constrained by the limitations of the resources (capital, labour, time, ideas, influences, etc.) that are available. It must decide where its scarce resources are best deployed. It is the purpose of this article to provide marketers in the financial services sector with some guidance on this decision.

An interesting perspective on this issue can be obtained by examining the emphasis given in this journal. Which areas of marketing are given the most emphasis by *IJBM* authors? An answer to this question was attempted by reviewing *IJBM* articles over a period of slightly more than four years (all issues 1987, 1988, 1989, 1990 and No. 1, 1991). The main topics only were recorded. This was found to be a most useful and revealing process. Some clear themes emerged and these are summarized in Table 1, along with illustrative examples under each main heading.

This does give an indication of the wide range of areas covered as well as of the topics which have most preoccupied *IJBM* authors (i.e. segmentation, techniques). However, the purpose of this article is to identify the marketing areas rated by practitioners as providing the most potential. The perspective on this of *IJBM* authors is interesting and they would be expected to address issues of concern to practitioners. However, the exact mix and weight given in the pages of *IJBM* will be unlikely to correspond exactly with that felt to be most appropriate by marketing managers. The views of practitioners must be sought.

This article therefore has two main purposes. The first is simply to list and describe the main areas of marketing activity in financial services, as seen by senior marketing managers. The second purpose is to prioritise these areas, this is indicate which areas should be given most attention because improvements are expected to yield the highest returns, in terms of improved company performance. Again it is the perspective of senior financial services marketing managers that is sought.

The manner in which these research objectives were implemented is described next in the methodology.

METHODOLOGY

The first stage required that a list of the areas of financial services marketing activity should be developed. It was intended to use the services and financial services marketing literature to do this. However, it soon became clear that this would produce a very lengthy list, too long to be used as a research instrument, nor would it guarantee the inclusion of the areas of particular relevance to current practitioners. This part of the study, the examination of the literature, was used therefore to identify seven general headings of marketing activity: product management, interdepartmental relationships, internal and external communications issues, technology, pricing issues, marketing techniques, and new product development.

The next stage required that senior marketing managers in the financial services sector be asked to elaborate on these seven general areas with the purpose of (1) confirming these overall areas of marketing activity, and (2) identifying particular areas which the managers considered important and which impinged on the company's performance.

Companies, from which managers would be interviewed, were selected on the basis of (1) whether they had a nationwide distribution network or customer base, (2) whether they were in the top 10 of their sector in terms of assets under management, and (3) whether they had an established marketing department under the direction of a marketing director or equivalent chief marketing executive (the targeted interviewee). It was assumed that this level of respondent would be most aware of and sensitive to the marketing issues affecting their company or industry and the effect of such issues on performance.

Interviews with six senior marketing managers from companies across the financial services sector were easily arranged. (Note that the study here is a part of a larger study across the entire services sector, not just financial services. Interviews with five other senior marketing managers (not in financial services) were also carried out and these five extra interviews were used to confirm and interpret the findings of the six financial services interviews). The interviews confirmed the appropriateness of the seven general headings but, most importantly, expanded on these headings to produce a list of 26 areas of marketing activity believed to affect overall company performance.

The second major part of the study required that these areas of marketing activity be prioritized. This would be accomplished via a mailing of a questionnaire to a sample of senior financial services marketing practitioners. But first the questionnaire had to be developed. Here a methodology used by Lupton and Tanner (1987) to assist organizational change was adapted to a marketing context. It is important to realise that some areas of marketing activity may be relatively easy to improve but have limited impact on performance, whereas others may be more difficult to improve but have more significant effect on performance. Therefore each area of marketing activity would be subjectively assessed on four, bipolar five-point scales, adapted from Lupton and Tanner (see

Table 1. Review of *IJBM* main topics.

Buyer behaviour	Factors affecting choice of retail banks and usage of financial services
	Choice of financial institution depending on financial services required
	Criteria used by financial officers to choose banks
	Cross-cultural comparison of attitudes towards and usage of credit cards
	Comparison of the characteristics of loyal versus non-loyal bank patrons
	Use of and attitude towards electronic banking services
Competition	Competition between financial service organisations and retailers or between banks and non-bank financial institutions
	Competition between regional financial centres
Country analysis	Assessment of the Singapore banking market
	Different approaches by foreign banks to the establishment of a multistate presence in the US
Image	Comparison of customer perceptions of banks versus building societies
	Attitude towards banks as a basis for differentiated product positioning
Legislation	Effect of the deregulation of financial markets on marketing strategies
	Implications of the Single Market in 1992
	Effect of the Financial Services Act (UK, 1986) on financial institution concentration
New product development	Use of marketing research to develop new products
	Formalising the new product development process
	Use of non-financial as well as financial criteria to evaluate new products
	Factors affecting the adoption of financial innovations
Organization	Forms of marketing organisation and their links to strategic direction
	The division of work between front-line and backroom staff
	Use of an information-tracking system to improve organisational co-ordination
	Adoption of a marketing orientation through a top-down–bottom-up planning process
Product management	Product management to support relationship building
	Product differentiation to appeal to distinct market segments
	The characteristics of successful new consumer financial products
	The impact of developments in information technology upon the range of products offered
Salesforce management	The key elements in the sales management job
	Use of the salesforce to implement strategy
	Management of relationships with corporate accounts
Segmentation	Segmentation on the basis of actual behaviour
	The need to develop subsegments
	Differentiated marketing activities to meet the needs of different commercial segments
	Use of different media to reach different segments
	Segmentation of the UK personal saving/investment market by saver motivations
	ATM cardholders and non-holders contrasted
Service quality	Competitive edge through service delivery
	Desired improvements in the delivery of banking services
	Determinants of service quality
	Development, implementation and evaluation of customer care programmes

Table 1. Continued.

Service quality (Cont.)	Factors affecting the degree of customer-orientation of a financial institution
	The relationship between internal and consumer satisfaction
Techniques	Frameworks to evaluate loan portfolios
	Sources of bias in product concept testing of financial services
	Speed of adoption of techniques in wholesale vs. retail banking
	Techniques to aid product design
	Use of decision support systems to profile assets
	Use of techniques to aid the development of competitive market strategies
Technology (impact of)	Impact of new technology on bank customers
	Comparison of home banking services
	Evolution of business/marketing strategies in close association with IT developments
	Diffusion theory explanation of the spread of home banking
	Factors discriminating between users and non-users of automated teller machines
	The need to assess market needs as well as technical feasibility
	Use of expert systems

Figure 1). These scales measure each area's current as well as potential impact on performance as well as the potential for achieving improvement in the particular marketing area. The scales are:

- *First scale* called 'current effect on performance' directly measures the effect that each marketing area is currently having on performance. It is a measure of the status quo.
- *Second scale* ('scope for improvement') measures the extent to which it is considered that an area could be improved, regardless of the impact this may have and also regardless of whether or not the capability exists to make the improvement. It is a measure of the extent to which performance in an area falls below the maximum possible.
- *Third scale* ('sensitivity to change') is an estimate of the sensitivity of organisational performance to improvement in each area of activity. It is an 'elasticity' measure.
- *Final scale* ('ease of change') is a measure of the ease with which change can be effected within a marketing area, but this time taking into account any possible constraints imposed by existing practices, organisational culture, organisational competences, etc.

The questionnaires were mailed to the senior marketing executive (named in most cases) of 49 financial services companies, asking the managers to rate the 26 areas of marketing activity on the four scales. The companies were UK-based, with a national presence but in the top 20 of their sector. Sectors sampled included retail and merchant banks (13), insurers (15), building societies (13), and other financial institutions, such as finance houses and leasing companies (9). A single mailing was used with no follow-up.

A total of 21 usable replies was obtained, a 43 per cent response rate which was considered acceptable, given the difficulty of the task requested and the size of the respondent's corporations. It can be said that the study represents a good cross-section of some of the UK's leading and most marketing-knowledgeable financial services organisations. (Some of the marketing managers, who did not complete the questionnaire, indicated that this was because their organisations were not yet sufficiently experienced in their use of marketing to provide accurate answers to the questions.)

Scale 1: Current effect on performance
The extent to which each area of activity impacts on
the company's overall financial performance.

```
Low                                     High
1        2        3        4        5
+--------+--------+--------+--------+
```

Scale 2: Scope for improvement
The extent to which the management of each area of
activity was considered to have room for improvement.

```
None                                    Much
1        2        3        4        5
+--------+--------+--------+--------+
```

Scale 3: Sensitivity to change
The extent to which overall performance would be affected by an
improvement on the dimension. A subjective measure of whether a small
improvement on the dimension would result in a large improvement
in performance or vice versa.

```
Low                                     High
1        2        3        4        5
+--------+--------+--------+--------+
```

Scale 4: Ease of change
The ease with which a desirable improvement in the management of each
area could be effected, given the company's present culture.

```
Very hard                           Very easy
1        2        3        4        5
+--------+--------+--------+--------+
```

Figure 1. Response scale definition.

AREAS OF MARKETING ACTIVITY

The interviews with the marketing managers produced 26 areas of marketing activity affecting company performance in the financial services sector (see Table 2).

A number of issues were raised concerning product management, particularly the completeness of the product line and the extension, proliferation and deletion of products (variables 18, 4, 5 and 6). Unlike goods, addition or deletion of financial services cannot be based on straightforward indicators of performance such as sales per unit area. Furthermore, the long-term relationship or contractual nature of many financial products may prohibit deletion. Non-profitable products may have to be supported because of this. For instance, once introduced, a typical life insurance product has to be supported until it matures, even if few such policies were sold (probably making it unprofitable to support). Conditions can vary over the lifetimes of such products, which may be tens of years. A

Table 2. Description of areas of marketing activity.

Marketing area	Abbreviation
1. Determining 'best' price	Pricing
2. Advertising and promotion strategy	Promotions
3. Advertising split between intermediaries and end users	Ad split
4. Managing product improvements and extensions	Prod. extension
5. Managing product proliferation	Prod. proliferation
6. Managing product deletion	Prod. deletion
7. Involvement with the development of corporate strategy	Corp. strategy
8. Managing the salesforce	Salesforce
9. Utilising technological developments	Technology
10. Cooperating with other departments	Co-operation
11. Marketing's working relationship with personnel management	Rel. personnel
12. Marketing's working relationship with financial management	Rel. finance
13. Marketing's working relationship with operations management	Rel. operations
14. Marketing's working relationship with computing management	Rel. DP
15. Training of customer contact staff	Staff training
16. Managing customer contact staff generally	Staff management
17. Developing new products	NPD
18. Maintaining a complete product line	Prod. line
19. Introducing products ahead of the competition	Launch 1st
20. Designing 'unique' products	Unique products
21. Using marketing research	Mktg research
22. Using concept testing	Concept testing
23. Segmenting the market	Segmentation
24. Economic modelling	Econ. modelling
25. Branding of products	Branding
26. Positioning products	Positioning

policy taken out in the relatively inflation-free 1930s, paid up in the 1940s, and payable on death (perhaps in the 1990s) may be worth less to the insurance company than the cost of administration. Legislation forces changes and proliferation. The cancellation of tax relief on life assurance meant that consumers who increased their cover were paying different rates for essentially the same product. The additional record keeping required increased administration and mailing costs. The proliferation of intangible, difficult to compare products, sometimes crossing sector boundaries, introduces elements of confusion in the minds of both customers and staff (Easingwood, 1986; de Brentani, 1989), as well as adding to the problems of maintaining large databases. Proliferation also increases the product knowledge requirements at the branch, agency and broker levels as well as increasing the need for ongoing training.

Another set of issues involves the relationship of marketing with the rest of the organisation (variables 7 and 10–16). Interaction between the marketing department and operations, finance, data processing and personnel departments, as well as inter-departmental cooperation in general, were all raised as issues affecting overall performance. In those organisations, with a relatively new marketing department, the dominant culture tended not to be marketing, and marketing was sometimes not able to contribute so widely as it wished, i.e. to the training and management of contact staff, to input to corporate strategy and planning. Marketing managers saw the contact staff role as critical. The width and depth of the typical product line placed considerable demands on the contact staff's knowledge which is required to complement marketing, advertising and product initiatives.

Issues of communication were also raised (variables 2 and 3). Many financial services organisations incorporate large networks of intermediaries in their distribution channels. Hence they have two target groups for their communication efforts and with it the need for separate but consistent communication strategies. This separation also leads to complex budget allocation decisions across target audiences and media type.

The rapid pace of technological change created concerns over how best to achieve the maximum benefit from technology or how it could be used to gain competitive advantages (variable 9). As one insurer explained: a customer base of 2.5 million and the processing of 200 000 policies, 800 000 claims, and 2.4 million letters and memos per year means that effective information technology is a necessity just for survival. The boon of technology can also be a bane. The development of new products frequently requires considerable programming input from the data-processing department and so new product designs or changes to existing products cannot always be effected as rapidly as marketing would like. This can affect the chances of being first to market. It also necessitates good working relationships between the marketing and Data Processing (DP) department with the former not expecting the impossible from the latter.

Determination of the 'best' price (variable 1) for a financial service was the main issue raised under the general heading of pricing policy. A particular problem presented was the low awareness that consumers of financial services generally have of the pricing structure and the price paid for a particular service. This situation is likely to be aggravated by current trends in financial services pricing, i.e. customers apparently being paid to use a financial service such as an interest-bearing account; tied agents not having to reveal commission structures compared with independents who do, under the requirements of the Financial Services Act. Such actions alter the consumers' perceptions and expectations of the value of and cost of financial services. Another pricing difficulty is the allocation of both fixed and variable costs between multiple products, perhaps sharing development programmes/channels/outlets.

Knowledge/implementation of the various marketing techniques available varied considerably. Issues discussed were those of positioning (product and corporate), branding, concept testing, marketing research, segmentation, and econometric modelling (variables 21–26). Companies with large internal marketing research departments, not surprisingly, were the most frequent users of marketing techniques. Others appeared to rely on external consultants, whilst the use of marketing techniques for some companies was occasional and erratic. All the managers indicated that they expected to use such techniques more in the future.

Another topic was that of new product development, including the process of new product development, the difficulties of creating unique or hard-to-copy services and being first with a new product (variables 17, 19 and 20). There was a consensus that new meant new to the company as opposed to new to the customer. Examples are banks and insurers moving into estate agencies and building societies becoming tied agents for insurers. The only examples mentioned of 'new to the world' products were the invention of unit trusts (which created opportunities for a range of unit-linked 'new' products) and the introduction of ATMs. There was general agreement that creation of new and/or hard-to-copy financial services is very difficult. This explains the importance given to 'being first to market', although some companies espoused a policy of being a 'fast second'.

A fairly frequent concern was that the marketing department funding was too low.

Finally, a separate but important area of marketing activity is the management of the salesforce.

MARKETING ACTIVITY FACTORS

The literature and interviews produced a list of 26 marketing area activities. Interpretation of a large database such as this, comprising many variables, is often assisted by use of factor analysis. Factor analysis identifies groups of variables that are intercorrelated and places them into 'factors'. Unfortunately, it was not possible to perform factor analysis on so many variables (26) with just 21 completed questionnaires. However, this study was part of a larger investigation looking at other services besides that of financial services and as part of that study identical information was collected from an additional 15 major UK services companies. Factor analysis was possible for the combined sample (size 36) and the results are presented in Table 3. The groupings of the variables into the factors is thus obtained using the larger sample (albeit with 58 per cent financial services), but all results reported in the article represent the scores from the financial services companies only.

The six major areas of marketing activity affecting corporate financial performance are thus:

- *NPD strategy:* This factor has a strong new product development focus including the development of new products, launching them first, positioning them, maintaining a complete product line and offering unique products.
- *Customer interface:* Includes not just the obvious company/customer interface variables (management and training of contact staff and relations with operations) but also some of marketing's tools for reaching the customer (branding; advertising) and understanding the customer (marketing research). This factor is thus a broad indicator of the company/customer interface dimension.
- *Marketing department influence:* Represents marketing's high level influence, i.e. input to corporate strategy, general cooperation with other departments.
- *Width of product line:* This includes the management of the product range (proliferation and deletion), plus the management of the salesforce, as it is the salesforce that has to understand the product range and explain it to customers (difficult if the product range is too wide or changes frequently).
- *Depth of product line:* The effectiveness of product line extensions depends on relationships with data processing and on good communications with appropriate markets.
- *Pricing policy:* Pricing by segment is seen as the main issue in the pricing area.

The average scores for each factor on 'current effect on organizational performance', 'scope for improvement', 'sensitivity to change' and 'ease of change' are presented in Figure 2. It can be seen (Figure 2a) that the two factors currently considered to have the most impact on company performance are customer interface and marketing influence—topics currently also of interest to researchers in the services sector (i.e. First International Research Seminar in Services Management, 1990).

However, it is the other three measures (scope for improvement, sensitivity to change,

Table 3. Financial services: average scores and rankings.

Factor name	Factor loading*	Area of marketing activity	Current effect on performance Average	Rank	Scope for improvement Average	Rank	Sensitivity to change Average	Rank	Ease of change Average	Rank
NPD strategy	0.79	V17 NPD	3.90	1	3.76	4	3.76	3	2.43	22
	0.84	V19 Launch 1st	3.48	9	3.71	6	3.86	1	2.10	25
	0.61	V26 Positioning	3.00	18	3.52	11	3.14	19	2.81	14
	0.85	V18 Prod. line	3.42	12	3.42	15	3.16	17	2.32	23
	0.79	V20 Unique products	2.86	20	3.29	19	3.38	11	1.76	26
		Factor 1 average	3.33		3.54		3.46		2.28	
Customer interface	0.62	V16 Staff management	3.70	2	3.80	3	3.65	6	2.55	20
	0.82	V15 Staff training	3.62	6	3.95	1	3.81	2	2.57	19
	0.61	V13 Rel. operations	3.67	5	2.95	22	3.25	16	3.30	2
	0.63	V02 Promotions	3.24	15	3.52	12	3.38	9	2.95	10
	0.58	V21 Mktg research	3.38	14	3.57	9	3.00	20	3.33	1
	0.80	V25 Branding	3.10	17	3.10	21	3.30	13	3.10	7
		Factor 2 average	3.45		3.48		3.40		2.97	
Marketing department influence	0.84	V07 Corp. strategy	3.57	8	3.57	10	3.67	5	2.76	17
	0.79	V10 Co-operation	3.38	13	3.62	7	3.38	10	2.57	18
	0.60	V12 Rel. finance	3.19	16	3.29	18	3.33	12	2.81	13
		Factor 3 average	3.38		3.49		3.46		2.71	
Width of product line	0.58	V08 Salesforce	3.43	11	3.75	5	3.70	4	2.45	21
	0.82	V05 Prod. proliferation	2.90	19	3.10	20	2.50	23	3.10	6
	0.77	V06 Prod. deletion	1.90	26	2.90	23	2.05	26	2.95	11
		Factor 4 average	2.74		3.25		2.75		2.83	

Depth of product line	0.51	V04 Prod. extension	3.67	4	3.62	8	3.29	14	3.10	8
	0.42	V14 Rel. DP	3.43	10	3.90	2	3.48	8	2.29	24
	0.79	V03 Ad split	2.67	22	2.88	24	2.71	21	2.76	15
		Factor 5 average	3.25		3.47		3.16		2.72	
Pricing policy	0.86	V01 Pricing	3.70	3	3.35	17	3.48	7	3.14	5
	0.51	V23 Segmentation	2.76	21	3.38	16	3.29	15	3.29	3
		Factor 6 average	3.23		3.37		3.38		3.21	

* Principal components, varimax rotation, Kaiser normalisation using a sample size of 36 (21 from financial services and 15 from other, non-financial service sectors).
† Note that one factor included a group of variables (technology, relationship with personnel department, concept testing and econometric modelling) that appear to have little in common. These variables were assessed to have little effect on any of the scales and so this factor is excluded from the discussion.

ease of change) that provide an indication of the future potential for each factor. It can be seen that the three factors thought to offer the most scope for improvement (marketing influence, NPD strategy and customer interface, Figure 2b) are the same three factors producing the most impact on corporate performance if improved (Figure 2). However, they are not easily changed within the existing corporate constraints (especially NPD strategy).

There is a quite different attitude to pricing strategy. It is seen as the easiest factor to improve, has good impact on corporate performance if improved (Figure 2d) and provides reasonable scope for improvement. It would thus appear to be a priority area for attention. However, detailed discussion of implications is presented below, which also shows how a single measure (combining scales 2, 3 and 4) can assist this process.

IMPLICATIONS

Interpretation of the findings for management attention is helped by presenting the data on two scatterplots. Figure 3 shows 'current effect on performance' versus 'scope for improvement'. Marketing activities located in the upper right quadrant (quadrant 1) already have considerable impact on company performance and offer scope for improvement, in the opinions of the participating financial services marketing managers. An approximate ranking of the marketing areas can be obtained by multiplying the two scores. Marketing areas in the first quadrant are:

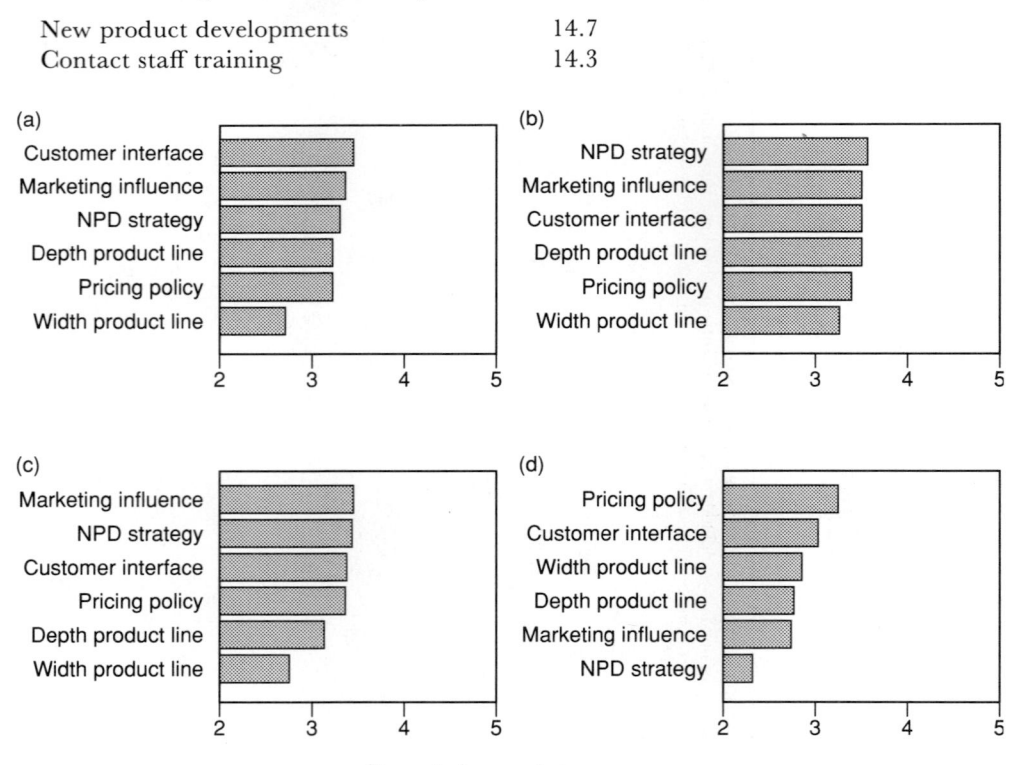

New product developments	14.7
Contact staff training	14.3

Figure 2. Average factor scores.

Scope for improvement

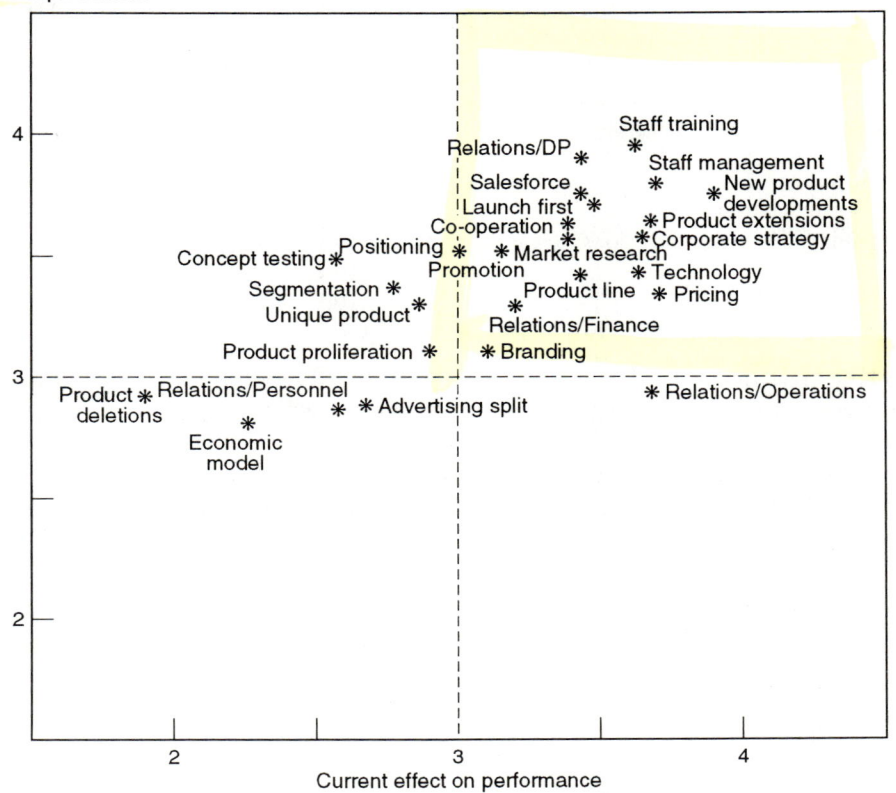

Figure 3. Performance/scope for improvement matrix.

Contact staff management	14.1
Relations with DP department	13.4
Product improvements and extensions	13.3
Launch first	12.9
Managing the salesforce	12.9
Input to corporate strategy	12.8
Utilising technological developments	12.4
Determining best price	12.4
Co-operating with other departments	12.2
Using marketing research	12.1
Complete product line	11.7
Advertising of promotions strategy	11.4
Positioning of products	10.6
Relations with finance	10.5
Branding	9.6

All the above areas are seen as already impacting on overall financial performance and yet offering scope for improvement. The suggestion is that improvements here might well

40 FINANCIAL SERVICES MARKETING

produce better corporate performance via the high input already achieved. A second plot, of 'sensitivity to change' versus 'ease of change', is revealing. Marketing areas in the first quadrant are considered to be relatively easy to change and to have a high relative impact on corporate performance. Areas in the first quadrant (together with the value of the product of the scales) are:

Pricing	10.9
Segmentation	10.8
Relations with operations	10.7
Branding	10.2
Product extensions	10.2
Marketing research	10.0

These areas deserve to be given priority by financial services marketing managers. They are relatively easy to change and also have a high relative impact on performance.

As can be seen from Figure 4, most marketing areas (69 per cent) fall in quadrant 2 (i.e. have a marked effect on corporate performance but are difficult to change) or in quadrant 4 (i.e. easy to change but having little effect on corporate performance). Thus, whilst there are many areas that are considered to have a considerable current impact on performance

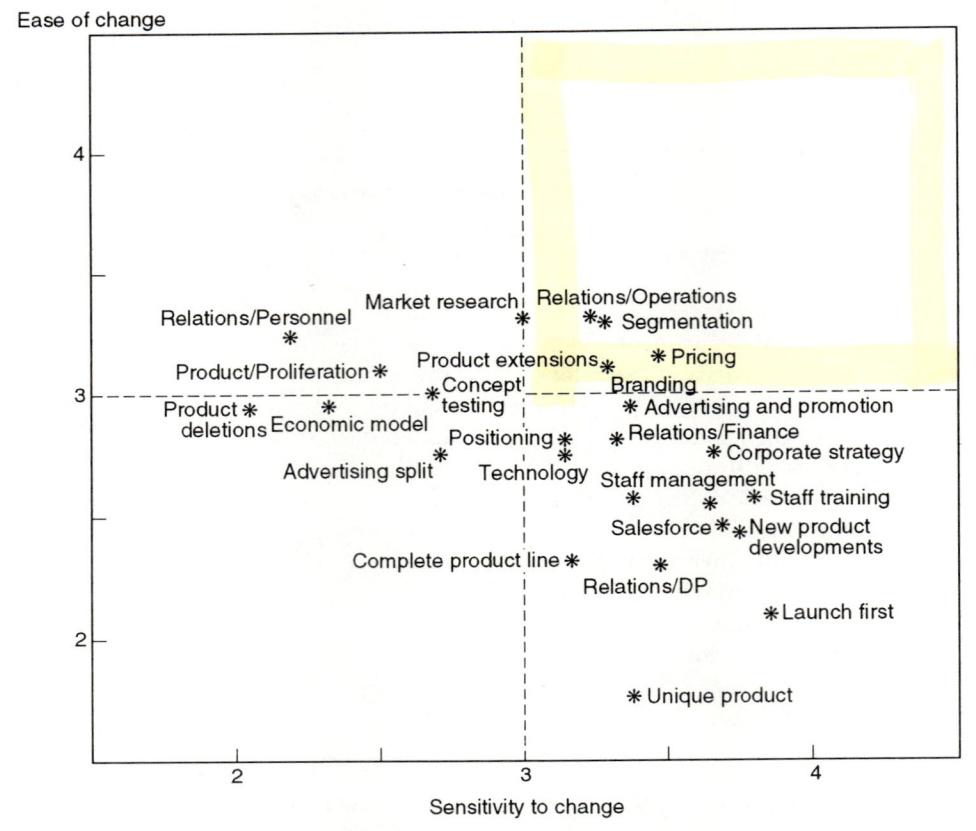

Figure 4. Sensitivity to change/ease of change matrix.

and have scope for change, relatively few are considered likely to have a high impact on performance if improved and also to be easily improved.

A single measure is therefore proposed called 'potential':

$$\text{Potential} = (\text{Scope for improvement}) \times (\text{Sensitivity to change}) \times (\text{Ease of change}) \times 0.8$$

By multiplying by 0.8 potential has a maximum score of 100. A neutral score of 3 on each factor would produce a potential score of 21.6. Note that a multiplicative form is used because of the need to have the simultaneous presence of the three factors.

High values indicate areas that score reasonably well on all three components (i.e. impact on company performance, offer scope for improvement, can be improved within the existing corporate culture). Such areas ought to be prime candidates for management attention and action. Table 4 shows each area's score on potential. The area with the highest potential scores in financial services are:

- Management of contact staff training
- Management of product extensions
- Determining 'best' price
- Segmentation
- Involvement in determining corporate strategy.

Table 4. 'Potential' scores and ranks.

Area of marketing activity	Potential Score	Rank
V01 Pricing	29.28	3
V02 Promotions	28.14	8
V03 Ad split	17.25	22
V04 Prod. extension	29.44	2
V05 Prod. proliferation	19.22	21
V06 Prod. deletion	14.03	26
V07 Corp. strategy	28.93	5
V08 Salesforce	27.20	10
V09 Technology	23.81	18
V10 Co-operation	25.17	13
V11 Rel. personnel	16.27	23
V12 Rel. finance	24.62	16
V13 Rel. operations	25.31	12
V14 Rel. DP	24.82	15
V15 Staff training	30.97	1
V16 Staff management	28.29	7
V17 NPD	27.50	9
V18 Prod. line	20.01	20
V19 Launch 1st	24.01	17
V20 Unique products	15.66	24
V21 Mktg research	28.57	6
V22 Concept testing	22.25	19
V23 Segmentation	29.20	4
V24 Econ. modelling	15.23	25
V25 Branding	25.37	11
V26 Positioning	24.89	14

Better performance in these areas ought to lead to better company performance according to our sample.

Clearer directions for management action can usually be found by looking at factor scores. This is because the factors aggregate individual variables. Thus, for instance, a factor scores high on 'potential' only if on average its constituent variables also score high. This indicates a clearer emphasis than a high score for one variable only. Figure 5 shows the average scores on potential for each factor.

The factors are discussed in turn:

- *Pricing policy:* Has the highest score on 'potential' (Figure 5). Pricing is seen as offering good scope for improvement (Figure 2b) which would impact on company performance (Figure 2c). However, unlike the other factors, it is seen as relatively easy to improve within the existing corporate restraints (Figure 2d) and it is this that produces the high 'potential' score. Thus, pricing seems to be a priority area in financial services. Better pricing can be achieved and will produce better company performance. This is reinforced by noting that both variables belonging in this factor (determining the best price and segmentation) are in the top five on 'potential' score.
- *Customer interface:* This factor (which is a broad measure of the company/customer interface from the management of customer contact staff to the marketing tools, such as branding and marketing research for approaching and influencing the customer) has the second highest score on potential behind pricing. It is seen as offering scope for improvement (Figure 2b) and will impact on company performance (Figure 2c), very similar to pricing. However, it is seen as harder to change than pricing (Figure 2d). Overall it has slightly less 'potential' than pricing. Even so, we regard the rating on this factor as an indication that marketing managers are reasonably optimistic that efforts in this area will be repaid by improved company performance. It is a large and complex area and it is not surprising that change is expected to be harder to win.
- *Marketing influence:* This factor (marketing's high level influence), like customer interface, is seen as offering scope for improvement and will impact on company performance (Figures 2b and 2c). However, it is seen as harder to effect change in this area within the company climate and so its potential is lower than that of customer interface.
- *Depth of product line:* There is good scope for improvement on this factor (product extensions assisted by DP) as demonstrated in Figure 2b, but the organisation's performance is less sensitive to improvements on this dimension (Figure 2c) and, in

Factor	Score
Pricing policy	36.6
Customer interface	35.1
Marketing influence	32.7
Depth product line	29.8
NPD strategy	27.9
Width product line	25.3

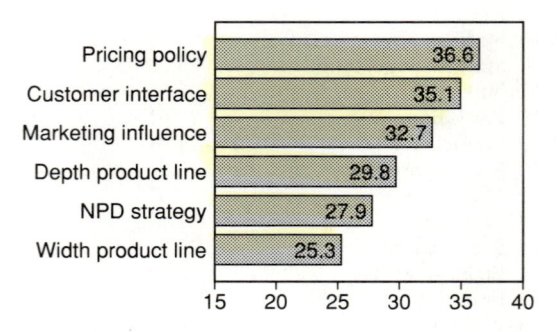

Figure 5. Factor scores on 'potential'.

addition, improvements are not expected to be easily won (Figure 2d). Hence 'potential' is lower.
- *NPD strategy:* The importance of this factor (developing new products, launching them first, positioning them, maintaining a complete product line, offering unique products) is certainly recognized. There is good scope for improvement and any improvements would feed through to improved company performance (Figure 2b and c). However, NPD strategy is seen as the most difficult area in which to effect improvements (Figure 2d) within the constraints of the company and its environment. It is this that causes its low 'potential' score. Thus NPD strategy must receive some priority, given its potential impact, but it would be unrealistic to expect improvements to be easily won or to materialise in the short term.
- *Width of the product line:* This factor (product proliferation and deletion) is given the lowest 'potential' score. It deserves the lowest priority from financial services marketing managers. The main reason for this is that improvements in this area are thought to have the least effect on company performance (Figure 2c) and, in addition, there is less scope for improvement (Figure 2b) and change is not particularly easily won (Figure 2d).

CONCLUSIONS

This article has described the perceptions that marketing managers in the financial service sector have of the activities they perform that are most deserving of priority attention. Marketing managers were asked to evaluate a number of areas of marketing activity on the extent to which each area offered scope for improvement, on the sensitivity of organizational performance to improvements in the areas, and on the degree to which it would be possible to improve performance in each area, given prevailing circumstances. A single measure of opportunity provided by each area called 'potential' was also developed. Interpretation of the information was helped by reducing the individual areas of marketing activity to a smaller number of factors. Pricing, followed by customer interface and marketing influence, were thought by the marketing managers to be worthy of priority attention. Improvements here would be most likely to result in better company performance.

It is useful also to compare the priorities expressed by the marketing managers with the emphasis found in the literature review. Although such a review, picking out only the main themes from each article, is of course a rather subjective and summary activity, there are some similarities in emphasis. The general area of the interface with the customer, including service quality, is frequently addressed in the literature and is also seen as an area of high potential by the managers (customer interface is the second highest rated factor).

Organisational issues are addressed in the literature as well as given priority by the managers (i.e. marketing influence factor). However, there are also some examples where the literature and the managers seem further apart. For instance, marketing managers give pricing the highest priority, but this topic has only occasionally been the main focus of *IJBM* articles. There are also examples of gaps in the opposite direction, i.e. areas that are emphasised in the literature but given low priority by the managers. An example is technology, the subject of many articles but given fairly low priority (18th place) by the marketing managers. Another example is NPD which the literature does address but is actually given the lowest priority by the managers. However, the reason the managers give NPD low priority is not because they think it unimportant—they do not—but because they think improvements are not easily made in this area. Part of this assessment is undoubtedly caused by competitive factors, but part is also caused by the difficulties of achieving change within the constraints of the organisation. In fact the managers considered that many marketing areas offered scope for improvement and furthermore that improvements made would feed through to better company performance. The difficulty, in many cases, was one of achieving improvements within the prevailing company culture.

This does mean that researchers and writers on service marketing in the financial services sector will increasingly need to address issues of change. 'Pure' marketing contributions may not be so highly valued. This observation merely emphasises the non-separability of marketing from other management areas (i.e. operations, human resource management) in services and in financial services that has been recognised for some time (i.e. Grönroos, 1990). Marketing writers must pay particular attention to 'making marketing happen' issues (Piercy, 1991). Perhaps the situation may be helped by increased incorporation of ideas from the organisational change literature (i.e. Lupton and Tanner, 1987) into the marketing framework.

REFERENCES

Bitner, M. J. and Zeithaml, V. A. (1987), 'Fundamentals in Services Marketing' in Suprenant, C. (Ed.), *Add Value to Your Service*, Proceedings of 6th Annual Services Marketing Conference, American Marketing Association, Chicago, Illinois, pp. 7–12.

de Brentani, U. (1989), 'Success and Failure of New Industrial Services', *Journal of Product Innovation Management*, Vol. 6 No. 4, December, pp. 239–58.

Easingwood, C. J. (1986), 'New Product Development for Service Companies', *Journal of Product Innovation Management*, Vol. 3 No. 4, December, pp. 264–75.

First International Research Seminar in Services Management (1990), Proceedings edited by Jackson, S., Bateson, J. and Chase, R., Institut D'Administration des Entreprises, Aix-en-Provence.

Grönroos, C. (1990), *Service Management and Marketing*, Lexington Books, Lexington, Massachusetts.

International Journal of Bank Marketing, Vol. 5 (1987), Vol. 6 (1988), Vol. 7 (1989), Vol. 8 (1990) and Vol. 9 No. 1 (1991).

Lupton, T. and Tanner, I. (1987), *Achieving Change: A Systematic Approach*, Gower, London.

Piercy, N. (1991), *Market-Led Strategic Change: Making Marketing Happen in Your Organisation*, Thorsons, London.

4

Problems of Integration and Differentiation in the Management of 'Bancassurance'

Glenn Morgan

This article examines the development of 'bancassurance' operations in the UK. It considers the competitive and regulatory pressures which have contributed to these developments. It argues that there is a continuum in terms of the integration of banking and insurance. In the UK case, full bancassurance remains the prerogative mainly of the retail banks; the majority of building societies remain as 'tied agencies' which do not allow the full strategic integration which is at the core of bancassurance. However, there are strong indications that the larger societies see these problems and intend to move to full bancassurance, a process that may be assisted by the entry of European insurers as partners in this process. 'Putting bancassurance into operation' is a complex process as insurance selling continues to be seen as a distinctive skill needing to be differentiated from traditional deposit-taking functions. The paper reviews three cases which differ markedly in terms of how they seek to balance the conflicting pressures of integration and differentiation. In the final section, it emphasises the need to create integration as fundamental to the customer's experience of bancassurance.

INTRODUCTION

The last decade has seen many changes in the organisation of the financial services industry in both Europe and the UK. An important aspect of this process of change has been the closer integration of banks and insurance companies. In France, the resulting institutional linkages are referred to as 'bancassurance', in Germany the term used is 'Allfinanz'. In the UK, the emergence of the phrase 'financial services' reflects the breakdown of old barriers between banking and insurance and their replacement by integrated institutions offering a range of services (Salomon Bros., 1990).

This article seeks to clarify what is meant by 'bancassurance'. The first part of the paper argues that only a specific sort of integration between banking and insurance should be considered 'bancassurance'. In this sense, at present there are only a handful of institutions in the UK that can be accurately termed 'bancassurance', though recent regulatory and competitive changes mean that these numbers will probably increase over the next few years. The second part of the article argues that 'bancassurance' can be organised in a variety of ways and presents evidence from three institutions that are publicly recognised as 'bancassurers' and shows their different approaches to selling insurance products through their branch networks. In the final section, the development of bancassurance in the UK over the next decade is considered in the light of the different models available for managements to draw on.

THE NATURE OF BANCASSURANCE

Whilst the term 'bancassurance' is now commonly used, its meaning is less often clearly specified. The approach taken here is that financial institutions can be placed along a continuum denoting the degree to which they have moved towards bancassurance. In other words, it is not a case of an institution either being a bancassurance institution or not, but rather the degree to which it has adopted bancassurance characteristics. At its most developed, bancassurance refers to a financial institution with a branch network which in addition to its money transmission and lending services also sells its own insurance and investment products to its branch customers. It is therefore characterised by a holding company structure in which an insurance company and a deposit-taking institution coexist. Furthermore, it is not just that the two coexist but that their strategies are integrated. In particular, the customer base of the deposit-taker becomes the target of the insurance company arm's sales, marketing and product development.

Moving away from this full-fledged model, there is the model of the institution which is predominantly deposit-taking but which sells the product of one particular insurer through its branch network. In this context, the insurer is a legally separate entity but there is a stable contractual tie between the deposit-taking institution and the insurer. In strategic terms, both organisations keep their options open. The legal contract can be renegotiated; both sides continue to pursue their own independent strategies outside this contract even though integration may be close at an operational level, where the insurer sets up a special administrative unit to deal with business from the branch institution, for example.

Third, there is the situation where the deposit-taker sells insurance and investment products but has neither its own insurance company nor a legally contractual tie to a particular insurer. In this instance, sales of insurance and investment may be very important to the deposit-taker but no attempt has been made to 'backward-integrate' into the insurance area. Finally, at the opposite end of bancassurance is the situation where a deposit-taker has no insurance business at all or a very insignificant proportion.

In general terms, the logic of bancassurance can be explained quite simply. A deposit-taking institution normally has a branch network; before moves towards bancassurance, the network sells banking products (i.e. mainly money transmission services, savings accounts and loans). As the institution moves towards bancassurance, it begins to sell both banking and insurance products. Since the core infrastructure costs associated with running a branch network remain the same in both cases, there is an assumption that

| No Insurance Business | No Ties (Deposit Taker Independent) | Tied (Insurer Independent) | Holding Company (Full Bancassurance) |

Figure 1. The bancassurance continuum (from the point of view of the deposit taker).

selling more products (banking products plus insurance products) will increase overall productivity and therefore overall company profitability. Built into this assumption are a further set of assumptions:

- that the costs of selling insurance products are not so great as to offset potential productivity gains, e.g. that the deposit-taker does not have to employ so many new staff at such a high rate of salary to sell insurance products that costs rise in line with revenue and productivity gains are nil.
- that selling insurance products will not be at the direct expense of banking products, e.g. customers simply switch money out of high interest accounts into bonds or insurance policies, causing income from banking-related products to fall, and meaning that overall productivity gains are non-existent.
- that trying to sell two distinctively different types of product within one framework does not create so much tension and conflict that costs of management time to control these problems and the adverse impact on overall company selling far outweigh any positive gains.

Bancassurance in the UK

In the UK, the assumption that bancassurance will have a positive impact on deposit-taking institutions has become particularly powerful because of the way the competitive and regulatory environments have developed. For example, banks' core businesses of money transmission and lending were becoming progressively less profitable over the decade owing partly to the introduction of free banking and interest-bearing cheque accounts, and partly to bad lending decisions (to Third World countries, property developers and unstable conglomerates such as Brent Walker and Robert Maxwell) (Channon, 1988). Whilst efforts could be made to reduce costs, e.g. through introducing new technology and rationalising branch structures, the real need was to find new substantial sources of revenue. Investment and insurance products were one of the favoured solutions to this need (Ennew *et al.*, 1990; Howcroft, 1991; Stephenson and Kiely, 1991; Thwaites, 1991).

Although the banks had sold insurance products for some years, there was not a clear strategy for developing this business until the 1980s. Instead they maintained a differentiation between their branch networks and their insurance selling arms. For example, a number of banks had set up their own insurance companies in the 1970s but rather than linking these closely to their existing branch network, they encouraged their insurance salesforce to operate like the direct sales forces of specialist insurance companies (TSB was the major exception to this, establishing a form of 'bancassurance' in the 1970s). In particular, they were separate from the branch network and existing customer base and were supposed to go prospecting for new customers, using the cold-calling techniques characteristic of companies such as Allied Dunbar. Inside the branch, selling insurance products was a minor part of the role of the branch manager who might sell some products from the bank's own insurance company, but was also quite willing to sell products from completely separate companies, if that was felt to be in the interests of the customer. The bank in fact might earn more commission from the sale of a product from another company than it would from the sale of its own insurance company's product. Thus an insurance company might be owned by a bank but the degree of strategic integration would be very low, the two companies operating almost autonomously.

Within the building society sector, sales of insurance products were invariably related to the provision of mortgages. Societies would generally be linked to a panel of insurance companies and customers would be sold policies linked to their house purchase on the basis of judgements about the most appropriate company given the particular circumstances of the client and the commission being offered to the society. The switchover from repayment to endowment mortgages in the mid-1980s as a result partly of changing government tax regulations greatly increased the significance of these links. Over the 1980s, the proportion of endowment mortgages rose from 20 per cent to 80 per cent, with the societies' commission income from endowments increasing significantly. This process of diversification out of repayment mortgages into insurance-based products was enhanced by the Building Societies Act 1986 which allowed societies to diversify in a controlled manner (Ennew et al., 1990; Ingham and Thompson, 1992). One aspect of this was the potential to expand insurance business into non-mortgage-related areas either by selling the products of insurance companies or by setting up their own insurance company. Thus whilst the building societies were some way behind the banks in terms of their involvement in insurance, they were beginning to move in the same direction.

By the mid-1980s there was an increasing overlap between the activities of banks, insurance companies and building societies. As yet, however, with the odd exception, there was very little in the way of an explicit strategic integration of banking and insurance activity which is the characteristic of 'bancassurance'. The spur to this was the Financial Services Act 1986 (hereafter FSA). Whilst there were many elements involved in the Act (Morgan and Knights, 1990), the most pertinent aspect for present purposes concerns the principle of 'polarisation'. Financial intermediaries such as brokers, banks and building societies tended to have links with a number of insurers. In the opinion of Professor Jim Gower, who had been asked by the Thatcher government to look into the question of investor protection, the advice which the intermediaries gave to their clients tended to be 'tainted' by their wish to maximise their commissions from the sale. He argued that the customer needed to be better informed about the relationship between the insurer and the adviser. This was to occur in two ways. First, there should be a distinction between those advisers who were able to offer advice about all the different companies and products in the market (and were therefore 'independent advisers', not tied to any particular company) and those advisers who were representing one particular company and only offering the client advice from that limited product range (known as company representatives). This involved a polarisation; an individual was either an independent intermediary *or* a company representative. He/she could no longer be in between, i.e. deal with a limited range of insurers. In theory, the customer should know the difference between the two types of adviser, the implication being that the 'rational investor' would rather deal with an independent adviser than a company representative.

The second point, which was designed to reinforce this, was that the advice of the independent adviser should not be tainted by commission factors. Whilst Gower recommended that this could be done through a maximum commissions agreement which would constrain all companies from paying excessive commissions, subsequent rulings by the Office of Fair Trading (OFT) that this would constitute restraint of trade led to a switch of policy towards disclosure. In other words, the independent would have to reveal how much commission was being paid by the insurance company. In theory, the client could then decide whether this could have 'tainted' the advice received. Whilst the principle of disclosure has been established there have been ongoing debates concerning its exact nature and its application to the company representative sector.

The FSA had an immediate impact on the banks and building societies because they could no longer continue their practice of offering advice from a panel of insurers. They had to decide whether to go independent or tied. Of the main banks, Lloyds, Barclays and TSB already had their own insurance companies and the Midland soon decided to set one up with help from Commercial Union. They all decided to tie their branch networks formally with their insurance companies. In other words, the only FSA-regulated products which they sold through their branches would be those of their own insurance companies. Following the FSA, then, all of the main banks (except NatWest which opted for independent status) moved more directly into the bancassurance field. They each owned an insurance company, the products of which were sold through their bank branch networks.

For the building societies, things were more complicated. None of them owned an insurance company at this stage and the amount of cash either to purchase an existing company or set one up from scratch was prohibitively expensive. Under the Act, however, they were able to tie with an existing insurance company and become appointed representatives of that company. Alternatively, they could become independent intermediaries offering advice on all companies. At first, many of the building societies went independent. They believed this chimed in better with their existing practices, maintained their independence and offered good commission payments.

From the point of view of the insurance companies, however, the situation appeared dangerous. Their former outlets through the banks looked destined to shrink significantly and now they were having to compete more fiercely for building society business. If they could create ties with the bigger building societies, this would at least secure them one part of the market. They therefore offered higher commissions to societies willing to tie directly with them. On top of this, the insurance companies would take over more of the costs of regulation and training under the FSA in the event of a tied agreement. For building societies struggling with the costs and complexities of independent advice, this became an offer too good to refuse. Gradually, more and more of the societies made ties with insurance companies, until only the Bradford and Bingley and the Yorkshire of the largest societies retained their independent status.

By 1990 the high streets of Britain were characterised by two groups. On the one hand, there were a very small number of large independent intermediaries such as the NatWest and the Bradford and Bingley, where the banking/deposit function was augmented by a financial advice system but with no direct tie to an insurance company. On the other hand, there were the emerging bancassurance operations which in turn were characterised by two major forms. In one form, the insurance company was actually owned by the bank (or building society; by 1990 three societies, the Britannia, the National and Provincial, and the Woolwich, had either bought or set up their own insurance company). In the other form, the two organisations retained legal independence but had created a contractual tie whereby the society sold the products of the insurance company through its branch networks.

Since 1990 there have been further changes, mainly characterised by a move towards tighter integration of banking and insurance. In 1992 NatWest announced that it was to set up its own life company (in conjunction with the insurers Clerical and Medical who will hold a 5 per cent stake). From 1993 its branch network would be tied to the new NatWest Life and it would therefore cease providing independent advice through its branch network though it would continue to offer it through a separate subsidiary. The Royal Bank of Scotland has made a similar move through setting up Royal Scottish Assurance with Scottish Equitable (with 51 per cent owned by RBS and 49 per cent owned by Scottish Equitable). Abbey National (formerly a building society and now a bank) has purchased an insurance company, Scottish Mutual, to develop products which it will sell through its branch network. Its previous tie with the insurance company Friends Provident is not to be renewed. The Halifax Building Society has recently sought powers from its members to set up its own life company in the future, which might mean the end of its tie to Standard Life.

In conclusion, the trend towards full bancassurance is now well established in the UK context. The move towards integration has been clear since the Financial Services Act and the contractual ties which characterised the early links particularly in the building society sector are gradually being replaced in the largest societies by ownership links, thus allowing a much stronger coordination of strategic decision-making between the insurance and the banking organisations.

BANCASSURANCE IN OPERATION

The trend which had been identified in the previous section has been well recognised and understood for some time. What is less well understood is that there are significant differences in the way in which the full bancassurance model actually operates in practice. In this section, following some introductory comments, short case-studies of the different ways in which the bancassurance model has been developed will be presented.

Banks, building societies and insurance companies are legally distinct entities. In their core business areas and in terms of authorisation to trade, the three sets of institutions are controlled by different regulators; the banks are regulated by the Bank of England under the Banking Acts, the Building Societies by the Building Society Commissioner, and the insurance companies by the Department of Trade and Industry under the various Insurance Acts. All three sets of institutions are also regulated under the Financial Services Act. Whilst they can be contractually tied or linked together within one holding group, they cannot legally merge into one organisation.

Within a bancassurance operation, it is possible to distinguish two core activities. One concerns the production, administration and service of insurance/investment products. This is the function which only the insurance company can undertake. The second activity concerns the distribution, marketing and sale of the insurance product. Here lies the core strategic question for companies seeking to move into the bancassurance area. Who is to control the distribution, marketing and selling of the insurance product—should it be the bank/building society or the insurance company? Since the point of the bancassurance operation is to sell to the existing clients of the bank and utilise the branch network more efficiently, there is a prima facie argument that it should be the bank. However, there is an equally strong argument that the selling of insurance and investment products is a specific skill distinct from banking, which needs managing differently (Knights and Morgan, 1990; Morgan, 1990; Burton, 1991). Therefore, the distribution, marketing and selling needs to be predominantly controlled by the insurance company. The more one approaches the full bancassurance model, the more urgent it becomes that these arguments are resolved. Indeed, one could say that opting for the bancassurance model is not in itself a solution to anything; rather it is the starting point for debate. How can the bancassurance model be turned into a profitable venture for any particular company? The temptation may be to pursue bancassurance for its own sake as a strategic ploy that will increase the size of the company and improve the career prospects of the individual. As Papasavvas and Parmee have commented,

Personal ambition, perhaps in the genuine guise of ambition for one's company or society, is, in our view, a significant driving force in many bancassurance ventures . . . The risk is that ambition might cloud the vision and distort judgement . . . partnership might be forged on the grounds of image and self-esteem rather than solid business grounds. (Papasavvas and Parmee, 1992: 13)

Thus the question is how companies implement the basic bancassurance framework. An examination of three cases of financial institutions which have sought to resolve these issues illustrates both the range of possibilities and the range of difficulties which are fed.

Case 1: ShilCo

ShilCo has a branch network and owns an insurance company (ShilInCo). ShilInCo products are sold almost entirely to Shilco customers. Although some products are sold through direct marketing and independent financial advisers (IFAs), this is only a very small part of total business and ShilInCo's marketing and product development are increasingly co-ordinated with the needs of ShilCo itself. ShilCo branch staff are divided between ordinary cashiers and customer service representatives (CSRs). Any enquiries about insurance or investment products are referred to CSRs who establish in general terms the sorts of products which the customer needs. If these relate to general insurance products or mortgages, the CSR will conduct a full interview and, if possible, make the sale. If the customer's needs are related to FSA-regulated products, i.e. investments, then the customer will be referred to a representative of the insurance company ShilInCo. The representative of ShilInCo will actually have a small office space in the branch and will have a diary kept which will indicate when he/she will be in the branch. The ShilInCo representative will discuss the client's needs in the branch and may make a sale. More likely, however, is that an appointment will be made at the client's house and the sale will be made there. Other leads will be generated by the branch manager writing direct to clients with advice about the insurance and investment facilities offered by the company and either inviting them into the branch to see the ShilInCo rep or informing them that the ShilInCo rep will be visiting them at their home at a specified time.

All the ShilCo staff are paid on a normal salary structure, with only a small commission element. As a branch they are targeted in a number of ways, including insurance premiums and leads generated for the ShilInCo sales representative. The ShilInCo person, however, is paid by commission only. Although employed by ShilInCo and provided with a car and various other benefits such as private health care, non-contributory pension and subsidised mortgage, salary is determined by the number, size and quality of sales made. The ShilInCo rep will be set targets for business and be expected to achieve them. SilCo managers argue that insurance and investment selling involves different skills to normal money transmission and lending products and therefore it requires a dedicated salesforce and a specialist management system with different remuneration structures and target mechanisms from those appropriate to branch staff. It does, however, believe that the two groups can work together harmoniously in the same physical environment and with the same customers.

ShilCo is often quoted as a fine example of how bancassurance can work in the UK. Yet behind this image, there have been a number of problems. These arise basically from the cultural clash between insurance and deposit-taking which is institutionalised in the structural separation of the branch employees and the insurance sellers. ShilCo staff at all levels have at various times resented the insurance sellers for a number of reasons, including their high earnings and their instrumental and at times high-handed attitude towards branch employees and customers. Furthermore, there was a perception within the ShilCo senior management that at a time when they were under intense pressure to cut costs both in branches and head-office, the insurance company was still spending on ostentatious new buildings and presenting itself as highly profitable (since it was, in accounting terms, getting the use of the branch facilities for nothing). These difficulties (together with changing market conditions) led at one period to a significant decline in productivity. Following a number of senior management meetings and reorganisations, relations between the Shilco and the insurer have been restructured. Shilco is now much more clearly the more powerful entity with the insurer serving the needs of the branch network as defined by ShilCo staff. Whether this will overcome all the problems given the continued structural divide between the branch employees and the insurance sellers is for the future to decide, though it is important to emphasise that ShilCo is still amongst the most profitable of the bancassurance operations in the UK.

Case 2: BulCo

This company also owns an insurance company (BulInCo) whose products it sells to its customer base through its branch network. As with ShilInCo. BulInCo products are sold primarily to BulCo's existing customers and therefore product development and marketing is increasingly coordinated between the two companies. Unlike ShilCo, however, BulCo attempts to keep its specialist insurance salesforce outside the branch environment. As with ShilCo, the initial contact is expected to be with cashier staff. These staff seek to screen out customers with the potential to buy investment and insurance products. Unlike ShilCo, however, in BulCo, customers can be referred either to specialist sellers within the branch (who are employed by BulCo) or to specialist sellers outside the branch (who are employed by BulInCo).

Within the branch, there is an in-house salesforce as well as a number of advisers who travel locally between branches. These sellers are authorised to sell FSA products. They receive a standard bank structured salary with a marginal commission element. In career terms, they learn selling as one of the elements of modern retail financial services practice and although they specialise, they may still find themselves doing routine cashiering tasks if necessary.

The out-of-branch salesforce is run by BulInCo. Unlike ShilInCo representatives, there is a basic salary but this is only small and commission earnings are expected to predominate. Recruitment, training and coaching is undertaken by specialist sales managers. A further distinction from ShilInCo reps is that BulInCo reps, although allocated to branches, are not expected to locate themselves there and wait for lead referrals and sales opportunities. Instead, the branch manager and the staff will seek to make appointments for the representative at the potential client's home. In theory, the rep may come into the branch to meet the manager and the staff but only to develop a friendly relationship, not to directly meet clients, though there is a temptation for them to spend time in the branch meeting customers as well as staff.

BulCo then have two potential sales channels—one is that of the specialist insurance company salesforce, the other is that of their own specialists within their branch. Branches are set targets for business under the various categories of product and managers have a certain autonomy as to how to distribute potential leads within the two salesforce categories. In general terms, it is expected that more complex products such as pensions and bonds will be sold by BulInCo reps, whilst more straightforward products are sold in the branch. However, branch managers have a certain autonomy about how to manage this balance so long as they are achieving their overall targets.

In the case of BulCo, the branch environment is 'uncontaminated' by any outside influence. BulInCo still draw on branch leads but they work predominantly outside the branch. The interface between Bulco and BulInCo occurs through the lead generation process which can be via telephones and letters rather than as a direct face-to-face interaction.

The problems for BulCo revolve around its customer base. The organisation is increasingly sales driven; employees in the branches as well as in the insurance salesforce are targeted to sell. Every person the customer comes into contact with will be trying to sell. Customers may come to resent this and purposely avoid the branch. From the employee's point of view, the pressure to sell means that there may be resistance to passing on leads. Until one's own targets have been met, why pass prospects to somebody else, even if that other person may be more experienced and skilled? BulCo wants to make sure that its customers are not experiencing over-selling but are on the other hand meeting with the appropriate type of salesperson from the range of possible sellers. It is also determined to drive down costs, particularly in terms of its branch network, and to make its heavy investment in BulInCo profitable. Thus although again from the outside, BulCo is perceived to be a bancassurance success, there remain many difficult issues to be resolved.

Case 3: ColCo

ColCo operates a third distinctive model. It too owns an insurance company (ColInCo) whose products it sells through its branch network. In the past, ColInCo products have been sold by branch staff who have been given special training. These staff receive leads from cashiers and then try to sell insurance-based products to branch customers. In career terms, they are part of the normal grading structure within ColCo and receive no commission for their sales. Working in the selling function is seen as necessary to proceed up the hierarchy of ColCo. In material terms, however, there is no immediate incentive for an individual staff member to take on the task. Sales are primarily conducted in the branch and there is little home visiting. The time, skills and incentives required to sell the more complex pension and investment products are not therefore provided.

ColCo's management feel that as a result they are not utilising their bancassurance possibilities to the full. They have therefore decided to set up a specialist salesforce to sell insurance products to their customer base. This salesforce will receive leads from the branch staff which it will follow up through home visits. It will be paid a basic salary (higher than BulInCo) with commission on top. Unlike BulInCo, however, the specialist salesforce will not be employed by the insurance company. On the contrary, they will be managed and controlled by ColCo. Although ColCo recognise that they will have to bring in specialist salesforce management skills, they nevertheless wish to keep ultimate control by integrating the salesforce within ColCo itself. Thus the insurance company remains effectively a manufacturer (of insurance products), whilst ColCo is the distributor and seller of the products.

The issues for ColCo revolve around two problems. First, does it produce sufficient business to make a specialist salesforce worthwhile? A specialist salesforce paid by salaries and commissions is an expensive proposition; will it bring in enough new business to be a worthwhile investment? Secondly, can it be managed in such a way that it does not create a disruptive effect on the already existing branch selling system?

In summary, these three cases indicate the wide range of possibilities that are open even when an institution has opted for the full bancassurance model. At one end (ShilCo), nearly all the selling of FSA-regulated insurance products is done by a salesforce from a separate company; at the other end, the salesforce is controlled by the branch network provider (ColCo); and in the middle there are effectively two salesforces, one controlled by the insurance company (BulInCo) and one controlled by the network provider (BulCo). It is worth noting that there is a further possibility which is embodied in the ColCo case i.e. where there is no separate salesforce at all and the branch staff simply 'add on' selling to their other tasks.

THE FUTURE FOR BANCASSURANCE

These analyses indicate that there is a twofold movement occurring in the development of bancassurance in the UK—one at the level of inter-organisational integration, the other at the level of intra-organisational integration.

Inter-organisational integration

In general, it appears that bancassurance is increasingly occurring through the creation of integrated financial services institutions, where a holding company owns both an insurer and a branch network. If coherence and control of the company–customer interface is essential to bancassurance, the sort of loose relationship which characterises the tied agent position is probably inherently unstable in the long run. Neither party is in the position to control it fully. The bancassurance provider wants products which fit its perception of customer needs. It therefore wants to drive the insurance provider towards particular levels of service and product development which may not fit the insurer's strategy. For example, the bank or building society may demand dedicated high levels of service for its own customers which would involve increased costs for the insurer and reduce the attractiveness of the link to them. On the other hand, the bancassurance provider is putting at risk their own brand and their own customers by linking in with the insurer.

Thus where the insurer slips below certain standards, the bancassurance provider receives a substantial proportion of the odium. An example of this has occurred recently where the Nationwide Building Society has faced criticism owing to the poor performance of endowment mortgages managed by its tied insurer, the Guardian Royal Exchange. From the point of view of managing their most valuable resource, their customer base, financial service companies are likely to become less and less happy with the tied arrangement. It can therefore be expected that more companies will move towards the full bancassurance model of integration at the level of ownership.

This is not to say that the tied agent position will rapidly go out of existence. Given the large number of smallish building societies which remain in the UK and which are currently tied, this is unlikely to be the case. For these societies, it would be an expensive proposition to set up their own life companies, particularly since it is not clear how much 'insurance' business needs to be generated in order to make it profitable. Small operators may do as well to stick to tied agent status rather than set up or buy their own company since there are economies of scale involved in the provision of insurance products which only come into operation when large amounts of business are going through the system. Conversely, large operators who are currently tied are likely to find increased pressure on them to set up their own operation if they wish to achieve a co-ordinated approach to bancassurance.

It is of interest to note that this in turn may offer opportunities for foreign insurance companies to get into bancassurance in the UK. Deposit-takers in the UK hovering on the brink of setting up their own insurance company or uncomfortable with their dependence on a tie with a UK insurer may be persuaded into a merger or takeover with a foreign insurer willing to invest in the development of a full bancassurance operation. Whilst there are a number of legal and regulatory barriers which would need to be overcome, it would not be altogether surprising in the light of the moves to a Single European Market in the financial services to see the creation of major new bancassurance operations in the UK through the bringing together of an existing branch network with the capital and skills of an insurer from outside the UK (Morgan, 1992).

Intra-organisational integration

The creation of a bancassurance group is only the first step. The next problem is how to create an integrated approach to the customer which maximises the advantages of selling insurance through a branch network. All the cases considered indicated a strong belief in the need to maintain a specialised insurance salesforce. Thus bancassurance is not simply a case of selling more products through the same people as before. Inevitably, this raises problems as to how far specialist sellers should be differentiated from other branch employees, in terms of salaries, careers, management controls, physical location. ShilCo has gone furthest in this process of differentiation whilst at the same time locating the two groups together, thus creating severe problems for management in overcoming potential conflicts. ColCo is at the opposite end in that its salesforce will not be managed and controlled by a different company. Institutions face the problem of simultaneously integrating *and* differentiating. They need to integrate because from the customer's point of view a coherent and consistent view of the organisation is necessary if a long-term relationship is to be developed. They need to differentiate because different skills are needed in selling insurance to being a deposit-taking institution. The closer they integrate—i.e. create one management structure and one set of cultural values, minimise career and salary differentials—the more consistent the customer experience *but* the less likely the organisation is to achieve high sales (because the employees lack the specialist skills, management and incentives that traditionally drive insurance salesforces). The more they differentiate (i.e. by creating specialist sales management and representatives with their own careers, incentive schemes and training programmes), the more likely the salespersons as individuals are to achieve high sales targets *but* the less likely the organisation as a whole is to create a coherent, consistent and long-term relationship with the customer.

For the foreseeable future it appears that there will be a number of ways of resolving these tensions. One important criterion for any particular organisation moving towards bancassurance will be to ensure that it builds on its existing values and culture. Therefore, those institutions which are already strongly sales oriented may find it easier to create a differentiated specialist salesforce. Those organisations which are needing to develop such a culture in the first place may be better off emphasising an integrated approach. However, as a general point, it appears that bancassurance operations are likely to centre more on creating differentiation *within* an integrated strategy rather than vice versa. This is because bancassurance depends upon the idea that the customer purchases a wide range of products from one organisation. The organisation must create a consistent relationship with the customer, one in which the customer feels comfortable about doing all his/her financial 'shopping' in the one bancassurance 'supermarket'. Therefore the strategy is based fundamentally on 'integration' of products, services, marketing and brand image. Within this there can be specialisms and differentiation but they must be controlled in such a way that integration is not damaged. Building from tight integration to gradual differentiation may therefore be more consonant with the overall goal of bancassurance than creating a differentiation and then trying to 'manage it backwards' to become integrated. Thus it can be expected that over the next few years, bancassurance managers will be concerned to balance integration with differentiation but with the emphasis on creating a structure which ensures consistency and coherence of experience on the part of the customers.

CONCLUSIONS

In conclusion, this article has argued that bancassurance will become more predominant in the UK over the next few years. Even in the current recession, banks and building societies see this as a priority. So long as lending and money transmission operations remain difficult areas in which to make profits, successful insurance selling can act as a counterweight.

There will be a move out of tied agency operations towards integrated financial services holding companies with branch networks and insurers giving strategic direction by an integrated decision-making process at group level. This process may be speeded up by the entry of European insurers taking over existing branch networks and creating new bancassurance operations. This trend will go along with a variety of approaches to the actual organisation of selling within the branch network. However, the tendency is likely to be that selling practices will be closely integrated with deposit-taking functions in order to ensure coherence and consistency of experience for customers. Specialist salesforces will remain but management will be concerned to ensure that they do not become separate from the culture and customer orientation of the branch network. Bancassurance is the future for retail financial services but creating a successful operation is a complex task for management.

ACKNOWLEDGEMENT

The author acknowledges the financial support of TSB plc and Huthwaite Research Group in conducting the research on which this paper is based. Thanks are also due to former colleagues at the Financial Services Research Centre, Manchester School of Management, UMIST, for their comments, especially David Knights, Fergus Murray and Andrew Sturdy.

REFERENCES

Burton, D., 1991, 'Tellers into Sellers?', *International Journal of Bank Marketing*, Vol. 9, No. 6, pp. 25–9.
Channon, D., 1988, *Global Banking Strategy*, London, Wiley.
Ennew, C., T. Watkins and M. Wright, 1990, 'The New Competition in Financial Services', *Long Range Planning*, Vol. 23, No. 6, pp. 80–90.
Howcroft, B., 1991, 'Increased Marketing Orientation: UK Bank Branch Networks', *International Journal of Bank Marketing*, Vol. 9, No. 4, pp. 3–9.
Ingham, H. and S. Thompson, 1992, 'Structural Deregulation and Market Entry: The Case of Financial Services', Working Paper: Manchester School of Management, UMIST.
Knights, D. and G. Morgan, 1990, 'Management Control in Sales Forces: A Case Study from the Labour Process of Life Insurance', *Work, Employment and Society*, Vol. 4, No. 3, pp. 369–89.
Morgan, G., 1990, 'The Management of Sales Forces', *Personnel Review*, Vol. 19, No. 3.
Morgan, G., 1992, 'Globalisation of Personal Financial Services', *Service Industries Journal*, Vol. 12, No. 2, pp. 193–209.
Morgan, G. and D. Knights, 1990, 'The Financial Services Act', Research Report: Financial Services Research Centre, UMIST.
Papasavvas and D. Parmee, 1992, 'Banks, Building Societies and Insurers: The Whole Greater than the Parts?', Paper presented to the Staple Inn Actuarial Society, March 1992.
Salomon Bros., 1990, *Multinational Money Center Banking: The Evolution of a Single European Banking Market*, London, Salomon Bros.
Stephenson, B. and J. Kiely, 1991, 'Success in Selling—The Current Challenge in Banking', *International Journal of Bank Marketing*, Vol. 9, No. 2, pp. 30–8.
Thwaites, D., 1991, 'Forces at Work: The Market for Personal Financial Services', *International Journal of Bank Marketing*, Vol. 9, No. 6, pp. 30–5.

Part II

Consumer Behaviour

CONTENTS

Introduction to Part II 61

5 Consumer Buying Behaviour in Financial Services: An Overview 64
S. McKechnie, *International Journal of Bank Marketing* (1992), **10** (5), 4–12.
6 Retail Financial Services Segmentation 78
R. Speed and G. Smith, *The Service Industries Journal* (1992), **12** (3), 368–383.
7 The Youth Market for Financial Services 91
B. R. Lewis and G. H. Bingham, *International Journal of Bank Marketing* (1991), **9** (2), 3–11.
8 Mapping Customer Segments for Personal Financial Services 106
T. S. Harrison, *International Journal of Bank Marketing* (1994), **12** (8), 17–25.

Introduction to Part II

As marketing management has developed in the financial services industry, increasing attention has been given to researching and understanding customer needs and expectations in order to broaden and deepen customer bases, and to maintain customers—thus creating loyalty and longer term relationships. It is particularly important to appreciate how the distinguishing characteristics of services impact on consumer behaviour, and to consider how increasingly sophisticated market segmentation techniques allow financial services institutions to develop and position their offerings.

The distinguishing characteristics of services, especially intangibility, heterogeneity and inseparability of production and consumption, have implications for consumer behaviour. For example, consumers may have problems in acquiring effective information on product offerings and elements of customer service, be it through the branch, by post, by telephone, from personal contact or via print media. Branches of banks and building societies have varying promotional displays of leaflets describing accounts, loans and other services; and many now also have financial services advisors available to customers. In addition, direct mail, focused on both continuing and new offerings, is a prevalent feature of financial services marketing communications.

As availability of appropriate or potentially effective information is variable, consumers often also have difficulties in making comparisons between services and/or organizations based on this information. They may also have difficulty in evaluating service encounters; with an organization, its personnel, environment and/or technology.

Consequently, consumer information search in relation to financial services providers and/or their services is usually typified by a preference for and/or reliance on internal sources of information such as previous experience and the experience of others, e.g. friends, relatives, work associates. This is indicated, for example, in the research of the 1970s and 1980s focused on account opening and choice of bank. So, financial services may be described as high in experience qualities and low in search qualities.

With respect to comparison of organizations and/or services, consumers are likely to be considering a smaller evoked set (than in product markets) and evaluations are often made after consumption rather than before. As a result, companies may be interested to measure the fit or 'gap' between consumer expectations prior to decision-making, and their subsequent perceptions of performance of a company and its services and customer service.

Further, consumer loyalty is easier to achieve than in many product markets. If consumers are generally satisfied with a financial services institution, then loyalty will prevail with respect to that service provider, rather than to a particular service, that the organization hopes will provide them with opportunity for selling more services to the same consumer(s). Consumer loyalty builds with successful encounters with the same bank, building society, insurance company, etc.

An additional aspect of consumer behaviour in financial services relates to consumers' participation in service production and delivery, for example: interactions with an ATM or with telephone banking operations which require input of information with respect to needs; providing personal information for loan or mortgage applications; discussing personal circumstances with financial services' employees with respect to obtaining advice or drawing up a will. Thus, the consumer becomes involved in a number of service encounters with the organization, its employees, environment and technology, which impact on perceptions of the organizations and its services.

The article by Sally McKechnie 'Consumer Buying Behaviour in Financial Services' is wide in scope. Firstly, she considers the implications of the characteristics of services, in understanding financial services buying behaviour, with reference to a number of services marketing theorists. This is followed by a review of key buyer behaviour literature from the USA and Europe, focused on the consumer decision-making process, in both personal and organizational markets. A number of key models are summarized, together with their critics. This conceptual material is followed by the main thrust of her article, which is a review of 21 empirical research studies into consumer buying behaviour in financial services. McKechnie provides a flavour of the nature of the research investigations and their key findings. She concludes that there is still progress to be made in the development of a conceptual framework which deals with issues of buyer behaviour in financial services.

The organizations in the financial services industry are now highly aware of the techniques available and possibilities for market segmentation, and a number of them are becoming increasingly sophisticated in the approaches that they take, which may include assessment of the relative profitability of particular segments. The second article in this section is from Richard Speed and Gareth Smith, which is also a review paper focused on segmentation within financial services. Speed and Smith draw attention to the distinction between 'a priori' segmentation research where the researcher decides on a basis for segmentation (e.g. age, sex, stage in family life cycle, social class), and *'post hoc'* segmentation where segments are determined on the basis of clustering of respondents on a set of relevant variables (e.g. benefits, needs, attitudes). They review 38 studies from the USA and UK, completed during the 1970s and 1980s, which they divided into three groups according to the research methods used: normative research taking a case study approach; research using frequency data on segments characteristics (usually 'a priori'); and research using multivariate analysis techniques (usually cluster-based segmentation). They also offer a number of suggestions to improve the rigour of segmentation research (e.g. with respect to validation and consideration of segment stability over time) and to improve its value to practitioners; together with strategies for future research—which, for example, take into account the capabilities (and resources) of companies when identifying segments (e.g., the availability and costs of customer data-bases), and the positioning of products for segments (e.g. based on price, quality, attributes).

The third article, by Barbara Lewis and Graham Bingham focuses on Consumer Attitudes in the Youth Market for financial services. Banks in the UK, had in the 1970s, identified a segment of particular interest as the student market, in the anticipation that students become, in the long term, loyal and profitable customers. Subsequently, research evidence and practice has led to banks and building societies focusing more widely on a 'youth market' to include all school leavers, who are not necessarily a homogeneous group. Lewis and Bingham collected data from a sample comprising school children, those in further education, at university, and on government training schemes. They were asked about their financial services needs and behaviour (e.g. with respect to opening accounts, response to promotional offers and inducements, and financial services used); and attitudes to borrowing and with respect to perceptions of staff, levels of service, image, and satisfactions and dissatisfactions. Evidence was provided of differences in response between age and status groups, which have implications for the development and marketing of financial services to the youth market.

Tina Harrison has developed substantial expertise in understanding and researching segmentation in financial services. In her article, 'Mapping Customer Segments for Personal Financial Services', she stresses that many segmentation studies do not measure size or profitability of segments, nor consider determinants of buying behaviour, e.g. customer perceptions, attitudes and motivations towards financial services. In her exploratory qualitative research, interview data was collected with respect to a number of attitudinal and behavioural variables together with demographic information. Analysis included mapping of respondents with respect to perceived knowledge, confidence, interest and understanding of financial services, with their degree of financial maturity; and the resulting identification of four customer segments—'financially confused', 'apathetic minimalists', 'cautious investors' and 'capital accumulators'. The segments appeared to exhibit distinct attitudes, motivations, financial objectives and behaviour, with implications for potential profitability.

5

Consumer Buying Behaviour in Financial Services: An Overview

Sally McKechnie

Over the last decade there has been a growing interest in the field of services marketing and in the financial services sector in particular. Much of the literature to date has been concerned either with the extent to which services marketing requires a separate approach from the marketing of physical goods or with identifying specific marketing strategies to deal with the problems posed by the unique characteristics of services. In effect, most of the current studies of services marketing approach the problem from the perspective of the seller. By contrast, the issue of consumer behaviour has been relatively under-researched. Although a number of empirical studies have been undertaken, there has been little progress in developing a conceptual framework through which consumer buying behaviour for services may be understood.

Since relatively little has been published on buyer behaviour for services, it is necessary to turn to more general buyer behaviour literature to gain insights into possible techniques and approaches that might be applied in future conceptual and empirical research in this field. This article aims to examine the current status of buyer behaviour literature, so that some of this work can be synthesized with the generic literature on services marketing, as well as specific literature on financial services, in order to consider the nature of buying behaviour for personal and corporate financial services. The second section reviews briefly the recent development of services marketing and describes the distinguishing characteristics of services in general and financial services in particular. The next section reviews and appraises the main comprehensive models of consumer and organizational buying behaviour, and considers their applicability to financial services. In the fourth section the importance of understanding both sides of the buyer-seller interaction process for financial services transactions is examined, along with the implications this has for relationship marketing. Finally, conclusions are drawn from this overview of consumer buying behaviour in the financial services and recommendations are made for further research.

CHARACTERISTICS OF SERVICES AND THEIR IMPLICATIONS FOR BUYER BEHAVIOUR

The academic literature on services marketing has developed from a number of sources (e.g. Bateson, 1977; Eiglier and Langeard, 1977; Gummesson, 1979; Lovelock, 1981;

Shostack, 1977) and was described by Zeithaml *et al.* (1985) as being based on three assumptions: first, that factors existed which distinguished services from goods; second, that these factors posed special problems for service marketers not faced by goods marketers; and third, that services marketing required services marketing solutions. Services are typically distinguished from goods on the grounds of intangibility, inseparability, heterogeneity and perishability, and while goods and services are not polar extremes, these characteristics tend to dominate in services and create problems for services marketing. Although less explicitly recognized in the literature, the characteristics of services, including financial services, will also have an important impact on buyer behaviour. Thus any attempt to understand the purchase decision-making process must recognize the ways in which buyer behaviour can be affected by these characteristics.

Intangibility is the main distinguishing feature, since services are processes or experiences rather than physical objects and therefore cannot be possessed (Bowen and Schneider, 1988; Lovelock, 1981; Shostack, 1977). Furthermore intangibility can be double-edged in the sense that services are not only impalpable but also difficult for consumers to grasp mentally (Bateson, 1977). Consequently at the pre-purchase stage services are more difficult for consumers to evaluate than goods, since any evaluation will be low in search qualities, which are tangible attributes and can be considered in advance. Conversely, services are high in experience qualities, which refer to attributes which can only be assessed after purchase or during consumption. Furthermore, many professional or specialist services will also be high in credence qualities, which are attributes which cannot even be assessed after purchase and consumption (Zeithaml, 1981). Thus for many consumers, for example, any evaluation of financial advice given or product recommendations made must be based on trust in the financial adviser. As a consequence of intangibility, the ways in which services are evaluated, particularly at the pre-purchase stage, are likely to differ from goods, and this area needs further consideration in understanding buyer behaviour for services.

The second factor distinguishing services from goods is inseparability. The fact that services are processes or experiences means that essentially they must be produced and consumed simultaneously. This leads to a third distinctive feature, namely perishability: services cannot be stored for some future time period, hence the need for short distribution channels so that they can be produced on demand (Bateson, 1977). The inseparability of production and consumption in services make production and marketing interactive processes (Gronroos, 1978). The front-line service employees play an important 'boundary spanning role' in the production of services, as do the consumers themselves in their capacity as 'partial employees' (Bowden and Schneider, 1988). Therefore in understanding buyer behaviour it will be important to consider the interaction between buyer and supplier. Since services depend on input from both service employees and consumers for their production, the quality of the service output very much depends on the nature of the personal interactions of these parties. This makes the potential for variability in the service performance high, which leads to the final distinctive characteristic of services, namely heterogeneity.

In addition to these distinguishing features of services there are two more which are present in financial services, namely fiduciary responsibility and two-way information flows between buyer and seller. Fiduciary responsibility refers to the implicit responsibility of financial services organizations for the management of their customers' funds and the nature of the financial advice supplied to their customers. In financial services transactions a set of promises is essentially being exchanged between the buyer and the seller. From the buyer's point of view much depends on what exactly is being promised and the likelihood of such promises being delivered (Lewis and Chiplin, 1986). In the case of long-term savings plans, for example, it is often difficult for consumers to evaluate these promises that are given in the absence of full information. Decisions on whether to purchase such services are more likely to be based on experience and credence qualities as there are fewer search qualities (Zeithaml, 1981). Before any financial resources change hands consumers must have confidence and trust not only in the financial institution concerned but also in its personnel. Apart from relying more on information from personal sources, consumers are likely to consider factors such as the size, longevity and image of the financial services organization as indicators of whether any promises made are sound and likely to be fulfilled. The establishment of trust can also bring about a degree of inertia in buyer-seller relationships. Since an irreversible amount of time and effort is required by an individual in order to acquire the necessary experience and information on which to assess an institution's reliability, it is usually the case that once satisfied, a consumer is more likely to remain with that institution than incur the costs of searching for and vetting alternative suppliers.

As far as two-way information flows are concerned, what is unique about financial services, is that rather than being concerned with one-off purchases, they involve a series of regular two-way transactions between buyer and seller usually over an extended period of time (for example through the issue of account statements or customer visits to branches or ATM usage). As a by-product of the normal operation of these transactions a great deal of up-to-date private and confidential customer information is captured, which can subsequently be used to maintain and develop relationships with existing customers as well as attracting new ones.

UNDERSTANDING CONSUMER BUYING BEHAVIOUR

Understanding the nature of consumer buying behaviour has been a key component of research in marketing for some considerable time. If organizations are to be able to anticipate likely customer reactions to their marketing strategies and influence them where appropriate, it is crucial that they understand the needs and motivations of their customers and prospects.

Most of the literature on services marketing has, however, focused on the development of taxonomies of services and the unique characteristics of services when compared with goods. Murray (1991) pointed out that in spite of the recent attention which had been paid to the field of services marketing and the ensuing efforts to develop conceptual models and managerial paradigms, relatively less attention was being given to developing an understanding of consumer buying behaviour for services, particularly search behaviour in the purchase decision process. Although there is a substantial body of literature on buyer behaviour, the focus of attention in this literature is on consumer and industrial products. The key task is therefore to identify whether the main buying behaviour theories that already exist, can also be applied to financial services.

Much of the conceptual work has centred around the view of consumer buying behaviour as a decision process consisting of a number of discrete but interlinked stages. Probably the best example of this is the Engel-Kollat-Blackwell model (Engel *et al.*, 1991) which breaks the decision-making process into five stages: problem recognition; information search; evaluation of alternatives; purchase decision; and post-purchase behaviour. A similar approach was adopted by Nicosia's (1966) model of consumer decision making and also the Howard-Sheth (1969) model. In essence these models were built around the decision-making process succinctly summarized by Strong's (1925) mnemonic AIDA, standing for awareness, interest, desire and action. This model is one of a group of response hierarchy models, which appears in the adoption and diffusion literature. These models are based on the assumption that buyers will pass through a cognitive, affective and behavioural stage when there is a high degree of involvement with a product category which is perceived to have a high degree of differentiation of products within it (Kotler, 1991). There is also some evidence of similar approaches being used in organizational buying behaviour: for example, the Robinson *et al.* (1967) 'Buy Grid' model which analyses buying decisions across a series of sequential 'buy phases' for different types of buying situation; as well as the models by Webster and Wind (1972) and Sheth (1973).

However, this general type of approach has been subject to criticism. The consumer buying behaviour models mentioned above were criticized by Tuck (1976) on the grounds that they could not be tested and lacked specificity of variables. Foxall (1991) noted that they were all founded on a rational decision sequence which assumed too rational a consumer and did not offer any empirically testable hypotheses. Similarly organizational buying behaviour models were criticized by Turnbull (1991) for assuming a discrete and ordered process, since there was evidence to suggest that stages in the process could occur simultaneously or out-of-sequence depending on the buying situation. A further problem with these models is that they are all typically concerned with one-off purchases rather than recurrent ones.

An alternative conceptual framework was suggested by Baker (1983). His composite model of buyer behaviour is based on Kotler's (1972) framework of four major motivation models (namely Marshallian, Pavlovian, Freudian and Veblenian), which comprise four different disciplinary explanations of choice behaviour, together with sex key concepts which were considered to be most helpful in understanding influences which affect choice (namely selective perception; hierarchy of needs; hierarchy of effects; post-purchase dissonance; buy tasks and buy phases; and characteristics of goods). While this model still has the underlying notion of the decision to buy as the outcome of a discrete and sequential process, it endeavours to synthesize key variables in order to provide a useful framework for marketers and academics alike to structure their thoughts and actions around a particular problem so that successful strategies can be developed. Baker (1983) recognized, however, that it would be unrealistic to expect any model to encapsulate completely the complexity and dynamic nature of the buying process, and stated that an additional variable was required to act as a catalyst for the model to work: the specialized knowledge and experience of persons familiar to the specific product-market interface being studied.

The need to recognize the importance of the buyer-seller interface was addressed by the IMP (Industrial/International Marketing & Purchasing) group of researchers. Their model of organizational buying behaviour represented a major departure from the approaches made to date. This model sets out to conceptualize industrial marketing and purchasing as an interactive process which takes place within the context of long-term relationships between buyers and sellers. It was because of the centrality of this relationship to the buying process that it was necessary to study the two activities jointly rather than simply look at each aspect separately. The underlying rationale of the model represents a significant shift from the more traditional view of marketing which considers a marketer actively managing a marketing mix to match the needs of passive customers in an atomistic market (Ford, 1990). Such a view was considered by Ford (1980) as being unrealistic in industrial markets, since buyers and sellers formed interactive relationships with each other which developed as a process over time.

The interaction model is built on four factors: first, both buyer and seller being active participants in the market; second, the buyer-seller relationship being frequently long term, close and involving a complex pattern of interaction between and within each company; third, links between both parties often becoming institutionalized into a set of roles that each party expects the other to perform; and, finally, close relationships often being considered in the context of continuous raw materials or component supply. In essence it considers the role of marketing to be the establishment, development and maintenance of relationships between buyer and seller companies (Hakansson, 1982). The constituent components of the model are the interactive process, the participants involved, the environment within which the interaction takes place and the atmosphere affecting or affected by the interaction. As a conceptual framework it enables deeper insight not only into the components of the organizational buying decision-making process, but also the ways in which these components interact with one another.

In his recent review of organizational buying behaviour literature Turnbull (1991) pointed out that although the IMP model portrayed the complex nature of the organizational buying process, 'no single model adequately explained all the complexities of this process; a universal pattern of relationships had yet to be found in order to build a comprehensive model'.

CONSUMER BUYING BEHAVIOUR IN FINANCIAL SERVICES

As the previous section shows there is a wealth of conceptual material concerned with how buyers make decisions. This is supported by a large volume of empirical work, most of which was developed in the context of studying the purchases of physical goods rather than services. By contrast in the services marketing and financial services marketing literature the conceptual and empirical work is not as well developed. The reasons for this may be three-fold: first, this may be due to a problem with the conceptual models themselves in that they do not lend themselves to empirical testing (see Tuck, 1976; Foxall, 1991); second, it is not clear whether these models are necessarily the most appropriate conceptual frameworks to use in any case; and third, there has been a lack of appropriate measures of salient dimensions for testing concepts in services marketing situations (Teas et al., 1988). There is little, if any, theoretical work on how consumers buy services. Although Zeithaml (1981) examined how consumer evaluation processes differed between goods and services, this was not done in the context of a general model.

The lack of an acceptable theoretical framework has not inhibited empirical work and there has been a variety of studies of buying behaviour for both personal and corporate financial services. The results of the main studies are summarized in Tables 1 and 2.

It is apparent from Table 1 that empirical work has tended to shy away on the whole from testing conceptual frameworks. Instead, the focus has been on specific issues in relation to buying behaviour such as factors affecting the choice of bank and usage of financial services, customer loyalty, customer expectations and perceptions and service quality.

Financial services marketers need to understand how consumers decide on which suppliers to deal with and which brands to select. In their study of how consumers categorized banks and the effect demographic differences had on this process, Laroche and Manning (1984) found that although banks tended to be recognized by name, there was no clear association of brand concept with this, and that a correlation existed between demographic differences and this process. The study of the relationship of ethnicity and consumer behaviour by Joy et al. (1991) was significant in that it extended previous work on consumer goods to financial services and recognized the importance of the construct of ethnicity in this context.

On the whole, these empirical studies highlight the importance of factors such as confidence, trust and customer loyalty. Some of the common choice criteria in bank selection are dependability and size of the institution, location, convenience and ease of transactions, professionalism of bank personnel and availability of loans. It would appear from this that the personal consumer is more interested in the functional quality dimension of financial services (i.e. how the service is delivered) rather than the technical quality dimension (i.e. what is actually received as the outcome of the production process) (see Gronroos, 1984). This is not surprising given the difficulties consumers have in evaluating services (Zeithaml, 1981): because of the intangibility, inseparability and heterogeneity of services, there are fewer tangible cues to base decisions on prior to purchase and therefore greater reliance is placed on experience qualities after purchase or during consumption, and even credence qualities since consumers may find it extremely difficult to assess

Table 1. Personal financial services buying behaviour.

Author(s)	Field of study	Geographic area	Key finding(s)
Joy et al. (1991)	Link between ethnicity and use of financial services	Canada	Ethnicity should be considered as a construct having strong potential impact on consumption
Leonard and Spencer (1991)	Importance of bank image as a competitive strategy for increasing customer traffic flow	USA	Preference for banks amongst students as providers of financial services; greater confidence in large to medium-sized banks; importance of courtesy of personnel, competitive deposit rates, loan availability

Table 1. Continued.

Author(s)	Field of study	Geographic area	Key finding(s)
Lewis (1991)	International comparison of bank customers' expectations and perceptions of service quality	UK/USA	Very high expectations of service quality and high perceptions of service received, yet gaps did exist
Lewis and Bingham (1991)	Needs, attitudes and behaviour of youth market for financial services	UK	Youth market not homogeneous in terms of needs and behaviour
Meidan and Moutinho (1988)	Bank customer perceptions and loyalty	UK	Banks should develop ATM usage; financial institutions should review basic banking services, e.g. considering a service package, customer loyalty a function of more than one single variable
Jain et al. (1987)	Customer loyalty in retail banking	USA	Customer loyalty is a useful construct; bank non-loyal segment swayed by economic rationale, whereas greater emphasis placed on human aspects of banking by bank loyal segment
Laroche et al. (1986)	Factors influencing choice of bank	Canada	Importance of location convenience, speed of service, competence and friendliness of bank personnel
Furlong and Ritchie (1986)	Consumer concept testing of personal financial services among corporate employees	Canada	Clear preferences on nature and delivery of financial services, sometimes at odds with professional perceptions
Martenson (1985)	Consumer choice criteria in bank selection	Sweden	Random decisions by a third of respondents; importance of bank location, availability of loans, bank where salary paid through, and parental influences
Arora et al. (1985)	Choice criteria used in financial institutions	USA	Common criteria for bank and savings/loan customers, e.g. dependability of institution, convenience and ease of transactions, variety of services and size of institution
Laroche and Manning (1984)	Information processing activity of consumer bank selection	Canada	Existence of a 'foggy set' of bank brands rather than a 'hold set'
Kaynak and Yucelt (1984)	Comparison of attitudinal orientations of US and Canadian credit card users	USA/ Canada	Similar patterns in attitudes to owning and using a credit card

Table 2. Corporate financial services buying behaviour.

Author(s)	Field of study	Geographic area	Key finding(s)
File and Prince (1991)	Purchase dynamics of SME market and financial services	USA	Existence of three distinctive sociographic segments adopting innovations in bank services: return seekers, relevance seekers and relationship seekers
Chan and Ma (1990)	Corporate customer buying behaviour for banking services	Hong Kong	Great importance attached to banks understanding their clients' attitudes in order to serve them better
Yorke (1990)	Interactive perceptions of suppliers and corporate clients in marketing of professional services	UK/Canada/Sweden	Need to consider atmosphere in which relationship is being conducted to build picture of mutual perceptions of parties into medium- to long-term planning activity
Turnbull and Gibbs (1989)	Relationship between large companies and its lead and closest substitute bank	South Africa	Predominant bank selection criteria: importance of quality of service, quality of staff and price of services; split banking common
Teas et al. (1988)	Measurement of four important aspects of the long-term commercial bank and commercial customer relationship: banker's customer knowledge, personal working relationship with bank, banker's reactive and proactive behaviour	USA	Banks should take an active interest in the welfare of their commercial customers to be in a better position to develop long-term relationships with them
Turnbull (1983)	Relationship between banks' corporate customers and their sources of financial services	UK	Small/medium-sized companies do not always consider major UK banks as an appropriate source for all financial services
Turnbull (1982a)	Purchase of international financial services by medium/large-sized UK companies with European subsidiaries	UK	Greater effort required to understand the nature of customer needs and bank/customer relationships through detailed application of interaction theory
Turnbull (1982b)	Role of branch bank manager in bank services marketing	UK	Lack of customer orientation amongst bank branch managers
Turnbull (1982c)	Use of foreign banks by UK companies	UK	High concentration of decision making and extent of split banking; crucial importance of development and maintenance of a company–bank relationship

in hindsight whether they entrusted the right organization with the management of their financial resources.

The main areas covered by the publications summarized in Table 2 are the commercial bank/commercial customer interface in terms of the interaction process, mutual perceptions held, long-term relationships, factors affecting choice of bank and usage of international financial services and the need for customer orientation.

The application of some organizational buying behaviour models to the purchasing of international financial services was attempted by Turnbull (1982a), who concluded that no single model adequately explained all the complexities of these purchases. Nevertheless he pointed out that certain aspects of these theories seemed to lend themselves well in this respect. First, the application of the interaction model by the IMP group seemed to be particularly appropriate. Although this model is concerned with the sale and purchase of industrial goods, it may have been the case that is was considered to be appropriate to the sale and purchase of corporate financial services on the grounds that the latter also involved organizational buying behaviour, rather than because of any adaptability the model might have for services of any kind. Addressing the importance and nature of relationships between companies and banks, the interaction model examines factors which influence search and decision processes, in particular the 'atmosphere' in which these relationships are conducted. Second, consideration was given to the application of the stages of the purchase process put forward by Robinson *et al.* (1967) and Brand (1972), which led to the conclusion that the financial purchasing process largely followed these sequences. Finally, it was observed that the organizational factors in the Webster and Wind (1972) model also seemed to be appropriate. The buying centre concept from this model was also applied in another study (Turnbull, 1982c) which identified a low number of people directly involved in the decision-making process. In this same study the importance of developing and maintaining company–bank relationships was considered, and it was recognized that (although already widely accepted in US banks) customer contact bank employees played a key role in establishing relationships with new clients. The importance of company–bank relationships was stressed even further by Turnbull and Gibbs (1987) in their discussion of the concept of 'financially responsive relationship management' and the interactive process this entails, as well as the substantial benefits to be gained for both parties concerned. Based on more recent research it was claimed that the commercial banks which would succeed over the next ten years would be those which developed systems of financial responsiveness and whose customer contact officers and senior management had a better understanding of corporate customer buying behaviour (Turnbull and Gibbs, 1989). Although the long-term success of any service depended on the buyer–seller relationship, Yorke (1990) pointed out that most of the literature that had appeared on the relationship definition of marketing had looked at this from the perspective of the seller and not the individual or corporate buyer. He explicitly advocated the adaptation of the interaction model as being appropriate for the purchase of services, particularly corporate rather than personal services; and stressed the important implications it has for professional supplier firms. Acknowledging the wide recognition of the importance of establishing long-term working relationships in services marketing, Teas *et al.* (1988) concluded from their empirical research that commercial customers had favourable attitudes so long-term bank relationships where the bank behaved as follows: they were responsive to these customers' requests, initiated interaction with their customers, were knowledgeable about their customers' business and business needs, and developed close informal working relationships with their customers.

FUTURE DIRECTIONS

Although, as the previous section has indicated, there is a growing body of empirical literature, there is still some progress to be made in the development of a conceptual framework which deals with issues of buyer behaviour in services. While a range of general buyer behaviour frameworks exists, there are advantages in the formulation of theories at a lower level of abstraction to deal with more specific services issues (Blois, 1974). In this context, it would appear that while the application of the IMP framework to corporate financial services is particularly interesting, there are potentially useful insights to be gained from the more general application of this approach to financial services. The main reason for this is that the IMP model is the only buying behaviour model which explicitly covers relationships and interactions. It addresses the interactive process which takes place between the buyer and the seller in an exchange situation, and bases this not just on a single transaction but a series of transactions over time which enables a relationship to be formed between the two parties.

In services marketing, where there is a complex interface between the buyer and the seller, it is clear that the traditional marketing mix approach does not fully cover the relationships that exist between consumers and service providers and the task of managing the total customer/firm personnel interaction process (Booms and Nyquist, 1981; Gronroos, 1990). Although Foxall (1991) criticized consumer behaviour models for implying high consumer involvement and then indicated the recent development of alternative low involvement theories, it is the case that as far as consumers of services are concerned they are indeed actively involved in shaping up a service offering due to the inseparability of production and consumption.

Since the importance of buyer–seller relationships was only recognized relatively recently, there has been very little coverage of this topic in the literature either on buying, selling or behaviour. An important contribution was made to the latter by Watson (1986), who offered two conceptual frameworks: one model examining the steps involved in building a relationship; another model describing the communication tasks required at each stage of the process of relationship building. More recently it is interesting to note that Donaldson (1990) describes the interaction approach to selling as one of five approaches to the sales function and its management, and devotes a whole chapter to examining buyer–seller interaction.

Buyer–seller interactions have a great impact on the future buying behaviour of customers and on word-of-mouth communications about the services concerned. Consequently much importance needs to be given to the 'boundary-spanning role' performed by front-line service employees, and the need to ensure direct control of the environment in which these personnel work in order to set and maintain satisfactory standards of service quality (see Bowen and Schneider, 1988). The relationships that are formed between buyers and sellers need to be built on mutual trust and commitment if they are to be developed and maintained in the long term. For services generally they can be broad or narrow in scope and continuous or discrete in nature.

Having examined the potential usefulness of the interaction model for services in general, consideration is now given as to whether the same can be said for financial services in particular. By their very nature financial services tend not to be one-off purchases but ones which are required on a recurring basis (Turnbull and Gibbs, 1987) with the result that there is a clear need for financial services suppliers to establish initial relationships with their prospects while at the same time maintaining and developing long-term relationships with existing customers. Furthermore, financial services are based on customer trust and confidence not only in the organization supplying these services but also particularly in the customer contact employees themselves. Turnbull and Gibbs (1982c) in their study emphasized the importance of the interaction between the salesperson and the client, and that the salesperson, because of the nature of banking services (i.e. intangibility, complexity, uncertainty and great importance to buying organization), was often perceived as the item of purchase itself.

Financial services organizations operate in a high contact business where the nature of buyer–seller interactions and the establishment of long-term relationships based on confidence and trust have real implications for successful retention of customers and recruitment of prospects. A recent survey of senior financial services marketers revealed that, after pricing policy, they perceived the interface with customers as the second most important area of marketing activity as well as the area of second highest potential for improving company performance (Easingwood and Arnott, 1991). These findings were supported by Stephenson and Kiely (1991) who recommended that in the selling of banking services, the emphasis should shift from the promotion of an institutional image to concentration on the crucial boundary-spanning role played by customer contact personnel, since they not only sell and perform these services but are also equated by customers with the service.

CONCLUSION

From this overview it is apparent that there is a noticeable absence of any general conceptual framework that describes how consumers buy services in general, let alone financial services in particular. Although there have been many useful, albeit somewhat fragmented, insights into aspects of consumer buying behaviour in this context, there is a real need for marketing theories and concepts to be developed specifically for services. Rather than develop a specific set of ideas and approaches for financial services, it would appear that the framework adopted by the interaction approach already has potential for general application in services as well as financial services. However further research needs to be done and suggested areas would include the following: the application of the IMP model to services in general and personal financial services in particular; and the development of concrete measurement tools for the empirical testing of this applied model.

REFERENCES

Arora, R., Tamer Cavusgil, S. and Nevin, J. R. (1985), 'Evaluation of Financial Institutions by Bank versus Savings and Loan Customers: An Analysis of Factor Congruency', *The International Journal of Bank Marketing*, Vol. 3 No. 3, pp. 47–55.

Baker, M. J. (1983), *Market Development*, Penguin, Harmondsworth.
Bateson, J. E. G. (1977), 'Do We Need Service Marketing', in Eiglier, P., Langeard, E., Lovelock, C. H. and Bateson, J. E. G. (Eds), *Marketing Consumer Services Report No. 77–115*, Marketing Science Institute, pp. 1–30.
Blois, K. J. (1974), 'The Marketing of Services: An Approach', *European Journal of Marketing*, Vol. 8 No. 2, pp. 137–49.
Booms, B. H. and Nyquist, J. L. (1981), 'Analysing the Customer/Firm Communication Component of the Services Marketing Mix', in Donnelly, J. H. and George, W. R. (Eds), *The Marketing of Services*, AMA Proceedings, Chicago, pp. 172–7.
Bowen, D. E. and Schneider, B. (1988), 'Services Marketing and Management: Implications for Organizational Behaviour', *Research in Organizational Behaviour*, Vol. 10, pp. 43–80.
Brand, G. T. (1972), *The Industrial Buying Decision*, Cassell/Associated Business Programmes, London.
Chan, A. K. K. and Ma, V. S. M. (1990), 'Corporate Banking Behaviour: A Survey in Hong Kong', *The International Journal of Bank Marketing*, Vol. 8 No. 2, pp. 25–31.
Donaldson, B. (1990), *Sales Management: Theory and Practice*, Macmillan, Basingstoke.
Easingwood, C. and Arnott, D. (1991), 'Management of Financial Services Marketing: Issues and Perceptions', *The International Journal of Bank Marketing*, Vol. 9 No. 6, pp. 3–12.
Eiglier, P. and Langeard, E. (1977), 'A New Approach to Service Marketing', in Eiglier, P., Langeard, E., Lovelock, C. H. and Bateson, J. E. G. (Eds), *Marketing Consumer Services Report No. 77–115*, Marketing Science Institute, pp. 31–58.
Engel, J. F., Blackwell, R. D. and Miniard, P. W. (1991), *Consumer Behaviour*, 6th edn, The Dryden Press, USA.
File, K. M. and Prince, R. A. (1991), 'Sociographic Segmentation: The SME Market and Financial Services', *The International Journal of Bank Marketing*, Vol. 9 No 3, pp. 3–8.
Ford, D. (1980), 'The Development of Buyer-Seller Relationships in Industrial Markets', *European Journal of Marketing*, Vol. 14 No. 5/6, pp. 339–53.
Ford, D. (1990), 'Introduction: IMP and the Interaction Approach', in Ford D. (Ed.), *Understanding Business Markets: Interaction, Relationships and Networks*, Academic Press, London.
Foxall, G. R. (1991), 'Consumer Behaviour', in Baker, M. J. (Ed.), *The Marketing Book*, 2nd ed., Butterworth-Heinemann, Oxford.
Furlong, C. B. and Ritchie, J. R. B. (1986), 'Consumer Concept Testing of Personal Financial Services', *The International Journal of Bank Marketing*, Vol. 4 No. 1, pp. 3–18.
Gronroos, C. (1978), 'A Service-orientated Approach to Marketing of Services', *European Journal of Marketing*, Vol. 12 No. 8, pp. 588–601.
Gronroos, C. (1984), 'A Service Quality Model and its Marketing Implications', *European Journal of Marketing*, Vol. 18 No. 4, pp. 36–44.
Gronroos, C. (1990), 'Relationship Approach to Marketing in Services Contexts: The Marketing and Organizational Behaviour Interface', *Journal of Business Research*, Vol. 20, pp. 3–11.
Gummesson, E. (1979), 'The Marketing of Professional Services—An Organizational Dilemma', *European Journal of Marketing*, Vol. 13 No. 5, pp. 308–18.
Hakansson, H. (1982), 'An Interaction Approach', in Hakansson, H. (Ed.), *International Marketing and Purchasing of Industrial Goods*, John Wiley, Chichester.
Howard, J. A. and Sheth, J. N. (1969), *The Theory of Buying Behaviour*, John Wiley, New York.
Jain, A. K., Pinson, C. and Malhotra, N. K. (1987), 'Customer Loyalty as a Construct in the Marketing of Banking Services', *The International Journal of Bank Marketing*, Vol. 5 No. 3, pp. 49–72.
Joy, A., Kim, C. and Laroche, M. (1991), 'Ethnicity as a Factor Influencing Use of Financial Services', *The International Journal of Bank Marketing*, Vol. 9 No. 4, pp. 10–16.
Kaynak, E. and Yucelt, U. (1984), 'A Cross-Cultural Study of Credit Card Usage Behaviours: Canadian and American Credit Card Users Contrasted', *The International Journal of Bank Marketing*, Vol. 2 No. 2, pp. 45–57.
Kotler, P. (1972), *Marketing Management: Analysis, Planning, Implementation & Control*, 2nd ed., Prentice-Hall, Englewood Cliffs, NJ.
Kotler, P. (1991), *Marketing Management: Analysis, Planning, Implementation and Control*, 7th ed., Prentice-Hall, Englewood Cliffs, NJ.

Laroche, M. and Manning, T. (1984), 'Consumer Brand Selection and Categorisation Processes: A Study of Bank Choice', *The International Journal of Bank Marketing*, Vol. 2 No. 3, pp. 3–21.

Laroche, M., Rosenblatt, J. A. and Manning, T. (1986), 'Services Used and Factors Considered Important in Selecting a Bank: An Investigation across Diverse Demographic Segments', *The International Journal of Bank Marketing*, Vol. 4 No. 1, pp. 35–55.

Leonard, M. and Spencer, A. (1991), 'The Importance of Image as a Competitive Strategy: An Exploratory Study in Commercial Banks', *The International Journal of Bank Marketing*, Vol. 9 No. 4, pp. 25–9.

Lewis, B. R. (1991), 'Service Quality: An International Comparison of Bank Customers' Expectations and Perceptions', *Journal of Marketing Management*, Vol. 7, pp. 47–62.

Lewis, B. R. and Bingham, G. H. (1991), 'The Youth Market for Financial Services', *The International Journal of Bank Marketing*, Vol. 9 No. 2, pp. 3–11.

Lewis, M. K. and Chiplin, B. (1986), 'Characteristics of Markets for Personal Financial Services', in Carter, R. L., Chiplin, B. and Lewis, M. K. (Eds), *Personal Financial Markets*, Phillip Allan, Oxford.

Lovelock, C. H. (1981), 'Why Marketing Management needs to be Different for Services?', in Donnelly, J. H. and George, W. R. (Eds), *The Marketing of Services*, AMA Proceedings, Chicago, pp. 5–9.

Martenson, R. (1985), 'Consumer Choice Selection in Retail Bank Selection', *The International Journal of Bank Marketing*, Vol. 3 No. 2, pp. 64–74.

Meidan, A. and Moutinho, L. (1988), 'Bank Customers' Perceptions and Loyalty: An Attitudinal Research', *European Marketing Academy Proceedings*, pp. 472–93.

Murray K. B. (1991), 'A Test of Services Marketing Theory: Customer Information Acquisition Activities', *Journal of Marketing*, Vol. 55, January, pp. 10–25.

Nicosia, F. N. (1966), *Consumer Decision Processes*, Prentice-Hall, Englewood Cliffs, NJ.

Robinson, P. J., Faris, C. W. and Wind, Y. (1967), *Industrial Buying Creative Marketing*, Allyn & Bacon, Boston.

Sheth, J. N. (1973), 'A Model of Industrial Buyer Behaviour', *Journal of Marketing*, Vol. 37 No. 4, October, pp. 50–6.

Shostack, G. L. (1977), 'Breaking Free from Product Marketing', *Journal of Marketing*, Vol. 41 No. 2, April, pp. 73–80.

Stephenson, B. and Kiely, J. (1991), 'Success in Selling—The Current Challenge in Banking', *The International Journal of Bank Marketing*, Vol. 9 No. 2, pp. 30–8.

Strong, E. K. (1925), *The Psychology of Selling*, McGraw-Hill, New York.

Teas, R. K., Dorsch, M. J. and McAlexander, J. H. (1988), 'Measuring Commercial Bank Customers' Attitudes toward the Quality of the Financial Services Marketing Relationship', *Journal of Professional Services Marketing*, Vol. 4 No. 1, pp. 75–95.

Tuck, M. (1976). *How Do We Choose?*, Methuen & Co. Ltd, London.

Turnbull, P. W. (1982a), 'The Purchasing of International Financial Services by Medium- and Large-sized UK Companies with European Subsidiaries', *European Journal of Marketing*, Vol. 16 No. 3, pp. 111–21.

Turnbull, P. W. (1982b), 'The Role of the Branch Bank Manager in the Marketing of Bank Services', *European Journal of Marketing*, Vol. 16 No. 3, pp. 31–6.

Turnbull, P. W. (1982c), The Use of Foreign Banks by British Companies', *European Journal of Marketing*, Vol. 16 No. 3, pp. 133–45.

Turnbull, P. W. (1983), 'Corporate Attitudes towards Bank Services', *The International Journal of Bank Marketing*, Vol. 1 No. 1, pp. 53–66.

Turnbull, P. W. (1991), 'Organizational Buying Behaviour', in Baker, M. J. (Ed.), *The Marketing Book*, 2nd edn, Butterworth-Heinemann, Oxford.

Turnbull, P. W. and Gibbs, M. L. (1987), 'Marketing Bank Services to Corporate Customers: The Importance of Relationships', *The International Journal of Bank Marketing*, Vol. 5 No. 1, pp. 19–26.

Turnbull, P. W. and Gibbs, M. L. (1989), 'The Selection of Banks and Banking Services among Corporate Customers in South Africa', *The International Journal of Bank Marketing*, Vol. 7 No. 5, pp. 36–9.

Watson, I. (1986), 'Managing the Relationships with Corporate Customers', *The International Journal of Bank Marketing*, Vol. 4 No. 1, pp. 19–34.

Webster, Jr, F. E. and Wind, Y. (1972), 'A General Model of Understanding Organizational Buying Behaviour', *Journal of Marketing*, Vol. 36, April, pp. 12–19.

Wind, Y. and Thomas, R. J. (1980), 'Conceptual and Methodological Issues in Organizational Buying Behaviour', *European Journal of Marketing*, Vol. 14 No. 5/6, pp. 239–63.

Yorke, D. A. (1990), 'Interactive Perceptions of Suppliers and Corporate Clients in the Marketing of Professional Services: A Comparison of Accounting and Legal Services in UK, Canada and Sweeden', *Journal of Marketing Management*, Vol. 5 No. 3, pp. 307–23.

Zeithaml, V. A. (1981), 'How Consumer Evaluation Processes Differ between Goods and Services' in Donnelly, J. H. and George, W. R. (Eds), *The Marketing of Services*, AMA Proceedings, Chicago, pp. 186–90.

Zeithaml, V. A., Parasuraman, A. and Berry, L. L. (1985), 'Problems and Strategies in Services Marketing', *Journal of Marketing*, Vol. 49, Spring, pp. 33–46.

6

Retail Financial Services Segmentation

Richard Speed and Gareth Smith

In the light of the increasing importance of market segmentation in the retail financial services industry, this article reviews past research in the area. The article argues the need for research to move forward rather than repeat the kind of studies now being carried out by companies. The way in which academic research might provide a methodological model is discussed and areas for the future development of segmentation research are suggested.

Market segmentation has been a fertile area for financial services marketing research for many years. This research has covered many possible segmentation approaches and varies widely in its methodological approach. This article reviews this research and discusses the methodologies used.

The adoption of segmentation strategies within the financial services industry is one of the signs of the development of marketing within financial service companies. The adoption of these strategies means that companies are now carrying out segmentation research for themselves, and that academic segmentation research must move forward if it is to contribute to industry practice. Areas in which academic research into financial service segmentation might be developed in future are discussed.

SEGMENTATION IN FINANCIAL SERVICES

Since the seminal work of Smith (1956), market segmentation has been recognised as a powerful strategy. By concentrating on meeting the needs of homogeneous groups within a larger, heterogeneous market, companies have been able to increase profitability and reduce the competition they face. Their customers get a product better suited to their requirements. The car market is an excellent example of a market where segmentation has been to the benefit of both customer and company. Companies such as Mercedes and Rolls Royce have concentrated on the luxury-oriented segment, Ferrari and Porsche on a performance-oriented segment and Volvo on a safety-oriented segment. Mass manu-

---

Richard Speed is at The Management Centre, Kings College, London, Kensington Campus, Campden Hill Road, London W8 7AH.
Gareth Smith is at the Loughborough University Business School, Loughborough, Leicestershire, LE11 3TU.

facturers also segment their market, producing a range of cars with differing features in an attempt to meet the needs of different segments.

Marketing permeated into the traditional world of banking and financial services later than it did into consumer and industrial goods, and segmentation strategies have only recently been put into practice. Academic research into the possibilities of market segmentation for banks has been carried out since the early 1970s, although the early work was primarily American, reflecting the fact that the US financial services industry has historically been some way ahead of its UK counterpart in adopting marketing techniques. Because of the difference in the organisation of the banking systems it is debatable how easily such American research can be transferred to the UK.

As competition in financial service markets has increased, companies have increasingly adopted a segmentation strategy. They have moved from strategies of trying to attract non-users to attempting to increase the use of their products by existing customers and attempting to increase the exclusiveness of their relationship with the customer. The banks' adoption of a life-stage approach to their customers typifies this use of segmentation. Having realised that customers' financial needs differ as they pass through life, the banks have broadened and deepened their product ranges. The broadening of the product range has extended the coverage of the population, bringing products for children, teenagers and students. The deepening of the product range has seen the introduction of a greater variety of services for each group: first-time buyer mortgages, insurance and personal loans for the young, equity release products and high interest savings products for the elderly. Recently Midland Bank have taken things a stage further by introducing branded multi-service accounts, arising from a segmentation of the market on the basis of 'confidence with which individuals tackle all their financial affairs'; and 'the degree of authority expected from the bank' (Gavaghan, 1989). Midland's accounts are targeted at segments that might be identical in terms of age and status, moving segmentation in financial services closer to that found in consumer goods markets.

In reviewing the research into market segmentation in retail financial service markets, the four criteria for effective segmentation suggested by Kotler (1988) provide useful benchmarks. These are: measurability—the size and purchasing power of the segment must be able to be assessed; substantiality—the potential profit from the segment must be sufficient; accessibility—the firm must be able effectively to reach and serve the segment; and actionability— the firm must be able to generate effective programmes to attract that segment. Using these criteria, the research that has been carried out in this area can be reviewed.

A TYPOLOGY AND EVALUATION OF SEGMENTATION RESEARCH

Green (1977) suggested that segmentation analysis could be classified into two types. These are a priori and 'cluster-based' (also called *post-hoc*). The difference between these two methods is explained by Wind (1978). A priori segmentation is one where the researcher

Decides on a basis for segmentation, such as product purchase, loyalty customer type or other factor. The survey results show the segments' estimated size and their demographic, socio-economic, psychographic and other relevant characteristics. (Wind, 1978; p. 317)

Cluster-based segmentation is one where

Segments are determined on the basis of clustering of respondents on a set of 'relevant' variables. Benefit, need and attitude segmentation are examples of this kind of approach. As in a priori segmentation studies, the size and other characteristics (demographic, socioeconomic, purchase and the like) of the segments are estimated. (Wind, 1978)

In a priori segmentation cases are allocated to segments on the basis of characteristics the researcher has chosen, in cluster-based segmentation the cases are allocated on the basis of a similarity identified by a technique chosen by the researcher. An example of a priori segmentation research would be a study comparing the financial needs and attitudes of post-18 students and their peers in employment. An example of cluster-based segmentation would be a study of all school leavers, divided into groups according to similar financial needs or attitudes.

Several authors have written polemical articles discussing segmentation in financial services (Gwin and Lindgren 1982; Yorke, 1982; Brown, 1983; Evans and Beckman, 1984; Wills, 1985). Most of these authors seek to explain the ideas and methods of segmentation for the benefit of financial service companies, and the criteria for success.

The published research can be divided into groups according to the methodology used. One group seeks to describe approaches that can be adopted in seeking to address the needs of particular market segments, suggesting products and features that might be successful or how segments might be identified. This research in normative, taking a case study approach, reporting what one company has done or what companies might do. This research is concerned with the actionability of the segment, being entirely qualitative. It serves as a source of ideas for programmes, and further market testing would be necessary to establish its usefulness. Table 1 lists examples of this type of research.

A second section of the literature, nearly all dealing with a priori segmentation, has a more quantitative element to it, generally providing an assessment of the characteristics of the segment. This type of research normally provides frequency data on demographics, attitudes to the product or choice criteria, combining this with recommendations on how to respond to this data. The problems with this data arise from two areas—measurability and substantiality. Because the data investigates only the characteristics of the selected segment, it does not attempt to measure the profitability or size of the segment against the remainder of the market. Further research is therefore necessary to support action targeted at the chosen segment. The fundamental problem with a priori segmentation is that there is no necessary link between the segments selected by the researcher and buyer behaviour. For example, it may be possible to describe differences between voter's behaviour on the basis of age or social class, but these are not determinants of voting behaviour.

A sub-section of this research not only examines customer attitudes and characteristics against a chosen criteria, such as age or brand choice, but also recognises that the author is

Table 1. Segmentation research taking normative approach.

Research	Segmentation basis	Data used	Method
Doyle and Newbould (1975) UK	Usage of building society	Account usage	Non-empirical
Gee (1975) USA	Women	Case study	Non-empirical
Goodfellow (1987) USA	Selection criteria	Qualitative data	Non-empirical
Marrs (1984) USA	Age	Case study	Non-empirical

dealing with a dependent/independent variable relationship and so tests the significance of the relationship between the pre-selected dependent variable and the independent variables. Methodologies for this type of research include chi squared, T tests and regression analysis. Table 2 shows research analysing segments using frequency data on segment characteristics, and that which test the significance of frequency findings.

Research using multivariate techniques is usually concerned with cluster-based

Table 2. Segmentation research using frequency data.

Research	Segmentation basis	Data used	Method	Type
Arbeit and Sawyer (1974) USA	Users and non-users	Attitudinal data Demographic data	Frequency data	A priori
Hood and Walters (1985) USA	Established bank customers	Demographic data Bank usage Attitudinal data	Frequency data	A priori
Johnson and Sullivan (1981) USA	Bank loan users vs. finance company	Attitudinal data Demographic data	Frequency data	A priori
Langrehr (1981) USA	NOW account users and non-users	Bank usage Demographic data	Chi-squared test	A priori
Lewis (1982a) UK	Students	Qualitative	Frequency data	A priori
Lewis (1982b) UK	Weekly cash paid	Qualitative	Frequency data	A priori
Martenson (1985) Sweden	Bank used	Attitudinal data Choice criteria	Frequency data	A priori
Mason and Mayer (1974a) USA	High/low income	Image measures Choice criteria	Frequency data	A priori
Mason and Mayer (1974b) USA	Types of institution	Image measures Choice criteria	Frequency data	A priori
Reynolds and Wells (1978) USA	Frequent savers	Psychographic data Bank usage	Frequency data	A priori
Riggall (1979) USA	Selection criteria	Choice criteria	Frequency data	Cluster-based
Stanley et al. (1979) USA	High income	Demographic data Socioeconomic data Attitudinal data	Frequency data	A priori
York and Hayes (1982) UK	Working women	Attitudinal data Demographic data	Frequency data	A priori
Burnett and Wilkes (1985) USA	Age	Demographic data Psychographic data Bank usage	Chi-squared and MANOVA of banking attitudes against age	A priori
Stanley et al. (1985) USA	Age	Bank usage Demographic data	Chi-squared	A priori
Taylor and Bergiel (1984) USA	Multiple institution usage	Bank usage Demographic data	t-test, chi-squared	A priori

Table 3. Segmentation research using multivariate analysis.

Research	Segmentation basis	Data used	Method	Type
Arora et al. (1985) USA	Bank vs. savings & loan customers	Choice criteria	Principal components factor analysis	A priori
Awh and Waters (1974) USA	Users and non-users of charge-cards	Socio-economic data Demographic data Attitudinal data	Discriminant analysis	A priori
Fitts and Mason (1977) USA	Users and non-users	Attitudinal data Demographic data Socio-economic data	Multiple regression analysis Canonical correlation analysis	A priori
Kinnaird et al. (1984) USA	Account usage	Benefit measures Psychograph data	Determinant attribute analysis Factor analysis	A priori
Pool (1974) USA	Usage of ATMs	Demographic data Bank usage Attitudinal data	Discriminant analysis	A priori
Anderson, Cox and Fulcher (1976) USA	Selection criteria	Choice criteria Socio-economic data	Determinant attribute analysis K-means clustering	Cluster-based
Burnett and Chonko (1984) USA	Selection criteria	Demographic data Bank usage Socio-economic data	Factor analysis to determine similar usage patterns Chi-squared to test demographic significance	Cluster-based
Calantone and Sawyer (1978) USA	Stability of segments	Attitudinal data Psychographic data	Factor analysis Howard and Harris algorithm (k-means) Clustering	Cluster-based
Clancey and Roberts (1983) USA	Credit card usage	Attitudinal data Bank usage Psychographic data Demographic data	Tested 130 possible segmentation bases for ability to discriminate. Many methods used	Cluster-based & a priori
Fry et al. (1973) USA	Loyalty	Bank usage Socio-economic data Geographic data	Regression analysis	Cluster-based
Jain et al. (1987) USA	Loyalty	Bank usage Attitudinal data	Correlation analysis Multiple regression to test demographic significance Canonical correlation analysis also used	Cluster-based

Table 3. Continued.

Research	Segmentation basis	Data used	Method	Type
Laroche and Taylor (1988) Canada	Selection criteria	Awareness of institutions Bank usage Demographic data	Determinant attribute analysis Factor analysis (principal components)	Cluster-based
Laurent (1979) USA	Perceived image	Attitudinal data Demographic data	Determinant attribute analysis Multi dimensional scaling	Cluster-based
Matthews and West (1986) UK	Attitudes to girobank	Demographic data Attitudinal data Socio-economic data	Factor analysis (principal components) Ward's method clustering	Cluster-based
Morgan (1978) USA	Use of overdrafts	Demographic data Financial data Socio-economic data	K-means clustering	Cluster-based
Moutinho and Meidan (1989) UK	Selection criteria	Attitudinal data Demographic data	Factor analysis	Cluster-based
Reese and Stanton (1984) USA	Selection criteria for black bank customers	Choice criteria Socio-economic data	Determinant attribute analysis Complete linkage cluster analysis	Cluster-based
Robertson and Bellinger (1977) USA	Selection criteria	Financial data Media usage	Factor analysis Ward's method clustering	Cluster-based

segmentation, because the identification of segments requires some measurement of similarity. Because there is no split in the data into dependent and independent variables, clustering techniques are used to identify homogenous segments. Two types of techniques are used in this process. The first are used to generate suitable data for measuring similarities among cases. Popular techniques are factor analysis and determinant attribute analysis. The second set of techniques are used to determine similarity of cases. Techniques used in this sort of research include various cluster analysis techniques, factor analysis, regression analysis and multi-dimensional scaling. The advantages of cluster-based segmentation are in measurability and substantiality, since so long as the appropriate data has been collected, the entire population is represented in the survey and can be compared. A major problem with cluster-based segmentation is indicated by the wide range of techniques that can be used to generate segments. Differences in the assumptions underlying the various techniques used to identify segments means that differences occur in the segments identified. It is difficult therefore to determine whether or not the segments identified are 'natural clusters' and whether they truly identify similar buyer behaviour in financial services. The resulting segments are also likely to be less accessible than those identified by a priori methods purely on the basis of socio-economic or demographic characteristics.

Some research concerned with a priori segmentation has used multivariate techniques, such as discriminant analysis and regression analysis, to test the strength of the relationship between independent and dependent variables. Table 3 shows research which uses the multivariate techniques outlined for segmentation research (see Punj and Stewart (1983) for a discussion of the various clustering techniques mentioned).

A MODEL FOR FIRMS

Examining the research carried out into financial services, it is immediately apparent that the research reported has varied widely in both the chosen methodology and the rigour of the analysis. As the experience of companies in segmentation research grows, poor quality academic research in methodological terms can only serve to distance academics and practitioners. Thus, as the use of segmentation strategies becomes more common, one role of academic research is to offer the practitioners a model for their own studies. The points noted below would, if followed, improve the rigour of segmentation research and therefore improve its usefulness to practitioners:

(1) If segmentation is carried out on an a priori basis, with the prior selection of the dependent variable, then the researcher needs to identify which of the independent variables significantly distinguish between the segments. This can be done using regression of discriminant analysis. A study of this type is reported by Clancey and Roberts (1983). They examined 130 possible segmentation bases for the credit card market, finding 25 of these had a high ability to discriminate. Joseph and Yorke (1990) report part of a study taking this approach, examining 'various segmentation bases and their ability to identify variables which "best" act as discriminators for a product/service' (Joseph and York, 1990, p. 772).

(2) A priori segmentation can be improved by testing alternative dependent variables and segment stability. For instance, Burnett and Wilkes (1985) carried out a priori segmentation using age of customers as the basis for segmentation and also tested the needs of the sample against wealth. They concluded that age was not as good a predictor of financial service needs as wealth. This additional analysis would improve the assessment of segment homogeneity.

(3) Validation of any segmentation is important. Those based on quantitative analysis can be validated by a wide variety of methods. Techniques available include the hold-out method, where part of the sample is used to generate segments and the remainder to validate them by repeat analysis, the Monte Carlo method, where random numbers are used as a validation, and the jack-knife and bootstrap methods where the original sample is reused in validation (Cooil, Winer and Rados, 1987). Validation by hold-out allows some assessment of the accuracy with which characteristics have been ascribed to a priori segments (Wind, 1978, p. 328). Cluster-based segmentation in particular needs careful validation. Cluster analysis can be carried out using a variety of techniques based on different proximity and similarity measures. The divergent assumptions underlying these techniques can lead to wide variations in findings. Cluster analysis validation is usually carried out by comparing

the results of using a variety of techniques on the sample (see Wishart, 1987, pp. 18–20, for a recommended method of validation).

A further point about the published research is that very little consideration is given to the stability of the segments over time (an exception is Calantone and Sawyer, 1978). If choice criteria vary over time then a programme aimed at that segment may be unsuitable; and if demographics or media habits change, then accessibility will be reduced as the programme will be aimed at the wrong customers. Longitudinal studies of segment stability provide a means of tracking the target segment and therefore increase the actionability of the segment.

STRATEGIES FOR FUTURE RESEARCH

Now that market segmentation has become accepted and followed as a strategy within the financial service industry, the need for educational or exemplary research is diminished. The sophistication that is now developing in financial service marketing illustrates this. The financial service organisations now conduct their own research to identify segments and to make such a strategy executable. The key issue for academic marketing researchers is how to take segmentation research forward, rather than repeat analyses which are now commonplace within the companies. Wind (1978) has pointed out the need for academic segmentation research to reflect management's information needs. Having demonstrated the usefulness of segmentation to the companies, academic researchers must now re-examine the practical problems of a segmentation strategy and move on to examine methods of increasing the effectiveness of segmentation. This not only requires the more sophisticated quantitative analysis discussed above but also a consideration of some of the underlying issues.

In past research, if any practical segmentation strategy was proposed then it had usually been wholly shaped by the characteristics of the identified segment. The next stage of segmentation research must be to take a more holistic view of the segmentation process. To do this, market segmentation research must begin to examine possible segmentation strategies in relation to other aspects of the market and the company's position within it. Companies are dealing with a heterogeneous target market within which a target segment might be identified. In attempting to develop optimum segmentation strategies, research should begin to take account not only of the target market but the implications of a company's capabilities and the impact on non-target customers.

Company capability

It is frequently pointed put that the capabilities of a company are a constraint on its choice of strategy (see, for instance, Ansoff, 1984). This is equally true of a segmentation strategy. Once a profile of the possible target segment has been developed it is only useful if it is within the company's capabilities to profit from targeting that segment. An important issue in determining whether a segment is exploitable is the costs of a segmentation strategy. Fortunately the rise in importance of segmentation strategies has come at a time when the information systems of financial service companies are undergoing a major improvement. Companies now have a better idea of which of their products their customers use, and can identify multiple users. They are moving towards a position where they can identify the costs of supplying their products and calculate return made for a given level of activity. Of course, most of the information on costs and profitability is commercially confidential, but researchers can address both the costs of the products required to service a target segment and the likely returns from the given target customer in the model they develop. By gathering data on product usage rates and average balances and premiums, for instance, and including these in the profiles of the segments, researchers can extend the benefits offered to practitioners by providing better information on the substantiality of the segments. Clancey and Roberts (1983) followed this approach in the credit card study discussed earlier, and were therefore able to conclude their assessment of the 'optimal' segmentation with a potential sales and profit analysis for each segment identified.

Given the improved systems for determining costs, it should be noted that there are still many problems with customer databases in financial services. The most obvious one is that the only time detailed information is taken from customers is on first taking out a product. For many customers this was years ago, and the information taken is now useless. The financial services companies now know a good deal about customers' financial habits, but they have very little information about the demographics and attitudes of their customers. Given the interest of banks in particular in selling new services to their existing customer base, the clear identification of segment membership is of major importance. The current strategy is based on selling to warm leads by encouraging customers likely to buy the new service to identify themselves through response coupons, etc., before selling is attempted. If the membership of a segment within the bank's customer base that is most likely to buy, for instance, the bank's new insurance products can be established, then the likely success of such a strategy is increased.

Financial service companies already use geodemographic systems such as FinPin, Acorn and MOSAIC to supplement their existing customer database. This is particularly useful for direct mailing of customers. Recently however new techniques addressing this problem have been developed. One such technique is data fusion (Rothman 1988; Baker et al., 1989). This is a method for statistically joining different sample surveys covering different subject areas with different respondents to produce a complete data set including, for instance, data on exposure to all media, classification data, attitudinal and lifestyle data and product and brand usage data. The cost of gathering such a data set in a single operation would be prohibitive. As Baker et al. point out, 'this is clearly an impossible questionnaire to construct, let alone ask people to answer'. So far, the principal use of data fusion has been to improve measures of advertising effectiveness (Douglas, 1990). Such a technique presents researchers with an opportunity to develop segmentation studies based on a combination of one or more of the major public and commercial databases and a survey of the company's customer base, providing considerably greater detail than could ever be gathered by a survey of the customer base alone. Research of this sort would lead to improved customer profiling and hence greater segment accessibility.

Product positioning

Another aspect of the segmentation process that could be enhanced by research is the implementation of segmentation strategies, how to position products for segments. Kotler (1988, p. 308) defines positioning as 'designing the company's image and value offer so that the segment's customers understand what the company stands for in relation to its competitors'. There are many dimensions to positioning products, and this discussion concentrates on the use of different marketing mixes.

Aaker and Shansby (1982) have provided a guide to positioning products using strategies based on attribute, price/quality, use of application, product user, product class and competitors. Brief consideration of financial service promotion reveals positioning strategies that exemplify all these strategies. Illustrations are given in Table 4. Insurance products in particular are positioned on the basis of attributes, e.g., flexibility, telephone helplines. Many investment and interest-bearing current accounts are positioned on the basis of price and quality in terms of the interest paid, a good case being Girobank's accounts. Standard Life's investment record allows it to position on this basis. The payment option credit cards present are the basis of the usage positioning strategy of both Barclaycard and Access. Coutts is a good example of positioning on the basis of product class. A Coutts account is positioned alongside Porsche cars as an indicator of success and wealth.

Positioning on the basis of the product user is used with lifestyle segmentations, such as that of Midland and also Halifax Card Cash. Positioning by reference to competitors has been used by some of the smaller banks and building societies. Nationwide Anglia positioned Flexaccount by reference to the clearing banks' current accounts and the Co-operative Bank have advertised using the copy 'The Co-operative Bank. Why Bank with one that isn't?'

As Aaker and Shansby point out:

Positioning usually means an overt decision is being made to concentrate on only certain segments. Such an approach requires commitment and discipline because it's not easy to turn your back on potential buyers. Yet, the effect of generating a distinct meaningful position is to focus on the target segments and not be constrained by the reactions of other segments. (Aaker and Shansby, 1982, p. 61)

The need for effective positioning strategies to consider segments in isolation presents a particular problem in traditional branch-delivered financial services. Companies such as Unilever can produce a vast range of products that are marketed as free-standing brands, with a minimal association with the parent company. However, any branch-distributed financial service is inevitably associated with the company, because the branch is the sole

Table 4. Examples of positioning strategies in retail financial services.

Positioning strategy	Example
Attribute	G.A. Direct Line car insurance
	G.R.E. Choices pension
Price/quality	Girobank
	Midland Exchequer Accounts
	Standard Life
Use or application	Barclaycard
	Access
Product user	Halifax Card Cash
	Midland Vector
	Midland Meridian
Product class	Coutts Bank
Competitor	Co-operative Bank
	Nationwide Anglia Flexaccount

outlet for the product. Through this association branch-distributed products will also be associated with each other and cannot be positioned completely independently as Aaker and Shansby suggest. If a company follows a multiple segment strategy, then it will be attempting to position different products for different segments using a wide variety of segmentation variables. All these products will be associated with the company and with each other. There is a danger therefore that the positioning strategy for particular segments will impact detrimentally on other segments. The traditional approach has been to position the company, rather than products.

Many of the recent developments in financial services, such as direct mail, telephone and home banking, have acted to remove this problem. Midland's First Direct telephone banking service is a good example of a product that has been separated from the traditional branch system and been positioned independently of Midland itself. As the technology of financial services and the ability of companies to reach their target market improves, product positioning can only become more important.

Research into positioning in financial services is a natural progression from the segmentation research that has been carried out in the past. There are two aspects of positioning that might be addressed by research: the responsiveness of target segments to different positioning strategies and the impact of any positioning strategy on non-target segments. As this discussion has shown, there have traditionally been difficulties in positioning branch-distributed products for different segments, problems are not widely found in the consumer goods market. As the options available to financial service companies increase, research into targeting markets and position products for them will become a very exciting prospect indeed.

CONCLUSIONS

This article has sought to review research into segmentation in the retail financial services market and offer some suggestions for future areas of research. The adoption of segmentation as a strategy by companies in the industry means that companies are carrying out the kind of segmentation research that was previously the preserve of the academic researcher. Academic research therefore no longer has to be evangelical or educational, and can now serve as a methodological model for practitioners. It has been noted that to do this researchers must take care to validate and test their findings, and to identify clearly the relative strengths of segmentation variables.

To improve the contribution of research for practitioners, a more holistic approach to segmentation research has been suggested. If segmentation research takes more account of the capabilities of companies when identifying segments, then the resulting strategies are likely to be more successful. The two improvements outlined, incorporating the data necessary for profitability analysis into the segmentation profile and improving and combining data from different sources to improve companies' customer information base for segmentation purposes, both address issues currently very important to financial service companies. A further suggestion is to address the issues that follow segment identification by developing research on positioning financial services. It is argued that, by developing in these directions, financial service segmentation research can remain a fertile area for practitioners and researchers alike.

REFERENCES

Aaker, D. A. and Shansby, J. G., 1982, 'Positioning Your Product', *Business Horizons*, May–June pp. 56–62.
Anderson, W. I., Cox, E. P. and Fulcher, D. G., 1976, 'Bank Selection Decisions and Market Segmentation', *Journal of Marketing*, Vol. 40, January, pp. 40–5.
Ansoff, H. I., 1984, *Implanting Strategic Management*, London: Prentice Hall International.
Arbeit, S. and Sawyer, A. G., 1974, 'Applying Psychographic Analysis to a Retail Banking Market', *Magazine of Bank Administration*, Vol. 50, November, pp. 39–45.
Arora, R., Cavusgil, S. T. and Nevin, J. R., 1985, 'Evaluation of Financial Institutions by Bank versus Savings and Loan Customers: An Analysis of Factor Congruency', *International Journal of Bank Marketing*, Vol. 3 No. 3, pp. 47–55.
Awh, R. Y. and Waters, D., 1974, 'A Discriminant Analysis of Economic, Demographic, and Attitudinal Characteristics of Bank Charge-Card Holders: A Case Study', *Journal of Finance*, Vol. 29, pp. 973–980.
Baker, K., Harris, P. and O'Brien, J., 1989, 'Data Fusion: An Appraisal and Experimental Evaluation', *Journal of the Market Research Society*, Vol. 31. No. 2, pp. 153–212.
Brown, M., 1983, 'A Critical Appraisal of the Major Segmentation Procedures', *Admap*, July/August, pp. 386–91.
Burnett, J. J. and Chonko, L. B., 1984, 'A Segmental Approach to Packaging Bank Products', *Journal of Retail Banking*, Spring/Summer.
Burnett, J. J. and Wilkes, R. E., 1985, 'An Appraisal of the Senior Citizens Market Segment', *Journal of Retail Banking* Vol. VII No. 4, Winter, pp. 57–64.
Calantone, R. and Sawyer, A. G., 1978, 'The Stability of Benefit Segments', *Journal of Marketing Research* Vol. XV, pp. 395–404 and pp. 16–19.
Clancey, K. J. and Roberts, M. L., 1983, 'Towards an Optimal Market Target: A Strategy for Market Segmentation', *Journal of Consumer Marketing*, Vol. 1, No. 1, pp. 64–73.
Cooil, B., Winer, R. S. and Rados, D. L., 1987, 'Cross-Validation for Prediction', *Journal of Marketing Research*, Vol. XXIV, August, pp. 271–79.
Douglas, T., 1990, 'Hitting the Sale on the Head?', *Marketing Week*, 1 June, p. 17.
Doyle, P. and Newbould, G., 1975, 'New Marketing Strategies for Building Societies', *Admap*, February.
Evans, R. H. and Beckman, M. D., 1984, 'Psychographic Analysis: An Aid for Bank Management', *Magazine of Bank Administration*, Vol. 50, January, pp. 32–5.
Fitts, R. L. and Mason, J. B., 1977, 'Market Segmentation Research—An Application to Bank Services', *Omega* Vol. 5, No. 2, pp. 207–14.
Gavaghan, K., 1989, 'Banking on Choice', *Meridian Magazine*, Vol. 1, Midland Bank Publication.
Gee, N., 1975, 'Banks Tap the Women's Market', *Public Relations Journal*, Vol. 31, August, pp. 14, 16, 30.
Goodfellow, J. H., 1987, 'Consumer Perceptions and Attitudes Towards Savings and Investments' *International Journal of Bank Marketing*, Vol. 5, No. 3, pp. 32–48.
Green, P. E., 1977, 'A New Approach to Market Segmentation', *Business Horizons*, Vol. 20, pp. 61–73.
Gwin, J. M. and Lindgren, J. H., 1982, 'Bank Market Segmentation: Methods and Strategies', *Journal of Retail Banking*, Vol. IV, No. 4, pp. 8–13.
Hood, J. and Walters, C. G., 1985, 'Banking on Established Customers', *Journal of Retail Banking*, Vol. VII, No. 1, Spring, pp. 35–40.
Jain, A. K., Pinson, C. and Malhotra, N. K., 1987, 'Customer Loyalty as a Construct in the Marketing of Bank Services', *International Journal of Bank Marketing*, Vol. 5, No. 3, pp. 48–72.
Johnson, R. W. and Sullivan, A. C., 1981 'Segmentation of the Customer Loan Market', *Journal of Retail Banking*, September, pp. 1–7.
Joseph, L. and Yorke, D., 1990, 'Full Speed Ahead: Market Segmentation Research in the Personal Financial Services Sector', *Proceedings of the 19th European Marketing Academy Conference*, May, Innsbruck, pp. 769–81.

Kinnaird, D., Shaughnessy, K., Struman, K. D. and Swinyard, W. R., 1984, 'Market Segmentation of Retail Bank Services: A Model for Management', *Journal of Retail Banking*, Fall, pp. 53–63.

Kotler, P. 1988, *Marketing Management: Analysis, Planning, Implementation and Control* (Sixth Edition) New York: Prentice Hall USA.

Langrehr, F. W., 1981, 'Consumer Reactions to NOW Accounts', *Journal of Retail Banking*, December, pp. 7–15.

Laroche, T. and Taylor, T., 1988, 'An Empirical Study of Major Segmentation Issues in Retail Banking', *International Journal of Retail Banking*, Vol. 6, No. 1, pp. 31–8.

Lewis, B., 1982a, 'Students Accounts', *European Journal of Marketing*, Vol. 16, No. 3, pp. 63–72.

Lewis B., 1982b, 'Weekly Cash Paid Workers', *European Journal of Marketing*, Vol. 16, No. 3, pp. 92–101.

Marrs, C. H., 1984, 'Developing a Profitable Programme for the Senior Market', *Journal of Retail Banking* Vol. VI, Nos. 1 & 2, pp. 25–35.

Martenson, R., 1985, 'Customer Choice Criteria in Retail Bank Selection', *International Journal of Bank Marketing*, Vol. 3, No. 2, pp. 64–74.

Mason, J. B. and Mayer, M. L., 1974a, 'Differences Between High and Low Income Savings and Chequing Account Customers', *Bank Administration*, Vol. 50, June, pp. 48–64.

Mason, J. B. and Mayer, M. L., 1974b, 'Analysing Factors That Affect Bank Patronage', *Bank Administration*, Vol. 50, July, pp. 42–4.

Matthews, B. and West, A., 1986, 'Bank of Selection Criteria Reviewed: The Case of the National Giro Bank', *Marketing Education Group Proceedings of 19th Annual Conference*, Plymouth Polytechnic, July, pp. 589–602.

Morgan, F. W., 1978, 'Profitability Market Segmentation: Identifying Heavy Users of Overdraft Services', *Journal of Business Research*, Vol. 6, No. 2, pp. 99–110.

Moutinho, L. and Meidan, A., 1989, 'Bank Customers' Perceptions, Innovations and New Technology', *International Journal of Bank Marketing*, Vol. 7, No. 2, pp. 22–7.

Pool, A. A., 1974, 'Application of Discriminant Analysis in Formation of Promotional Strategy for Cash Dispensing Machines', *Journal of Bank Research*, Spring, pp. 13–19.

Punj, G. and Stewart, D. W., 1983, 'Cluster Analysis in Marketing Research: Review and Suggestions for Application', *Journal of Market Research*, Vol. XX, May.

Reese, R. M. and Stanton, W. W., 1984 'Further Segmenting a Minority Banks Customer Set', *Journal of Retail Banking*, Vol. VI. No. 4, Winter pp. 297–301.

Reynolds, F. D. and Wells, W. P., 1978, 'Lifestyle Analysis: A Dimension for Future-Oriented Bank Research', *Journal of Bank Research*, Autumn, pp. 181–5.

Riggall, J., 1979, 'What Counts with Bank Customers', *A.B.A. Banking Journal*, May, pp. 117–18.

Robertson, D. H. and Bellinger, D. N., 1972, 'Identifying Bank Market Segments', *Journal of Bank Research*, Vol. 7, pp. 276–83.

Rothman, K., 1988, 'Data Fusion and Single Source Surveys', *Admap*, July–August, pp. 39–41.

Smith, W. R., 1956, 'Product Differentiation and Market Segmentation as Alternative Marketing Strategies', *Journal of Marketing*, July, pp. 3–8.

Stanley, T. J., Berry, L. L, and Danko, W. D., 1979, 'Personal Service Versus Convenience: Perceptions of High Income Customers', *Journal of Retail Banking*, June, pp. 54–61.

Stanley, T. O., Ford, J. K. and Richards, S. J., 1985, 'Segmentation of Bank Customer by Age', *International Journal of Bank Marketing*, Vol. 3, No. 3, pp. 56–63.

Taylor, R. D. and Bergiel, B. J., 1984, 'Financial Services—Implications for Market Segmentation', *Mississippi Business Review*, XLVI No. 5, November, pp. 3–7.

Wills, G., 1985, 'Dividing and Conquering; Strategies for Segmentation', *International Journal of Bank Marketing*, Vol. 3, No. 4.

Wind, Y., 1978, 'Issues and Advances in Segmentation Research', *Journal of Marketing Research*, XV August, pp. 317–37.

Wishart, D., 1987, *Clustan User Manual* (Fourth Edition), St. Andrews: Computing Laboratory, University of St. Andrews.

Yorke, D. A., 1982, 'Definition of Market Segments for Banking Services', *European Journal of Marketing*, Vol. 16, No. 3, pp. 14–22.

Yorke, D. A. and Hayes, A., 1982, 'Working Females as a Market Segment', *European Journal of Marketing*, Vol. 16, No. 3, pp. 83–91.

7

The Youth Market for Financial Services

Barbara R. Lewis and Graham H. Bingham

INTRODUCTION

In recent years financial institutions have become increasingly sophisticated in their marketing planning, in particular with respect to market segmentation and targeting. Young people—students, school-leavers, etc.—have been the focus of research attention and resultant marketing activities; and their financial service needs, attitudes and behaviour change as a consequence of continuing environmental developments. The focus of this article is empirical findings from a recent survey among a youth-market sample, together with some implications for the marketing strategies of banks and building societies.

The environment

Environmental influences are well known to both marketing researchers and practitioners, and relate to demographic, legal and economic, social and cultural, and technological trends. The youth market is variously defined with respect to age; e.g. 15–24 year olds, 9.26 m in 1986—16.3 per cent of the UK population. This percentage is decreasing to approximately 14.2 per cent in 1991 and 11.9 per cent in the year 2000, although it will rise again thereafter. Thus the target group is at present becoming smaller, with an increasing proportion of students (between 1970 and 1985 the numbers in colleges of further education, universities, and polytechnics increased by 87 per cent for women and 33 per cent for men) who have delayed earning power and different financial service needs. Of the total 60 per cent are in employment, 21 per cent are students and 11 per cent are out of employment. When one considers the 'worth' of the youth market to financial service institutions, their disposable income is seen to be low (relative to adults) but their discretionary income and purchasing power are high: banks and building societies see immediate 'sales benefits' to be gained from attracting young people as customers and 'future revenues' which will be generated from loyal customers.

Other relevant environmental trends are: legal—the advent of the Building Societies Act and the Financial Services Act and consequent increasing competition for student and young persons' accounts; technological—relating to operations management, customer services and product development (e.g. ATMs, EFTPoS, home banking); and social and cultural—namely changing attitudes and behaviour across the whole population with regard to acceptance of credit, share ownership, etc.

Segmentation

Within their corporate and marketing strategies, the banks and, more recently, the building societies in the UK have segmented their markets and within the personal-account sector have considered various bases: geographic; demographic; psycographic to include life styles, personality and social class; and behavioural—benefits sought, usage patterns, etc. (see, for example, Reidenbach and Pitts, 1986).

With regard to the youth market, the banks and building societies target young people to 'catch them early' in the belief that their switching behaviour is limited, and that they will remain loyal and purchase additional financial services through their life cycle, i.e. because of their potential as future customers. Even if their long-term potential is in question, one can expect to cross-sell other products (e.g. mortgages, insurance services, personal loans) within a few years. Furthermore, in trying to reach the youth market one can look to Schiele's (1974) 'pond and stream' analogy, where adults would comprise a 'big pond'—a static marketplace where marketers go fishing for sales. In contrast, young customers are seen to be moving downstream from childhood into the big pond and the small moving stream is dynamic. Schiele suggests that fishing the stream requires a different approach from fishing the pond, e.g. one could secure an efficient catching device such as a new across a narrow point.

Research pertaining to the beliefs, attitudes and behaviour of the youth market focuses on a number of issues. In particular, Mintel (1988) provides evidence of a youth market, the members of which emphasise the importance of material possessions, are more concerned with consumption than saving, and for whom money is important for personal success. This is partly influenced by later marriage and the extension of a 'single-life cycle' with spending priorities which are fashion- and leisure-orientated. However, at the same time, young people want to be happy, fulfilled and healthy; they place importance on family relationships; they want to be seen as thoughtful, sensitive, caring and responsible; and they want to be seen as model citizens.

Issues in reaching the youth market are also highlighted by Mintel (1988). For example, they consider desirable 'appeals and images' and appropriate media, i.e. approaches which are typified in the various combinations of advertising and promotion used in recent years by both banks and building societies—to include specialised services, incentives and inducements.

Following consideration of previous research, present knowledge of the youth market and the marketing activities of financial service institutions designed to target young people, a number of research objectives were developed, namely to determine:

- needs, attitudes and behaviours of the youth market with respect to financial services and banks/building societies
- elements of satisfaction/dissatisfaction with experience of financial services
- the extent of loyalty towards financial institutions
- possible differences in needs, attitudes and behaviour between segments of the youth market, i.e. is the youth market homogeneous or not?

RESEARCH METHODS

Initially, three focus-group interviews were held to provide information with regard to young people's attitudes towards, beliefs about, and behaviours concerning financial service institutions, to include services they would need now and in the future (see Tynan and Drayton(1988) for a discussion of focus-group research methods and Bingham (1989) for the detailed findings). One group comprised seven students (aged 18–22 years) and the others ten and nine young people who were working (ages 16–20 years); all had an account at a bank or building society.

They talked at length about their needs, attitudes and behaviour, and a host of ideas emerged for incorporation into a structured, self-completion, survey questionnaire. The questionnaire itself moved through a number of pilot versions, tested with students and young people at school/college and working. In so doing, contacts were set up with various schools and colleges. The final questionnaire included 45 questions (210 variables for analysis).

The sample

At the time of the research the youth market was estimated to total approximately 6.9 m (Office of Population Census and Surveys, 1987), comprising those at school, 0.64 m (9.2 per cent); in further education, 0.47 m (6.8 per cent); in higher education—university or polytechnic, 0.52 m (7.5 per cent); working 4.45 m (64.2 per cent); and unemployed, 0.85 m (12.3 per cent).

Following consideration of various sampling methods to facilitate a self-completion questionnaire survey, co-operation was secured from a number of schools and academic institutions (e.g. colleges of higher/further education, universities and polytechnics) including those providing courses for Government Youth Training Scheme (YTS) participants and young workers on day-release. A total of 800 questionnaires was distributed in March 1989 through schools and colleges in the Greater Manchester area, to be returned, anonymously, to the researchers in reply-paid envelopes. Four-hundred and sixty-nine completed questionnaires were returned, a response rate of 58 per cent—of which 57 per cent were from males and 43 per cent from females.

The age distribution of respondents was narrower than one would have liked (49 per cent were aged 16–17 years; 28 per cent were 18–19 years; and 23 per cent were 20–24 years), but even so when the data were analysed, using MINITAB, a number of differences in response between age groups were evident.

Differences were also found depending on the young person's status which comprised: 29 per cent who were at school/sixth form; 16 per cent in a college of further education; 22 per cent at university/polytechnic; 18 per cent working and 14 per cent on a YTS scheme. Unfortunately, because of the sampling method chosen, young unemployed people were not included in the survey. Their responses most likely would have differed from their working counterparts and this omission may be remedied in any subsequent research among the youth market.

Other demographic data collected related to social class and accommodation. The sample was over-represented with respect to AB respondents—not unexpectedly, owing to the inclusion of a university/polytechnic group and the exclusion of unemployed youngsters. Further, 72 per cent lived in a parental home, 8 per cent in rented accommodation and 17 per cent in a student hall of residence. Only two respondents owned property and were, therefore, recipients of a mortgage.

Of the 152 working respondents (to include those on YTS schemes), 40 per cent were paid weekly in cash, providing evidence of the continuing widespread existence of this method of payment in the UK in contrast with most other European countries, and the consequent low need for current accounts at banks and building societies. A further 56 per cent of this group had their earnings paid directly into an account (29 per cent weekly and 27 per cent monthly): the need for a financial institution so as to gain access to their earnings was an important reason for opening a bank or building society account for a number of these people, and in some cases employers had exercised influence in the choice of bank/building society. The remaining 4 per cent of respondents were paid by cheque.

PRESENT ACCOUNT OWNERSHIP

An initial focus of questioning was present account ownership. The respondents had various combinations of deposit/savings, current and cashcard (no cheque-book) accounts at both banks and building societies (see Table 1).

Eighty-five per cent of respondents had some form of bank account, including 16 per cent who had only a deposit/savings account. So 69 per cent had a bank 'current' account, comprising 52 per cent with a traditional current account and 20 per cent with a cashcard account (3 per cent had both): cashcard accounts were established as recently as 1985 and are already successful in the youth market. In addition, 59 per cent had a building society account, including 39 per cent who had only a deposit/savings account: 4 per cent had a building society current account and 10 per cent a cashcard account—evidence that the building societies are starting to penetrate the youth market with new services/types of account.

Overall, 37 per cent of respondents had a deposit/savings account with a bank (close to the population norm) and 43 per cent with a building society. This latter percentage would be expected to rise, as many people see ownership of such an account as a preliminary step to obtaining a mortgage.

Consideration of the different age groups showed some variation in account ownership. Among the 16–27 year olds, 76 per cent had a bank account, including 52 per cent with a current or cashcard account. They had more primarily cashcard accounts, which are targeted at them, with no cheque-book. It is consequently difficult for banks to cross-sell other financial services to these people if they can and do make most of their deposits and

Table 1. Account ownership.

	Bank (%)	Building society (%)
Any account	85	59
Deposit only	16	39
Current account	52	4
Cashcard account	20	10
Deposit	37	43

withdrawals without entering a branch, a problem that is increasingly relevant for both banks and building societies. Among the 18–19 year olds, 91 per cent had a bank account (83 per cent a current or cashcard account); and, in the 20–24 years group, 95 per cent had a bank account (85 per cent being current or cashcard). Once over 18 year, young people can legally use a cheque guarantee card and, therefore, use of a current account and cheque-book would be expected to be widespread. The over-18s had few deposit/savings accounts, especially among students who tend *not* to save.

Split banking

An interesting research finding was that a high percentage of young people (22 per cent) had an account with more than one *bank*. The main reasons were several: some respondents mentioned locational convenience to home/work/college, the importance of which can never be underestimated, and which is also a factor in bank-switching behaviour (see later). Other respondents referred to the greater choice of services offered, more cash points, and the availability of more money—some university students had accounts at more than one bank to take advantage of free overdraft facilities: one wonders to what extent these people may be shopping around for the 'best' service. Another group mentioned free gifts, although these are not necessarily important to the youth market in general (see later).

These findings have implications for banks who have invested heavily in free gifts and incentives to attract young customers in the belief that they will remain loyal to one bank and purchase additional financial services during their life cycle. Free gifts may not be the best means of attracting customers, and one can raise the question whether or not banks should offer loyalty bonuses/gifts to young people in order to retain their accounts and business. Furthermore, the need for personal selling and building of long-term relationships will be greater with customers who use more than one institution, in particular when one bank is used for saving and another for a current account.

OPENING THE ACCOUNT

The next section of questioning concerned the opening of the respondent's main account, i.e. the one used most often, which involved a mixture of current, cashcard and deposit/savings accounts at banks, building societies and, in a handful of cases, post office savings accounts. Nineteen per cent of accounts had been opened by the time the respondents were 12 years old, and a further 23 per cent between 13 and 15 years—which highlights the potential benefits of attracting children's accounts, as many of them are used as the main account when the child becomes an adult.

The main reasons for opening an account related to: *saving* pocket-money, gifts, earnings from part-time or holiday jobs (usually school/sixth formers); *cashing* students' grant cheques; *cashing* work cheques; and having work cheques paid in. So the benefits sought from an account vary with the status of the young person, which might well be better emphasised in marketing communications.

Parents had some involvement in the opening of one-third of the accounts and, when asked to rate the importance of a number of influences on the choice of a bank or building society, respondents scored location (to home and work) and cashpoint availability—i.e. convenience—most highly, as shown in previous studies among both students and adults. Other important influences were the services offered, free banking, reputation and image, parental influence, and free overdrafts. The least important influences were advertising and free gifts.

In a subsequent question, respondents were asked about the relative influence of five factors in the choice of a new current account/bank. Overall, interest on account was ranked highest followed in order by free banking, cheque-books, free overdrafts and free gifts—seen to be relatively unimportant for all respondent groups.

Differences between respondent groups showed that university/polytechnic students attached less importance than others to interest on account, and more importance to free banking—no doubt as their account balances are typically low. Overall, the desire for free banking, interest on account and cheque-books varied between status/age groups, which has implications for the financial service packages offered to segments of the youth market: banks and building societies do need to consider the changing needs within the youth market.

Free gifts

The attractiveness of free gifts was pursued in a following question, with a monetary gift being seen as more attractive to all respondents than shop discounts, record vouchers, filo-fax, coach card, calculator or stationery (in order of preference). Further analysis showed that the attractiveness of various gifts was not homogeneous: coach cards were more appreciated by university/polytechnic students—as one would expect; working/YTS respondents are more attracted than others by shop discounts; college students liked free stationery; and the filo-fax appealed to college students and YTS trainees (but *not* to university/polytechnic students)—do they 'aspire to the messages' surrounding a filo-fax?

One may suggest that, because of the relatively low influence of free gifts in the buyer decision-making process, for the banks and building societies to continue to offer them rather than interest or free banking may be a misallocation of resources. However, this promotional activity will no doubt continue, but the financial institutions concerned need either to target their gifts to sections within the youth market, or maybe just to offer cash incentives.

Hypothetical banks

Promotional issues were the focus of one more question which was focused on account opening. The respondents were presented with the offering of five hypothetical banks (see Table 2) and asked which they would prefer if choosing a new bank. This method of questioning goes some way towards eliminating socially conforming answers with respect to the relative importance of promotions.

The most preferred bank was C, followed by A, D, B, E. Bank C was seen to be attractive because it had all the offerings other than a free gift. Bank A scored well because of the free banking and interest on the current account. Bank D was rated less highly because there was no interest on the account. Bank B suffered because of lack of a cheque-book. Bank E fared badly owing to the inclusion of bank charges—so it would appear that the youth

Table 2. The offerings from five hypothetical banks.

	Bank A	Bank B	Bank C	Bank D	Bank E
Free banking	Yes	Yes	Yes	Yes	Costs £30 per year
Interest on current account	3%	5%	4%	No	5%
Free gift	£15	£10	No	£20	£20
Interest-free overdraft	No	£100	£150	£200	£200
Cheque-book	Yes	No	Yes	Yes	Yes
Cashpoint card	Yes	Yes	Yes	Yes	Yes
Overall ranking	2	4	1	3	5

market would *not* prefer accounts that charge a monthly fee. It is doubtful whether or not the respondents ever calculate the costs and benefits of interest *vis-à-vis* charges: however, what is important is their perception of a 'good deal' from their bank or building society.

Analysis of respondent groups showed that school children/sixth formers preferred Bank B (to A, D, E) without a cheque guarantee card they lack the need for a cheque-book, and preferred Bank E to Bank D—they consider interest to be more important than free banking (as a result of fewer transactions?). Those in work/YTS trainees ranked Bank A second, a choice attributable to the interest, which is more important to them than a free overdraft. Once again, students appeared to have different priorities: students in both further and higher education ranked Bank D second, influenced by the combination of a £200 free overdraft and a large free gift, and now less bothered by lack of interest on a current account.

Overall, the research findings indicated that free banking interest on accounts and a cheque-book are more important than free overdrafts and free gifts when choosing a new current account. But also that it is the complete service package that is chosen, i.e. a service mix that should be tailored to the needs of each group within the youth market. Banks and building societies cannot simply offer one promotional item and hope to attract the entire youth market.

FINANCIAL SERVICES USED

Respondents were asked about the importance of a number of financial services, using a four-point scale from 'very important' to 'not at all important'. The basic services of current account, deposit account, cheque-book and cheque guarantee card, and cashpoint card were all felt to be very important, followed by credit cards. Limited importance was given to loans, overdrafts and mortgages—a *future* need. Retailer cards were, perhaps surprisingly, seen *not* to be important.

They were then presented with a list of 21 financial services and they indicated their use of them at both banks and building societies. Sixty-four per cent had at least one current account, 53 per cent used a cheque-book and 66 per cent had at least one cashpoint card. Fifty-five per cent had at least one deposit account and a further 19 per cent used a savings scheme(s)—which could indicate a need for investments with a higher return than would normally be received, but at the same time 'tying up' funds—this implies that a proportion of the youth market is willing to undertake longer-term investments.

Credit cards were used by only 17 per cent of respondents but a higher proportion of those who were eligible for one, and standing orders by 13 per cent. Four per cent had a loan and 14 per cent an overdraft (i.e. evidence of dissaving) and two people had a mortgage. Foreign exchange and traveller's cheques had been used by 28 per cent.

The services which were, essentially, *not* used by the youth market were found to be Euro-cards, stockbroking and unit trusts, home banking (limited trials only), pensions, insurances, and debit cards. When the characteristics of debit cards were described in the questionnaire 63 per cent of respondents stated that they would use this in the future, 18 per cent were unsure and 19 per cent replied that they would not use the service if it was made available to them. This is certainly a potentially attractive product for those under 18 years who cannot have a cheque guarantee card.

With regard to insurance products, for possessions, life and holidays, the banks and building societies have yet to make any progress within the youth market and indeed in the focus-group discussions participants felt they would probably go to a specialist insurance service institution.

When asked specifically where they would go first for various insurance products, mortgages and pensions, the main responses were

- Travel insurance: travel agent (68 per cent), insurance company (26 per cent) bank/building society (5 per cent).
- Car insurance: insurance company (95 per cent), bank/building society (4 per cent).
- Mortgage: bank (25 per cent), building society (74 per cent).

Overall, the banks were found to be dominant in supplying financial services to the youth market, although 59 per cent of respondents did have some form of building society account. Building societies do not appear, as yet, to be cross-selling services to the youth market—only partially explained by the number of 16–17 year olds with savings accounts who have not yet had the need or opportunity to use a wide range of financial services. However, even the banks would appear to have a considerable way to go to communicate to the youth market that they provide a wide range of financial services.

Attitudes to borrowing

Respondents were asking about preferred ways of paying for a variety of items from fast food, drinks, records, televisions, mail-order items, to cars, holidays, and for rent/mortgages. These were predominantly cash for low-cost items and also for some expensive items. One-third would be willing to use a credit card for television and holidays, although only 17 per cent had, as yet got one.

When asked about attitudes towards overdrafts, 212 (45 per cent) felt that overdrafts are acceptable in some cases; 119 (25 per cent) that they are a necessary service for young people, and 72 (15 per cent) that overdrafts provide an indication of good forward planning. However, 109 (23 per cent) felt that overdrafts were the result of bad financial management. Overall, there was an acceptance by the majority of the need for overdrafts but until now only 14 per cent had used one.

When questioned about present willingness to obtain a loan to purchase certain items, 45 per cent said they definitely or probably would get a loan to buy a car (higher among those at work than the student groups); other popular items were holidays, televisions, stereo systems, computers and furniture. However, there was some evidence of negative attitudes towards advertising of credit. Fifty per cent of respondents felt that banks and building societies should not promote loans and overdrafts to young people; 25 per cent were unsure and only 25 per cent felt that loans and overdrafts should be advertised.

So one may conclude that, whilst accepting the need for such services, the youth market has a great deal of opposition to financial institutions tempting young people to use them: indeed, during the group discussions some respondents felt that it was irresponsible of the banks to advertise overdrafts as a good thing and perhaps to induce mismanagement. Hence the banks and building societies need to tread cautiously when promoting loans and overdrafts.

Finally, in this section, some questions on money management were included. Sixty-one per cent of respondents believed they managed their money very well or well, 29 per cent thought they were fair managers, with only 11 per cent feeling they were poor or very poor at handling their money. Further, 73 per cent stated that they did not need advice on how to manage their money, i.e. they wished to be financially independent, 14 per cent said that they did need advice and 14 per cent did not know. From the group discussions it would appear that the student or young people's counsellors provided by some banks were seen simply as a first port of call if a problem arises; they were *not* used to provide financial advice.

PERCEPTIONS OF STAFF, SERVICE AND IMAGE

In the penultimate section of the questionnaire, the respondents were requested to indicate the direction and intensity of their opinions of staff, service and image as measured by a list of bipolar scales, which were scored from +2, +1, 0 to −1, −2. Their mean responses are shown in Figures 1, 2 and 3.

Perceptions of staff

Respondents had a very favourable impression of staff at their financial institution and staff qualities tended to be rated more highly than the level of service and overall image of bank or building society. It would seem that the efforts of financial institutions, through training and efforts of financial institutions, through training and customer care programmes, to provide competent staff, and to improve service levels, are being successful. Staff were seen to be competent, helpful, well-mannered and friendly. The lowest scores indicated a perception that staff are not so caring as they could be and do not always offer a personal service, which is counter to the image offered in some financial services advertising. Thus there would seem to be room for improvement with regard to these staff qualities. In addition, the bank's staff tended to be rated less highly than those of building societies, on most dimensions.

Perceptions of service

Service factors, other than staff qualities, were generally seen in a favourable light with the exception of speed of service; a number of respondents had perceptions of slow service and

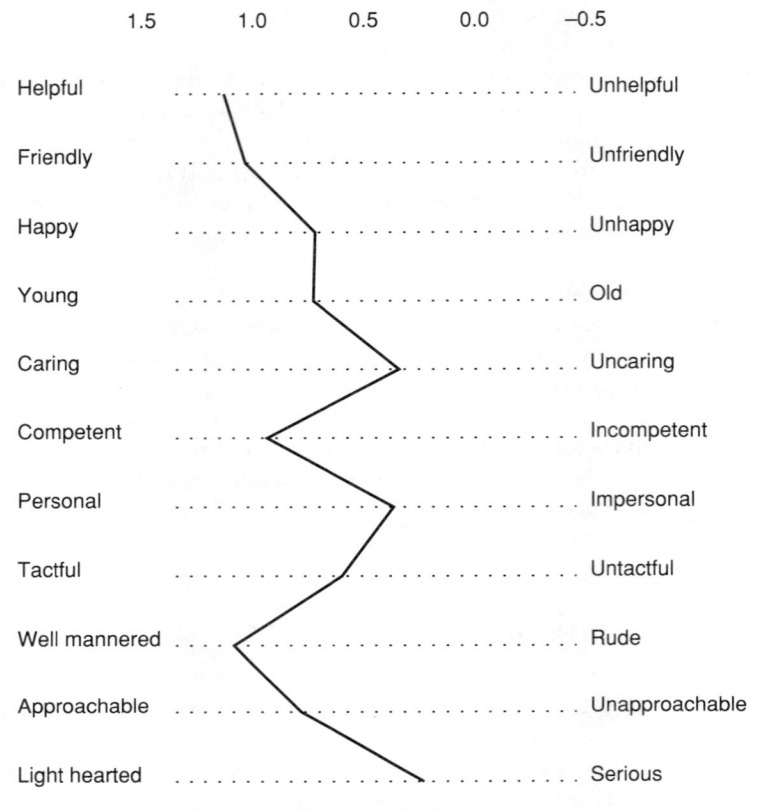

	1.5	1.0	0.5	0.0	−0.5	
Helpful						Unhelpful
Friendly						Unfriendly
Happy						Unhappy
Young						Old
Caring						Uncaring
Competent						Incompetent
Personal						Impersonal
Tactful						Untactful
Well mannered						Rude
Approachable						Unapproachable
Light hearted						Serious

Figure 1. Perceptions of staff (mean scores).

long queues—which was stated as a cause of dissatisfaction and possible switching. The banks and building societies scored most highly with regard to availability, accessibility, and convenience factors—all important in the choice of a financial institution.

With regard to communication of services (e.g. the new interest-bearing accounts) it may be argued that there is scope for improvement; if young people are fully informed about the services on offer, the amount of split banking might be reducible. A problem here is that in the group discussions a dislike for reading information leaflets and booklets provided by banks/building societies was indicated; can the organisations find more novel ways to communicate the services they offer?

Image of financial institutions

The image of the banks and building societies was fairly good, with respondents seeing them as clean, warm and bright. However, they were also seen to be uninteresting organisations and perhaps—not surprisingly—very similar, highlighting a perceived lack of differentiation between financial service organisations.

Building societies' staff, service and image were rated more highly than the banks ($p < 0.05$), a finding which poses a problem for the banks if they are to remain a dominant force in the youth market. For example, building societies were seen to be more convenient

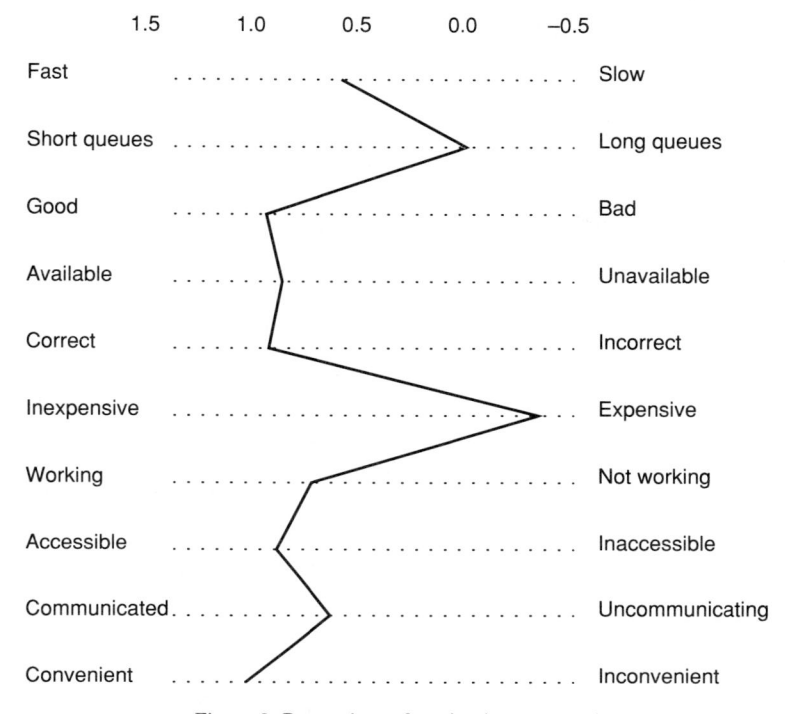

```
              1.5      1.0      0.5      0.0     −0.5
Fast                                                    Slow
Short queues                                            Long queues
Good                                                    Bad
Available                                               Unavailable
Correct                                                 Incorrect
Inexpensive                                             Expensive
Working                                                 Not working
Accessible                                              Inaccessible
Communicated                                            Uncommunicating
Convenient                                              Inconvenient
```

Figure 2. Perceptions of service (mean scores).

despite having fewer branches—probably owing to a combination of opening hours and their ATM facilitates.

SATISFACTIONS AND DISSATISFACTIONS

A final set of questions concerned satisfactions, dissatisfactions and switching behaviour. Seventy per cent of respondents strongly agreed or agreed with the statement 'the service offered by my bank/building society meets my current needs', 24 per cent neither agreed nor disagreed and only 6 per cent disagreed. Even so, a number of dissatisfactions were expressed, mainly relating to convenience and service levels. Twenty-two per cent of all respondents referred to queuing and 20 per cent to cashpoints running out of money. Other problems were charges (for 11 per cent), errors (9 per cent) and lack of information about new services (9 per cent). Dissatisfied customers expressed a high expectation of changing bank or building society, but those who were very satisfied were *not* likely to consider a change ($p < 0.01$)—as one would expect.

Switching Behaviour

Twenty-eight per cent (131 people) had already changed a bank or building society. University/polytechnic students had the greatest tendency to switch (36 per cent of them—and a higher percentage than found by Brockmann-Smith, 1979), which poses a

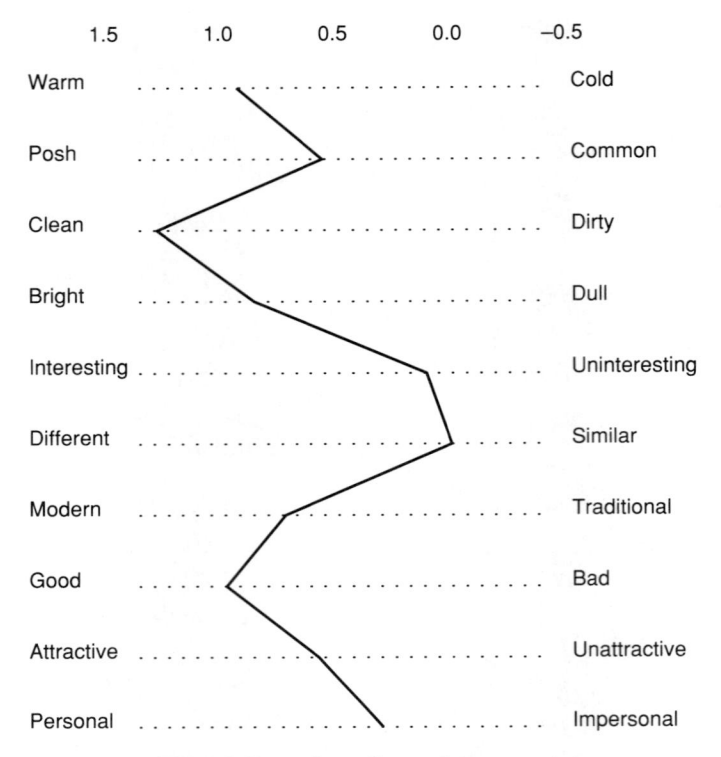

Figure 3. Perceptions of image (mean scores).

dilemma for financial institutions as this group is potentially a very profitable segment after they graduate and start work. However, it could be argued that young people are not locked into a particular institution until they start work.

The main reason for switching financial institution (see Table 3) was dissatisfaction with the service provided, and so it would appear that the banks/building societies are not meeting the demands of a section of the youth market. However, great emphasis has been placed on the service provided in the respondents' choice of financial institution and it

Table 3. Main reasons for switching bank/building society.

	%
Unhappy with service	26
Inconvenience of location	14
Moved to a different area	10
To get interest on account	9
Errors in service	8
Free banking	7
Free/larger overdraft	8
Refusal of a service	6
To get a free gift	6
Other	7

could be argued that young people today expect higher levels of service than their predecessors. What is evident is that young people will change their bank or building society if they are not satisfied with the service they receive.

Other reasons for switching behaviour were convenience-related factors, the desire for account interest, free banking and overdrafts, and free gifts. The increased importance of account interest in both initial choice of bank and as an influence in the decision to change institutions (compared with the previous findings of Brockmann-Smith 1979) could well be due to the recent legislative changes—as a consequence of which both banks and building societies offer interest-bearing accounts. The provision of current-account interest by some institutions may well have increased awareness of it and promoted the demand for it among a large section of the youth market, and so those institutions which have been slow to follow this trend may, as a result, have lost some accounts.

When respondents were asked it they were likely to change their bank or building society in the next five years, 32 per cent indicated that they definitely or probably will, and 37 per cent probably or definitely not: 31 per cent were uncertain. Past switchers were more likely ($p < 0.05$) to indicate possible changes (40 per cent of them) than those who had not changed so far: and 38 per cent of university/polytechnic students said they were likely to switch—higher than percentages reported by Brockmann-Smith, 1979). The most popular anticipated reasons put forward for possibly changing financial institutions were: to get interest on a current account (20 per cent), dissatisfaction with present bank/building society (19 per cent), move to a different area (17 per cent), change of job (16 per cent), to get a free overdraft (16 per cent) or to get a free gift (12 per cent).

These research findings lead one to suggest that banks and building societies cannot assume that young people will become loyal customers and that *some* will switch financial institutions whenever they feel there is a 'better offer' elsewhere. Such a group would be more likely to respond to promotional offers which the banks/building societies are using to attract new customers. These efforts will be wasted if young people do not remain loyal. A major challenge for the future is to try to retain existing youth-market customers as they enter more profitable stages in their life cycle.

CONCLUSIONS

The youth market for financial services is typified by increasing competition among the banks and building societies for a currently declining customer group who are becoming more aware, discerning and adaptable to change; this impacts on their needs, attitudes and behaviour with respect to financial services and institutions.

Almost all the survey respondents had at least one bank or building society account. Their reasons for opening accounts resulted from the benefits sought and the source of their income, and the influences on their choice of financial institution were dominated by locational convenience factors and the range of services produced, parental influence was found to be less than in early research among young people—a sign of independence and interest on accounts, free banking and overdrafts were more important than free gifts.

Usage of financial services was primarily related to basic services and accounts with limited use, as yet, of saving schemes and credit cards, and little use of loans and overdrafts and insurance services. There was some evidence of a cash-orientation, although a majority accepted the need for overdrafts and a willingness to obtain loans, but evidence of negative attitudes towards advertising of loans and overdrafts, i.e. young people accept the need for such services but oppose the idea of financial institutions tempting them to use credit. Perhaps the banks and building societies should tread more cautiously in this area. Furthermore, students' and young people's counsellors were used for basic problem solving rather than—as intended—a source of 'financial advice'.

In addition, the research findings indicate that the youth market is not homogeneous with respect to needs and behaviour. A number of differences emerged between age and status (at school, at work, or student) groups with respect to account ownership, services used, and value of promotional gifts and inducements. For example, 16–17-year-olds were the main recipients of cashcard accounts (no cheque-book) and their contact with the bank/building society was only really via the ATM which eliminates possibilities for cross-selling opportunities within the branch. For the 18+ year-olds an organisation could respond to heterogeneity in the market by providing, for example, one current account with low/no interest but attached favourable overdraft terms (for university/polytechnic students), and another account with high interest but no special overdraft facilities (for those in well paid employment).

The youth market appears to have generally very favourable perceptions of the staff in banks and building societies, but with room for improvement with respect to being 'caring' and offering 'personalised' service. Levels of service and overall image were not quite so high, with problem areas being queues/slow service and communication of services. In terms of satisfaction, the majority of respondents felt that their banks and building societies were meeting their needs, but a number were dissatisfied with convenience and service levels—and more than one in five had already switched from one financial service organisation to another. It would seem that expectations of service are very high and young people will switch financial service providers if they are not happy.

The financial awareness, knowledge and independence of young people were contributory factors to the extent of 'split banking'; one in five of the respondents had accounts at more than one bank, having been partially attracted by promotional activities including free gifts. The extent of split banking and bank switching among the youth market must provide some cause for concern for financial service organisations. They cannot assume that young customers will remain loyal and purchase additional services throughout their life cycle. The need for personal selling and building of long-term relationships within the youth market would seem to be high; should free gifts and bonus incentives be considered as rewards for customer loyalty and a means of customer retention rather than as a (partially unsuccessful) means to attract customers?

To conclude, it is possible to return to the pond and stream analogy (Schiele, 1974) which suggests that a 'net' approach should be used to 'catch' the youth market as they drift downstream from adolescence to adulthood. The research findings indicate that this is a simplification of reality and that a number of interrelated streams exist before young people reach the 'pond of adulthood', at which they are likely to be 'locked into' a financial service organisation. A variety of catching devices is needed in the various streams, depending on young people's needs and attitudes. Furthermore, the extent of split banking and institutional switching implies that no 'net' is perfect—and that a number of young people, depending on their age and status, and subsequent needs, will drift from one stream to another.

Furthermore, banks and building societies need to consider the costs and benefits of attracting young customers and to try to pinpoint the stage when a customer may be expected to become loyal, i.e. where the net should be cast. Typically, the cost of retaining a customer is less than that of attracting new business from other institutions. The future market shares of banks and building societies will depend on their ability to attract and retain the youth market. However, this market is not homogeneous with respect to needs, attitudes, and behaviour regarding financial services, and so different service mixes need to be developed to satisfy the subsegments.

REFERENCES

Bingham, G. H. (1989), *An Investigation of the Needs, Attitudes and Behaviour of the Youth Market, with respect to Financial Services*, unpublished Dissertation, Manchester School of Management, UMIST.
Brockmann-Smith, M. B. (1979), *Bank Marketing to Students*, unpublished Dissertation, Manchester School of Management, UMIST.
Mintel (1988), *Youth Lifestyles*, Special Report, Mintel Publications, London.
Office of Population Census and Surveys (1987), OPCS, St Catherine's House, 10 Kingsway, London WC2B 6JB.
Reidenbach, R. E. and Pitts, R. E. (1986), *Bank Marketing: A Guide to Strategic Planning*, Prentice-Hall, Englewood Cliffs, NJ.
Schiele, G. W. (1974), 'How to Reach the Young Customer' *Harvard Business Review*, Vol. 52, March–April, pp. 77–86.
Tynan, A. C. and Drayton, J. L. (1988), 'Conducting Focus Groups—A Guide for First-time Users', *Marketing Intelligence & Planning*, Vol. 6 No. 1, pp. 5–9.

8

Mapping Customer Segments for Personal Financial Services

Tina S. Harrison

INTRODUCTION

The financial services industry has undergone dramatic changes in the last decade altering both the structure of the industry and the way in which it operates. Deregulation in the 1980s with the introduction of the Building Societies Act (Brooks, 1989) has enabled building societies to operate more freely. They are now able to compete directly with the banks for the same customers. Consequently, the traditional domains of the banks and the building societies are now being eroded. The sector which is now emerging is one of financial services.

As a result of the relaxation of legal restriction, this sector has experienced product proliferation. The number and range of products on offer has increased greatly as financial institutions have aggressively attacked all segments of the market. Marketing has begun to increase in importance, although the urgency to adopt marketing concepts and strategies has not been apparent since market opportunities have been favourable.

The 1990s, however, have brought about a very different picture. Financial institutions are now facing rising costs, reduced consumer spending, market saturation, increased competition and the recession. Profit margins are being squeezed and financial institutions are being forced to rethink their marketing strategies in an attempt to maintain a competitive edge. In contrast to the expansion and diversification of the 1980s, financial institutions are now experiencing rationalization and streamlining of their businesses (Kitching, 1982). It has soon become apparent that financial institutions can no longer be all things to all customers. The importance of identifying profitable customer groups is increasing and market segmentation strategies, which recognize the importance of concentrating on the needs of homogeneous groups within a larger heterogenous market, are receiving greater attention.

FINANCIAL SERVICE SEGMENTATION

Much work has been conducted into the segmentation of retail financial services customer markets (see Speed and Smith, 1991, for a review of the literature). However, too much has been either too simplistic, too descriptive or merely replicative of similar research conducted by financial institutions themselves.

Segmentation methodologies fall into two areas. The first of these deals with a priori approaches to segmentation whereby a basis for segmentation is chosen, such as product ownership or usage, and results from the survey provide estimates of segment size and the characteristics in terms of demographics, socio-economics, etc. (Wind, 1978).

The majority of segmentation research in financial services has tended to be a priori in nature. The characteristics chosen have been largely demographic and in uni-dimensional form which has concentrated on only one variable at a time. In particular, variables such as stage in the family life cycle and social class have been utilized (see for example Baker and Fletcher, 1987; Mathews and Slocum, 1969; Meidan, 1984; Stanley et al., 1985). The stage in the family life cycle is an important consideration since it has been noted that individuals do have different financial needs and objectives as they progress through life. However, there are problems associated with such as approach to segmentation. A priori methods investigate only the characteristics of the selected segment; they do not attempt to measure the profitability or the size of the segment against the remainder of the market. Moreover, there is not necessarily a link between the segments selected and buyer behaviour. Thus, it is possible to describe differences between behaviour of customer segments on the basis of external characteristics, but these external characteristics are not necessarily the determinants of behaviour. It is the determinants of behaviour which are of importance.

The second approach, which has gained much less attention because of the need to employ sophisticated computer equipment, is that of *post hoc* segmentation. This method involves dividing a heterogeneous market into segments based on their homogeneous responses to a survey (Gwin and Lindgren, 1982). A very comprehensive review of the studies involving these techniques has been provided by Speed and Smith (1991). The majority of research in this area has tended to rely on cluster-based models which group individuals according to their homogeneous responses based on the inter-correlations between items. These models generate difficulty in accessibility to markets as there is often a weak link between the results produced by clustering and the characteristics of individuals in terms of demographics and socio-economics. A discriminant approach is more desirable, which discriminates between variables and highlights the relative importance a number of independent variables have on the dependent variable. The clustering approach, on the other hand, is unable to demonstrate this as it does not distinguish between dependent and independent variables, and since all variables in a cluster-based model are in effect dummy dependent variables.

UNDERSTANDING THE CONSUMER

It is apparent from reviewing the literature that segmentation studies in personal financial services have not been adequate. While past research in this area had provided detailed descriptions of customer groups in terms of their attitudes and financial behaviour, it has been unable to provide the essential information financial institutions are seeking: who are likely to be the profitable customers and how can they be located?

In order to provide the answers to these questions segmentation studies must be more holistic. The answer lies in gaining a greater understanding of the financial services customer and his/her behaviour. The traditional segmentation variables of age, stage in the family like cycle and social class have provided little insight into financial services customer behaviour. Furthermore, evidence suggests that these are now less than optimal bases in view of recent societal trends such as the changing structure of the family as a result of increased divorce rates, and the increasing number of individuals who choose not to marry (Wagner and Hanna, 1983; Derrick and Lehfeld, 1980; Leach, 1987; Cornish and Denny, 1989).

Research studies must focus on the financial services customer and the perceptions, attitudes and motivations he/she has towards financial services. Psychographic segmentation attempts to address these issues since it hinges entirely on the way the customer thinks (Wills, 1985). Psychographics look at 'the inner person rather than the outward expression of the person' (Beane and Ennis, 1987, p. 22). However, according to Ziff (1971), the definition of psychographics remains a controversial one and is perhaps a main contributory factor to much of the confusion that surrounds it. To some researchers psychographics refer to basic personality characteristics, whereas other definitions include attitudes, values and beliefs. In addition to this the general concept seems to be foreign to the traditional running of many financial institutions and is perhaps one of the reasons why psychographically-based research has not yet reached its full potential in segmenting the market for personal financial services.

Such as approach to market segmentation, which focuses on the customer and his/her mind set, is potentially very complex. In order to take full advantage of the factors which could affect take-up and usage of financial services it is necessary to develop a multi-dimensional model. This allows for a greater number of variables to be included in the study from which determinants of financial services behaviour can be identified and markets segmented.

In addition to this it is important to analyse the market segments in terms of the implications for potential profitability. Since adequate means of identifying profitable customers quantitatively are not available, a qualitative assessment of potential profitability is being used which provides an indication of the relative degree of income likely to be generated as a result of the customers' behaviour in the use of financial services. By nature financial services are not one-off purchases but involve a series of two-way transactions over an extended time period (McKechnie, 1992). It is this post-purchase period and the behaviour of the customer therein that is of importance in assessing potential profitability.

RESEARCH PROBLEM

The research outlined in this article is the initial stage of the development of a multi-dimensional model for segmentation in the personal financial services sector. The work presented here is based on a preliminary qualitative study which attempts to highlight variables for segmentation in the personal financial services sector which may prove to have deterministic power for financial services behaviour. A detailed quantitative study is currently under way to investigate the relative sensitivity of the variables chosen in identifying potentially profitable customer segments for financial services.

METHODOLOGY

Sampling procedure

Individuals were interviewed in detail about a wide range of financial services and products. The individuals were selected from the Register of Electors for a particular ward in the Manchester area which is known to contain a relatively heterogeneous population, thus accounting for a variety of different individual characteristics. Letters were mailed to 33 households selected at random from the register and follow-up telephone calls were made to arrange interviews. Forty-five per cent of the individuals from the households contacted agreed to an interview, thus giving a sample size of 15. Although this is a relatively small number, it was considered to be sufficient for an exploratory study of this kind. Interviews were conducted in the respondents' homes and lasted between one-and-a-half to two hours.

Test variables

The variables chosen in the study were selected on the basis of the limitations presented earlier in segmentation studies in the personal financial services sector. In an attempt to achieve a greater understanding of the financial services customer and how he/she uses financial services, several aspects of consumer buyer behaviour have been developed as segmentation variables. The following variables, in particular, have been considered to be of prime importance.

- Individuals' own perceived knowledge and understanding of financial services.
- Perceived confidence and ability in dealing with financial matters.
- Expressed level of interest (involvement) in financial services.

The variables were measured on the basis of the individuals' own self-assessment of how they perceive their own levels of knowledge, confidence and interest to be. Thus, the measurement tool was a subjective rating, although the majority of respondents found it useful to rate themselves also on a scale of 1 to 10.

In addition to the cognitive variables mentioned above it was also necessary to have some account of financial services usage for each respondent in order that the relationship between financial services consumption and knowledge, confidence and interest could be examined.

Financial services customers rarely have just one product, but rather are customers of a range of products or a 'package'. Thus, the relationship between the customer and the financial institution can become very complex as there are numerous points of contact. Therefore, rather than analyse the results in terms of discrete product holdership it was decided to adopt a technique to categorize individuals in terms of their financial consumption. A study by Kamakura *et al.* (1991) found that financial services consumption and service acquisition appears to occur in a hierarchical order from higher-liquidity, lower-risk products to those requiring greater resources and with lower liquidity. This enables both financial services and users to be positioned along a 'latent', difficulty/ability dimension which assumes that the more 'difficult' financial products require higher levels of investment 'ability' or maturity. Thus according to this concept, the ability (in financial terms) to become involved with any of the basic foundation products (i.e. current accounts, savings/deposit accounts, loans and mortgages) is necessary before the more 'complex' products, involving longer-term commitment, resources and risk are looked into.

This hierarchical movement between financial services is referred to as 'financial maturity', which hypothesizes that individuals move from lower-order to higher-order financial products and ownership of higher-order products presupposes ownership of lower-order products (or at least the ability to own them).

Running concurrently to this is the notion of financial objectives and the financial life cycle. Financial objectives or financial needs also form a hierarchy that evolves over time. Thus, individuals and households have a financial life cycle reflective of the needs and objectives which are of importance at particular stages in the family life cycle. For example, consider two groups of financial services (credit and loans, and savings and investments) which individuals and households acquire. Savings products can be viewed as a means of financing future consumption based on current earnings, whereas credit and loans products are viewed as methods of financing current consumption based on future earnings. Both take-up and ownership of these products have been hypothesized to depend on financial needs or objectives and ability to acquire (Katona, 1960). For example, such objectives could be to save (borrow) for the sake of emergencies, maintaining liquidity, making major purchases, children's education, retirement, growth in capital value or generating future income (Kamakura et al., 1991). Certain needs/objectives assume that others have already been or are capable of being met.

Figure 1 illustrates the hierarchy of financial needs/objectives. The diagram shows the movement of financial services customers from the base of the pyramid to the tip. There is a general observation that individuals move from the less risky assets to the more risky ones.

The hierarchy of financial objectives is very similar to the hierarchy of needs proposed by Maslow (1970) which states that the lower, basic needs pertaining to human survival must be met before the higher needs, which are not directly related to human survival but relate to life enhancement and quality of life. In terms of financial services consumption the question of resource allocation is of importance. It is, therefore, expected that basic objectives such as liquidity, cash reserves and insurance are satisfied before allocating funds for higher-order products. However, similar to Maslow's hierarchy of needs, the extent and rapidity of the upwards movement varies from individual to individual as a result of a number of factors.

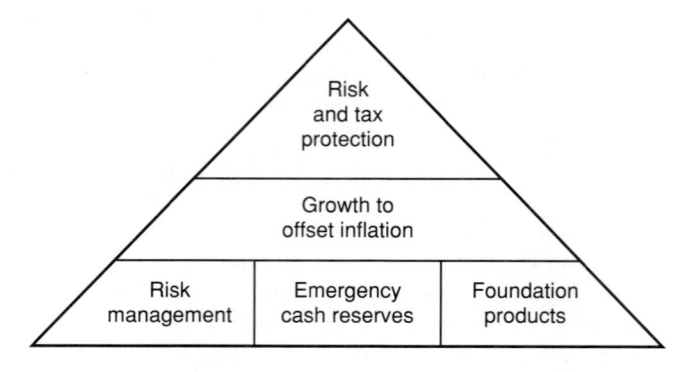

Figure 1. Hierarchy of financial needs.

Analysis of the data

The analysis consists of mapping the 15 respondents in the sample on a two-dimensional map (see Figure 2) constructed from the variables mentioned above. The vertical axis, labelled perceived knowledge, takes account of the individuals's own subjective assessment of how much they feel they know about financial services. It also takes account of how confident the individual feels about his/her level of knowledge. Respondents were also asked to verify their verbal account of how knowledgeable they feel by placing themselves on a scale of 1 to 10, where 1 is not at all knowledgeable and 10 is extremely knowledgeable. Thus the map illustrates high and low perceived knowledge where low = 1–5 and high = 6–10.

The horizontal axis measures the 'degree of financial maturity' as defined by Kamakura *et al.* (1991). Based on the previous discussion of hierarchical financial objectives and the complexity of the financial product the following scale of financial maturity is being used:

Financial Maturity Scale
(1) *Foundation products:*   Cheque account (and related services).
                                  Savings/deposit account.
                                  Credit card.
                                  Mortgage.
                                  Loans.
(2) *Risk management and cash reserves:* Life assurance.
                                  Endowments.
                                  Pension plan.
                                  Time deposits/TESSAs.

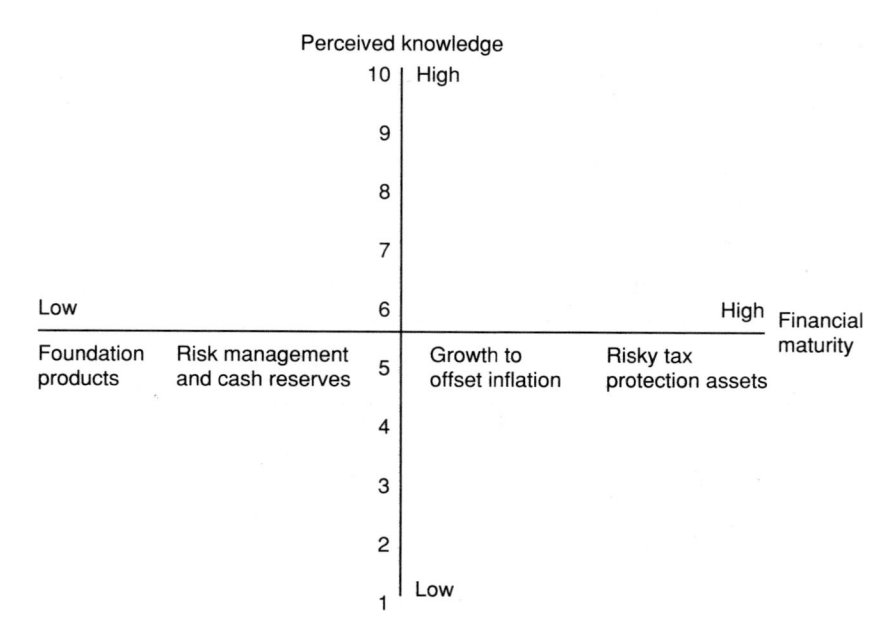

Figure 2. Two-dimensional segmentation map.

(3) *Growth to offset inflation:* Stocks and shares.
Unit trusts.
Personal Equity Plans.
(4) *Risky, tax protection assets:* Government bonds.
(Adapted from Kamakura et al., 1991.)

Financial maturity is also measured as low and high, where low financial maturity is defined by individuals having current usage of any of the foundation products and risk management and cash reserves. High financial maturity is exhibited by those individuals who are involved in more risky, tax-protection assets and whose objectives are growth to offset inflation.

Findings

The findings (illustrated in Figure 3) highlight four financial services customer segments based on their level of knowledge and understanding of financial services and on their degree of financial maturity. The segments are labelled 'financially confused', 'apathetic minimalists', 'cautious investors' and 'capital accumulators' which reflect the characteristics of the individuals in each of the segments. Each segment is characterized by particular attitudes towards financial services, perceptions of financial services, financial services behaviour and also degree of future orientation. There are also differences in financial objectives and motivation and the implications each segment has for potential profitability. A brief description of each segments characteristics follows.

Financially confused

This group is characterized by a low level of perceived knowledge and a low level of financial maturity. Thus, individuals in this segment have a nominal involvement with financial services. The majority of products used by this group tend to be foundation

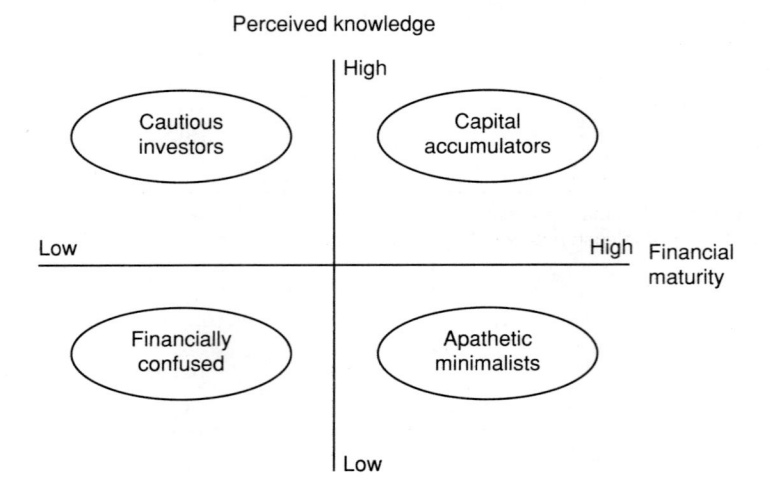

Figure 3. Financial services consumer segmentation.

products such as cheque accounts, savings, loans and mortgages. Individuals do not claim to be very knowledgeable about financial services, least of all about the one(s) that they themselves have and use.

A common feeling of this segment is one of apathy towards financial services. The level of interest it very low, which may be a prime factor driving perceived knowledge since although respondents claim to know very little, at the same time they feel they do not need to know very much because they believe that they are unlikely to ever have a need for many financial products.

The four respondents which fell into this segment seemed to divide themselves evenly into sub-segments based on their differences in the types of foundation products used and their attitudes towards them. Obviously, these sub-segments are very small and cannot be taken as conclusive evidence of financial services customer behaviour. Nevertheless, they do provide an insight into the possibilities that there are for further segmentation within broadly defined segments.

The first sub-segment (financially confused savers) is characterized by a very limited use of foundation products with no use of credit and loan facilities and only a small amount of savings. Attitudes towards borrowing and loans are definitely unfavourable. However, whenever such financial services have been used it has been with caution and reservation. A possible reason for such negative attitudes could be a result of a strong fear of debt and worry of not having enough money. This has resulted in a small amount of savings with the short-term objective of 'emergency cover'. Individuals in this group are also extremely cautious and wary of shares and other financial products perceived by them as being too 'risky'.

The second sub-segment (financially confused borrowers) exhibits a much wider use of foundation products, particularly loans and credit facilities. Not surprisingly, these individuals express no strong negative attitudes towards borrowing and the use of loans and have no reservations about the use of credit/borrowed money. However, the future orientation of these individuals is also rather short term due to an apathetic view of savings and investments and short-term objectives of borrowing money.

Apathetic minimalists

This segment is characterized by a fairly low level of perceived knowledge of financial services, although a quite high level of financial maturity is exhibited. Thus, despite the lack of knowledge individuals feel they have, they do own fairly complex and high involvement financial services such as stocks and shares and unit trusts and PEPs.

Similarly to the financially confused segment, the five respondents who fell into this segment of the map could be divided into two groups characterized by saving-dominant responses (two individuals) and credit-dominant responses (three individuals); the former exhibiting very limited use of foundation products, with particular emphasis on savings, and the latter showing a much wider use of foundation products, in particular loans and credit services. A prime reason for this could be due to the stage in the family life cycle into which respondents in each of these two subsegments fall. The saver-dominant sub-segment is comprised of individuals in either the bachelor or empty nester stage of the life cycle (Wells and Gubar, 1966). Hence, they are unlikely to have dependants and financial commitments in terms of family and mortgages. Thus, these groups are less likely to exhibit a need for loans and credit facilities.

The credit-dominant sub-group is comprised of individuals largely in the full nest stage of the life cycle (Wells and Gubar, 1966). Thus, by definition these individuals will have families and dependants to support and mortgages to pay. They are, therefore, more likely to have a need for borrowing since expenditures at this stage of the life cycle are very high relative to income, and opportunities for saving are much fewer.

Despite the differences in the use of foundation products exhibited by the two subsegments, there do not appear to be any strong negative attitudes towards loans and the use of credit. However, the saver-dominant sub-segment does seem to have a definite fear of getting into debt which has possibly led to extreme caution in the use of loans. Furthermore, these respondents feel that loans should only be used in an emergency, which would suggest a reactive approach to borrowing.

'individuals utilize loans to achieve their aims in life'

The credit dominant sub-group does not appear to suffer from this fear of debt. The behaviour of this segment is also different with regard to the usage of credit and is also slightly more extravagant. This segment exhibits a rather proactive approach to borrowing and individuals will utilize loans and credit to achieve their aims in life.

As well as the feeling that knowledge of financial services is very low, this segment also appears to have a very low level of interest in financial matters. In fact, it seems that individuals in this segment do not attach very much importance to financial services at all which could be a primary factor affecting motivation.

Individuals also reported low levels of confidence in their knowledge of financial services as well as in their ability to deal with financial services. There was a general feeling that advice would need to be sought on particular services. As a result of this they appear to be willing to entrust third parties with their decisions and delegate the responsibility to someone else—a financial institution. This would also explain the fairly high degree of financial maturity exhibited by this group as take-up of the complex products held by respondents was instigated by financial advisors.

A further explanation for the high degree of financial maturity could be found in the type of products owned by these individuals. In terms of the shares reported, the majority were from the recent government privatization issues. A report conducted by Financial Research Services (1988) indicates that there has been an influx of new investors to the stocks and shares market via the various privatization issues which has made share buying more accessible to a wider range of individuals and has heralded a shift from the traditional up-market profile of this type of investor. Thus, it may be argued that this somewhat 'simplified' method of share buying requires less financial sophistication than other forms of share buying and is essentially an 'easier' method of buying shares.

Cautious investors

The three respondents in this segment perceive themselves to have very good knowledge of financial services and yet they exhibit only a moderate degree of financial maturity concentrating mainly on savings and investment items but ignoring those which they perceive as being too risky.

In terms of the use of foundation products there is wide usage by this group, including loans. They are not afraid of loans and have no fear of debt, neither do they have any strong attitudes towards loans and the use of them. However, if this segment were to borrow money, they would look for what they consider to be the 'cheapest' alternative. This would usually involve using interest-free credit from a retailer, borrowing from an insurance policy or using a charge card. Usage of credit card does not fall into this group of perceived cheaper alternatives. Consequently there appears to be a dislike for credit card usage from this segment. The problem is not with the credit card itself, as the convenience offered by the credit card is seen favourable. However, cost in terms of interest is considered to be too high to use on a regular basis. Thus, credit cards used by this segment experience only selective use.

In terms of the higher involvement, more complex financial products held by this segment, the emphasis is on 'safer' savings items, particularly in the form of insurance or private pensions. The cautious nature of these individuals seems to cause them to avoid such investments as PEPs, shares and unit trusts with a definite aversion for speculation and the risk attached to it.

The knowledge and financial sophistication of this group appears to be influenced by occupations in professional/business capacities. This too may be a reason for the high level of interest individuals in this segment exhibit towards financial services and related matters.

A further observation of this group is their future orientation. In contrast to the financially confused, who take a rather short-term view of their futures and have mainly short-term objectives of saving for emergencies, this group have much longer-term financial objectives. Thus, they are not worried or opposed to tying their money up in an investment, just as long as it is perceived by them to have very little risk attached to it. Respondents are particularly aware of the importance of making provisions for their futures; thus they re-evaluate their financial situations periodically.

Capital accumulators

This segment is characterized by a very high level of perceived knowledge and understanding of financial services as well as a high degree of financial maturity. Thus, the three individuals in this segment have complex, high-involvement financial products such as unit trusts and PEPs about which they feel very knowledgeable and confident.

In many respects the respondents in this segment are very similar to those in the cautious investors segment with one major exception, the capital accumulators are not averse to speculation and are, in fact, favourable towards the products perceived by the other segments to be high risk.

In general, this segment exhibits very selective use of the foundation products with a distinct lack of credit/loan usage. Again, this could be due to the age of respondents and the stage in the family life cycle, as the segment is comprised largely of respondents who are either in or near retirement age, have finished paying their mortgage and have no dependants.

While there did not appear to be any strong attitudes towards loans and the use of credit it was not viewed as very favourable. The prime reason seemed to be not fear of getting into debt but, similarly to the cautious investors, the expense incurred through interest payments. Consequently, in cases where credit was used, 'cheaper' alternatives would be sought such as interest-free credit from a retailer, in the case of major purchases, or the use of credit cards, to take full advantage of deferred payment, and credit card balances would always be paid in full so that no interest cost is incurred.

Similarly to the cautions investors this segment also has a strong future orientation which seems to be reflected in the type of products used. The value of interest on savings and investments and income generation through financial investments is of greater importance than easy access to funds.

'Analysis has suggested four customer segments'

As with the cautious investors, the high levels of perceived knowledge of financial services and, indeed, the high level of interest in financial matters could also possibly be as a result of occupations in financial and business-related fields.

CONCLUSIONS AND IMPLICATION

The analysis has suggested four customer segments for financial services on the basis of customers' own perceived knowledge, confidence and interest in financial services and the relative degree of financial maturity, defined by the type and complexity of financial services currently in use by the respondents. Each of the four segments is distinct in terms of the financial objectives exhibited, motivations for financial services usage and attitudes and behaviour towards financial services. Both the financially confused and the apathetic minimalists take a rather short-term view of their futures. The financially confused segment is primarily concerned with saving for emergencies but otherwise has negligible use of financial services. The apathetic minimalists have slightly higher perceived knowledge of financial services and much higher financial maturity. However, the degree of financial maturity appears to be the result of successful selling on the part of financial institutions. This segment is very trusting and willing to take the advice of financial advisors. Hence, an easy sales target.

The capital accumulators have a similar degree of financial maturity to the apathetic minimalists. The difference between the two is that the former have made a conscious effort to become involved in the higher-risk products and are in fact motivated by the perceived benefits offered by these products. The apathetic minimalists would otherwise not have bought such high involvement financial products if it had not been for the advice given.

The cautious investors are very much like the capital accumulators in that they are very future orientated and their financial objectives are very long term. The difference is that the former prefer to avoid high-risk products and opt for 'safer' investment type products, although both segments are in favour of tying money up and high returns are more important than easy access.

At this stage it is not possible to draw conclusions as to whether customer's own perceived knowledge, confidence and interest in financial services are determinants of financial services behaviour or indeed potential profitability. However, it does appear that segments defined according to these variables do exhibit distinct attitudes, motivations, financial objectives and behaviour. It also seems that, based on the behaviour exhibited by the segments, there are opportunities for differing levels of potential profitability from each of the segments. Figure 4 hypothesizes the relative level of potential profitability from segments with low, medium and high perceived knowledge based on their behaviour towards financial services.

Figure 4 indicates that the segments with extremely low and extremely high perceived knowledge offer the lowest levels of potential profitability. The explanation for this is that

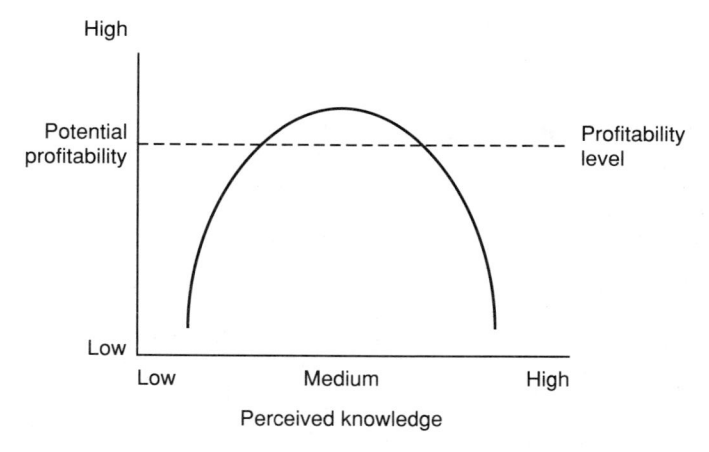

Figure 4. Conceptual segment profitability.

those with extremely low levels of perceived knowledge also seem to have very low levels of interest in financial services and do not seem to attach a great amount of value to financial services. As a result of this it appears that overall behaviour towards financial services is low and product usage is limited to a selective number of foundation products, mostly a savings account, a mortgage and a current account. The customers with a very high degree of perceived knowledge of financial services would also seem to possess a high level of financial sophistication. These individuals, therefore, know which products are best suited to their needs. They are also likely to approach an independent source which may not necessarily allow for fee generation for financial institutions.

The customers who fall into the category of moderate level of perceived knowledge and confidence in dealing with financial matters seem to offer the greatest opportunities from the financial institution's viewpoint in terms of potential profitability. The point at which this becomes crucial is unclear; so too are the reasons for this. However, it is suspected that individuals in this category may fall victim of lack of information or misinformation. Certainly, the results of this study have shown that certain respondents are easier sales targets than others which may provide opportunities for profit potential.

'certain respondents are easier sales targets than others'

It must be stressed that this is only preliminary work and further quantitative work is being conducted to further test the discriminatory power of the variables explained here. However, from the results of the qualitative work it could appear that individual perceived knowledge, confidence and interest in financial services could possibly form determinants of financial services behaviour and potential profitability. If this is the case they could prove to be valuable bases in segmenting the market for personal financial services.

REFERENCES

Baker, K. and Fletcher, R. (1987), 'OUTLOOK—A Generalized Lifestyle System', *Admap*, March, pp. 23–8.

Beane, T. P. and Ennis, D. M. (1987), 'Market Segmentation: A Review', *European Journal of Marketing*, Vol. 21 No. 5, pp. 20–42.

Brooks, A. L. N. (1989), 'Strategic Issues for Financial Services Marketing', *Management Decision*, Vol. 27 No. 1, pp. 40–7.

Cornish, P. and Denny, M. (1989), 'Demographics are Dead—Long Live Demographics', *Journal of the Market Research Society*, Vol. 31 No. 3, pp. 363–73.

Derrick, F. W. and Lehfeld, A. K. (1980), 'The Family Life Cycle: An Alternative Approach', *Journal of Consumer Research*, Vol. 7, September, pp. 214–17.

Financial Research Services (1988), 'Financial Research Survey', *Management Summary Reports*, Great Britain, April–September.

Gwin, J. M. and Lindgren, J. H. (1982), 'Bank Market Segmentation: Methods and Strategies', *Journal of Retail Banking*, Vol. IV No. 4, Winter, pp. 8–13.

Kamakura, W. A., Ramaswami, S. N. and Srivastava, R. K. (1991), 'Applying Latent Trait Analysis in the Evaluation of Prospects for Cross-selling of Financial Services', *International Journal of Research in Marketing*, Vol. 8 No. 4, November, pp. 329–49.

Katona, G. (1960), *The Powerful Consumer*, McGraw-Hill, New York, NY.

Kitching, D. W. C. (1982), 'Rationalising Branch Banking', *Long Range Planning*, Vol. 15 No. 1, pp. 53–62.

Leach, C. (1987), 'How Conventional Demographics Distort Marketing Realities', *Admap*, May, pp. 41–5.

Maslow, A. H. (1970), *Motivation and Personality*, 2nd ed., Harper & Row, New York, NY.

Mathews, H. L. and Slocum, J. W. Jr (1969), 'Social Class and Commercial Bank Credit Card Usage', *Journal of Marketing*, Vol. 33, January, pp. 71–8.

McKechnie, S. (1992), 'Consumer Buying Behaviour in Financial Services: An Overview', *International Journal of Bank Marketing*, Vol. 10 No. 5, pp. 4–12.

Meidan, A. (1984), *Bank Marketing Management*, Macmillan, New York, NY.

Speed, R. and Smith, G. (1991), 'Retail Financial Services Segmentation', *Service Industries Journal*, Vol. 12 No. 3, July, pp. 368–83.

Stanley, T. O., Ford, J. K. and Richards, S. K. (1985), 'Segmentation of Bank Customers by Age', *International Journal of Bank Marketing*, Vol. 3 No. 3, pp. 56–63.

Wagner, J. and Hanna, S. (1983), 'The Effectiveness of Family Lifecycle Variables in Consumer Expenditure Research', *Journal of Consumer Research*, Vol. 10, December, pp. 281–91.

Wells, W. D. and Gubar, G. (1966), 'The Life Cycle Concept in Marketing Research', *Journal of Marketing Research*, Vol. 3, November, pp. 355–63.

Wills, G. (1985), 'Dividing and Conquering: Strategies for Segmentation', *International Journal of Bank Marketing*, Vol. 3 No. 4, pp. 36–46.

Wind, Y. (1978), 'Issues and Advances in Segmentation Research', *Journal of Marketing Research*, Vol. XV, August, pp. 317–37.

Ziff, R. (1971), 'Psychographics for Market Segmentation', *Journal of Advertising Research*, Vol. II No. 2, April, pp. 3–9.

Part III

Product Innovation

CONTENTS

Introduction to Part III 121

9 Success Factors for New Consumer Financial Services 124
   C. J. EASINGWOOD and C. STOREY, *International Journal of Bank Marketing* (1991), **9** (1), 3–10.
10 Bank Customers' Perceptions, Innovations and New Technology 136
   L. MOUTINHO and A. MEIDAN, *International Journal of Bank Marketing* (1989), **7** (2), 22–27.
11 Insurance Product Development: Managing the Changes 147
   A. JOHNE, *International Journal of Bank Marketing* (1993), **11** (3), 5–14.

Introduction to Part III

Financial services organizations are trying, through their product offerings, to achieve product differentiation in a traditionally undifferentiated area. They are allocating resources both to present products through, for example, enhanced delivery systems, branding, employee commitment and customer service, and to developing new products/ services.

Product offerings include basic or core services (e.g. a checking account, insurance cover), with facilitating services which are required for consumption of the service (e.g. a cheque book and cheque guarantee card, an insurance policy) together with supporting services which are not required but which enhance the service and differentiate it from competition (e.g. ATMs, home banking). All this is what the customer receives. In addition, financial services organizations need to consider how their services are delivered or received, which is dependent on the augmented service offering. This includes the accessibility of the service (e.g. locational convenience, availability of advice), the extent of customer participation (e.g. provision of information including form filling), and the interaction between the organization (its personnel, systems, technology and environment) and the consumer.

Developing technology, for example, plays a key role in financial services and various aspects of delivery systems, thus providing more choice, convenience and economy for consumers. It is increasingly evident in: ATMs for cash and other services; self-service banks (e.g. the new Co-operative Bank branches with no personnel); electronic funds transfer at point of-sale; home/office banking via telecommunications and computer links for payments services; financial management systems; electronic letters of credit; provision of financial information to businesses; global cash management; expert systems; and SMART cards.

Personnel pay a role in customer service, advice services etc., and financial services organizations need to create a balance between 'high-tech' with depersonalization of service (and reduced opportunities for cross-selling) and 'high-touch' which facilitates interpersonal interactions with customers.

Branding in financial services has traditionally been associated with corporate names but is now increasingly evident with product offerings, e.g. Midland Bank have Vector, Orchard and Meridian accounts, each linked to a specific lifestyle group, and with home-banking services as First Direct, HOBS and Direct Line.

New financial services development is stimulated by deregulation of financial services, increasing customer needs and expectations, advances in technology and new forms of competition. New service developments ranges from: style changes (e.g. uniforms, interior of branches); improvements (e.g. updating products, longer opening hours); extensions to product range; new services (e.g. building societies moving into insurance services); to major innovations which lead to changes in consumer behaviour (e.g. home banking).

Minor product/service development may be incremental, inexpensive and of low risk, and the costs of developing and introducing major innovations in financial services may be low compared with manufacturing industry. But there are, nevertheless, potential losses from product/service failures with respect to factors such as wasted managerial efforts, adverse effect on company image, and reduced ability to introduce other new products/ services.

Many models of the new product development process are available, including a good one for services developed by Scheuing and Johnson (1989) and reported in the article by Johne. Key features of any scheme include planning for product changes, exploring ideas, screening and evaluation, development and launch. The characteristics of financial services, in particular their intangibility, have implications throughout the new product development process. For example, market research is difficult as consumers cannot 'see' product features, rather they are being asked to judge the anticipated benefits. In addition, 'testing' of financial services is not the norm, consumers are making a commitment (e.g. by taking out an insurance policy, making a will, arranging a loan).

Further, as patents are not possible, there is risk and ease of competitive entry and, therefore, a tendency for organizations to improve services and their delivery rather than to innovate. The concept of product warranties (i.e. guarantees) is not applicable in the normal way to financial services but, for example, investment schemes may have guaranteed payments, and all the major players have clearly developed and communicated Codes of Practice for particular customer segments.

Finally, in the light of existing products and possibilities for improvement, change and innovation, financial services organizations focus at a strategic management level on their product-market mixes. This is a key area of decision-making and outcomes vary between organizations (e.g. banks, building societies, insurance companies and retailers) with respect to their emphasis on retail *vis-à-vis* corporate and international markets, segments within these markets, and width and depth of their product/service range. Thus, they are paying attention to market development, market penetration, product development and/ or diversification.

The first article in this section is by Christopher Easingwood and Chris Storey, 'Success Factors for New Consumer Financial Services'. They developed, from the research literature and business press, 43 possible attributes associated with successful new financial services products, representing a range of marketing, organizational, technological and product dimensions. They also identified 125 new financial products directed at the consumer market, and asked the marketing managers for these products to rate the success of the products, and to estimate the extent to which the attributes helped or hindered the success of the products. Analysis identified nine clusters of attributes that were intercorrelated to produce factors or dimensions of success (or failure). Four of these were highly correlated with success—overall quality, differentiated product, product fit and internal marketing, and use of technology—and are factors that marketing managers should pay particular attention to.

Luiz Moutinho and Arthur Meidan in their article, 'Bank Customers' Perceptions,

Innovations and New Technology' report findings from a study which included investigation of bank customers' usage of new services such as electronic funds transfer and automatic teller machine systems, attitudes and importance ratings with respect to new bank products, and consumer perceptions of risk attached to ATMs. Factor analysis utilizing LISREL resulted in identification of four types of customers, with differing perceptions, attitudes and behaviour towards existing and new bank technology. The findings have implications for product development and associated marketing activities, for example with respect to segmentation, pricing strategies, advertising and promotion, and the mix of delivery systems.

The final paper in this section, 'Insurance Product Development', is from Axel Johne who has made a major research contribution, over the years, in the area of new product development. He discusses the need for successful product development to be assessed in terms of both supply based measures to appraise whether internal targets (e.g. profitability) are being met, and also with respect to market based measures—to appraise the extent to which market appeal and potential are being achieved. Johne also considers the relatively slow, but changing, adoption of marketing in insurance companies, but which includes attention to product innovation and positioning. Qualitative research data are presented from interviews in life and general insurance companies and relate to: the types of product development being pursued; key activities in the development process; organizational arrangements to handle development activities; the contribution of marketing specialists; and the contribution of top management. Johne concludes that insurance companies need to adopt both a proactive and an innovative approach to new product development, with an emphasis on exploiting market opportunities, more formalized control systems, and top management support.

9

Success Factors for New Consumer Financial Services

Christopher J. Easingwood and Chris Storey

The financial services industry is changing rapidly. There has been a general blurring of the traditional boundaries between banks, building societies and insurance companies due to changing regulations, new technology, new competitors and increasingly sophisticated consumers. Banks, building societies and insurance companies find their traditional services faced with increased competition. In order to survive companies must develop successful new products.

But there has been little research into the characteristics of successful new consumer financial products. Although it has been argued that the financial loss from product failure is low in the financial services sector (Davison et al., 1989), it is also true that there are hidden costs to failure, such as the cost of managerial effort wasted on weak products, a reduced ability to introduce other new products and the adverse effect of an unsuccessful new product on corporate image.

The research on success factors that has been published is mostly focused on industrial products. For instance Cooper (1986) and Cooper and Kleinschmidt (1987a) examine new industrial products and find that the quality of the execution of the new product development process (at all stages) is a main determinant of product success or failure. In a later work, Cooper (1988) also identifies product advantage (a superior product, a unique benefit or solves a customer problem), among other factors, as being important for industrial product success. In one of the few studies of new service development, Langeard et al., (1986) identified five key areas in this process: a unique service concept; a well-identified market segment; a specialised easy-to-duplicate delivery system; a narrow core offering; a clear, easy to remember service image. In another study of a services sector, this time of business to business services, de Brentani (1989) found that in addition to a formal new service development process 'successful service development requires that companies identify what buyers perceive as quality and incorporate these features into the service design' and 'new services need to be unique and truly innovative to achieve a major advantage in the marketplace'.

However, while these literatures (i.e. on product success factors, on new service development) provide some useful findings, it may or may not be the case that these findings transfer across unaltered to financial services and they are in any case not sufficiently specific for use in financial services (for instance to help in the design of a questionnaire on new financial products). The purpose of this research is then to describe the characteristics of successful new consumer financial products. More specifically, the purposes are:

- to identify the attributes that are associated with successful new financial products;
- to find out if these, possibly numerous, attributes cluster naturally into a smaller number of factors;
- to check if any of the attributes/factors are particularly associated with successful financial products.

METHODOLOGY

An outline of the methodology is presented in Table 1.

The first step required is the development of a list of possible attributes of successful financial products. The literature on product success factors (i.e. Cooper and Kleinschmidt, 1987b; Cooper, 1988) and the literature on new service development (Easingwood, 1986; Langeard et al., 1986; Reidenbach and Moak, 1986; de Brentani, 1989) were examined but, as explained above, these provided some guidelines only, but not enough detail with which to develop a list of success attributes for financial products. Recourse was therefore made to the popular business, financial and marketing press (*Banking Technology*, *Banking World*, *Business*, *Campaign*, *Director*, *Financial Adviser*, *Financial Weekly*, *Insurance Age*, *Investor's Chronicle*, *Marketing*, *Marketing Week*, *Money Management*, *Money Marketing* and *Precision Marketing*.) Issues from 1988 and 1989 were systematically examined for articles discussing financial products and note made of any attributes quoted as contributing to a product's success. This was a highly productive process yielding a total of 43 attributes representing a comprehensive range of marketing, organisational, technological and product dimensions (see Table 2).

It was then required to identify a number of new products to be used at the next stage of the study, the data collection stage. Marketing managers were to be asked to rate the products on the attributes. It was decided to include products that had been introduced in

Table 1. Methodology.

Purpose	Procedures
Identification of attributes possibly associated with successful new financial products	Examination of articles in the business press
Identification of new financial products (in the marketplace at least six months)	Examination of launch announcements in the financial press
Collection of data on the rating of the financial products on the attributes	Mailed questionnaire to marketing managers
Simplification and consolidation of data	Factor analysis
Association of attributes/factors with success	Correlation analysis, tests of significance

Table 2. New financial services attributes.

	Mean value of attribute[a]		Significance of difference[b]	Rotated factor loadings
	Successful products	Unsuccessful products		

(1) Targeting through direct mail				
The direct mail operation could select from existing customers.	6.1	5.2	+	0.89
The direct mail operation could access a large database.	6.1	4.9	++	0.88
The direct mail operation targeted the correct audience.	6.1	4.8	++	0.86
The direct mail operation was styled to the target audience.	6.2	5.7		0.85
The direct mail operation adopted a personalised approach.	5.9	5.3		0.79
The product was targeted at a clearly identified market niche.	7.1	5.9	++	0.39
The product could be adapted for each customer.	5.9	5.2		−0.38
(2) Overall quality				
There was quality in the delivery of the service.	7.0	5.0	+++	0.77
The product benefited from high quality in the after-sales service.	6.3	5.0	++	0.75
The organisation had a reputation for quality.	7.7	4.9	+++	0.74
There was a good fit between the product, its delivery system and the existing organisational structure.	6.8	3.2	+++	0.57
The product was considered a quality product compared to competitive products.	7.1	5.6	+++	0.55
The product had a strong brand image.	6.9	4.9	+++	0.55
The product had a supporting tangible element.	5.8	5.2		0.49
(3) Communication strategy				
The communication strategy was consistent with the company's other products/brands.	6.6	5.7	+	0.85
The communication strategy was consistent over time.	6.3	5.3	++	0.77
The communication strategy was effective in giving the product a unique image.	6.3	5.0	++	0.69
The communication strategy was consistent with the rest of the marketing strategy.	6.8	5.2	+++	0.56
The technology employed could assist in identifying changing customer needs.	5.1	5.2		0.48
The technology employed in the product, or the delivery system was innovative.	5.7	4.9	+	0.46
The communication mix was effective in raising consumer awareness.	6.2	4.9	++	0.45
(4) Product Fit and Internal Marketing				
Delivery was supported by an extensive branch network.	6.9	5.2	+++	0.77
The product extended or completed the product line.	6.9	5.9	++	0.75

Resources were used to inform staff prior to the product launch.	7.2	++	0.62
There was investment in the training of staff.	7.0	+++	0.58
(5) Use of technology			
The technology employed could assist in providing an individualised service.	6.1	5.2	+	0.78
The technology employed could assist in the management of the product.	5.9	4.9	++	0.66
The organisation was considered to be different from its competitors.	6.5	5.3	+++	0.54
The product allowed a long-term customer relationship to be built.	6.4	5.4	++	0.37
(6) Intermediary support			
Delivery was supported by access to an extensive network of intermediaries.	6.3	4.9	++	0.87
The effective use of intermediaries was supported by quality service to intermediaries.	6.2	4.7	++	0.85
The effective use of intermediaries was supported by the financial return to intermediaries.	5.9	5.2		0.73
The technology employed could be used to assist intermediaries.	6.0	5.4		0.59
(7) Market research			
The effective use of market research into customer needs improved the product.	6.1	5.4		0.75
Market research was used to test responses to product ideas.	5.8	4.9	+	0.73
The product was differentiated for different market segments.	5.5	5.0		0.56
Effective test marketing helped the product strategy.	5.2	4.7		0.55
The product could be continuously updated to meet changing customer needs.	6.1	5.2		0.45
(8) Differentiated product			
The product offered unique benefits to the customer.	6.9	5.7	+++	0.87
The product was the first of its type in the market.	6.0	5.1	+	0.69
The product was considered innovative.	7.0	5.8	+++	0.59
(9) Low price			
The product was relatively low priced.	6.2	5.7		0.72
The product was quickly conceived and implemented in response to a market opportunity or threat.	6.8	5.2	+++	0.38

[a] The value of the attribute was assessed on a 9-point scale from 1 (very much hindered the success of the product) to 5 (no effect) to 9 (very much helped the success of the product).

[b] +++ 1 per cent level, ++ 5 per cent level, + 10 per cent level.

the first half of 1989 so that the marketing managers would be in a position, at the time of the study, in the first half of 1990, to make a reasonable assessment of the strengths and weaknesses of the marketing strategy employed. The products to be included in the study were identified by searching for product launch announcements made in issues taken from the first six months of 1989 of *Financial Adviser*, *Insurance Age*, *Money Management* and *Money Marketing*. This process produced a sample of 125 new financial products directed at the consumer market.

The next stage involved the design of the questionnaire and its mailing to the marketing managers of the financial products. The questionnaire required that each manager assess the success of the product by estimating the extent to which the product had achieved its objectives using a 9-point scale from 1 (major failure) to 5 (neither success nor failure) to 9 (major success). Although it is recognised that this is a rather over-simplified measure of success it was thought adequate as it avoided various difficulties such as there possibly being a number of different reasons for launching the new product, difficulties in allocating the costs of shared delivery systems and difficulties in estimating cannibalisation of other products. The questionnaire also described each attribute in a short statement, and then asked the manager to estimate the extent to which the attribute described in the statement (or its lack) helped or hindered the success of the product. This again was measured on a 9-point scale, from 1 (very much hindered) to 9 (very much helped) with the mid-point (5) representing the neutral position.

'It is important to look at the influence of combinations of attributes'

The questionnaire was mailed to the marketing managers of the 125 products, with a total of 77 usable replies obtained, a response rate of 62 per cent. Of the products 64 were judged to be broadly successful (i.e. a score of 6 or more) and 13 were considered not to be successful (i.e. a score of 5 or less). This latter group is referred to as 'unsuccessful'. The attribute mean scores for 'successful' and 'unsuccessful' products are shown in Table 2.

However, success is influenced by many factors. The articles in the business press rarely mentioned particular attributes in isolation and so it is important to look at the influence of combinations of attributes. This can be done using factor analysis. This is a much-used statistical technique for simplifying large databases. Factor analysis proceeds by identifying clusters of variables (attributes in this example) that are intercorrelated and are thus component measures of a larger more aggregate dimension, called a factor. Thus a database with many variables is reduced to a smaller number of overall dimensions which are manageable and interpretable and yet contain most of the original information.

Factor analysis was run on the database of 77 cases with 43 variables or attributes*. Nine factors emerged. They are interpreted by examining their component variables, represented by the factor loadings (see Table 2). The factors are: targeting through direct mail, overall quality, communication strategy, product fit and internal marketing, use of technology, intermediary support, market research, differentiated product and low price.

'Successful targeting of financial services is achieved through direct mail'

The next section of the article describes each of these factors with some illustrations.

*Factor analysis (principal components, Varimax rotation, Kaiser normalisation) was performed. The Kaiser–Meyer–Olkin measure of sampling adequacy was 0.67 indicating that the data are suitable for factor analysis, in spite of the poor ratio of cases to variables. On examination of the skee plot of the eigenvalues it was decided to include factors with eigenvalues greater than 1.20. This produced nine factors accounting for 67 per cent of the variance.

SUCCESS FACTORS

Targeting through direct mail

The first factor represents the use of direct mail to target appropriate segments. This is partly a matter of having a large database and also having the capability to select members of the target segment from this database, but it is also a case of designing the product and the direct mail to appeal to the market niche. Interpretation of this factor suggests that successful targeting of financial services is achieved much more through use of direct mail than it is through use of targeted advertising.

The Automobile Association has 7 million members and a database containing one-third of UK households. It has used direct mail techniques to build up a portfolio of 2.5 million motor insurance policies, 500 000 home insurance policies and 400 000 life insurance policies (*Precision Marketing*, 1989c).

Overall quality

The second factor is very much a complication of quality components, including the quality of the product itself compared to competitive products and the quality of the delivery system plus the high quality of the after-sales service, as well as a good fit between the product, its delivery and the organisational structure. The after-sales service helps to generate long-term goodwill which increases the likelihood of cross-selling other products at a later date. It is sometimes said that product quality in financial services can be difficult to assess and because of this other factors are important. The data here seem to support this view as the quality factor also includes attributes that measure the reputation of the organisation itself, plus the strength of the brand image and surrogate tangible elements, such as plastic cards and documents, to build customer perception of quality.

There were many illustrations of this factor. Chase Home Loans is committed to keeping its mortgage rate in the bottom quarter of the market and also undertakes to pay compensation to brokers when mortgages are not processed within a specified time period. The Insurance Service claimed to complete car repairs the next day by dealing directly with the garage. Companies also trade on the strength of their reputation e.g. Marks & Spencer in unit trusts (*Insurance Age*, 1988, 1989, *Marketing*, 1988).

Communication strategy

The third factor represents the effectiveness of the advertising strategy. This is partly a matter of the advertising creating a special image for the product, but it is also very much to do with achieving overall consistency (consistency with the marketing strategy, consistency with the company's other products, and consistency over time). In addition, it does seem that the effectiveness of the communication strategy is linked to technology leadership (superior product technology, superior delivery system technology and the superior use of technology in identifying customer needs). Presumably the technology advantage provides a real competitive advantage around which to build an effective communication strategy.

'Technology can also be used as a point of differentiation for the organisation'

Midland Bank helped to ensure that the communication strategy for Vector was consistent with the overall strategy for the product by involving both the design consultancy and the advertising agency at an early stage in the product development process (*Marketing*, 1987).

Product fit and internal marketing

Factor 4 describes the support the product receives and its fit with the organisation. It appears that products that complement or extend the existing product line are more likely to receive the support of a well-trained branch network staff than products not fitting in with the organisation so well. This is not surprising when it is recalled that a high street bank may offer 200–300 services so that any new product that competes with these existing products will not receive much support.

Nationwide Anglia tried to increase its staff's comprehension of FlexAccount by inviting them to open an account prior to the product's launch. Midland Bank spaces its new product launches to avoid overloading staff with too much new information (*Marketing Week*, 1988, *Precision Marketing*, 1989a).

Technology

Factor 5 has a technological emphasis with technology used partly as a tool to help manage the account (i.e. as on a cost control tool) but also more positively to give value to the consumer such as by providing an individualised service. Technology can also be used as a point of differentiation for the organisation, and to aid in the development of long-term relationships.

The use of screen-based information systems has allowed Girobank to reposition itself as a telephone-based bank, attempting to attract those consumers who prefer banking by phone in the evening to going to a bank's branch during the day. Midland Bank is experimenting with computer software to identify those customers who have recently changed their behaviour and offers them a new more suitable account before, it is hoped, the customer actively searches elsewhere (*Precision Marketing*, 1988, *Precision Marketing*, 1989a).

Intermediary support

Companies using an intermediary network do not of course have direct control over the support given their products by the intermediaries. Factor 6 describes the action taken (quality service, good financial returns, assistance via technology) to encourage intermediaries to support the company and its products.

'Many companies operate "help" lines, support the intermediary with relevant information'

Many companies operate 'help' lines, support the intermediary with relevant information, help the intermediary to manage the business, etc.

Market research

Factor 7 represents the financial organisation's commitment to market research. This includes continuous monitoring of customer needs, product improvements based on the results of market research, the development of products suited to particular market segments as well as test marketing and evaluation of new product ideas.

'The currency mortgage was rated as one of the most innovative developments'

Research undertaken by Barclays identified a segment of users of banking services that has an 'in-built fear of credit running away with them' and therefore attempted to appeal to this segment by positioning their new credit card Assent as a card that helps the user to keep 'in control' (*Precision Marketing*, 1989b).

Differentiated product

Factor 8 clearly describes characteristics of the differentiated product: providing unique benefits, being first, being innovative. The currency mortgage offered by mortgage brokers, John Charcol, was rated as one of the most innovative developments of the year in retail banking. It lets property owners take out a mortgage in a foreign currency and thereby take advantage of lower overseas interest rates. This has proved popular as UK interest rates continue to rise, although the high level of risk limits its market (*Management Today*, 1988).

Low price

Factor 9 is a low price strategy, associated with a fast response to changing market conditions. It seems that it is particularly appropriate to develop a low price alternative when copying competitor products, there being little otherwise to distinguish between such products. Speed of response is also important when reacting to developments in the marketplace. For example, the Nationwide Anglia FlexAccount was conceived and implemented in less than a year in response to regulatory changes (*Marketing Week*, 1988).

Summary

In summary, it has been demonstrated that the 43 attributes associated with new financial product success can be grouped into nine summary factors. Some of the key points to emerge from this analysis are:

- Successful targeting of financial services is achieved more through the effective use of direct mail than it is through use of alternative elements of the marketing mix such as targeted advertising.
- Quality is a multi-dimensional factor comprising elements of the product, its delivery, the after-sales service, the reputation of the organisation, the branding of the product and the existence of tangible elements.
- The effectiveness of the advertising strategy is seen as driven by the consistency of the strategy: consistency with the marketing strategy, other products and over time.

- A competitive edge in technology can provide the basis of effective communication.
- Products that complement the existing product range are likely to receive staff support.
- Intermediaries are attracted by quality service, good financial returns and technological support.

DETERMINANTS OF SUCCESS

This article has described the attributes and factors that financial services managers must understand and manage when launching a new product. But how much can be said about the association of these attributes and factors with success? There are several ways of answering this question.

'Every attribute made some contribution to the success of the product'

Table 2 reports the average contribution of each factor towards the success of the financial services product. All attributes rated higher than 5 can be interpreted as having made some contribution at least, on average, to the success of the product, even if slight, and all attributes rated as 6 or higher can be interpreted as having made a positive contribution, on average, to the success of the product. Examination of Table 2 shows that all 43 attributes were rated higher than 5.0 for the successful products. Thus every attribute made some contribution to the success of the product, on average, even if the contribution in some cases was small. It is encouraging to note that 33 or the 43 attributes (77 per cent) were rated 6.0 or higher and thus assessed to have made a clear contribution to the success of the product.

A second approach to understanding the causes of success in this market is to compare the average value of each attribute for successful products versus unsuccessful products. In all but one case the average value was higher for the successful products than for the unsuccessful ones In 25 out of the 43 attributes (58 per cent) this difference between successful and unsuccessful products was statistically significant at the 5 per cent level or higher (at the 10 per cent level the difference was statistically significant in 31 of the cases, i.e. 72 per cent) and in 12 out of the 43 cases (28 per cent) the difference was highly significant (1 per cent level).

'Success in financial services is rarely due to the effect of a single attribute'

However, success in financial services is rarely due to the effect of a single attribute but is due to combinations of attributes. The correlations between the average factor score and the estimate of success were therefore calculated (see Table 3).

Four of the factors are highly correlated with success:

- overall quality
- differentiated product
- product fit and internal marketing
- use of technology

These findings broadly confirm results from literatures other than financial services (i.e. the product success factors literature, services marketing literature) that factors such as a differentiated product, product fit and competitive use of technology are associated with successful new products. However, the additional contribution is twofold. First, of course,

Table 3. Correlations with success.

Factor	Correlation coefficient
(1) Targeting through direct mail	0.10
(2) Overall quality	0.42*
(3) Communication strategy	0.12
(4) Product fit and internal marketing	0.27*
(5) Use of technology	0.23*
(6) Intermediary support	0.14
(7) Market research	0.11
(8) Differentiated product	0.35*
(9) Low price	0.10

* Significant at the 1 per cent level.

is that the association between some of these factors and product success has now been established and measured in financial services. Second, factors such as differentiation, quality, product fit and technology have been interpreted in a financial services context for the first time.

'Having a differentiated product is associated with successful financial products'

For instance, it has been found here that having a differentiated product (being first, being innovative) is associated with successful financial products, and this finding has its direct equivalent in the product success factors literature (Cooper, 1984a; Cooper and Kleinschmidt, 1987a). However, 'overall quality' (the product, the delivery system, after-sales service, the organisational reputation for quality), which is more highly correlated, is a new factor integrating a number of attributes described in the services marketing literature (e.g. the importance of the company-customer interface (de Brentani, 1989) and the importance of company reputation (Easingwood and Mahajan, 1989)).

'Product fit and internal marketing' (the new product complementing existing products and receiving support from the staff) is a new factor combining attributes identified in the product success factors literature (see Cooper, 1984b on 'product fit') with attributes identified in the services marketing literature (see de Brentani, 1989 on marketing new services to an organisation's own front-line personnel). Finally, the opportunity provided by technology to deliver a competitive edge has been discussed fairly widely (see Watkins, 1988 in financial services; Porter and Miller, 1985 more generally).

We consider these results to be most encouraging, especially as the study did not include many unsuccessful financial products. With more unsuccessful products included in the comparison it would be expected that the differences in attribute and factor scores between successful and less successful financial products would have been even more evident.

STRATEGIES

Finally, do financial services companies use similar strategies to support their products? To find out, a cluster analysis (Ward's Method) was run on the factor scores producing three clusters with very distinct profiles (see Table 4).

Table 4. Mean factor scores for clusters.

Factor	Clusters		
	I (n = 26)	II (n = 16)	III (n = 35)
(1) Targeting through direct mail	0.70	0.01	−0.53
(2) Overall quality	0.41	0.27	−0.43
(3) Communicating strategy	0.29	−0.46	−0.01
(4) Product fit and internal marketing	0.32	−0.12	−0.18
(5) Use of technology	−0.24	1.21	−0.38
(6) Intermediary support	−0.62	0.84	0.07
(7) Market research	0.11	0.19	−0.17
(8) Differentiated product	−0.11	0.18	0.00
(9) Low price	−0.12	0.13	0.03

The first cluster, with 26 cases, contained successful financial products (average success score of 7.2). The emphasis for products in this group is placed on targeting through direct mail and overall quality, with some, although rather less emphasis on a good product fit and internal marketing together with an effective communication strategy. Intermediaries are not used.

The second cluster of products are also successful (average of 7.4), but apart from this are very different from the first cluster. Particular emphasis is placed on effective use of technology in combination with (possibly in support of) intermediaries. Overall quality is slightly above average but there is little emphasis on communication strategies, possibly because of the intermediary emphasis.

'Quality, a differentiated product, product fit, internal marketing and use of technology are associated with success'

The last cluster is less successful than the first two groups (average success score of 6.4) and not surprisingly there are no factors with high positive scores and the average rating is particularly low on targeting through direct mail, overall quality and use of technology.

CONCLUSIONS

The research described in this article has identified a number of attributes that are associated with new financial product success. These basic attributes are grouped into nine distinct underlying factors. The research has shown that four of these factors, namely, overall quality, a differentiated product, product fit and internal marketing and use of technology are associated with success. The attributes forming each factor have also been described. Marketing managers must pay particular attention to the management of these factors if they are to introduce new financial products that are successful.

'Future work will look at a wider range of measures of success in financial services'

Future work will seek to integrate more completely findings from related areas such as the growing literature on product success factors, will look at a wider range of measures of success in financial services (Easingwood and Percival, 1990), and will seek to contrast successful financial products with a larger number of unsuccessful products.

REFERENCES

Banking World, December 1988, p. 13.
Cooper, R. G. (1984a), 'How New Product Strategies Impact on Performance', *Journal of Product Innovation Management*, Vol. 1 No. 1, pp. 5–18.
Cooper, R. G. (1984b), 'New Product Strategies: What Distinguishes the Top Performers', *Journal of Product Innovation Management*, Vol. 1, No. 3, pp. 151–64.
Cooper, R. G. (1986), 'New Product Performance and Product Innovation Strategies', *Research Management*, Vol. 29 No. 3, pp. 19–25.
Cooper, R. G. (1988), 'The New Product Process: A Decision Guide for Management', *Journal of Marketing Management*, Vol. 3 No. 3, pp. 238–55.
Cooper, R. G. and Kleinschmidt, E. J. (1987a), 'Success Factors in Product Innovation', *Industrial Marketing Management*, Vol. 16, pp. 215–23.
Cooper, R. G. and Kleinschmidt, E. J. (1987b), 'What Makes a New Product a Winner: Success Factors at the Project Level', *R & D Management*, Vol. 17 No. 3, pp. 175–89.
Davison, H., Watkins, T. and Wright, M. (1989), 'Developing New Personal Financial Products—Some Evidence on the Role of Market Research', *International Journal of Bank Marketing*, Vol. 7 No. 1, pp. 8–15.
de Brentani, U. (1989), 'Success and Failure in New Industrial Services', *Journal of Product Innovation Management*, Vol 6, pp. 239–58.
Easingwood, C. J. (1986), 'New Product Development for Service Companies', *Journal of Product Innovation Management*, Vol. 4, pp. 264–75.
Easingwood, C. J. and Mahajan, V. (1989), 'Positioning of Financial Services for Competitive Advantage', *Journal of Product Innovation Management*, Vol. 6 No. 3, pp. 207–19.
Easingwood, C. J. and Percival, J. (1990), 'Evaluation of New Financial Services', *International Journal of Bank Marketing*, Vol. 8 No. 6, pp. 3–8.
Insurance Age, October 1988, p. 26.
Insurance Age, Mortgage Supplement, March 1989, p. 9.
Langeard, E., Reffait, P. and Eiglier, P. (1986), 'Developing New Services' in Venkatesan, M., Schmalensee, D. M. and Marshall, C. (Eds), *Creativity in Services Marketing*, American Marketing Association, Chicago, Illinois.
Management Today, December 1988, p. 54.
Marketing, 29 October 1987, p. 43; 6 October 1988, p. 1.
Marketing Week, 1 April 1988, p. 50.
Porter, M. E. and Miller, V. E. (1985), 'How Information Gives You Competitive Advantage', *Harvard Business Review*, July–August, pp. 149–60.
Precision Marketing, 31 October 1988, p. 2; 16 January 1989a, p. 8; 8 May 1989b, p. 27; 3 July 1989c, p. 8.
Reidenbach, R. E. and Moak, D. L. (1986), 'Exploring Retail Bank Performance and New Product Development: A Profile of Industry Practices', *Journal of Product Innovation Management*, Vol. 3 No. 3, pp. 187–94.
Watkins, T. (1988), 'The Use of Information Technology in Insurance Marketing', *Marketing Intelligence & Planning*, Vol. 6 No. 2, pp. 21–6.

10

Bank Customers' Perceptions, Innovations and New Technology

Luiz Moutinho and Arthur Meidan

INTRODUCTION

Recent changes in the technology of financial services, suppliers and delivery systems have produced more assortment, convenience and economy for consumers. All these innovations have changed the face and format of the financial services industry by introducing new marketing patterns and practices.

Many factors have contributed to make financial services attractive and affordable. These include a progressive deregulation in banking; higher discretionary income; the two-income family; rising interest rates; the entry of non-banks offering non-regulated services; accessible telecommunications and accurate information; mass advertising and promotion of financial services, and new delivery systems (Meidan and Moutinho, 1988). In these circumstances, the roles of new product development, technology and innovations have become of paramount importance. Indeed, the banking industry has reacted with large numbers of new products which have an impact on both customers and on the financial institutions themselves.

NEW TECHNOLOGY AND INNOVATION

The future banking scenario will be profoundly different technologically from that of today. Recent product innovation in banking include:

- *Office/Home Banking.* Using a terminal, visual display unit and telecommunication link, a customer (personal or corporate) has access to a range of services, e.g. payment services, financial management services and reporting services within the home or office.
- *Electronic Letter of Credit.* This service enables corporate customers to open or amend a letter of credit in their office and transmit it to the bank instantly. It may stand alone as a single product or form part of the office banking package.
- *Provision of Financial Information.* Financial data and information that are frequently updated are broadcast to customers' terminals via cable. The service includes foreign currency and interest rates reporting, various rates forecasts, and prediction and commentaries. View Data and Reuters are typical examples.

- *Global Cash Management*. This service is made possible by the breakthrough in telecommunications technology which has facilitated the transfer of information over long distances. It is particularly useful for international corporations which have bank accounts worldwide. The service allows customers to transmit instructions about accounts or funds transfer electronically, and provides reporting facilities for global accounts, transaction deals (details of debit and credit entry) and foreign exchange deals. The customer can, therefore, minimise borrowing costs, maximise returns on surplus funds and hedge against interest rate or foreign exchange fluctuations.
- *Self-service Bank*. This is a bank office with limited staff but a whole range of fully automated terminals which allows customers to transact banking activities via self service, e.g. the lobby ATM of Verbraucherbank in West Germany.
- *ATM Cash Dispenser*. ATMs have prevailed in the UK for a number of years but the present trend is to build more functions into the quick cash dispenser. Moreover, to obtain sufficient transaction volume to justify its operating costs, some banks, e.g. National Westminster and Midland in the UK, are sharing their ATMs.
- *EFTPoS* is a cashless and chequeless means for shopping and payment at the point of sale. Its operation requires a debit card, a Personal Identification Number (PIN) and a PoS terminal that is connected with the bank's mainframe. Its main feature is that the customer's and retailer's accounts will be debited and credited respectively with the purchase amount at the same time.
- *The Smart Card*. This is a memory card with a traditional magnetic strip and a programmable micro-chip. Invented by a Frenchman (Roland Moreno) in 1974, it has been taken seriously by the world's banks and credit card companies only over the last five years or so. It operates in an off-line environment and its many uses include: ATM transactions, EFTPoS transactions, videotex and as a personal identification card. At present, it finds its major success in France, with government support.
- *A Total Systems Approach*. Packages or systems of financial services make sense for the consumer because they conveniently provide a total solution to the financial problems facing him/her. They make sense for the financial institution because built into the concept is an automatic vehicle for increasing the number of financial services used per customer. This is highly desirable because previous research has shown that the more relationships a customer has with the financial institution, the less likely he/she is to switch financial institutions.

The concept of predetermined packages of financial services can be worked a number of ways, depending on a financial institution's capabilities, imagination and market characteristics. For instance, a bank in a college town might develop one package for college-age consumers, another for young adult households, a third for middle-aged adults and a fourth for business accounts.

New technology is no longer a simple, supporting feature in the banking industry; it is not just a 'catalyst' in the development process either. It has specific implications for bank product development.

The objectives of the present study were to:

- determine the dimensions of bank customer's current usage of financial services, as well as the level of usage of new and more sophisticated bank services, in particular, those related to electronic fund transfer and automated teller machine systems;
- determine the importance which bank customers attach to some basic attributes of

more familiar bank services and their perceptions, attitudes and importance ratings with respect to some new bank products;
- evaluate the level of usage, importance and customers' perceived risk attached to ATMs, and
- evaluate the level and probability of bank switching as related to the level of satisfaction/dissatisfaction experience by the customer with regard to the bank's current offerings.

METHODOLOGY

In order to work out an interaction-based approach of bank customer behaviour, a theoretical framework was developed to evaluate the usefulness of the research design. This framework is depicted in Figure 1.

A stratified sampling procedure was used in this study. The research has been executed by sampling and interviewing 200 established bank customers. In addition to the 14 attitudinal statements towards banking, each one using a seven-point rating scale, the

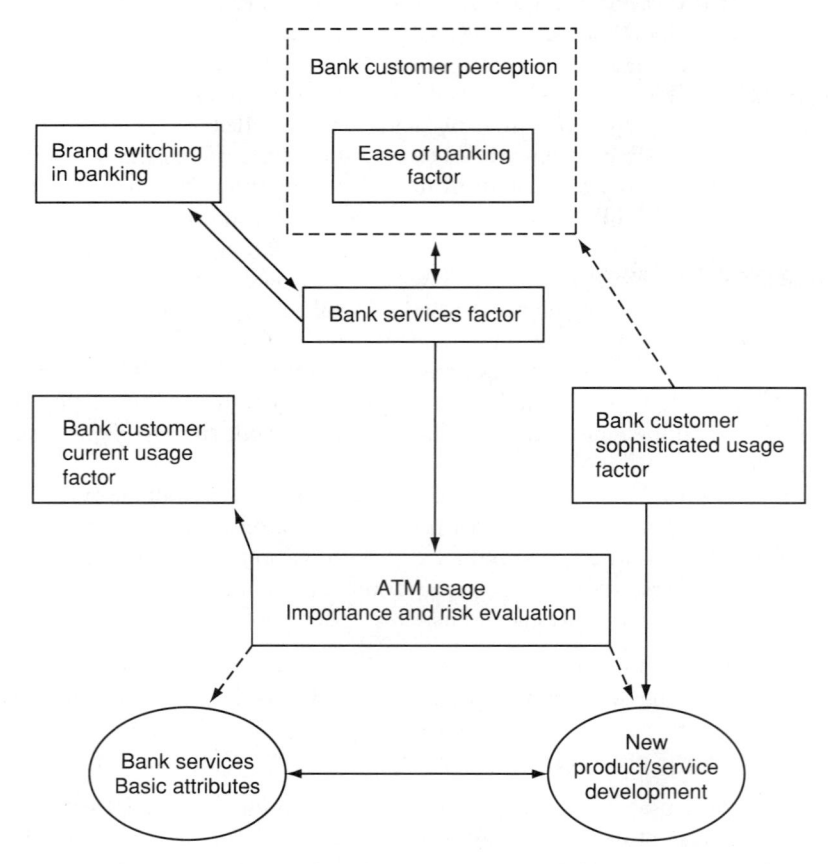

Figure 1. A theoretical framework for the study of bank customer perception and loyalty related to current bank usage and new product development.

questionnaire also contained 'filter' questions and demographic characteristics-related items. The two demographic variables used in this analysis were age and sex. The ratio of female to male respondents was 106:94. In terms of age brackets, the sample comprised: 18–35 age group, 26 per cent; 36–53 age group, 43 per cent; and 54 and over, 31 per cent.

Four groups of variables were selected as descriptors and independent variables, each operationalised by a number of items, with the exception of the variable concerned with 'new technology'. These groups of variables comprise bank services variables, ATM variables and bank loyalty variables. The groups of variables and their items are listed in Figure 2. The items were designed to measure bank marketing effectiveness in three essential areas:

(1) provision of existing and new banking services; the 'human factor' (helpfulness of staff) and pricing policy;
(2) usage rate, importance and perceived risk of ATMs, and
(3) bank switching, loyalty and usage patterns in relation to bank pricing and lending policies.

The variable NEWT 1 was related to the level of bank customer awareness with regard to 'smart' credit cards.

Factor analysis has been used to investigate whether the three plus one hypothesised groups of variables would result in corresponding and mutually independent factors. Following the principles of parsimony, splitting of factors ended when only one variable dominated on one factor. In traditional factor analysis models, both factor loadings and factor scores are indeterminate. In confirmatory factor analysis, the loading

Bank services
SERV 1 — New bank services
SERV 2 — Helpfulness of bank tellers
SERV 3 — Number and location of ATMS
SERV 4 — Banking fees
SERV 5 — Average wait in line/queue to see a teller

ATM usage
ATM 1 — Average wait in line/queue to use an ATM
ATM 2 — Importance of ATM to withdraw/deposit
ATM 3 — Importance of ATM to pay off credit cards
ATM 4 — Perception of safeness when using an ATM

Bank loyalty
LOYA 1 — Credit card interest rate effects on usage
LOYA 2 — Credit card interest rate effects on switching bank
LOYA 3 — Savings accounts interest rate effects on switching bank
LOYA 4 — Turn-down effect on switching bank

Technological awareness
NEWT 1 — Awareness of new 'smart' credit cards

Figure 2. List of research variables.

indeterminacy problem is overcome by restricting certain loadings (or factor variances) a priori.

The LISREL model provides an integral approach to data analysis and theory construction. This is accomplished by allowing simultaneous evaluation of both the measurement and causal (i.e. structural) components of a system. The casual component refers to the hypothesised structural relationships between the latent constructs. LISREL can easily handle errors in measurement, correlated errors and residuals, and reciprocal causation; and uses maximum likelihood estimation, which is a full information approach. This means that all of the parameters are estimated simultaneously.

The study variables were measured through the use of itemised rating scales which had a set of distinct response categories associated with the main 14 attitudinal areas of research. The different itemised rating scales implied an attitude continuum underlying the response categories. Furthermore, they essentially took the form of multiple-category questions. During the pre-testing of the questionnaire, it was found that an itemised rating scale would be easier to respond to and more meaningful from the respondents' perspective.

Personal interviews with established bank customers were carried out at three bank branches situated in different social strata locations. An introductory statement explaining the purpose of the study was used as an opener designed to secure respondents' co-operation. The selection of qualified respondents was made through a screening process based on their demographic and established bank customer profile. The measurement model can be described by two equations which specify the relations between endogenous latent and manifest variables and between exogenous latent and manifest (i.e. observable) variables, respectively. These equations bear a close resemblance to the basic factor-analytic model. Actually, the measurement component of the LISREL model can be viewed in terms of a confirmatory factor-analytic model.

The structural equation component of LISREL refers to the hypothesised exogenous and latent endogenous variables that characterise the causal system under study.

The objective of LISREL is to reproduce the observed co-variance matrix as closely as possible and to determine the goodness of fit of the model to the data. The χ^2-test compares the goodness of fit between the co-variance matrix for the observed data (S) and co-variance matrix ($\hat{\Sigma}$) derived from a theoretically specified structure (model).

The goodness-of-fit index (GFI) is a measure of the relative amount of the variances and co-variances jointly accounted for by the model. The computer program used in this research study was LISREL VI.

FINDINGS

Factor analysis utilising LISREL estimates (maximum likelihood method) resulted in four factors (underlying customer attitudes towards new and existing banking services) shown in Table 1 and described as follows:

(1) *'On-the-move' customers.* Individuals with high factor scores on this underlying attitude towards banking tend to be concerned about queuing and waiting in line, either when they want to use an automated teller machine (ATM) or see a bank teller, and place a great deal of importance on the utilisation of ATMs when withdrawing or depositing

money. They are usually considered to be 'heavy users' of ATMs. They also show a considerable amount of concern about the number and locations of ATMs. They are convenience-orientated bank customers.

(2) *'Hi-tech value/cost-oriented' customers.* Bank customers concerned with this factor place importance on the development of new bank technology. They are the only group aware of the new 'smart' credit cards. They perceive the use of ATMs as being safe and would also like to see ATMs providing extended services such as paying off credit cards. On the other hand, they show concern about the high costs of bank technology which ultimately would be passed on to customers through banking fees.

(3) *'Better-of-the same' customers.* Individuals with high factor scores on this underlying attitude towards banking tend to wish for the development of new bank services, although these relate more to an extension and improvement of existing bank products and services. They also place a great deal of importance on the 'human factor' in the delivery of bank services, such as the degree of helpfulness of bank tellers.

(4) *'Price-sensitive' customers.* Bank customers concerned with this factor place a great deal of importance on the interest rates charged by the bank. High interest rates will trigger a negative effect on these customers in terms of credit card usage and degree of bank loyalty. High interest rates on credit cards may even lead these customers to switch banks, as well as low interest rates on savings accounts. A 'turn-down loan' effect will most likely make them switch banks.

These four factors have an adjusted, goodness-of-fit index of 0.823 as indicated in Table 2. The resulting factors determined 82 per cent of total variance and co-variance of the

Table 1. Factor analysis and structure of bank customer attitudinal groups—LISREL estimates (maximum likelihood).

Variables	Factor 1	Factor 2	Factor 3	Factor 4
SERV 1	–	–	0.710 000	–
SERV 2	–	–	0.540 000	–
SERV 3	0.640 000	–	–	–
SERV 4	–	0.540 000	–	–
SERV 5	0.610 000	–	–	–
ATM 1	0.750 000	–	–	–
ATM 2	0.590 000	–	–	–
ATM 3	–	0.510 000	–	–
ATM 4	–	0.590 000	–	–
LOYA 1	–	–	–	0.410 000
LOYA 2	–	–	–	0.650 000
LOYA 3	–	–	–	0.450 000
LOYA 4	–	–	–	0.720 000
NEWT 1	–	0.420 000	–	–

Measures of goodness of fit for the whole model:
Chi-square with 149 degrees of freedom: 202.46 ($p = 0.002$).
Goodness-of-fit index 0.828.
Adjusted goodness-of-fit index 0.823.
Root mean square residual 0.110.

Table 2. Factor structure of bank services effectiveness, ATM usage and bank loyalty items—an alternative factor labelling: the bank service provider side.

Items	Factor 1 Current Usage	Factor 2 Cost/value of Technology	Factor 3 Ease of Banking
SERV 1	–	–	0.710 000
SERV 2	–	–	0.540 000
SERV 3	0.640 000	–	–
SERV 4	–	0.540 000	–
SERV 5	0.610 000	–	–

Items	Factor 1 Current Usage	Factor 2 Cost/Value of Technology
ATM 1	0.750 000	–
ATM 2	0.590 000	–
ATM 3	–	0.510 000
ATM 4	–	0.590 000

Items	Factor 4: Bank Switching
LOYA 1	0.410 000
LOYA 2	0.650 000
LOYA 3	0.450 000
LOYA 4	0.720 000

Reliability Estimate: % Variance and Co-variance = 82.

implemented items. Only factor loadings greater than +4.0 (cut-off point for the solution) were used in the interpretation of the factors. As shown in Table 1, the cross loadings of each item on the LISREL is significant at $p = 0.002$. The resulting factor structure for a specified four-factor solution supports the discriminant validity of the results, according to the loadings of the 14 questions on four separate factors (Table 1). The items with the highest correlations are descriptive of the 'on-the-move' bank customer's factor.

The factors derived are somewhat simpler than the hypothesised groups of independent variables of the research model.

The results of the factor-analysis procedure indicate that established bank customers can be differentiated by their perceptions, attitudes and degree of loyalty towards existing and new bank technology. Further research refinement and development may be necessary for determining their reasons for adopting or rejecting new bank technology.

The factors characterising 'hi-tech value/cost-oriented' and 'price-sensitive' bank customers, however, have practical implications for developing and marketing existing, improved and new bank services to these two groups. For instance, 'hi-tech value/cost-oriented' customers have high loadings on items emphasising new bank technology benefits. New services to be provided by EFT systems should be targeted towards this group. Furthermore, a flexible pricing policy to be implemented by the bank should have an optimal effect on them.

'Price-sensitive' customers have high loadings on items related to the bank's policy on interest rates. They represent a segment of the market with a high-price elasticity of demand. The bank should apply competitive price strategies in this case, in order to increase the credit card usage rate, the number of savings accounts, and to minimise the risk of bank switching.

BUILDING ON PAST RESULTS

Some of the findings in this study conflict with those of a prior study which concluded that price was not a major factor in bank choice (Lawson and Watt, 1983). However, other results, i.e. those related to the 'on-the-move' bank customers, in terms of availability and location of ATMs, convenience and avoidance of queues, coincide with those of previous studies (Lawson and Watt, 1983; Watkins, 1984; Arora et al., 1985; Matthews and Watt, 1986). Finally, the findings related to the 'better-of-the-same' customer group also coincide with those of a prior bank customer behaviour study (Laroche et al., 1986).

Table 2 shows the solution's factor structure, described according to an alternative labelling process. In this case, bank services effectiveness, ATM usage and bank customer loyalty variables are loaded into rotated factors, which were labelled according to a number of critical bank marketing policies:

(1) customer current usage of services;
(2) cost/value of new bank technology;
(3) ease of banking to EBCs, and
(4) bank switching.

Items concerned with the effectiveness of bank services have their highest loadings placed on the factors related to the current usage of services and the trend towards the ease of banking.

The loadings of ATM-related variables indicate that bank marketing managers should concentrate their attention on developing ATM current usage. This can be done through the provision of additional services, for example, by incorporating artificial intelligence (AI) devices. The results pertaining to bank loyalty variables are all related to the bank switching factor, as if they were confirming a natural assumption.

Incorporating of elements of the banking services supplier in this model of interaction based on segmentation proves to be an enrichment of the research design, compared with studying and measuring purely the perceptions, attitudes and behavioural patterns of bank clients. A clear advantage of this type of interaction-based market segmentation is the direct relation between marketing stimuli and descriptor variables (Vollering, 1984).

CONCLUSION AND IMPLICATIONS

The introduction of new products such as EFTPoS, home banking and ATMs have greatly decreased the interface of the bank with its customers. These products will not build customer franchises, but will lower the bank's direct involvement with the customer and may, in turn, affect patterns of customer loyalty (Howcroft and Lavis, 1986). Some of the possible marketing developments as a result of new technology and product innovation in banking are presented in Table 3.

Especially for home banking, customers can carry out simple banking transactions, such

Table 3. The impact of new technology on product development, bank customers and marketing policies.

Some recent new banking products (as a result of technology and innovation)	The impact on bank customers	Possible future bank marketing policies
(1) Office/home banking (2) Electronic letter of credit (3) Provision of financial information (4) Global cash management (5) Self-service banking (6) ATM—cash dispenser (7) EFTPoS (8) Smart card	(a) A decrease in the direct interface between the customers and the bank, i.e. depersonalisation (b) Lower direct involvement with the customer (c) Less customer loyalty to the bank (d) Difficulties in differentiating among various bank products	• Diversification of products and specialisation • Careful segmentation • Less branches but larger outlets; attempts to increase 'cross-selling' in branches • ATM to provide more functions • More non-traditional banking services including development of 'stand-alone' products • Fee income will form a larger part of banks' total income • More rational pricing, including more differential pricing policies • Promotions to assume greater importance

as bill settlement and account enquiry without visiting the branch at all. Even if the customer needs to withdraw cash (home banking does not allow cash withdrawal), he/she can resort to ATM or EFTPoS (for the latter service, a cash withdrawal facility may be provided at the retailer's discretion by 'overcharging' the customer a certain sum and giving the same sum to the customer in cash). Since customers do not necessarily have to visit the bank to conduct their financial affairs, the chance for the bank to 'cross-sell' its other services will largely be reduced. Indeed a trend of *depersonalisation* is emerging in the banking industry, and as such, its impact on the way in which banking business will be conducted is unknown. The implication for bank product development is that the trend is towards more '*stand alone*' products consisting of only one or a few associated services.

Moreover, it will become more difficult for customers to differentiate the services offered by one bank from those of another, as any technological advantage gained will be short lived; it is easily imitated or even emulated. The growing trend of *non-differentiation* among bank products, coupled with competition internal and external to the banking sector, has three main implications.

First, to contest successfully in a highly competitive environment, in which lines of demarcation among banks and between banks and other financial institutions are becoming blurred, banks should be willing to *concentrate* on appropriate activities. They can no longer afford to perform every operation and provide every service in every physical location (Hopper, 1986). It is necessary to increase specialisation at an ever-increasing pace. They must carefully segment their markets and use both branches and automated delivery systems to provide 'tailored' products to selected consumer groups. Career women, two-salary or multi-salary families, the over-50s market, and the high-balance, high net worth segment all warrant special attention (Howcroft and Lavis, 1986). Market segmentation by specialisation and differentiation will require the choice of a delivery system mix and will ultimately influence the cost structure and hence the bank's profitability and ability to operate successfully in the market.

Secondly, *fee income* will form a much larger part of the bank's total income. Existing and new products have to be rationally and competitively priced. Many services that have been provided free in the past will have to be charged and differential pricing will be used where possible (especially if there are no restrictive legislations imposed by the Office of Fair Trading) to encourage customers to use new products like EFTPoS, in which high transaction volume is essential to justify the economics of its operation.

Thirdly, when consumers find it increasingly difficult to distinguish one bank from another or from other financial institutions, *promotion* will assume greater importance. For instance, advertising and promotional phrases could appear on the screen of ATMs, home banking terminals and even on the debit or credit cards.

Furthermore, to justify the continuation of the *branches and ATMs*, banks will have to carry out new product development by providing a wider range of services and performing more functions. The number of branches will decrease, but many branches will be larger and will play a major part in serving the middle market of small businesses, farmer retailers and professionals. This will form part of the segmentation strategy, and the product range can be enriched by including more non-traditional bank services. The branches can sell much more extensively, ranging from ancillary services, such as insurance, portfolio management, tax management, leasing, factoring and pension schemes, to the more diverse information services such as travel, estate agency, legal advice, business and marketing research. At present, Barclays operates a 'Money Doctor' scheme which provides money management services and is especially useful to professionals. National Westminster and Lloyds offer Business Development Loans for small to medium businesses; and various loans and schemes are available for farmers to help them purchase machinery and agricultural equipment.

Similarly, the ATMs should perform *more functions*. For instance, some ATMs at present only enable customers to enquire on their account balance and withdraw cash. More functions similar to those provided by competitor banks, such as account transfer and requests for bank statements and cheque books, should be built in.

With the passage of time, society is becoming confronted with an accelerated shift from an industrial to an information technology-orientation. A new breed of consumer, who is more demanding and technologically aware, has emerged. With the changing expectations of consumers the skill levels of bank employees will have direct effects on bank performance. Banks will have to accept the inappropriateness of treating consumers as a mass market, if retail effectiveness is to be sharpened.

REFERENCES

Arora, R., Cavusgil, T. S. and Nevin, J. R. (1985), 'Evaluation of Financial Institutions by Bank versus Savings and Loan Customers: An Analysis of Factor Congruency', *International Journal of Bank Marketing*, Vol. 3 No. 3, pp. 47–55.
Hopper, M. (1986), 'Strategies for the Development of Electronic Systems', *Journal of Bank Research*, pp. 202–5.

Howcroft, J. B. and Lavis, J. (1986), *The New Revolution in Structure and Strategy*, Blackwell, Oxford, pp. 64–72; 173–82.

Laroche, M., Rosenblatt, J. A. and Manning, T. (1986), 'Services Used and Factors Considered Important in Selecting a Bank: An Investigation across Diverse Demographic Segments', *International Journal of Bank Marketing*, Vol. 4 No. 1, pp. 35–55.

Lawson, R. and Watt, A. W. (1983), 'Market Orientated Pricing for UK Banks', *International Journal of Bank Marketing*, Vol. 1 No. 2, pp. 53–67.

Matthews, B. P. and Watt, A. W. (1986), 'Bank Selection Criteria Reviewed: The Case of the National Girobank', in Cowell, D. and Collis, J. (Eds.), *Proceedings of the Marketing Education Group 19th Annual Conference 'Managing Marketing'*, Plymouth, July, pp. 589–602.

Meidan, A. and Moutinho, L. (1988), 'Bank Customers' Perceptions and Loyalty—An Attitudinal Study', *Proceedings of European Marketing Academy Conference*, Bradford University Management Centre, 6–8 April.

Vollering, J. B. (1984), 'Interaction Based Market Segmentation', *Industrial Marketing Management*, Vol. 13, pp. 75–80.

Watkins, T. (1984), 'Optimising Bank Service Provision: A Simulation Approach', *International Journal of Bank Marketing*, Vol. 2 No. 1.

11

Insurance Product Development: Managing the Changes

Axel Johne

INTRODUCTION

Both life and general insurers in Britain are today under pressure to strengthen their market offerings. This is a direct result of deregulation, which has brought with it increased competitive activities and will continue to do so under ongoing legislative changes within the European Community. Product innovation is also being stimulated by heightened customer expectations, advances in enabling technology, and by new forms of competition.

Traditional players now poach each other's customers. Not only this, but they themselves are vulnerable to new styles of competition from entrants like banks and building societies. In many insurance markets, old-style combative marketing is being supplemented by new-style competitive marketing in which companies fight for business in radically changed ways (Peters, 1990; McKenna, 1991). These competitive changes have powerful implications for established insurance companies which now face urgent decisions as far as the management of product development is concerned.

WHAT IS SUCCESSFUL PRODUCT DEVELOPMENT?

It is commonly assumed that a product development is successful if it meets objectives set by the supplying company. But, because companies have differing objectives and use different methods for measuring financial performance, there is disagreement over how product development success can be measured. There is also disagreement over what constitutes a product development. Some have argued that the tasks faced by suppliers define the nature of a development. This has led to the suggestion that there are two main types of product development—product improvement and new product development. Product improvement being concerned with updating existing products and new product development being concerned with quite new offerings (Johne and Snelson, 1990). We can call this approach the supply-based approach.

Other writers stress that the true nature of product development and whether it is successful can only be understood from the viewpoint of the market. The argument runs that it is customers' preferences which determine how offerings are received: appropriately targeted offerings are likely to be successful, while poorly targeted offerings are likely to be unsuccessful. Proponents of this viewpoint stress that what needs to be analysed is not the challenge with which a particular product development presents a supplier, but how different a development is in meeting the preferences of customers (de Bruicker and Summe, 1985; Quinn et al., 1990; Mathur, 1992). We can call this latter approach the market-based approach.

Fundamental to the market-based approach is the concept of the offering—that is to say, what has been developed for a target market. An example will bring this concept alive. Insurance offerings are made up of merchandise (cover) and support (service). Proponents of the market-based approach argue that it will be the mix of both which determines the level of demand. Market segments will respond differently. Some segments will want support and will be prepared to pay for it. Others will just want the basic cover.

In the case of many insurance offerings it has been left to brokers to add the support element. However, increasing numbers of companies now usurp the broker's function by selling direct. This is often the practice of new entrants, such as banks, which use their own distribution networks. A key question facing suppliers who do this is how much support to provide for the basic merchandise. If too little support is provided, inexperienced customers will feel hesitant in dealing direct. If too much support is provided, resources are wasted which could be applied to strengthening other elements in the marketing mix.

The market-based approach provides an effective method for assessing product development success. It is in specific markets that suppliers win or lose business, and therefore it is in markets that explanations for success or failure are to be found. Measuring success in target markets is, of course, quite different from the supply-based approach which uses internal measures. The distinction is important because frequently the internal hurdles used ignore market potentials.

We have deliberately spent time on the issue of product development success and how it might best be measured. Much academic research continues to rely on self-assessment by managers for classifying developments as successful or unsuccessful. Few researchers include controls to ensure that managers were aiming to fulfil similar objectives. The issue is important because reluctance on the part of analysts to state the objectives against which developments were undertaken can cause successes to be classified as failure and vice versa. For example, a company with high market or profitability hurdle rates will classify a product development as a failure if it fails to meet these, while another company with low hurdle rates will classify a similarly performing development as a success.

Market-based measures of product development success are powerful. An associated external measure of success is the degree to which a company is creating a market for itself on its own terms, rather than just competing on terms laid down by established industry players. This latter type of success can be achieved by destabilizing and reshaping an established market or, perhaps, even by opening up a completely new market, as was done by providing low-cost private motor insurance to customers direct through telesales (Johne, 1992).

While market share success registers that customers are responding positively to new offerings, it nonetheless represents an incomplete measure of success. The market-based measure tells us nothing about whether a supplier is managing to meet customers' preferences profitably (as opposed to doing customers a great favour). For this reason both measures must be considered together: the market-based measure to appraise the extent to which market potentials are being exploited; the supply-based measure to appraise whether internally determined targets are being met in the quest to maintain and develop the business.

The two measures of product development success pose marketing specialists with considerable challenges. Marketing specialists should, by virtue of their skills in accessing relevant information, be able to assist in developing offerings which have positive market appeal. Not only this, but marketing specialists have a responsibility to identify markets affording maximum opportunities. Additionally, they have responsibility in working together with other specialists to ensure success in terms of internal profitability. The extent to which marketing specialists can and do get involved in both these operational aspects depends on the extent to which marketing has been accepted in a company. It is this topic to which we turn next.

THE ADOPTION OF MARKETING IN INSURANCE COMPANIES

Table 1 shows different stages which one American author (Kotler, 1991) has suggested are typical in the slow learning of marketing in US banking. We shall see, later, that the adoption of marketing in British-based insurance companies appears to be following a similar pattern. Probably all British insurers now embrace marketing in the form of advertising, sales promotion and publicity. In companies at this first stage, marketing managers do just that—they are responsible for advertisements, sales promotions and publicity. Similarly, most insurance companies, and especially those which deal direct with customers (as opposed to relying on brokers), have now progressed through the second stage in adopting marketing—the smiling and friendly atmosphere stage—typified by Commercial Union's message: 'We won't make a drama out of a crisis'.

Greatly increased competition from established competitors and also from new entrants is forcing more and more suppliers of insurance to progress to the third stage in adopting marketing, where emphasis falls on developing new products. An internal slogan which typifies this stage is 'We must innovate in response to market changes, or we shall be overtaken by competitors'. All insurers approached in our study have now reached this stage in adopting marketing.

The next, higher, stage is the use of marketing expertise to position product developments in an optimal way. In this fourth stage, emphasis is on developing offerings (in terms of merchandise and support features) which are preferred above those offered by competitors. In the field of personal general insurance, some British insurers have now become skilled at applying this type of marketing to destabilize and reshape traditional markets. An example is provided by Direct Line, a new supplier established in 1985,

Table 1. Five stages in the adoption of marketing (from Kotler, 1991).

1. Marketing is advertising, sales promotion, and publicity.
2. Marketing is smiling and a friendly atmosphere.
3. Marketing is innovation.
4. Marketing is positioning.
5. Marketing is marketing analysis, planning, and control.

which is a wholly owned subsidiary of the Royal Bank of Scotland. Direct Line was one of the first motor insurance companies to cut out the traditional broker middleman to operate direct with customers using telesales techniques. In its first five years of operation it created over 300 000 new policyholders.

The fifth, and highest stage of marketing is when a company has installed effective systems for marketing analysis, planning, implementation and also control. When this has happened, marketing expertise is used to: (1) collect relevant marketing data; (2) analyse it for the purpose of positioning offerings appropriately; and (3) implement product change programmes profitably through planning and control. It is, of course, in this highest stage that marketing experts contribute not only to designing better positioned offerings, but also to their profitable introduction and management.

SAMPLE OF COMPANIES

There are literally hundreds of companies in Britain authorized to transact insurance business. Not all are active in the major areas of insurance. However, rivalry is increasingly tense, especially as a result of completely new entrants into the market. From the population of authorized companies identified from the *Insurance Directory & Year Book* (1992) a convenience sample of 10 general insurers and 10 life companies based in London and the south-east of England was selected. Both large and small companies were included.

Initial contact was made by letter addressed to the chief executive of the relevant part of each company followed by a telephone call to amplify the objectives of the study. The purpose of the telephone call was to obtain the company's co-operation and to identify the names of appropriate managers to interview. Fourteen general insurers were initially approached, of which 10 agreed to take part in the study. In the case of life companies the numbers were twelve and ten. The names of the co-operating companies are given Table 2.

The main data were obtained through face-to-face interviews conducted at the relevant operating site. It was not possible to control strictly for the job title of respondents. In some companies the chief executive was interviewed, in others less senior managers were interviewed holding a variety of titles, such as assistant general manager, business

Table 2. Companies which co-operative in the research.

Life insurers	General insurers
Barclays Life	Cornhill
Clerical Medical	Eagle Star
Confederation Life	Iron Trades
Colonial Mutual Life	Legal & General
Crown Life	London & Edinburgh
CCL Assurance	Minster
Eagle Star	Norwich Union
Equitable Life	Provincial Insurance
Prudential	Royal Insurance
Manufacturers Life	Sun Alliance

development director/manager, product development manager, marketing actuary. All respondents were, however, directly involved in product development decision taking. A tape recorder was used during interviews, with objections being raised by only two respondents to this form of data collection. When objection was raised written notes were made of the responses. Each face-to-face interview lasted, on average, one-and-a-half hours.

THE FOCUS OF THE STUDY

Prior analysis of theoretical and practical writings in the area of product development led us to focus data collection on five key issues. Because questions were not plucked out of the air, we were able to underpin them with hypotheses built up from the product and service development literature (Easingwood, 1986; Johne and Snelson, 1990; de Brentani, 1991; Cooper and de Brentani, 1991). The questions asked of respondents related to one or more of the following five key issues.

Issue 1

What types of development are currently being pursued? Our hypothesis was that there would be a preference for pursuing low-risk, incremental types of product development.

Issue 2

What are the key activities in the development process during which important decisions are made? Our hypothesis was that it is difficult to identify key activities because development is pursued in an informal and unsystematic manner.

Issue 3

What formal organizational arrangements are in place to handle development activities? Our hypothesis was that insurers do not adopt formal organization structures to deal with the development of new offerings.

Issue 4

What is the contribution made by marketing specialists? Our hypothesis was that marketing specialists play a minor role in the development of new insurance offerings.

Issue 5

What contribution does top management make? Our hypothesis was that top management fails to take on the role of 'envisioning, energizing and enabling the innovation programme'.

DISCUSSION OF FINDINGS

Data were collected in 1990 and in 1992. The findings for the general insurers are based on personal interviews conducted in 1990 and updated by follow-up telephone interviews in 1992. The data from suppliers of life insurance were collected in personal interviews in 1992. Findings are presented under the headings for each main issue. To respect confidences responses are not ascribed to individual company sources.

It must be stated at the outset that a common feature shared by all the sample companies (ten general insurers and ten suppliers of life insurance) was that each was currently undergoing changes in its business operation and orientation. Not surprisingly, these changes were more pronounced in some companies than in others. All companies co-operating in our investigation have now recognized the need to become more market oriented. A marketing manager in a large company offering general insurance explained the background to the current situation as follows:

In the 1980s we just could not cope with business that came to us through overall growth in the market. This has led some people even today to ask: 'Why change to a customer orientation when we have been successful in the past without it?'. What these people can't see, is that past success is no guarantee for future success.

The follow-up interviews with general insurers indicated that there has been increased acceptance of the importance of marketing. It is true that in some companies marketing has become heavily involved in pruning product lines, rather than in adding to them, but both in large and small companies there is now clear evidence of increased responsibilities having been given to marketing specialists for the purpose of exploring and exploiting product development opportunities. Further, in many companies top management is now prepared to involve itself in checking product development progress. These changes are going on now, and so we were not surprised to find control procedures in place in several general insurers which are now far more formal than in 1990.

In 1990 traditionalism and functional specialization were mentioned time and time again by general insurers as barriers to change. The issue was described boldly by the product development controller in a small company providing general insurance:

The main problem has to do with attitude. It's about tying to persuade technical experts, such as underwriters who have traditionally wielded all the clout around here, that their way is not the only way, and certainly not the most effective way for preparing for the future.

Overall, we found the approaches to and systems for managing product change to be more developed in companies offering general insurance. Three general insurers within the sample of ten have now taken very considerable steps in tightening their product development procedures. In one small company, in which top management involves itself fully, marketing and underwriters now co-operate closely from initial brainstorming sessions for identifying new product opportunities right through to launch. In this company development times have been reduced considerably from approval of an idea to launch.

There was also clear evidence in several general insurers of far more sophisticated approaches to analysing markets. A few companies are making extensive use of marketing maps in which target markets have been identified through careful segmentation analysis. These more sophisticated approaches had in some companies been introduced by consultants, while in others they had been developed internally. Increasing use of project or venture teams was also reported in general insurers, though in a number of companies these were obviously being used by top management as a mechanism to drive changes within and between traditional functional fiefdoms.

In the 10 life insurers we again found a situation of flux. While still predominantly led by the underwriting function, product development is increasingly being influenced by marketing inputs. This is happening as a by-product of strenuous attempts within companies to become more marketing oriented. To effect heightened market orientation new staff have been recruited. In most companies in the sample these new marketing specialists have not, as yet, been able to assume responsibility for driving product development. Instead, they are expected to work closely with underwriters when asked by them to do so, in order to ensure that developments are promoted appropriately on completion. In several companies actuaries involved in product development work have been given the new title of 'marketing actuary', to reflect their widened responsibilities.

Types of developments being pursued

In companies supplying general insurance, as well as those supplying life cover, the predominant types of development currently being undertaken concern the updating of existing products. At its most limited the updating of existing products involves changing aspects of the rating structure or altering the promotional mix. The director of operations and marketing in a small company offering general insurance summarized the situation in 1990 as follows:

Most of our product development is revamping/repackaging of existing products. Half of what we do is pure reaction to competitors' moves. Most of the other half is us trying to steal an edge in the short run. We do devote time and resources for the longer run. That's the futuristic bit—worrying about the sort of products we are going to need in five years' time. Unfortunately, this gets quite low priority because we have limited resources which tend to get drawn into immediate fire-fighting activities.

A number of factors were suggested as contributing to the predominant emphasis on incremental product developments. First, copying is a low-risk, inexpensive, activity. Second, because of the heavy reliance placed on selling through brokers, many companies perceive there to be little room for improving products apart from lowering the price. The frustration of the constraints imposed by selling through brokers was summed up by a marketing manager as follows:

If you sell through intermediaries as we do, you have the problem of having them between you and the end customer all the time. So we often ask ourselves: 'What's the advantage of coming up with something new, when there is always this filter between us and the customer?'

In the constrained circumstances in which companies selling through brokers perceive themselves to be operating, development initiatives frequently focus on targeting more accurately the preferences of specific socio-economic groupings, or types of business customers. A marketing manager expressed this rather neatly by saying: 'Really, anything new we do is a spin-off from an existing product range into another market niche.' A product manager for general products went further:

In terms of new lines of business, there are very limited opportunities in the insurance industry. True innovation in terms of a new kind of product are few and far between. Because of this, we concentrate on segmenting the market, rather than segmenting the products.

In 1990 not one respondent in general insurance would admit to us that their company had a regular programme of product development involving both updating existing lines and developing new lines. At that time the emphasis was on *ad hoc* initiatives. No evidence of programmes which involve making fundamental changes to the merchandise content or the support content was found. The situation was particularly marked in small companies, which all emphasized the need to continue to sell through the established broker network.

We found the situation markedly different in 1992. Three general insurers in the sample have now established classical marketing departments staffed predominantly by outsiders. Such departments are headed by a marketing director or manager supported by marketing specialists, especially including product managers. Product managers then typically assume responsibility for product improvement. For more radical product development, use is being made of business development managers whose job is to head teams of specialists from different internal business functions.

As one would expect, there is wide divergence in the way general insurers approach product development, and within the limited sample we cannot claim to have captured the total span. However, whereas in 1990 we found a situation in which reactive product development was the rule, in 1992 there is clear evidence in some companies of a far more systematic approach to progressing product developments. While we did find evidence of monitoring product development systematically in certain life insurers, the trend within these companies appears less advanced.

We must emphasize that our findings in this area need to be treated with caution, especially as far as the larger companies are concerned. In large companies, major initiatives such as selling direct, rather than through an established broker system, are not taken by those charged with day-to-day product improvement. However, despite the fact that our respondents were first and foremost concerned with managing improvements, they did express quite strange views on the subject of more fundamental product change. Indeed, there were marked differences in opinion on whether it was better to focus predominantly on copying competitors, as opposed to becoming more proactive in developing new offerings. Some felt it wasteful to develop new products continuously which could be readily copied. Others argued that leading with new and better offerings on a continuous basis represented the essence of competing successfully in the long term.

In a general insurer, a company which clearly appreciates the advantages afforded by product development, we heard the following statement:

We reflected on what each of our products was offering customers, and decided that the best way to create sustainable competitive edge was through beefing-up the support we provide. Accordingly, we have decided that we are no longer going to be a low cost supplier. We are going to ensure that our customers get better treatment from us than they do from out competitors. We feel that's the way we can differentiate ourselves. Product features can be copied quickly. It's in providing superior services we'll make sure we stay ahead.

It is clear that personnel in this company—a medium-sized one—have adopted a much wider view of product development opportunities. In this company, clearly articulated views exist on how offerings can be improved to stay in tune with changing market preferences. Not only this, but certain officers in this company see that by making radical changes to the way their offerings are delivered to customers, considerably greater shares of business can be captured. At the present time, management in this company is locked into detailed discussion with a range of technical specialists on how this can best be done.

Overall, as far as Issue 1 is concerned, we found that the emphasis was on low-risk, incremental types of product development in all the sample companies. This confirms our hypothesis. In large measure top management is responsible for this skewed approach to product development, which would appear the stem directly from a short-term orientation to investment. More radical product developments require larger and longer-term investment and, typically, involve higher risks, which most top managements approach with utmost caution.

Key activities in the development process

All serious research in the product development area has shown that completing a new offering successfully does not happen instantaneously. Typically, a number of supporting activities need to be undertaken. For example, first there may be a need to sift out ideas for possible new developments against objectives; thereafter, exploratory research may be needed prior to projecting profits and comparing alternatives. Often, it is only then that development work starts in earnest, and even thereafter the new product might not be launched before a test market exercise has been completed.

A large number of development models have been advanced in the area of manufactured products (Booz, Allen & Hamilton, 1982; Crawford, 1987; Cooper, 1988; Johne and Snelson, 1990). Researchers in the area of services development have advanced similar models (Donnelly *et al.*, 1985; Johnson *et al.*, 1986; Scheuing and Johnson, 1989). Of the services development models the normative model advanced by Scheuing and Johnson (1989), shown in Table 3, is the most comprehensive.

Many researchers have argued that systematic attention to development tasks contributes to success, or at least to the avoidance of failure. Yet whether development tasks should be attended to in sequential order, as opposed to some being undertaken simultaneously, remains open for debate. Several authors (Takeuchi and Nonaka, 1986; Dumaine, 1989; Smith and Reinertson, 1991) have stressed that while simultaneous or parallel working is wasteful of resources (because some tasks are duplicated), it allows developments to be completed faster. They show, for example, that faster, less efficient development can be profitable, especially in markets in which early adopters are prepared to pay a premium price.

Table 3. Scheuing and Johnson's (1989) model of service development.

1. Formulation of objectives and strategy.
2. Idea generation.
3. Idea screening.
4. Concept development.
5. Concept testing.
6. Business analysis.
7. Project authorization.
8. Service design and testing.
9. Process and system design and testing.
10. Marketing programme design and testing.
11. Personnel training.
12. Service testing and pilot run.
13. Test marketing.
14. Full-scale launch.
15. Post-launch review.

As well as deciding how much parallel working to countenance through teamwork, companies need to decide whether one standard way is appropriate for the different types of offering which can be developed. The issue here is whether different organizational arrangements are needed for completely new offerings as supposed to making improvements to existing offerings. In this respect, in accordance with the contingency approach to management, some analysts have argued that completely new product development is best managed differently from making ongoing improvements (Johne and Snelson, 1990).

Whereas, in 1990, in general insurance companies, there had been limited evidence of the use of formal guidelines for progressing individual developments, we found the situation changed in 1992. Three general insurers have new introduced formal monitoring systems, while in others the merits of so doing are under active discussion at the present time. In life insurers, only very rudimentary systems were in evidence, but several companies are currently actively contemplating changes in this area of their operations.

For the purpose of analysing the systems currently being used, we focused attention on the following five key activities:

(1) Planning product changes.
(2) Idea exploration.
(3) Screening and evaluation.
(4) Physical development.
(5) Launch.

Our aim was to ascertain how systematically each separate activity is undertaken. This issue is important, for previous research has suggested that systematic attention to key product development tasks is strongly associated with success (Booz *et al.*, 1982; Cooper and Kleinschmidt, 1986; Cooper and de Brentani, 1991; Edgett and Jones, 1991; Johne and Snelson, 1990).

As far as planning product changes are concerned there is evidence of increasing attention being paid to this within the context of overall planning systems. In both life and general insurers we found important changes under active consideration. The situation was particularly changed in certain general insurers compared with the situation in 1990. Most life companies and general insurers now undertake what is commonly referred to as 'fundamental reviews of the product portfolio'. Such ongoing monitoring and analysis against broader market opportunities is most commonly conducted annually, wither by the corporate planning department or by representatives of marketing.

Responses concerning the second key activity—idea exploration—provided further important insights. A common reply was that there are no really new insurance products and that product development is merely a matter of putting together different policies with a few frills to make them attractive to different market segments. A product manager responsible for general insurance used the following words:

In insurance terms there are very few new products. So what we tend to find ourselves doing is segmenting the market.

The sentiments behind these words illustrate the limited way in which ideas are often considered. In most of out discussions emphasis was placed predominantly on the merchandise element of the offering, with little or no attention being paid to how this can be supported differently for specific market segments. In the case of companies which sell through brokers, it was not uncommon to find great reliance on these for ideas. However, some life insurers and some suppliers of general insurance are now taking important independent initiatives in reading markets. We found this to be the case predominantly in companies selling direct. A number of such companies are now taking part in joint market research programmes with other suppliers into end-user attitudes and behaviour. As a result, some respondents claimed that they had made some very interesting and surprising discoveries about how existing markets might be reconceptualized and served better.

The third key activity—screening and evaluation—was found, in 1990, in general insurers, to be undertaken in an *ad hoc* fashion. In 1992, in several general insurers, as well as in a few life companies, this activity is now undertaken far more systematically. There is, however, a reluctance on the part of most companies to use explicit formal criteria for evaluating developments. To a large degree this is to be expected when developments are of the incremental, or 'me-too' type, which are commonly undertaken without a formal feasibility study. One respondent explained the reasons for this in racy terms:

For developments where we are responding to competitive action in the market, the proper routine will often be ignored. In such cases—and it's all too frequent for my liking—we are responding to cries of anxiety from the front line. So we have to make very quick decisions.

In 1990 we found that screening and evaluation criteria were poorly defined in most general insurance companies. When assessment criteria existed their form and content were frequently not shared across the company. In 1992 we found that in several general, as well as in some life companies, it is marketing departments which are making strenuous efforts to rectify the situation.

While there is clear evidence of greater involvement by top management in some companies, there is still widespread non-involvement in screening decisions. We would venture to comment that non-involvement on the part of top management in screening makes a pretty dangerous cocktail with regard to future business prosperity. Under a *laissez-faire* regime, marketing criteria frequently take second place to financial considerations and also to the level of technical and systems synergy looked for. The dominance of the latter factors can lead to the development of low risk, incremental product improvements. While this can give the illusion of active product development, it can spell long-term disaster if some competitors undertake more radical product developments (Gluck and Foster, 1975; Foster, 1986).

As far as the fourth key activity is concerned—physical development—we found that, while in all traditional insurance companies co-ordination is still undertaken by underwriters, the situation is changing in favour of marketing, or at least to include marketing. In two general insurers we found sophisticated project management software systems in use which enable development tasks to be attended to sequentially. In all companies which adopt a co-ordinated team approach to development, we found that the core team was responsible for physical development, with extra specialists brought in as and when required.

The fifth key activity—launch—was found to be formally and tightly controlled in the majority of life and general insurance companies. Companies typically launch on a national basis because of a widespread belief that test marketing is uneconomic because if gives the game away to competitors. The importance of involving others in the company for gaining commitment was stressed using the following words:

Promotional campaigns are given a high profile so that everyone knows what's happening in advance. A third of what you do in product development is promoting to your own people. If the sales force are not on your side, then it's never going to get into the marketplace successfully.

Overall, as far as Issue 2 is concerned, we are able to confirm the hypothesis that it is, indeed, difficult to identify key activities. Most developments are still pursued in an informal and unsystematic manner. Yet, there are clear indications that this situation is changing. More systematic development processes and more rigorous methods for monitoring progress are currently being introduced by consultants in a number of companies. In other companies staff with experience of marketing fast-moving consumer goods have been recruited for assisting in this area.

Formal organizational arrangements

Companies have widely differing organizational mechanisms at their disposal for developing offerings. A commonly used method is to ascribe responsibility for product development to product managers. However, as many companies have found to their cost, these managers are usually so busy fighting fires with present products, that they have little time for new products. To overcome this problem, some companies have created permanent new product managers. New product committees may also be used as semi-permanent organizational devices to review and approve proposals. While committees serve an important co-ordinating role, they can seriously slow down decision making, especially when departmental representatives seek to preserve sectional interests, rather than focusing on exploiting market opportunities fast. Despite their disadvantages, we found committees to be the predominant organizational mechanism for progressing developments in both life and general insurance companies.

To overcome problems associated with subordinating functional interests to business interests, some companies have established interdisciplinary new venture teams. Their purpose is to force important developments through the bureaucracy. We found evidence of such new venture teams in both life and non-life companies, but frequently their remit was wider than product development. In some companies their purpose included process innovation. We found this to be the case particularly in companies in which top management preferred to delegate responsibility for innovation.

We found no real evidence of new-style organizational arrangements, such as self-managing teams. One life company is currently going through the traumas of introducing matrix-based structures which simultaneously accommodate specialist functional inputs, geographical sales and distribution territories, as well as target markets. Overall, however, the picture remains one of functional structures built on rigid hierarchical lines of control.

When one considers the dominant culture of the companies in the sample, and the types of developments most frequently undertaken (improvements as opposed to completely new offerings), it is not surprising that terms such as 'product champion' were but rarely heard. In the majority of companies in the sample, changing the offering was seen as a process requiring a methodical and routine approach. Once the broad parameters had been agreed between underwriting and marketing, individuals were drawn in to contribute on the basis of their position and specialist skills, rather than any distinct personal qualities such as enthusiasm or creativity. This was stressed by the business development manager in a large company:

I will use the systems manager and underwriting manager, the reason being that if they are going to run their own subgroups, then they need to have the authority to pull that subgroup together and make it work. Therefore, it's not really a team brought together for its expertise, it's a 'power team' which can make things happen and get the job done.

Our findings overlap with those of Easingwood (1986) who found that few service suppliers adopt radical organizational structures, because it is comparatively rare for them to be involved in the development of really new offerings. Overall, as far as Issue 3 is concerned, our hypothesis about the lack of formal organizational arrangements was not supported by the findings. In our sample a clear preference emerged in favour of managing developments through permanent new product committees comprising a mix of functional specialists.

Contributions by marketing specialists

The traditional skill base of insurance companies has been underwriting. In the past it has been excellence in underwriting as well as investment expertise which has been the key to sustained profitability. As has already been stressed, in almost all companies underwriters retain their traditional power as far as initiating product development is concerned. This has serious implications for the types of development which are being undertaken, or perhaps put more accurately: the types which are not being undertaken.

In large part, the failure to envisage more radical amendments to the offer is a direct result of poor market information usage. In small companies, in particular, marketing information systems and the use of formal market research is still underdeveloped. The corporate planning manager of a small general insurance company explained the situation in the following way:

We are in the early stages of using market research. This is an innovation in itself. In the past we tended to design products based on what we thought customers need, rather than finding out what they really want.

The marketing actuary of a medium-sized life company stated:

Our understanding of the market basically comes from conventions and meetings that we go to within the industry, and we do receive information regularly from the insurance press.

It would be inaccurate to give the impression that all companies lack formal market research information. At least one life company in the sample has now established a strong department dedicated solely to collecting and disseminating market research information internally. In this company extensive use is made of salesforce feedback. As far as salesforce feedback is concerned, it is again dangerous to generalize. In some companies marketing and sales co-operated actively in identifying opportunities for new products, in others there is enmity between 'newfangled' marketing and old-established sales.

Overall, as far as Issue 4 is concerned, our hypothesis concerning the role played by marketing specialists is not supported. Marketing specialists were found to make increasing contributions to product development in many life insurers and in general insurance companies, even if they did not take the leading role. Unfortunately, marketing expertise is not being used to its full effect. Often, marketing's contribution is restricted to merchandise amendments and promotional amendments aimed at particular market segments. In the absence of greater demands from top management for contributions aimed at exploiting market potentials more purposefully, it is unlikely that full use will be made of the marketing expertise which is now in place.

Contributions by top management

Our hypothesis concerning top management involvement was supported by the findings. We found such involvement low in the case of the predominant type of development undertaken—product improvement. As a general rule, this type of product development is left to underwriters or product managers to get on with as part of their normal duties.

We must emphasize, however, that our investigation concentrated on updating offerings, rather than new offering development. It may be that top management is more closely involved in completely new developments, which may is some companies be pursued through separate organizational mechanisms, such as new business development departments. The extent to which this is the case required further research.

It was stressed to us by several respondents that when aims were articulated by top management, these are typically expressed in terms of sales targets over what had been achieved in the past. The issue was highlighted by a new product manager in a life company as follows:

Our corporate strategy is based on sales projections. We work backwards from these. Our task becomes one of reflecting on the type of new products needed to meet particular targets. Our strategy, therefore, is grounded in the past rather than in the future.

As far as we were able to judge, few top managers in the companies we sampled, provide the sort of top management support that Tushman and Nadler (1986) speak of in 'envisioning, energizing and enabling' an innovation programme. Hence, as we have indicated, initiatives are most commonly left to technical specialists. Unfortunately, mainly because of the lack of interest and direct involvement by top management, marketing specialists who get involved in the later stages of product development are not able to lead in suggesting ways in which market opportunities might be exploited to the full. This problem is particularly acute in companies—the vast majority—in which underwriters and systems specialists continue to have a dominating influence over the types of products to be developed.

DISCUSSION

It has been argued that the financial loss from failed product development in financial services is low (Davison *et al.*, 1989). However, such a suggestion assumes that development costs can be ascertained accurately. Although not specifically commented on in this article, many respondents stressed difficulties in accurately attributing costs to products, let alone to specific product developments. We can, therefore, confidently assume that the true costs of managerial time wasted on less than successful product development is rarely known precisely.

During the 1980s many insurance companies in the UK enjoyed high returns on capital as a result of buoyant equity and property markets. In many cases, investment gains offset any insurance losses handsomely, meaning that sometimes insufficient attention was paid to operating efficiencies. The early 1990s have seen a dramatic fall in returns on capital. Further, the UK equity market is no longer buoyant and property prices have also declined. With anticipated new competition from abroad following the Single European Market in 1993, all insurance companies now operate in a far more abrasive competitive climate. Today, operating costs do matter, and far greater importance is attached to efficient product development.

In order to understand the nature of the changes now under way in companies, it is necessary to look behind the trappings for evidence of substantive changes. A critical factor determining the nature of change in organizations is top management. On the basis of the data collected it appears that top insurance management still remains reluctant to articulate strategies which spell out clearly to organizational members expectations as far as product development is concerned. In the absence of clearly communicated competitive game plans it is questionable whether the grafting on of efficient product development practices from other industries will achieve anything but limited success. Our interviews indicated that in many companies individuals are now well aware of the type of changes needed. But, what is not at all clear is the order in which changes can best be introduced, and the way in which changes can best be managed within environments still dominated by technical experts and controlled on a hierarchical basis.

CONCLUSIONS

The increasing competitiveness of the insurance marketplace now requires companies to change their offerings more frequently than before. Ideally, companies will need to adopt both a proactive and an innovative approach to developing new products. This will entail a change of emphasis away from exploiting asset strengths to exploiting market opportunities. It will almost certainly require assets to be used differently than before. This type of change—to higher risk and higher investment activities—will require emphatic support from top management. Further, the successful implementation of innovative strategies will almost certainly require far more formalized systems for control purposes.

In many companies, particularly in the case of new entrants like banks, the quest for sustainable competitive advantage will centre on developing offerings which cannot readily be copied in their entirety. Quinn (1985) has argued that innovative companies anchor their visions of what is possible to the practical realities of the marketplace and ensure that this is achieved through two main mechanisms. First, a strong market orientation at the very top of the company. Second, an organization which forces purposeful interaction between technical and marketing specialists. While technical systems problems are likely to continue to feature strongly in insurance product development, greatest long-term payoff is likely to result from innovative interpretations of market opportunities (Easingwood and Mahajan, 1989). Achieving these types of changes will require insurers to make increasingly challenging alterations to their operations.

REFERENCES

Booz, Allen & Hamilton (1982), *New Products Management for the 1980s*, Booz, Allen & Hamilton, New York, NY.
de Brentani, U. (1991), 'Success Factors in Developing New Business Services', *European Journal of Marketing*, Vol. 25 No. 2, pp. 33–59.

de Bruicker, F. S. and Summe, G. L. (1985), 'Make Sure Your Customers Keep Coming Back', *Harvard Business Review*, Vol. 63 No 1, pp. 92–8.
Cooper, R. G. (1988), 'The New Product Process: A Decision Guide for Management', *Journal of Marketing Management*, Vol. 3 No. 3, pp. 238–55.
Cooper, R. G. and de Brentani, U. (1991), 'New Industrial Financial Services: What Distinguishes the Winners', *Journal of Product Innovation Management*, Vol. 7 No. 2, pp. 75–90.
Cooper, R. G. and Kleinschmidt, E. J. (1986), 'An investigation into the New Product Process: Steps, Deficiencies and Impact', *Journal of Product Innovation Management*, Vol. 3, pp. 71–85.
Crawford, C. M. (1987), *New Product Management*, Irwin, Homewood, IL.
Davison, H., Watkins, T. and Wright, M. (1989), 'Developing New Personal Financial Products— Some Evidence on the Role of Market Research', *International Journal of Bank Marketing*, Vol. 7 No. 1, pp. 8–15.
Donnelly, J. H., Berry, L. L. and Thompson, T. W. (1985), *Marketing Financial Services*, Irwin, Homewood, IL.
Dumaine, B. (1989), 'How Managers Can Succeed through Speed', *Fortune*, Vol. 13, February, pp. 30–5.
Easingwood, C. J. (1986), 'New Product Development for Service Companies', *Journal of Product Innovation Management*, Vol. 4, pp. 264–75.
Easingwood, C. J. and Mahajan, V. (1989), 'Positioning of Financial Services for Competitive Advantage', *Journal of Product Innovation Management*, Vol. 6, pp. 207–19.
Edgett, S. and Jones, S. (1991), 'New Product Development in the Financial Service Industry: A Case Study', *Journal of Marketing Management*, Vol. 7, pp. 271–84.
Foster, R. N. (1986), *Innovation: The Attacker's Advantage*, Macmillan, London.
Gluck, F. W. and Foster, R. N. (1975), 'Managing Technological Change: A Box of Cigars for Brad', *Harvard Business Review*, Vol. 53 No. 5, pp. 139–50.
Insurance Directory & Year Book (1992), Vol. I and III, Buckley Press Ltd, London.
Johne, F. A. (1992), 'New Style Product Development', *Management Decision*, Vol. 30 No. 2, pp. 8–11.
Johne, A. and Snelson, P. (1990), *Successful Product Development: Lessons from American and British Firms*, Basil Blackwell, Oxford.
Johnson, S. C., Scheuing, E. E. and Gaida, K. A. (1986), *Profitable Service Marketing*, Irwin, Homewood, IL.
Kotler, P. (1991), *Marketing Management: Analysis, Planning Implementation and Control*, Prentice-Hall, Englewood Cliffs, NJ.
McKenna, R. (1991), 'Marketing Is Everything', *Harvard Business Review*, Vol. 91 No. 1, pp. 65–79.
Mathur, S. S. (1992), 'Talking Straight about Competitive Strategy', *Journal of Marketing Management*, Vol. 8, pp. 199–217.
Peters, T. (1990), 'Get Innovative or Get Dead', *California Management Review*, Vol. 33 No. 1, pp. 9–36.
Quinn, J. B. (1985), 'Managing Innovation: Controlled Chaos', *Harvard Business Review*, Vol. 63 No. 3, pp. 73–84.
Quinn, J. B., Doorley, T. L. and Paquette, P. C. (1990), 'Beyond Products: Service-based Strategy', *Harvard Business Review*, Vol. 90 No. 2, pp. 58–67.
Scheuing, E. E. and Johnson, E. M. (1989), 'A Proposed Model for New Service Development', *Journal of Services Marketing*, Vol. 3 No. 2, pp. 25–34.
Smith, P. G. and Reinertson, D. G. (1991), *Developing Products in Half the Time*, Van Nostrand Reinhold, New York, NY.
Takeuchi, H. and Nonaka, I. (1986), 'The New Product Development Game', *Harvard Business Review*, Vol. 64 No. 1, pp. 137–46.
Tushman, M. L. and Nadler, D. A. (1986), 'Organizing for Innovation', *California Management Review*, Vol. 28 No. 3, pp. 74–92.

Part IV

Customer Care and Service Quality

CONTENTS

Introduction to Part IV 165

12 Developing an Instrument to Measure Customer Service Quality in Branch Banking 169
   N. K. AVKIRAN, *International Journal of Bank Marketing* (1994), **12** (6), 10–18.
13 Service Quality: Relationships Between Banks and Their Small Business Clients 183
   A. M. SMITH, *International Journal of Bank Marketing* (1989), **7** (5), 28–35.
14 Service Quality: Recent Developments in Financial Services 198
   B. R. LEWIS, *International Journal of Bank Marketing* (1993), **11** (6), 19–25.

Introduction to Part IV

The provision and delivery of financial services involves a variety of interactions between an organization, its personnel and customers, and a consequent need to 'care' for the customer. The concept of service quality includes service to the customer (providing what is required and being 'nice' to the customer), delivery/operations, relationships with customers, and internal relationships between employees and management. In developing service quality strategies, financial services organizations are managing services, systems, environment and people.

The need for service quality is driven by customers, employees and a changing business environment:

- Customers, be they personal or corporate, are increasingly aware of alternative financial services and providers, and of rising standards of service(s). Thus, their expectations rise and they become more critical of the quality of service received. In addition, knowledge of the costs and benefits of keeping customers relative to attracting new ones draws companies' attention to looking after present customers, responding to their needs and problems, and developing long-term relationships.
- Looking after employees is also an opportunity for financial services organizations. As companies become large, they may also become anonymous and bureaucratic. Communications may deteriorate and relationships may suffer. Further, in a recession climate, cost-cutting exercises and reorganizations can impact on staff morale, motivation and performance. However, companies are realizing that commitment to employees brings rewards.
- The financial services environment is characterized by economic, legal and technological changes. For example, the laws resulting in deregulation have increased competition and brought retailers into the industry. In a competitive environment, companies react by emphasizing operations and financial efficiency and/or more focused product and market strategies. Additionally, they can focus on service quality in their corporate and marketing strategies. Superior service may be seen as a mechanism to achieve differentiation and a competitive advantage.

With a focus on service quality, financial services organizations can expect a number of benefits:

- Customer loyalty through satisfaction. Looking after present customers can generate repeat and increased business and may lead to attraction of new customers from positive

word-of-mouth communication. Customer retention is more cost effective than trying to attract new customers. Cost savings also accrue from 'getting things right the first time'.
- Increased opportunities for cross selling. Comprehensive and up-to-date product knowledge and sales technique among employees, combined with developing relationships with customers, enables staff to identify customer needs and suggest relevant new 'products'.
- Employee benefits may be seen in terms of increased job satisfaction and morale and commitment to the company, successful employer–employee relationships and increased staff loyalty; which contribute to reducing staff turnover and the associated costs of recruitment, selection and training. Committed and competent employees will also make fewer mistakes (and, in turn, lead to fewer customer complaints) and so contribute to further cost savings.
- In addition, good service enhances corporate image and may provide insulation from price competition. Overall, successful service leads to reduced costs and increased productivity and sales, market share, profitability and business performance.

Service quality initiatives are high priorities in many financial services organizations, with expenditure seen as long-term investment for future growth and profitability. The development of service quality programmes requires, firstly, an awareness and understanding of the interactions between an organization and its customers and employees, i.e. service encounters or moments of truth, which impact on customers in terms of their impressions and evaluation of the service experienced and on employees with respect to their motivation, performance, jobs and rewards. Thus, the first major feature is, typically, to identify the key components or dimensions of service quality from customer and employee research, i.e. their needs and expectations which relate to:

- the services being offered: both core services with facilitating and supporting services, and the augmented service offering to include the service process and interaction between customers and the organization.
- delivery systems and procedures which operate efficiently and effectively, and which are responsive and reliable.
- delivery environment that includes both physical design and access aspects, and also emotional or atmospheric impact, which is experienced by both customers and employees.
- technology which is integral to financial services, the environment and delivery; advances having made major contributions to facilitating customer–company exchanges and increasing levels of service.
- employees: their role in the creation and provision of service quality cannot be overstated and includes their personal qualities, ability to understand and satisfy customer needs, and their skills and knowledge.

A second feature is to measure the importance of service quality dimensions, including assessment of customers' expectations of financial services providers and perceptions of actual service performance/delivery, using SERVQUAL and other tools in order to identify service quality 'gaps'. But also, to have an awareness of the associated measurement problems.

Thus, key elements of any programme are the development of services to meet customer needs, systems and procedures that are customer and employee focused, and a suitable delivery environment; and making the best use of technology in services, systems and environment to ensure speed, accuracy and efficiency.

Also integral to the success of any service quality programme is a focus on internal marketing, i.e. the internal customer (employee), and an investment in people. This is the realm of human resources management and the development of personnel policies to include recruitment, selection and training, and associated appraisal, rewards and recognition.

When a financial services provider has assessed key variables of customer care/service quality, translated them into service standards and systems, and recruited and trained employees, it then has to 'manage its promises', i.e. manage the delivery process. This includes paying attention to potential failure points, developing service guarantees (i.e. Codes of Practice in banking), and procedures for service recovery. Further, monitoring the programmes involves developing systems to research and evaluate customer satisfaction and dissatisfaction, and employee performance and satisfaction.

Finally, in order for a financial services provider to be successful with its service quality programmes, there needs to be management commitment to service quality and the creation of an appropriate culture. The organizational culture may require changes to achieve employee orientation to the company and everyone's orientation to the external customer. This change starts at the top; the service quality process begins with senior management's commitment to employees and customers, ideally with strong and visible leaders.

Three articles are included relating to service quality issues: one is concerned with developing a measuring instrument in the personal account sector, the second focuses on relationships in the small business sector, and the third provides an overview of several pieces of service quality research.

Measurement of customer service quality in branch banking is the focus of the article by Necmi Avkiran who develops a multi-dimensional instrument to measure customer perceptions of service quality. Avkiran discusses SERVQUAL and its recent refinements, together with a number of criticisms of the tool, before embarking on the development of a more practical framework with sound psychometric properties. This progressed through a rigorous research design involving multiple stage pretesting and piloting prior to a main survey of bank customers. Testing of construct and convergent validities was employed and response bias was also assessed. The main factor analysis led to the identification of four dimensions of service quality, namely, staff conduct, credibility, communication, and access to teller services.

Banks are increasingly seeking to attract and retain small businesses and increase their share of this market through their marketing activities including increasing their understanding of the clients' businesses, and the provision of specialist advice services. Anne Smith, in her paper, 'Service Quality: Relationships between Banks and their Small Business Clients', set out to identify the elements of service that determine the quality of bank service to small businesses, and to assess the relative importance of these elements. Elements of good bank service were found to be related to the efficiency of staff or the banks' systems and procedures, the personal quality of staff, the qualities of the bank manager, and the general support from the flexibility of the bank. In contrast, elements of poor service and dissatisfaction were found to be: inefficiency of staff (owing to labour turnover, movement of personnel, lack of knowledge, etc.) and/or bank systems and procedures; errors; perceived lack of support, understanding and flexibility from the bank; bank charges/pricing policies; qualities of the manager or other key contact personnel; insufficient information; the decision-making process; and queuing with personal customers. With respect to expectations of bank service, the most important aspects were found to be: accuracy and competence; confidentiality and trustworthiness; reliability; and speed in all aspects of bank service. Of least importance were tangible elements of service.

In the last article in this section, 'Service Quality: Recent Developments in Financial Services', Barbara Lewis provides a review of some of the seminal research into service quality issues, in particular with respect to definitions, determinants and measurement; and highlights a number of investigations in the financial services industry which relate to the perspectives of managers, customers and employees. The management perspective came from an early study of UK service industries in which the objectives, activities and advantages of customer care/service quality programmes were investigated. The customer perspective covers both the personal account and small business sectors, with key elements and dimensions of service quality being identified. The employees' perspective introduces the concept of internal marketing and the role of human resources management in service quality, and is demonstrated in two studies—one carried out in banks and building societies in the UK where the success of early customer service programmes was limited, and a second conducted in a bank in Cyprus where initiatives have been more fully developed. Lewis emphasizes the need for continuing customer care/service quality activities to take into account changing customer needs and expectations, the need for an integrated approach to service-quality embracing marketing, operations, human resources, and financial managers, and also the concern to update and refine measurement techniques. She concluded with suggestions for a continuing research agenda.

12

Developing an Instrument to Measure Customer Service Quality in Branch Banking

Necmi Kemal Avkiran

The purpose of the research is to develop a utilitarian multi-dimensional instrument that can be applied to measuring *customer service quality* as perceived by branch bank customers. The objective is to end up with a parsimonious set of items. The focus of the study is on retail operations as embodied by the branch. The project has been hosted by a major Australian trading bank with a large branch network.

Homogeneity of retail banking products forces customer service quality to emerge as a principal factor to be analysed in competitive strategies. A recent telephone interview survey throughout the state of Victoria (Quadrant Research Services, 1992) identified 'poor customer service' as the most frequently given reason by consumers for considering moving accounts. LeBlanc and Nguyen (1988) cite that costs of mediocre quality in service industries can be as high as 40 per cent of revenues. Thus, customer service quality is expected to be a major determinant of branch performance and potential.

A rigorous research design has been implemented, encompassing multiple-stage pretesting, piloting and a final stage drawing upon a sample size of 791 completed questionnaires. Data collected has been triangulated by using exit interviews, telephone interviews and mailed questionnaires. Additional empirical probing of instrument validity was achieved through testing for construct and convergent validities. Response bias was also tested.

CONCEPTUAL FRAMEWORK

The conceptual definition of customer service quality developed by Parasuraman *et al.* (1988) is adhered to, namely:

Perceived service quality is a global judgement, or attitude, relating to superiority of the service, whereas satisfaction is related to a specific transaction.

Those interested in further discussion of definition of service quality should refer to Parasuraman *et al.* (1988, pp. 15-17) and LeBlanc and Nguyen (1988, pp. 8-11).

LeBlanc and Nguyen arrived at a 37-item instrument based on data collected from credit union customers. A better known general service quality instrument is

SERVQUAL by Parasuraman *et al.* (1986, 1988, 1991). SERVQUAL, composed of 22 items, was developed by data collected across five separate service categories, one of which was retail banking. Major amendments were made to the approach used by Parasuraman *et al.* in their SERVQUAL instrument as explained in the following paragraphs.

Assessment of customer service quality defined by Parasuraman *et al.* as resulting from a comparison of expectations with perceptions on quality features requires two statements to assess each item. Carman (1990), Babakus and Boller (1992) and Brown *et al.* (1993) raise doubts about the psychometric properties and feasibility of Parasuraman *et al.*'s approach to measurement. For example, perceptions of quality can be expected to be influenced by the expectations generated by the service setting. On a practical level, how does one capture expectations prior to delivery of service and capture perceptions at the end of the service encounter? Also, Wall and Payne's (1973) study on deficiency scores indicates a tendency for respondents consistently to set expectations higher than perceptions, which can be construed as a psychological constraint. For the above reasons and to make the questionnaire more manageable, each item was surveyed directly (see Appendix). As Babakus and Boller (1992) succinctly put it '. . . the task would be simpler for respondents and the format would prevent potential problems with the difference scores'. The continuing academic debate on difference scores can be followed in papers by Brown *et al.* (1993) and Parasuraman *et al.* (1993).

Although traditionally scale development literature suggests some use of negatively worded items on questionnaires to reduce acquiescence bias (e.g. Churchill, 1979, p. 68; Likert, 1932), others in the field advocate omission of negative items (Babakus and Boller, 1992; Howell *et al.*, 1988; Lewis and Mitchell, 1990; Wason and Johnson-Laird, 1975). Parasuraman *et al.*'s original study on service quality required use of negatively worded items; however, in 1991, part of their proposed refinements included use of positively worded items only. Negatively worded items are considered difficult to comprehend (particularly in the context of Likert-type scales), can invoke negative connotations, and can lead to method factors, casting doubt on the validity of the instrument. In the presence of arguments both for and against inclusion of negative items, it was deemed appropriate to test for acquiescence bias, where acquiescence bias is defined as a 'respondent's tendency to concur with a particular position' (Zikmund, 1991).

The other amendment to Parasuraman *et al.*'s approach is the direct assessment of importance for the service quality items. An importance score was generated for each item, giving higher diagnostic and prescriptive value to the construct by providing a more refined measure, and helping to further segment the customer base according to customers' needs (Keirl and Mitchell, 1990) in the presence of socio-economic data. To test questions required to gather such data and gain a better understanding of ParaBank's customers, part B of the main stage questionnaires included socio-economic questions.

The following dimensions were conceptualized (see Appendix for items) (concise definitions for D1, D2 and D6 in Parasuraman *et al.*, 1988).

- *D1: Responsiveness* (items 1–4)—willingness to help customers and provide prompt service.
- *D2: Empathy* (items 5–10)—caring, individualized attention which the branch provides for its customers.
- *D3: Staff conduct* (items 11–15)—civilized conduct and presentation of branch staff that will project a professional image to the customers.

- *D4: Access* (items 16–19)—ease of access to branch staff either physically or on the telephone.
- *D5: Communication* (items 20–23)—verbal and written communication between branch staff and customers.
- *D6: Reliability* (items 24–27)—ability to perform the promised service dependably and accurately.

It should be noted that the proposed conceptual framework is not a replication of Parasuraman *et al.*'s work on SERVQUAL. Nevertheless, their now well-recognized work and the criticisms it has attracted are acknowledged in an effort to arrive at a more practical framework with sound psychometric properties.

RESEARCH DESIGN

The general procedure followed (adapted from Churchill, 1979; Parasuraman *et al.*, 1988) in developing the customer service quality instrument is summarized below:

(1) Define construct.
(2) Identify domain, i.e. dimensions.
(3) Generate items on dimensions.
(4) Collect data.
(5) Purify instrument.
(6) Collect fresh data from a sample on a set of items to emerge from the previous step.
(7) Further purify instrument.
(8) Evaluate reliability, dimensionality and validity of instrument.

In developing the measurement instruments, results of the first stage scale purification by Parasuraman *et al.* (1986) was used as the starting point. The 34-item instrument was customized for the bank and further refinement attempted; findings from a qualitative study commissioned to establish *quality service standards* (Dangar Research Group, 1991) were used in reviewing the suitability of the original SERVQUAL items to the host bank's branches. The instrument was pretested. The respondents were screened by inquiring whether they normally banked at that particular branch; in an effort to capture a minimum exposure to branch services, data were collected by administering questionnaires to a sample of branch customers who had been with the branch for at least three months.

Pretesting had three discernible stages, namely, vetting of the questionnaire by fellow researchers, self administering of the questionnaire items by 40 university students, and further qualitative assessment of the questionnaire items by the consultative panel formed within the host bank, and other practitioners. For the purpose of testing for acquiescence bias, the second stage of pretesting was composed of two different versions of the same questionnaire i.e. first version with four negative items and second version with eight negative items. It was hypothesized that the mean composite score from each version would not be significantly different if there were no acquiescence bias. In the absence of empirical evidence for acquiescence bias, it is reasoned that there would be no need to include negative items.

The instrument was piloted in nine branches through exit interviews; these branches were chosen with care to include variations in geographic location and size. A total of 159 completed questionnaires were collected; to maintain randomness among the cases, the fifth customer leaving the branch was approached with the exit questionnaire.

The main survey was administered through the customers of 20 randomly chosen branches; data collection methods were triangulated (Denzin, 1978; Sudman and Bradburn, 1984) by employing exit interviews, telephone interviews and mailed questionnaires. Seven-hundred-and-ninety-one completed questionnaires were returned; this figure is consistent with Crouch's (1984, p. 142) observation that 'Minimum sample sizes for quantitative consumer surveys are of the order of 300 to 500 respondents'. A sample size between 500 and 1,000 is considered very good to excellent where factor analysis is to be undertaken (Comrey, 1973).

Each quality item was surveyed directly on a five-point Likert-type scale e.g. 'politeness of branch staff' is 'much worse than I expected' to 'much better than I expected'. All response options were verbally labelled; results of tests carried out by Alwin and Krosnick (1991) support this practice. Similarly, a five-point importance scale followed each quality scale, possible responses ranging from 'not important' to 'very important' in the pilot stage (see Appendix). Homogeneity of importance scores for each item across cases was probed by examining coefficients of variation; the purpose of this exercise was to omit importance scales in the main survey stage should the scores prove to be homogeneous, hence making the questionnaire more manageable. In such a case, the research design calls for weighting of quality item scores with mean importance scores (Carman, 1990); mean of importance weighted item scores will provide a measure of customer service quality along each dimension of the construct (average of dimension means giving an overall measure).

To assist in further testing of validity of the instrument additional questions were posed in the main survey stage, namely:

- What is your overall quality rating of your branch? (OVERALLQ).
- Would you recommend your branch to a friend? (RECOMMEND).
- Did you ever complain about your branch services? (COMPLAIN).

(Designated variable names are shown in brackets).

The above three questions were used to assess empirically the convergent validity of the instrument. Construct validity was further assessed by administering a shuffled version of the questionnaire and by triangulation (Straub and Carlson, 1989). The following validity hypotheses were formulated:

H_0 There is no significant difference between scores of respondents answering the regular and those answering the shuffled versions (construct validity).

The aim is to determine whether sequencing of questionnaire items has any significant influence on scoring by respondents.

H_0 Correlation between OVERALLQ and SCOREQ is O (convergent validity), where SCOREQ = sum of scores across all items.

H_0 There is no significant difference between the scores of respondents answering Yes to RECOMMEND and No to COMPLAIN, and those answering No/Yes (convergent validity).

With the first hypothesis, a positive correlation is expected to be observed; with the second hypothesis, a significantly higher mean score is expected with respondents returning a Yes/No combination. A discussion of the advantages of stating hypotheses in the null form can be read in *Advanced Questionnaire Design* by Labaw (1985).

Coefficient alphas were calculated as a measure of reliability based on internal consistency (Churchill, 1979; Peter, 1979). According to Nunnally (1978, p. 230), 'Coefficient alpha sets an upper limit to the reliability of tests constructed in terms of the domain-sampling model. If it proves to be very low, either the test is too short or the items have very little in common'. Factor analysis was employed to verify dimensionality of the overall instrument.

RESULTS AND ANALYSIS

In pretesting, Wilcoxon scores (rank sums) non-parametric test results on sum of scores across all items (defined as variable SCOREQ) for each respondent supported the null hypothesis that the mean composite score from each negatively worded version was not significantly different (see Table 1). In this light and in view of other arguments against use of negative items presented above, it was decided to abandon negative wording in later stages.

Pilot stage

Homogeneity of importance scores for each item was tested by computing coefficients of variation (see Table 2). The coefficients were low, indicating homogeneous importance scores. Hence, it was deemed appropriate to abandon the importance scale in the main survey stage, recommending use of mean importance scores on each item as weights when the instrument is applied for measuring customer service quality at a branch (see Table 3).

Before further statistical analysis, frequencies were generated on the questionnaire items to vet the integrity of data entered. In purifying the quality scale, coefficient alphas were calculated first. Twenty-seven items made up the six conceptualized dimensions (see Appendix). The standardized alpha for the scale was recorded at 0.9132. Examining the

Table 1. Wilcoxon scores (rank sums) for variable SCOREQ classified by variable CASEID.

CASEID	N	Sum of scores	Expected under H_0	Standard deviation under H_0	Mean score
4	20	415	410	36.9181354	20.75
8	20	405	410	36.9181354	20.25

Wilcoxon two-sample test (normal approximation)
$S = 415 \quad \mathcal{Z} = 0.121891$ *Probablity* $> |\mathcal{Z}| = 0.9030$
t-test approximate significance $= 0.9036$
Kruskal–Wallis test (χ^2 approximation)
$\chi^2 = 0.01834 \quad df = 1$ Probability $> \chi^2 = 0.8923$
Note $S =$ sum of scores of the smaller sample
$\mathcal{Z} =$ Z-statistic

Table 2. Coefficients of variation on importance scores.

Variable	Coefficient of variation	Variable	Coefficient of variation
MANAGER	0.24	CLARITY	0.22
LEARN	0.26	INFORMED	0.24
SERVWHEN	0.23	TELEPHONE	0.19
PERSONAL	0.20	GREET	0.21
ACCTYPES	0.24	SYMPATHY	0.20
NEATNESS	0.21	COMPUTER	0.17
ADVICE	0.20	HELP	0.18
SECURITY	0.16	PRIVACY	0.17
STAFFNUM	0.15	LOAN	0.17
PROMISES	0.16	POLITE	0.16
CONCERN	0.16	APOLOGY	0.17
PROMPT	0.16	TELLERS	0.17
QUEUES	0.16	KNOWLEDGE	0.14
MISTAKE	0.14		

Mean: 0.19. Standard deviation: 0.03.

'Alpha if Item Deleted' column indicated that deletion of items would not raise the standardized scale alpha. At the dimension level, alphas ranged from 0.4730 to 0.7576; this suggested a possible misfit of some variables in their conceptualized dimensions. It was time to take a closer look at the dimensionality of the scale through factor analysis.

The 27 variables were factor analysed using Principal Axis Factoring (PAF) on SPSS; six factors were extracted, which coincided with the number of conceptualized dimensions. However, the unrotated factor matrix was difficult to interpret owing to the majority of the variables loading on Factor 1. Final statistics showed that 52.2 per cent of variance was explained by the six factors. The factor matrix was rotated orthogonally (using Varimax). From Table 4, it can be seen that this resulted in an easy-to-interpret matrix, where those variables loading 0.5 or above were retained (LeBlanc and Nguyen, 1988; Lesser and Kamal, 1991); deleted variables are marked with an asterisk. In order to test whether the observed factor structure was an artefact of the sample size, a second PAF

Table 3. Mean importance scores.

Variable	Mean	Variable	Mean
MANAGER	3.79	CLARITY	3.85
LEARN	3.89	INFORMED	3.90
SERVWHEN	3.91	TELEPHONE	3.93
PERSONAL	3.94	GREET	3.97
ACCTYPES	3.98	SYMPATHY	4.02
NEATNESS	4.04	COMPUTER	4.14
ADVICE	4.15	HELP	4.21
SECURITY	4.22	PRIVACY	4.23
STAFFNUM	4.23	LOAN	4.24
PROMISES	4.25	POLITE	4.26
CONCERN	4.26	APOLOGY	4.27
PROMPT	4.28	TELLERS	4.29
QUEUES	4.31	KNOWLEDGE	4.33
MISTAKE	4.36		

Table 4. Orthogonally rotated factor matrix (first PAF).

Variable	F1	F2	F3	F4	F5	F6
POLITE	0.71671					
SECURITY	0.69689					
GREET	0.68190					
NEATNESS	0.66742					
PRIVACY	0.53075					
COMPUTER	0.51206					
PERSONAL	0.49419					
SYMPATHY	0.42851					
ACCTYPES		0.67406				
INFORMED		0.64632				
SERVWHEN		0.55838				
LEARN		0.53005				
ADVICE		0.52809				
KNOWLEDGE		0.52527				
CLARITY		0.52365				
APOLOGY			0.87695			
CONCERN			0.76605			
MISTAKE			0.67112			
PROMPT				0.74106		
HELP				0.58653		
QUEUES				0.48794		
LOAN					0.69335	
MANAGER					0.55659	
PROMISES					0.47321	
TELEPHONE					0.39353	
STAFFNUM						0.57890
TELLERS						0.50152

with Varimax rotation was carried out on the reduced item pool (22 items), in effect increasing the cases-to-variable ratio. Results indicate that the structure of the matrix was principally retained, implying that the factor structure was independent of sample size (see Table 5).

Comparing the conceptualized dimensions to the groups of variables loading on factors necessitated re-evaluation of dimensions. Although some variables maintained their membership, others had changed groups. In light of the factor structure, dimensions were rearranged as follows (see Table 6):

- *F1: Staff conduct*—civilized conduct and presentation of branch staff that will project a professional image to the customers.
- *F2: Communication*—fulfilling banking needs of customers by successfully communicating financial advice and serving timely notices.
- *F3: Credibility*—maintaining staff-customer trust by recognizing and rectifying mistakes.
- *F4: Responsiveness*—willingness to help customers and provide prompt service.
- *F5: Access to branch management*—the ease of contacting branch management, say, for applying for a loan.
- *F6: Access to teller services*—the adequacy of number of staff serving customers throughout business hours and during peak hours.

Table 5. Originally rotated factor matrix (second PAF).

Variable	F1	F2	F3	F4	F5	F6
POLITE	0.74436					
GREET	0.72796					
SECURITY	0.68543					
NEATNESS	0.66825					
PRIVACY	0.52240					
HELP	0.50626					
COMPUTER	0.50375					
ACCTYPES		0.68420				
INFORMED		0.64426				
SERVWHEN		0.60514				
ADVICE		0.54419				
CLARITY		0.53523				
LEARN		0.53517				
KNOWLEDGE		0.53263				
APOLOGY			0.89930			
CONCERN			0.76619			
MISTAKE			0.68561			
PROMPT				0.81225		
LOAN					0.78442	
MANAGER					0.52937	
STAFFNUM						0.63144
TELLERS						0.51654

Table 6. Orthogonally rotated factor matrix.

Variable	F1	F2	F3	F4
POLITE	0.81581			
GREET	0.66407			
HELP	0.66165			
PROMPT	0.57949			
NEATNESS	0.55758			
APOLOGY	0.52020			
CONCERN	0.51834			
PRIVACY*	0.43102			
MISTAKE		0.63066		
SECURITY		0.57149		
INFORMED		0.54765		
CLARITY*		0.48655		
MANAGER*		0.48421		
COMPUTER*		0.46626		
LOAN*		0.39137		
ACCTYPES			0.74177	
ADVICE			0.61505	
LEARN			0.61237	
KNOWLEDGE			0.51623	
SERVWHEN			0.50303	
TELLERS				0.77704
STAFFNUM				0.70722

*Variables loading less than 0.5.

Factorability of the correlation matrix (strength of linear association among variables) also merits comment. Initial examination of the correlation matrix revealed a substantial number of correlations to be larger than 0.3 in absolute values which, according to Tabachnick and Fidell (1989), indicates factorability. After the second Varimax rotation, Barlett's test of sphericity was 1512.5872 at an observed significance level of 0, allowing rejection of the hypothesis that the population correlation matrix is an identity matrix i.e. zero correlations. However, it should be noted that Barlett's test is sensitive to the sample size and has a tendency to give significant results with large samples even when correlations are very low. Tabachnick and Fidell recommend its use when there are less than five cases per variable. In the analysis, there were 159 cases; with 22 variables, this translates into approximately 7.23 cases per variable, a number close to Tabachnick and Fidell's guidelines. Kaiser–Meyer–Olkin (KMO) measure of sampling adequacy yielded 0.84578, considered as 'meritorious' by Kaiser (1974). KMO is computed to compare the magnitudes of the observed correlation coefficients to that of partial correlation coefficients.

The iterative process continued by re-calculation of coefficient α for the smaller item pool of 22 variables. The standardized α for the scale showed a small drop to 0.8933 (higher α coefficients can be observed with larger item numbers, Norusis, 1992). In this instance, the observed drop is presumably due to elimination of eight items. Nevertheless, the scale α is an improvement over 0.87 reported by Parasuraman *et al.* (1988) for their bank, following the second stage of scale purification with 22 items. Among the six factors, α now ranged between 0.6235 (*F6*) and 0.8713 (*F3*), implying higher internal consistency for the revised variable groups.

Main stage

The 22 variables were factor analysed with principal axis factoring on the data set recoded to approximate an interval scale i.e. 1 to 5 scores from the questionnaire were changed to 0 to 4 (all other tests were run on the unmodified data set). As in the pilot stage testing, the factor matrix was rotated orthogonally. Table VI shows the four factors that emerged, those variables loading less than 0.5 marked with an asterisk for deletion. The KMO measure of sampling adequacy had risen to 0.95093 and variance explained increased to 54.3 per cent.

Overall, factorial membership of the variables is similar to that of the pilot stage but more discriminating. COMPUTER now belongs in *F2* which can intuitively be better explained. Refined operational definitions of construct dimensions can be stated as:

- *F1: Staff conduct*—responsiveness, civilized conduct and presentation of branch staff that will project a professional image to the customers.
- *F2: Credibility*—maintaining staff-customer trust by rectifying mistakes, and keeping customers informed.
- *F3: Communication*—fulfilling banking needs to customers by successfully communicating financial advice and serving timely notices.
- *F4: Access to teller services*—the adequacy of number of staff serving customers throughout business hours and during peak hours.

Calculation of coefficient α for the 22-item variable pool yielded α of 0.9392 and standardized α of 0.9397, a considerable improvement over the pilot stage. Recalculation of α on the final 17-item pool to emerge from factor analysis resulted in α of 0.9242 and standardized item α of 0.9249. The slight drop can be explained by the removal of five items, none of which was indicated for deletion on the 'Alpha if Item Deleted' column in reliability analysis. In this instance, the trade-off is between instrument reliability and dimensionality. Coefficient α generated for each factor after deletion of five items were higher and in a smaller range compared with pilot stage findings (0.8014 for $F3$ and 0.8845 for $F1$), indicating improved and more comparable dimensional reliabilities. It is worth noting that in both runs of coefficient α, the standardized values were very close to their corresponding α, indicating comparable item variances.

The hypotheses formulated to evaluate the validity of the instrument (see 'Research Design') required a number of tests. Mann–Whitney U-test was used to compare the scores from the regular and shuffled versions of the questionnaire (see Table 7). The two-tailed probability returned by SPSS, 0.1410, implies that the null hypothesis cannot be rejected at the significance level of 5 per cent. This can be regarded as evidence for construct validity. Further evidence can be found by looking at coefficient alphas on each data collection method (triangulation); mailed questionnaires returned the highest standardized α at 0.9418, followed by telephone questionnaires at 0.9336, and exit interviews at 0.9001. Since the three different applications of the same questionnaire resulted in similar reliability measures, it can at least be argued that the necessary condition for instrument validity is present.

As an extension of construct validity, convergent validity was also tested by examining the correspondence between answers to the question on overall quality rating (OVERALLQ) and sum of scores across all items (SCOREQ). Spearman's ρ of 0.6048 supports the main contention behind convergent validity that the observed results are not an artefact of the instrument i.e. there is a high correlation with results from instruments designed to measure the same construct (Churchill, 1979). Convergent validity was further probed by examining the instrument scores of respondents answering Yes to RECOMMEND and No to COMPLAIN, and vice versa. As expected, the mean of the average score (i.e. mean of variable SCOREQX) was significantly different with a higher mean on the Yes/No combination (see Table 8).

Testing for response bias in data collected through mailed questionnaires required computation of separate α on the first two-thirds and the last one-third of responses returned; the standardized α emerged as 0.9381 and 0.9420 respectively. The difference is small enough to indicate there was no significant response bias.

Table 7. Mann–Whitney U–Wilcoxon rank sum W test.

Mean rank	Cases	SCOREQ by VERID	
407.58	408	VERID = 1.00 regular	
383.66	383	VERID = 2.00 shuffled	
Total	791		
U	W	Z	2-tailed P
73406.5	146942.5	−1.4720	0.1410

Table 8. *t*-test for independent samples of yes/no response combinations.

Variable	Number of cases	Mean	SD	SE of mean
SCOREQX				
Yes/no 1 (Y/N)	522	3.2127	0.588	0.06
Yes/no 2 (Y/N)	100	2.5018	0.413	0.041

Mean difference = 0.7109
Leven's test for equality of variances: $F = 15.290$
$p = 0.000$

t-test for equality of means

Variances	*t*-value	df	Two-tail significance	Standard error of difference	95 percent confident interval for difference
Equal	11.55	620	0.000	0.062	(0.590, 0.832)
Unequal	14.62	185.59	0.000	0.049	(0.615, 0.807)

CONCLUSIONS

The outcome is a parsimonious, easy-to-use set of items tapping into the customer service quality as perceived by the customers (as opposed to branch staff or bank management). The six dimensions conceptualized at the start with 27 items were empirically reduced to 17 items across four discriminating factors. The observed factors are well-defined as evidenced in the rotated matrix. The dimensions to emerge are *staff conduct, credibility, communication*, and *access to teller services*. The instrument's reliability, dimensionality and validity have been empirically tested; the results are encouraging both in their own right and when compared with other studies.

The study is the first of its kind targeting branches of an Australian commercial bank, with emphasis on retail operations. Equally significant is the instrument investigating the importance of each quality item, providing a more refined measure compared to instruments without importance weights. The emergence of this instrument is particularly timely for Australia and for other countries in a similar position, where deregulation of the banking industry (and the accompanying fiercer competition) is manifesting itself in the form of branch network rationalization for the major commercial banks. A direction for further research would be to replicate this study outside Australia.

In addition to integrating the findings of this study into branch performance measurement, applications of the instrument can be further expanded to segmenting the customer base in accordance with customers' needs by attaching socio-economic items; diagnosing problem service areas by examining scores across dimensions and items; and, considering importance scores in formulating solutions for problem areas.

ACKNOWLEDGEMENT

The study described in this article is part of the author's PhD research activities. The editorial assistance provided by Dr Lindsay Turner of Faculty of Business, Victoria University of Technology, is gratefully acknowledged.

REFERENCES

Alwin, D. F. and Krosnick, J. A. (1991), 'The Reliability of Survey Attitude Measurement', *Sociological Methods and Research*, Vol. 20, August, pp. 139–81.

Babakus, E. and Boller, G. W. (1992) 'An Empirical Assessment of the SERVQUAL Scale', *Journal of Business Research*, Vol. 24, May, pp. 253–68.

Brown, T. J., Churchill, G. A. Jr and Peter, J. P. (1993), 'Improving the Measurement of Service Quality', *Journal of Retailing*, Vol. 69 No. 1, Spring, pp. 127–39.

Carman, J. M. (1990), 'Consumer Perceptions of Service Quality: An Assessment of the SERVQUAL Dimensions', *Journal of Retailing*, Vol. 66, Spring, pp. 33–55.

Churchill, G. A. Jr, (1979), 'A Paradigm for Developing Better Measures of Marketing Constructs', *Journal of Marketing Research*, Vol. 16, February, pp. 64–73.

Comrey, A. L. (1973), *A First Course in Factor Analysis*, Academic Press, New York, NY.

Crouch, S. (1984) *Marketing Research for Managers*, Butterworth-Heinemann, London, UK.

Dangar Research Group Pty Limited (1991), 'Quality Service Study', April–May.

Denzin, N. K. (1978), *Sociological Methods: A Sourcebook*, 2nd ed., McGraw-Hill Book Company, New York, NY.

Howell, R. D., Wilcox, J. B., Bellenger, D. N. and Chonko, L. B. (1988), 'An Assessment of the Role Conflict and Ambiguity Scales', in Frazier, G. *et al.* (Eds), *Efficiency and Effectiveness in Marketing*, American Marketing Association, Chicago, IL, pp. 314–9.

Kaiser, H. F. (1974), 'An Index of Factorial Simplicity', *Psychometrika*, Vol. 39, pp. 31–6.

Keirl, C. and Mitchell, P. (1990), 'How to Measure Industrial Service Quality', *Industrial Marketing Digest*, Vol. 15 (first quarter), pp. 35–46.

Labaw, P. (1985), *Advanced Questionnaire Design*, Abt Books, Cambridge, MA.

LeBlanc, G. and Nguyen, N. (1988), 'Customers' Perceptions of Service Quality in Financial Institutions', *International Journal of Bank Marketing*, Vol. 6 No. 4, pp. 7–18.

Lesser, J. A. and Kamal, P. (1991), 'An Inductively Derived Model of the Motivation to Shop', *Psychology and Marketing*, Vol. 8 No. 3, pp. 177–96.

Lewis, B. R. and Mitchell, V. W. (1990), 'Defining and Measuring the Quality of Customer Service', *Marketing Intelligence and Planning (UK)*, Vol. 8 No. 6, pp. 11–7.

Likert, R. (1932), 'A Technique for Measurement of Attitudes', *Archives of Psychology*, No. 140.

Norusis, M. J. (1992), *SPSS for Windows: Professional Statistics*, Release 5, SPSS Inc.

Nunnally, J. C. (1978), *Psychometric Theory*, 2nd ed., McGraw-Hill, New York, NY.

Parasuraman, A., Zeithaml, V. and Berry, L. L. (1986), 'SERVQUAL: A Multiple-item Scale for Measuring Customer Perceptions of Service Quality', Working Paper No. 86–108, Marketing Science Institute, August.

Parasuraman, A., Zeithaml, V. and Berry, L. L. (1988), 'SERVQUAL: A Multiple-item Scale for Measuring Consumer Perceptions of Service Quality', *Journal of Retailing*, Vol. 64 Spring, pp. 12–40.

Parasuraman, A., Zeithaml, V. and Berry, L.L. (1991), 'Refinement and Reassessment of the SERVQUAL Scale', *Journal of Retailing*, Vol. 67 No. 4, Winter, pp. 420–50.

Parasuraman, A., Zeithaml, V. and Berry, L.L. (1993), 'More on Improving Service Quality', *Journal of Retailing*, Vol. 1. 69 No. 1, Spring, pp. 140–7.

Peters, J. P. (1979), 'Reliability: A Review of Psychometric Basics and Recent Marketing Practices', *Journal of Marketing Research*, Vol. 16, February, pp. 6–17.

Quadrant Research Services (1992), 'A Tracking Study of Attitudes to the Integration of the Commonwealth Bank and the State Bank of Victoria', 18 May, Victoria.

Straub, D. W. and Carlson, C. L. (1989), 'Validating Instruments in MIS Research', *MIS Quarterly*, Vol. 13, June, pp. 147–69.

Sudman, S. and Bradburn, N. (1984), 'Improving Mailed Questionnaire Design', in Lockhart, D. C. (Ed.), *Making Effective Use of Mailed Questionnaires*, Jossey-Bass, San Francisco, CA.

Tabachnick, B. G. and Fidell, L. S. (1989), *Using Multivariate Statistics*, 2nd ed., Harper Collins Publishers, London.

Wall, T. D. and Payne, R. (1973), 'Are Deficiency Scores Deficient?', *Journal of Applied Psychology*, Vol. 58 No. 3, pp. 322–6.

Wason, P. C. and Johnson-Laird, P. N. (1975), *Psychology of Reasoning: Structure and Content*, Harvard University Press, Cambridge, MA.
Zikmund, W. G. (1991), *Business Research Methods*, 3rd ed., HBJ College Publishers, Orlando, FL.

APPENDIX: THE INSTRUMENT

1	2	3	4	5
Much worse than I expected	Worse than I expected	About what I expected	Better than I expected	Much better than I expected

1	2	3	4	5
Not important	Slightly important	Moderately important	Important	Very important

1. 'Willingness of branch staff to help me' is   [HELP]
2. 'Promptness of service from branch staff' is   [PROMPT]
3.* 'Concern shown by branch staff if queues get too long' is   [QUEUES]
4. 'Branch staff helping me learn how to keep down my banking costs' is   [LEARN]
5. 'Branch staff greeting me when it's my turn to be served' is   [GREET]
6.* 'Respect for privacy of my financial affairs when I am standing at the counter' is   [PRIVACY]
7. 'Personal attention I receive from branch staff' is   [PERSONAL]
8. 'Branch staff being sympathetic when I have problems' is   [SYMPATHY]
9. 'Expression of genuine concern if there is a mistake in my account' is   [CONCERN]
10.* 'Branch staff making me feel at ease when applying for a loan' is   [LOAN]
11. 'Politeness of branch staff' is   [POLITE]
12. 'Neat appearance of branch staff' is   [NEATNESS]
13. 'Ability of branch staff to apologise for mistake' is   [APOLOGY]
14. 'Branch staff's knowledge of bank's services and products' is   [KNOWLEDGE]
15. 'Quality of advice given about managing my finances' is   [ADVICE]
16. 'Number of open tellers during the busy hours of the day' is   [TELLERS]
17.* 'Ease of contacting the branch manager' is   [MANAGER]
18.* 'Ease of getting through to the branch on the telephone' is   [TELEPHONE]
19. 'Number of staff behind the counter serving customers' is   [STAFFNUM]
20. 'Branch staff telling me about the different types of accounts and investments available' is   [ACCTYPES]
21. 'Branch staff telling me when services will be performed' is   [SERVWHEN]
22.* 'Clarity of correspondence I receive from my branch' is   [CLARITY]
23. 'Branch staff keeping me informed about matters of concern to me' is   [INFORMED]
24.* 'Branch staff keeping their promises to me' is   [PROMISES]

25. 'Ability of branch staff to put a mistake right' is [MISTAKE]
26. 'Feeling of security in my dealings with the branch staff' is [SECURITY]
27.* 'Ability of branch staff to get information quickly from the computer' is [COMPUTER]

(Deleted items are marked with an asterisk. Variable names used in SPSS are indicated in brackets).

13

Service Quality: Relationships Between Banks and Their Small Business Clients

Anne M. Smith

During the 1980s the UK clearing banks have undertaken, or are planning, widespread and intensive customer programmes with the objective of improving the quality of service which their customers receive. The most often-cited reason for this (as reported earlier in this special issue) is to retain their existing customer base and, to a lesser extent, to attract new customers with the overall objective of increasing sales and profitability. An additional feature of the 1980s is the banks' drive to attract small businesses, exemplified by the high incidence of advertising campaigns and an increasing proliferation of product and other information aimed at this sector. This raises the question, by what criteria does the small business owner/manager measure the quality of service received in a banking relationship and, consequently, how can the banks improve the service which they offer in order to retain what may well be growing and increasingly profitable businesses?

Reported here are some of the findings of a research study which explored the determinants of service quality as perceived by small businesses. This involved personal interviews in 50 companies in the Greater Manchester/Stockport area. A brief overview of previous research into small businesses' satisfactions/dissatisfactions with their bank, together with the opinions of bank representatives, are also included.

SMALL BUSINESSES' REQUIREMENTS OF THEIR BANK—PREVIOUS RESEARCH

Previous research has indicated four key areas of bank service which the small business considers to be important and which can cause customer dissatisfaction: bank personnel, the organisation and structure of the clearing banks, pricing policy, and product offerings.

For the small business, characteristics of the bank representative are rated highly both when choosing a bank and in a banking relationship (see, for example, Dunkelberg and Scott, 1983; Buerger and Ulrich, 1986; Forum of Private Business, 1988). 'Knows you and your business' has been described as a factor of considerable importance, as has 'one person handles needs', 'easy access to loan officer', 'knowledgeable personnel' and 'personable employees'. However, a major criticism levelled by small businesses is the apparent inability of bank staff to understand their business, particularly when loans are requested, and to make informed judgements relating to the potential and needs of the client firm.

A major organisational factor affecting the efficiency of UK banks is the oligopolistic market structure within which they operate. This adversely affects the small firm, since not only is non-price competition a feature but also the size of the banks 'requires a degree of bureaucracy and remoteness of the few policy makers at the centre from the thousands of branch managers and assistant managers in the field' (Bannock, 1981). Speed of decision making, inflexibility and inaccessibility of the decision maker have thus been criticised by small businesses (see, for example, European Bankers' Small Business Seminar, 1984).

Lack of price competition and high perceived risk by the banks create major problems encountered by many small firms—high interest payments, bank charges, collateral requirements and problems in raising initial or additional finance. Further, small businesses are not well informed about bank charging structures (Peterson and Shulman, 1987; Forum of Private Business, 1988).

Finally, while small businesses do not rate highly a wide range of financial services, and while product requirements may be 'relatively simple', to the small business owner/manager who has neither the time nor the expertise of the corporate treasurer, these may represent complex issues. There is evidence that small business requires more and better quality information (Bannock, 1984; Paisley College, 1987); that product feature needs vary between firms of differing sizes (McKibbin and Gutmann, 1986); and that product needs have existed in this market for some time which the banks have only just begun to address (McClure, 1985; Bannock, 1984).

THE BANKS' VIEW

During 1988, interviews were undertaken by the author with senior representatives of nine UK clearing banks in order to establish:
- how the banks service this sector in terms of organisational structure, product offerings, pricing policy, etc;
- how the banks respond to reported customer dissatisfactions.

All bank representatives stated that their bank was actively seeking to increase its share of the small business market. Intense competition in other areas had increased the attractiveness of this sector which, due to high levels of unemployment coupled with government policy aimed at encouraging small businesses, is an expanding market. Additionally, a proportion of these businesses will grow into larger and, for the banks, increasingly profitability firms. The ability to attract and retain small businesses is therefore in the long-term interests of the banks. A substantial increase in competition was reported, in contrast to the view of the small business market which acknowledged very little increase in competitive activity by the banks (Forum of Private Business, 1988).

The major changes which are apparent according to the banks are: repackaging and branding together with more off-the-shelf products; simplified pricing and some price competition; more high profile status and increased usage of advertising and other promotional methods; links with government policy; an improvement in professionalism and changing attitudes of the bank manager; and segmentation of the market.

Definitions of a 'small business' varied to some extent, but a usual cut-off point was that of £1 million turnover per annum. Many of the UK clearers have been involved in major reorganisation and restructuring, which has typically involved a split between corporate and personal business, and the concentration of specialist personnel in corporate banking centres. The main point of contact for the small business owner/manager continues to be the bank manager. However, a number of banks are increasing the number of in-branch specialists and mobile personnel who are available for consultation, and ascribing responsibility for the small business sector at various levels of management. Additionally, a number of banks are taking steps to 'shorten the sanctioning trail' and thus accelerate the decision-making process.

Bank representatives did feel that small business proprietors encounter a number of problems when dealing with the banks. However, accusations of high interest rates and bank charges, and excessive collateral requirements, were considered to be unjustified. Two general points were that:

- the banks had to operate in the best interest of all their clients, business and personal, in addition to their shareholders;
- if the small business owner/manager did not have enough confidence in his/her own venture to be willing to offer collateral, then how could the banks justify offering funds?

Criticisms relating to lack of understanding and knowledge on the part of the bank personnel were acknowledged. However, it was stressed that the role of the bank manager was to assess business potential and be knowledgeable of relevant bank products, but not to understand the nature of all businesses dealt with. Increased understanding of the client's business through 'calling' and from regular meetings and referrals to specialists was encouraged. It was also stated that individual bank managers varied in their own expertise and skills.

Other acknowledged criticisms which were considered to be justified in some cases, or for other banks, related to: the banks are too busy and have too many customers; not enough facilities in the branch, e.g. for paying in money; the bank manager does not have enough time for meetings or visiting the client on his/her premises; inaccessibility of the manager; it is difficult to speak to someone who is the decision maker and who understands; lack of continuity; customers are not kept informed of what is going on; the banks are not receptive; and customers are afraid of approaching the bank manager.

THE RESEARCH STUDY

The author is involved in a research project concerned with quality service and the small business/bank relationship, which is one component of a major customer care/quality service research programme. The objectives of the current study are:

(1) To identify those elements of service which determine the quality of bank service to the small business client.
(2) To measure the level of perceived quality of service by comparing expectations and performance across those elements.
(3) To examine the buying process of small firms with regard to search behaviour and choice criteria.

The findings reported in this article relate to the first objective, i.e. the identification of service elements which are of importance to the small business in its dealings with the bank. The overall assessment of the level of service received and the unprompted reasons for that assessment are discussed together with respondents' ratings of the importance of 55 service factors. These factors were derived from a number of sources which include: an examination of both the service quality literature (see, for example, LeBlanc and Nguyen, 1988; Parasuraman et al., 1985, 1988); previous research relating to small businesses' requirements of their bank; group interviews with personal customers; and pilot interviews with small business owners/managers.

Interviews were conducted between April and July 1989 among 50 small companies from a wide range of manufacturing and service industries in the Greater Manchester/ Stockport area. Initially, 100 companies were selected from data compiled by Dun and Bradstreet, contacted by letter and a follow-up telephone call. Sixty firms agreed to participate in the research, 27 declined because the owner 'did not have the time', and the remaining companies had moved, ceased trading or been involved in takeovers, etc. (see Smith, 1989, for further details of sample response and characteristics).

The final interview schedule comprised 50 firms whose owners/managers were available during the time allocated for the fieldwork. The sampling procedure had included only companies with a reported annual turnover of less than 1 million. However, due to growth, takeover, etc, twelve firms had an annual turnover of between 1 and £2 million and four companies had turnovers of over £2 million.

In 26 firms the owner or one of the owners who had set up the business was interviewed; in 15 firms the interviewee had inherited or bought the business and in one other the original owner/managing director was interviewed soon after the firm had been taken over by another company. In eight firms it was the employee who was responsible for dealing with the bank who was interviewed, e.g. the company secretary, accountant/ financial manager, office manager.

FINDINGS

Respondents were asked how they would rate the overall level of service which they receive from their current bank. Seventeen (34 per cent) replied—very good; 16 (32 per cent)—good; 15 (30 per cent)—acceptable; and two believed the level to be poor. They then described the particular aspects of service which they felt were good, and what they felt was poor or could be improved.

Elements of good bank service

Favourable comments generally related to the efficiency of staff or the bank's systems and procedures; the personal qualities of staff; the qualities of the bank manager; and the general support from and flexibility of the bank itself (see Table 1).

A major source of satisfaction was the quality of the bank manager, or in a minority of cases, some other key contact figure. In some instances it was the availability of the bank manager, in others it was his interest in and understanding of the business or his ability and supportiveness.

It is possible to see the manager without having an appointment, or the assistant manager if he is not available—they don't put you off. We have been with them a long time; they understand the needs of the business.

At present we have the best relationship we have ever had. It's the involvement of the bank manager that matters. We might move with him if he goes.

Efficiency as a key source of satisfaction was more often in terms of staff efficiency, rather than systems/procedures.

They are a very efficient administration . . . can't fault the staff; they are very professional.

If we want anything sent out, people always find it for us immediately; if they can't they telephone; it is a first class branch.

A total of 28 firms made some comment regarding bank staff (other than the manager), with four describing both efficiency and personal qualities and 13 regarding such qualities as helpfulness, pleasantness and politeness of staff as their major attribute.

People are friendly; you can have a laugh which was not the case at our previous bank.

It is a good relationship and we have friendly discussions—they know me, I know them. The girl on the counter is more important than the bank manager.

Staff at the branch give the impression that they are working together. When they see a queue they come to the desk and help. Even the assistant manager will come to the counter.

Ten firms, of which seven did not mention individual staff or bank managers, described their satisfaction with the bank as a whole, the willingness to support the business and flexibility of arrangements.

Flexibility—if what you want doesn't suit the rule book, they can change it.

Other factors which were considered to comprise good service were products and/or systems which bank staff had suggested and which had been found useful; the availability of information concerning their accounts; and for one firm the design of a branch which had recently been modernised.

Elements of poor bank service

Seventeen firms rated the overall service which they received from their bank as acceptable or poor; however, all but three of the 50 firms mentioned aspects of bank service which they considered to be poor or needed improvement (see Table 2). The major sources of dissatisfaction were the inefficiency of staff and/or of bank systems and procedures and the related factor of errors.

Table 1. Elements of good bank service.

Service factor	No. of mentions*
Qualities of the bank manager/other key contact	17
Efficiency	17
Staff—personal qualities	15
Support/flexibility of bank	10
Other	6

* Totals exceed 50 since interviewees gave multiple responses.

Table 2. Elements of poor bank service.

Service factor	No. of mentions*
Inefficiency	25
Errors	18
Support/flexibility of the bank	12
Bank charges	14
Qualities of the bank manager/other key contact	12
Insufficient information	10
Decision-making process	9
Queuing	7
Other	11

*Totals exceed 50 since interviewees gave multiple responses.

'Major sources of dissatisfaction were the inefficiency of staff and/or of bank systems and procedures'

Inefficiency

Half of the sample criticised the banks for inefficiency. Thirteen described this in terms of inefficiencies of the bank's systems and procedures and twelve related to staff. Seven (less than half of the sample were involved in a significant amount of overseas trade) of these firms specifically criticised their bank for their inability to deal with foreign transactions effectively and here two related to staff and four to bank systems.

Of those who criticised the efficiency of bank personnel, it was occasionally for slow service in the branch or for dealing with telephone enquiries where the caller would be 'passed from department to department' but more often it was for failing to carry out the instructions of the customer:

They take your money but they don't look after it. There might be £40 000 or £50 000 in the current account. We had an arrangement with the bank to move money to a deposit account . . . When the assistant manager left, they stopped doing it . . . forgotten.

Five firms specifically mentioned the failing on the part of bank staff to inform the client when one of their customer's cheques had not been honoured in spite of repeated requests.

They are very poor at carrying out instructions. If you write and ask them to do something they do it for about a month and then they stop. When customers send a cheque which is not honoured it goes back and forth three or four times. We have told them to send the cheque back to us straight away; the customer can have gone bankrupt while that cheque is toing and froing. We said that if a cheque was presented twice, send it back to us. They did this for a while then again started re-presenting the cheque four times.

A number of interviewees felt that a high turnover of staff or 'switching them around' caused problems, and in other cases the absence of a particular member of staff had resulted in the customers' instructions not being carried out. Inefficiency due to lack of knowledge was mentioned in the context of foreign transactions and product knowledge.

No expertise at local branch for foreign transactions. If anyone leaves, we have to train them ourselves.

The bank produces an awful lot of nice glossy brochures, e.g. about computer links between banks and business, etc. . . . but when you ask someone at the bank they can't tell you anything about it.

'Others also criticised the bank for creating work for the customer'

Fourteen firms criticised their bank's systems and procedures. Again, the system for dealing with discredited cheques was mentioned and the speed with which this and other matters were dealt with. Respondents complained that bankers' drafts, cheque books, statements, etc, had to be ordered in advance and even then they were not always available when the customer went to collect them. One company owner stated that:

There is no sense of urgency in the banking system as a whole and too much paperwork.

Others also criticised the bank for creating work for the customer:

When the bank makes errors, it sometimes takes quite some time and requires written confirmation from the company when it is a bank problem in the first place, i.e. more work for the company secretary.

They won't automatically change money from current to deposit account. We have to send a letter of transfer every time . . . why can't they do this automatically?

A few firms commented on the clearing system itself and wanted to know why transfers from one branch of the same bank could take a number of days.

So when it's in neither account . . . where is it? The bank's using it, that's where it is.

Of those firms which criticised the banks for their dealings with foreign transactions it was again the speed of transaction and communication within the bank which was considered to be a problem.

Anything to do with international business is not good enough. This business needs quick responses to international dealings. Many firms are moving out of the centres of cities because of rates, etc. This means that they have to deal with small branches which do not have the specialists, expertise or discretion. If letters of credit have to be sent through the system this takes time and many errors have been made. The banks have a tremendous communication system, so why is communication between head office, regional office and the branches so slow?

Errors

An additional aspect of the inefficiency mentioned by over one-third of respondents was that of errors made by bank staff. These included errors in cash, inaccurate debiting and crediting of accounts, and sending statements to the wrong address.

Support/flexibility of the bank

Nearly one-quarter of the sample was critical of the bank's attitude towards small businesses. Lack of support manifest in the bank's unwillingness to lend money, particularly to growing firms, and high collateral requirements was often mentioned, as was the contrast between the bank's attitude towards lending to them and to students/ LDC lending—for example:

We might move to Argentina or Brazil, then they might lend us money and not expect to get it back!

The unwillingness or inability of the bank to understand business propositions and the problems faced by a small business were also mentioned. Further criticisms were concerned with what was described as the 'complacency of the banks':

It's more like a confessional than a commercial operation. It's only another business, after all, that we are dealing with. Yet people feel they have to be subservient.

The bank is using our money. They don't give us the service that we give to our customers. They feel safe in their fortress.

The banks have an underlying attitude of arrogance and complacency. They accept without argument that a bank is necessary to business. I wish I could manage without one. They don't aggressively compete. There is aggressive advertising to lend money and make profits from their facilities but they would rather tell you what they can't do when you are a customer. They are not interested in customer satisfaction.

Bank charges

Bank charges were, as expected, a major source of dissatisfaction and were mentioned by 14 firms at this stage. The level of bank charges was not originally to be included as a service factor (see Appendix) since this is the price which the customer pays for the service rather than an element of the service itself (for discussion of the relationship between price and quality see, for example, Gardner, 1970; Jacoby et al., 1973). However, since opinion of the level of bank charges can be an explanatory factor of overall service satisfaction this was included.

Major dissatisfactions with the banks' pricing policy were:

- charging customers who were in credit
- charging an arrangement fee for overdraft facilities, particularly where the customer might not even use this.

The banks were described as 'a bit worse than Shylock' for their policy of 'charging for everything' and at an 'extortionate rate'. The practice of their bank of reducing charges 'at the drop of a hat' as a result of a customer query was considered to be unacceptable by a number of companies which felt that their bank was 'plucking a figure out of the air and doubling it'. Other companies had found to their surprise that bank charges were negotiable and wondered why they had not been informed of this; others complained that charges were non-negotiable.

Two other related factors which are discussed later and which are considered to be elements of quality service are the extent to which bank charges are explained to the customer and, in the event of bank charges being increased/imposed, whether the customer is informed of this.

'If the firm was not borrowing money the bank had no interest in them as a customer'

Qualities of the bank manager/other key contact

Of the twelve firms that mentioned the bank manager, seven were criticising bank managers in general and four firms had never seen their current, and in some cases previous, manager. One respondent heavily criticised the current bank manager who was the successor to a number of good managers and was a potential cause of his company changing banks in the near future.

General criticism often involved the view that there were good and poor managers and a number of respondents had experienced both. The willingness of the manager to support the business, understand business problems, and to be available and interested in the business, were considered to be differentiating factors.

For those respondents who felt that they did not have a key contact this was a major cause of dissatisfaction and a prevalent view was that if the firm was not borrowing money the bank had no interest in them as a customer:

My main concern is that there is no relationship between the bank manager and the company. I don't even know his name. He has never contacted us although he has been there for seven years.

Insufficient information

Ten firms were not satisfied with the information which they received from the bank, excluding frequency of statements. The major complaint was that bank charges were not fully explained and would not be itemised even on request.

If we understood the principle of charges, we could reduce them by arranging our affairs differently. Sometimes there is a covering letter but never a breakdown.

. . . then there is the mystery bank charges. They will not tell us when we ask what rate we are paying. You have to find out yourself about costs, rates, products . . . A lot of booklets are not relevant and the manager doesn't explain.

Some firms also criticised the bank for not suggesting products which were relevant to them, e.g. higher interest accounts which were available, or systems, such as wages transfers which would be less costly and/or less work for the customer:

The bank should keep us up to date with the best ways of investing our money. We have had to initiate new products ourselves. The personal touch has gone out of business altogether because of computerisation. When we have had large sums of money in our account they should have noticed; it is immoral to let us leave money in an account when it could be earning money for us.

In two cases the bank had failed to inform the customer of changes in bank procedures/policy, and this was a major source of dissatisfaction. In one instance bank charges had been imposed on a customer with a credit balance without prior consultation or warning and in the other, the company had almost lost a major customer because the bank had failed to honour a cheque which had not been countersigned (previously the bank staff would have telephoned the drawer for authorisation).

The decision-making process

Nine firms criticised the decision-making process of the banks either in terms of time taken to agree facilities (two); discretion of the key contact (three), or both (four).

The trouble with small branches is the discretion of the bank manager. The businessman has to sell his idea to the bank manager who then has to sell it to the regional office, etc. The businessman would prefer to sell his own ideas himself, since he can answer the questions. There should be an opportunity for the client to talk to someone who does have the authority.

We need a specialist corporate adviser—banking is a minefield now for someone who is busy. You know what you want and go to the bank, usually seeing someone at a lower level; by the time it has been passed up the channel and they have said no to you, you have to start all over again. Half of the difficulty is knowing what the ground rules are and what is within the discretion of the person you are seeing. You need an adviser who knows what you can get. You also need someone at a senior level within the bank who can analyse the company requirements and deal with them. It may be better going directly to the regional manager.

Queuing

Seven respondents mentioned queuing as an element of poor service and four of these related to peak periods such as lunchtimes. However, many respondents rarely visited the branch themselves for business banking and would therefore not encounter this (sixteen interviewees dealt with counter staff in the branch less than once a month and four others never went into the branch for business banking).
'Accuracy, confidentiality, reliability and speed were ranked as the most important elements'

Other elements of poor service

Other factors mentioned by respondents were lack of car parking facilities and unfriendly, unhelpful, miserable staff. One criticised a new branch which was described as dirty, poorly lit, poorly heated and dark and others, lack of interest on current account; paying-in slips which had to have all details completed manually which caused errors to be made; the attitude of bank staff who expected the customer to understand the jargon and procedures involved in foreign transactions. Finally, one company had asked the bank to check on a customer who was rumoured to be heading for bankruptcy, and had received two letters on the same day—one from the bank stating that the customer was 'good for his money' and another from the liquidator informing him that 'the firm had been declared bankrupt'.

Small business' expectations of bank service

Having described their reasons for initial ratings of the level of service received from their current bank, respondents were then asked to consider 55 factors and to assess the importance of each factor as an element of bank service. Their responses are listed in the Appendix and show that, for the small business, accuracy, confidentiality, reliability and speed were ranked as the most important elements, and in some cases higher than the level of bank charges or interest rates (a minority of firms did not pay bank charges and were net depositors with the bank).

The three factors relating to accuracy or competence were all ranked highly reflecting the dissatisfactions expressed earlier relating to errors. Confidentiality and the trustworthiness of the manager (the latter being the highest ranked factor relating to the bank manager) were also rated highly, emphasising the importance of security in dealings with the bank. Reliability, both in terms of head office support for the branch and of staff 'doing what they say they will do', and accuracy are of great importance to the small business. Speed in all aspects of the bank service—decision making, transactions, dealing with customers both in the branch and by telephone, and resolution of problems and queries were ranked highly, reflecting the need for responsiveness and competence in a banking relationship. Having to queue in the branch was the least important speed-related factor; however, as mentioned previously, a number of interviewees do not visit the branch for business banking.

Of least importance were the cosmetic or tangible elements of service: the physical appearance of the branch and bank personnel and bank stationery/products were of little or no importance to the majority of respondents. A wide range of products and the content of leaflets and brochures were less important than the bank managers' propensity to convey product information, although the latter was not rated highly despite the need for this having been expressed earlier by some respondents.

'Of least importance were the cosmetic or tangible elements of service'

Apart from trustworthiness and speed of decision making, the most important factors pertaining to the bank manager were felt to be an understanding of the business, and having the authority to make decisions which affect the business. Having an interest in the customer's business, availability and personal qualities were also seen to be important. For bank staff, efficiency and reliability were the key factors. Their product knowledge and personal qualities were considered of less importance than similar bank manager related factors but were nonetheless ranked highly by a number of the respondents.

Other factors of importance to the small business were availability and frequency of information concerning their account, a clear definition and explanation of bank charges, and flexibility and responsiveness on the part of the bank to individual customer needs.

CONCLUSION

The small businesses involved in the study rated accuracy, confidentiality, reliability and speed-related factors highly in their assessment of what they expected in terms of service from their bank. This was reflected in their initial assessments of elements of good and poor service where efficiency and inefficiency were described as major causes of satisfaction or dissatisfaction.

The majority of firms felt that they were receiving good or very good service from their banks; however, nearly all firms could describe elements of service which they felt were poor and could be improved. These were most often related to inefficiencies in systems and procedures or of staff and the related factor of errors.

Further analysis will relate the small business' perceptions of bank performance across the 55 service factors in order to ascertain whether or not a comparison of expectation and performance across those factor can adequately explain the overall assessment of service levels.

REFERENCES

Bannock, G. (1981), 'The Clearing Banks and Small Firms', *Lloyds Bank Review*, October, pp. 15–25.
Bannock, G. (1984), *Surveys of Forum Members—New Insights into Small Business*, Forum of Private Business.
Buerger, J. E. and Ulrich, T. A. (1986), 'What's Important to a Small Business in Selecting a Financial Institution', *The Journal of Commercial Bank Lending*, October, pp. 3–9.
Dunkelberg, W. C. and Scott, J. A. (1983), 'Small Business Evaluates its Banking Relationships', *The Banker's Magazine*, November/December, pp. 40–46.
European Bankers' Small Business Seminar, Proceedings (1984), *Key Issues in Small Firm Lending*, March.
Forum of Private Business (The) (1988), *Small Businesses and Banks: A Two Nation Perspective*. The Forum of Private Business.
Gardner, D. M. (1970), 'An Experimental Investigation of the Price/Quality Relationship', *Journal of Retailing*, Vol. 46 No. 3, pp. 25–41.

Jacoby, J., Olsen, J. C. and Haddock, (1973), 'Price, Brand Name and Product Composition Characteristics as Determinants of Perceived Quality, *Journal of Applied Psychology*, Vol. 55 No. 6, pp. 570–9.

LeBlanc, G. and Nguyen, N. (1988), 'Customers' Perceptions of Service Quality in Financial Institutions', *International Journal of Bank Marketing*, Vol. 6 No. 4, pp. 7–18.

McClure, J. W. (1985), 'Improving Relations with Small Business', *ABA Banking Journal*, Vol. 77 No. 3, March, pp. 44–5.

McKibbin, G. and Gutmann, J. (1986), 'The Marketing of Financial Services to the Small Business Sector—A Research Based Approach', *Marketing Intelligence and Planning*, Vol. 4 No. 3, pp. 46–57.

Paisley College of Technology (1987), *Saturation Survey Report, September 1986*, Technology and Business Centre, Paisley College of Technology, February, unpublished.

APPENDIX: SMALL BUSINESS' EXPECTATIONS OF BANK SERVICE

Service factor	Overall* rating	Very important	Important	Of some importance	Of no importance
Information about your account is accurate	139	39	11	—	—
Your banking information is treated as confidential	139	39	11	—	—
Accuracy of written communication, e.g. bank statements	137	38	11	1	—
Promises made by bank staff (bank manager) are upheld by head office	133	36	12	1	1
Low bank charges	133	37	9	4	—
Low interest rates	131	37	8	4	1
A bank manager (or other key contact person) who is trustworthy	131	36	10	3	1
A bank manager (or other key contact person) who makes decisions quickly	131	33	15	1	1
Other bank personnel who do not make errors	130	34	12	4	—
Staff can be relied on to do what they say they will do when they say they will do it	129	29	21	—	—
A bank manager (or other key contact person) who understands your business	128	36	7	6	1
Information concerning your account is readily available to you	128	28	22	—	—
Easy access to the decision makers when telephoning	127	27	23	—	—
A bank manager (or other key contact person) who has the authority to make decisions which affect you and your business	126	32	14	2	2
Transactions are dealt with quickly	126	26	24	—	—
Bank charges are clearly defined and explained	126	28	20	3	—
Other bank personnel who are efficient and deal with customers quickly	124	27	20	2	—
Problems/queries are resolved quickly	123	24	25	1	—
The bank is flexible and responsive to individual customer needs	121	25	22	2	1
Telephone queries are dealt with quickly and efficiently	120	21	28	1	—
Willingness to lend money	117	28	14	5	3
Telephone calls are answered quickly and lines are free	115	17	31	2	—
A bank manager (or other key contact person) who is readily available for consultation when you want to see him/her	115	21	24	4	1
A bank manager (or other key contact person) who is interested in your business and your business problems	114	22	21	6	1

APPENDIX (Continued)

Service factor	Overall* rating	Very important	Important	Of some importance	Of no importance
Frequency of written communication, e.g. bank statements	112	19	24	7	—
A bank manager (or other key contact person) who is approachable, i.e. is pleasant, friendly and polite	112	22	19	8	1
There are facilities for privacy when dealing with bank staff	110	20	21	8	1
Written communication is easily understandable	108	17	24	9	—
Low collateral requirements	107	23	13	12	2
A bank manager (or other key contact person) who take the time to discuss your business	106	17	23	19	1
Other bank personnel who are approachable, i.e. are pleasant, friendly and polite	100	12	26	12	—
A bank manager (or other key contact person) who has up-to-date knowledge of bank products	99	16	19	13	2
Having special facilities for the business person in the branch	97	14	20	15	1
Car parking facilities near to the bank	95	16	17	13	4
Location of bank is convenient	94	10	26	12	2
Not having to queue in the bank	92	11	21	17	1
Physical safety when dealing with the bank	91	15	14	18	3
Opening hours which are convenient to you	90	9	26	11	4
A bank manager (or other key contact person) who will visit you on your own premises when required	89	10	23	13	4
The bank employs up-to-date technology and equipment	89	9	24	14	3
A business-like atmosphere within the bank branch	86	5	27	17	1
Other bank personnel who are knowledgeable about bank products	86	8	22	18	2
A bank manager (or other key contact person) who knows you personally, e.g. could address you by name outside the bank	83	14	11	19	6
A bank manager (or other key contact person) who offers helpful suggestions/advice on running your business	80	9	17	19	5
A bank manager (or other key contact person) who takes the time to explain and discuss bank products	80	6	19	24	1

A bank manager (or other key contact person) who is aware of local business conditions	80	5	25	15	5
A bank manager (or other key contact person) who keeps you informed concerning relevant products which become available	76	6	18	22	4
Not having to queue with personal customers	72	10	16	10	14
Other bank personnel who are interested in your business and your business problems	65	3	13	30	4
Other bank personnel have a smart appearance	55	2	14	21	13
A wide range of products are available	53	2	6	35	7
The physical appearance of the branch, decoration, colour, furniture, etc.	52	3	8	27	12
Leaflets/brochures, etc., are informative	52	1	7	35	7
A bank manager (or other key contact person) who has a smart appearance	40	2	9	16	23
The design, colour, etc., of bank stationery/products, e.g. cheque book	26	1	3	17	29

Overall rating: Very important = 3; important = 2; of some importance = 1.

14

Service Quality: Recent Developments in Financial Services

Barbara R. Lewis

INTRODUCTION

I was pleased to be asked to contribute to this special issue of the *IJBM*, in particular, as I had the privilege of being the first editor. During the 1970s I had been researching bank marketing issues with support from a major clearing bank and, subsequently, was able to provide material with a colleague for a special issue of the *European Journal of Marketing* (Turnbull and Lewis, 1982). Shortly afterwards the *IJBM* was launched and I accepted the challenge to be editor. This was stimulating and rewarding in terms of attracting leading academics and practitioners to form an Editorial Advisory Board and, in turn, articles from colleagues and contacts around the world.

Our editorial policy was to focus on strategic and research issues facing banks in both personal and corporate/international markets. This was a period of time when banks and competing financial institutions were becoming more professional in their marketing orientation, responding to challenges in their business and economic environment, and taking account of legislative change and technological developments. In my seven years as editor we published 151 articles from around the world: the UK, USA, Canada, Australia, Western Europe, the Middle East and the Far East. Topics were diverse: a third were focused on strategic issues or consumer images, attitudes and behaviour; one-third were concerned with specific elements of the marketing mix; a number on segmentation, the impact of technology and personnel matters; and some relating to bank marketing in developing countries. Several articles touched on issues relating to customer service and quality, and the role of employees in successful marketing strategies (e.g. Buswell, 1983; and LeBlanc and Nguyen, 1988).

In my last issue as editor, I had the opportunity to review the early research evidence and discussion with respect to service quality (Lewis, 1989b). In this current article, I am able to pick up the threads from my previous article and comment on some of the core literature from the USA, Scandinavia and the UK, which covers service quality definition and measurement. In addition, a number of examples are provided from researches carried out in the financial services industry. The latter part of this article then moves on to more prospective concerns with respect to the measurement of service quality and a number of research and strategic priorities which emerge from the present economic and competitive environment.

SERVICE QUALITY: DEFINITIONS AND MEASUREMENT

During the last decade considerable attention has been given by researchers in the USA, Scandinavia and the UK to definitions of service quality, its determinants and measurement. There has also been a variety of applications by both academics and practitioners in the financial services industry.

Albrecht and Zemke (1985) and Czepiel et al. (1985) highlighted the importance of service encounters, i.e. the direct interactions between service providers and their customers—both internal and external, indicating that the quality of encounters is essential in the evaluation of the quality of service experienced by customers. At the same time Berry et al. (1985, 1988) and Grönroos (1984) offered definitions such as: 'perceived service quality is a global judgement or attitude relating to service and results from comparisons by consumers of expectations of service with their perceptions of actual service performance'. If there is a shortfall then a service quality gap exists which providers wish to close.

Dimensions of service quality relate to both *core* and *augmented* service offerings (Grönroos, 1987) and have been widely researched. Some of the key contributions come from Lehtinen and Lehtinen (1982, 1991), who focus on process quality as judged by consumers during service, and output quality as judged after a service is performed; and Grönroos (1984) who discusses the technical (outcome) quality of service encounters—i.e. what is received by the customer, and the functional quality of the process—i.e. the way in which the service is delivered, together with the corporate image dimension of quality—the result of how customers perceive a company.

Parasuraman et al. (1985, 1988) offer the most widely reported set of service quality determinants: tangibles, reliability, responsiveness, communication, credibility, security, competence, courtesy, understanding/knowing the customer, and access. Subsequent factor analysis and testing by Parasuraman et al. (1988) condensed these into five categories (tangibles, responsiveness, reliability, assurance and empathy). Further, a significant UK contribution comes from Johnston et al. (1990) and Silvestro et al. (1990) who identified 15 dimensions of service quality which they categorized as hygiene, enhancing and dual-threshold factors.

The research of Berry and his colleagues also led to the service quality gap model (Parasuraman et al., 1985; Zeithaml et al., 1988). They had defined service quality to be a function of the gap between consumers' expectations of a service and their perceptions of the actual service delivery by an organization (Gap 5) and suggested that this gap is influenced by four other gaps or shortfalls:

- *Gap 1*: Managers' perceptions of customers' expectations may be different from actual customer needs and desires, i.e. managers do not necessarily know what customers (both internal and external) expect from a company.
- *Gap 2*: Even if customer needs are known, they may not be translated into appropriate service specifications/standards and systems.
- *Gap 3*: This is referred to as the service performance gap and occurs when the service

which is delivered is different from management's specifications for service, owing to variations in the performance of personnel—employees not being willing or able to perform at a desired level.
- *Gap 4*: What is said about the service in external communications is different from the service that is delivered, i.e. advertising and promotion can influence consumers' expectations and perceptions of service.

The (continuing) research of Berry and his colleagues is presented in two books: Berry and Parasuraman (1991): and Zeithaml *et al.* (1990). In addition to the service quality gap model they developed, from the dimensions of service quality they had identified, their SERVQUAL questionnaire (Parasuraman *et al.*, 1988). This has 22 pairs of Likert-type scales, the first 22 items are designed to measure customer expectations of service for a particular service industry and the following 22 are intended to measure the perceived level of service provided by a specific organization.

Service expectations: e.g. 'Customers should be able to trust bank employees', 'Banks should have up-to-date equipment'
strongly agree . . . . strongly disagree
       1   2   3   4   5   6   7

Perceptions: e.g. 'I can trust the employees of my bank', 'My bank has up-to-date equipment'
strongly agree . . . . strongly disagree
       1   2   3   4   5   6   7

SERVQUAL has been incorporated by researchers investigating service quality in a number of industries. It has been used to assess expectations and perceptions with respect to various determinants of service quality.

FINANCIAL SERVICES RESEARCH

Service quality research in the financial services industry has focused largely on consumer expectations and perceptions, i.e. Gap 5, in relative isolation from the other service quality gaps although, increasingly, research data are collected from management and employees as well as external customers. The published evidence can be considered from the perspectives of customers, management and employees.

Customers

An early example was the experience of a British bank (Buswell, 1983). Customers responded to attitude statements to assess the quality of service they received in relation to knowledge of staff, communications, expertise of staff, willingness to lend, and branch design. The bank was able to develop benchmarks and a system which had the ability to reveal changes in service at a particular branch over time, and to distinguish between branches at the same point in time.

LeBlanc and Nguyen (1988) focused on service quality in Canadian financial institutions and discussed six factors that explain perceived service quality: degree of customer satisfaction, contact personnel, internal organization, physical environment and instruments, corporate image, and personnel–customer interaction during the service encounter.

Lewis and Smith (1989) investigated the personal customers of banks and building societies in the UK and assessed their expectations and perceptions of 39 service quality criteria which related to four dimensions: physical features and facilities, reliability, the staff they came into contact with, and responsiveness to needs. Respondents had come to expect better service from their bank or building society in recent years and many believed that service had improved. There was a great deal of satisfaction with the overall service received, but the assessment of service quality gaps indicated dimensions of quality which could be improved.

A related project (Lewis, 1991), an international comparison of retail customers of banks in the USA and UK, provided evidence of cultural differences in attitudes and behaviour which impact on expectations and perceptions. Overall, US customers appeared to be less satisfied with the quality of service they received than their UK counterparts.

The UK banks' interest in small businesses led to the research by Smith (1989, 1990a, b) in which she investigated, from in-depth interviews, relationships between banks and small businesses. Key areas of service were found to relate to bank personnel, organization and structure of the banks, pricing policies and product offerings. In addition, 55 service factors were incorporated into structured questions for respondents to rate their expectations and their perceptions/satisfactions—to identify gaps in small business-bank relationships.

The management perspective

The views of top management were pursued by Smith and Lewis (1988, 1989) in 31 major UK organizations spanning financial services, retailing and leisure. The objective was to focus on service quality programmes and the ways in which the customer care philosophy permeated organizations from top management to customer contact staff. One aspect of the research was to identify what the management thought were the key elements which comprise good quality/customer service, i.e. what external customers expect from the company. The main suggestions related to: staff personal qualities and knowledge, speed and efficiency, systems and procedures, retail design, technology, and product range.

The managers were subsequently questioned about their customer care training programmes which were designed to move companies towards a service-oriented culture by breaking down barriers and improving internal communications. Advantages were seen to be creating an atmosphere of all working towards a common goal, understanding the work of others, and encouraging all staff to have responsibility and authority for achieving corporate objectives—which includes empowering employees to exercise judgement and creativity in responding to customer needs. Subsequent fieldwork found the organizations to be more successful with respect to external markets (Lewis and Smith, 1989) than with regard to their internal customers, i.e. employees (Lewis, 1989a).

The employees' perspective

The ability of an organization to ensure that the service delivered meets the specifications set, depends on the performance of *all* employees who must be *willing* and *able* to deliver the desired levels of service. Employees' contributions in meeting customer needs, and thus influencing customer perceptions of service, cannot be overstated. Success depends, first, on an understanding of 'internal marketing' in which employees are viewed as internal customers and jobs as internal products (Berry, 1980; Grönroos, 1981, 1985), to include internal market research and segmentation (Berry, 1981). Success also requires appropriate personnel policies for recruitment, selection, training and rewards for all employees—both customer contact and back-room staff. Personnel issues are presented by Lewis and Entwistle (1990) who also focus on relationships between customer contact and back-room staff; operations and non-operations staff; and between staff and management. In addition, in relation to Gap 3, Zeithaml et al. (1988) refer to the importance of teamwork, employee–job fit, technology–job fit, perceived control, appropriate control systems, and avoidance of role conflict and ambiguity.

The need for internal marketing and enlightened personnel policies is increasingly accepted, and is demonstrated in two studies. Employees in the banks and building societies researched by Lewis (1989a) provided opinions with respect to internal service encounters and relationships, perceptions of customer service in their organizations, training for customer service, and areas for service quality improvement. Overall, a number of deficiencies were found with respect to personnel initiatives and customer service training activities, resulting in problems with interpersonal relationships within the organizations and with staff knowledge.

Second, an investigation by Koula (1992) in a Central European bank, included interviews with senior management and a survey of employees. The management realized the importance of a motivated workforce and of its personnel in the delivery of service, and the employees appeared to have both requisite capabilities and confidence in themselves to perform well. There was also evidence of a good teamwork spirit, and good interpersonal relationships and communications between customer-contact and non-contact employees. However, some gaps were evident between management and personnel perceptions which impact on morale and motivation, quality of work, and subsequently, on the quality of service provided to external customers. For example, there was some evidence of role ambiguity—some staff being uncertain about what was expected of them, policies and procedures which limited the freedom of some staff, role conflict—although confident in their capability to satisfy customers, some felt overworked, and differences in opinion with respect to the objectives of the control and reward systems, which impact on motivation and performance. Overall, a number of areas for potential improvement in internal marketing, especially in research, were identified.

A current project is focused on banks in a Scandinavian country. Recent severe economic pressures have led to government interventions and control and significant rationalization and restructuring (including lay-offs) among the major banks. Even so, service quality initiatives are a management priority and management and employee attitudes toward service quality are the focus of the research investigation.

SERVICE QUALITY CONCERNS FOR THE 1990s

Financial services providers in the UK and elsewhere have, to date, spent considerable managerial effort and time on creating an awareness of customer service and service quality, and invested millions of pounds in developing service quality initiatives—in particular their 'customer care' training programmes. Nevertheless, there remains considerable scope for further awareness and initiatives in a number of directions. These relate to variable and changing customer expectations, the need for an integrated approach to service quality, and the development of mechanisms to monitor progress—especially service quality measurement tools.

Changing needs and expectations

Customer needs and expectations are, naturally, subject to change as a function of circumstances and experience. Also experience with one service provider (e.g. staff in a hotel or restaurant) may influence expectations of others (e.g. in a bank). In addition, consumers are increasingly aware of the alternatives on offer and rising standards of service and so their expectations of service and quality are elevated and they are increasingly critical of the quality of service they experience. Higher levels of performance lead to higher expectations and so companies can never be complacent about levels of service.

Further, consumers have *zones of tolerance* (Parasuraman *et al.*, 1991), the difference between *desired* and *adequate* expectations. The desired level of service expectations is what consumers hope to receive, a blend of what 'can' and 'should' be, which is a function of past experience. The adequate level is what is acceptable based on an assessment of what the service 'will be'—the 'predicted' service—and depends on the alternatives which are available. Tolerance zones vary between individuals, service aspects and with experience, and tend to be smaller for outcome features (e.g. accuracy of a bank statement) than for process dimensions (e.g. the greeting from a bank clerk). In addition, if options are limited, desires may not decrease but tolerance zones may be higher. Conversely, if more alternatives are available (e.g. competitive banks and building societies) it is relatively easy to switch and tolerance zones are more limited. Consequently, financial services organizations need to monitor customer expectation levels—both adequate and desired—on an ongoing basis.

An integrated approach to service quality

Service quality standards and specifications must obviously respond to consumer requirements and success necessitates an integrated approach from marketing, operations, human resources and financial managers. In particular, attention needs to be given to systems and procedures which are customer and employee focused and which are responsive, flexible and reliable. Other dimensions include technology, retail design and personnel development.

In relation to service standards a current competitive activity in the service sector is to offer Unconditional Service Guarantees (Hart, 1988). This is not yet prevalent in the financial services industry but UK banks now each have a Code of Practice in which they outline their commitment to customers, advise them of their rights and possibly provide 0800 telephone numbers for customer service/advice/queries and complaints. For example: 'We want our relationship to be a partnership based on confidence and trust', and 'Our commitment is to deliver to you a sound banking relationship without compromising on traditional standards of honesty and fair dealing'.

Hart (1988) summarizes key considerations relating to service guarantees which should get everyone in an organization to focus on good service, and to strive for zero defects in service delivery, i.e. to get things right the first time. As a result, banks and other financial service providers have developed service delivery systems and structured personnel policies to try to provide consistent high quality service. But problems do occur (e.g. employees may be sick or absent) and mistakes will happen (e.g. a lost cheque-book or an incorrect statement). The challenge for financial service organizations is to *recover* the problem or mistake and get it *very* right the second time. Service recovery may be defined as:

the process of returning an aggrieved/dissatisfied customer to a state of satisfaction with the company/service and making a special effort to get things right for the customer when something is wrong.

Grönroos (1988) refers to service recovery as the sixth dimension of service quality; Hart *et al.* (1990) focus on the 'fixing' of customer problems; and Schelesinger and Hesketh (1991) discuss the personnel implications of service recovery—in particular with respect to the empowerment of front-line employees in the service recovery process. Service recovery is important to companies as it has economic value, can increase customer loyalty, can assist in identifying organizational problems, and can improve overall service quality awareness.

Monitoring service quality: refinement of measurement techniques

A third area of concern relates to the tools and techniques employed to monitor service success and failure. It is clear from a review of the evidence that difficulties exist in the measurement tools utilized to assess expectations and satisfactions. In particular, there are a number of criticisms of the SERVQUAL scale: the absence of weighting of variables—which inherently vary in importance; the use of negatively worded statements which is confusing for customers; apparent (to the respondent) repetition of scales; the incorporation of two separate lists of statements—to measure expectations about companies in general and perceptions about a specific organization; the number of dimensions being assessed; and the timing of measurement activities—before, during or after a service encounter (see Babakus and Boller, 1991; Carmen, 1990; Lewis, 1990; and Lewis and Mitchell, 1990). Parasuraman *et al.* (1991b) now acknowledge some of these problems and have offered (limited) refinements to SERVQUAL.

Rating scales

There are further problems to be encountered when consumers complete multi-attribute rating scales. For example: the over-use of extremes, lack of verbal labels for some scale points, and ambiguous interpretation of mid-points of unlabelled scales (Smith, 1992). In addition, Lewis and Mitchell (1990) suggest that the seven-point Likert scale used in SERVQUAL may camouflage subtle variations in consumer expectations and perceptions and they offer a graphic positioning scale to increase accuracy—taken up by Orledge (1991) who also incorporated a bi-polar semantic scale rather than a Likert (agree-disagree) scale. She was assessing the opinions of students with respect to their banks' and building societies' provision of service including loan/overdraft facilities. They were asked for each aspect of service to indicate how well banks and building societies in general should perform by marking an E on the scale. On the same scale they were asked to indicate how their bank or building society performs by marking a P. For example:

narrow range of services . . . E . . . P . . . wide range of services,
employees are unapproachable . . . E . . . P . . . employees are approachable
customers always have to queue . . . E . . . P . . . customers never have to queue.

Further, Babakus and Boller (1991) highlight that SERVQUAL assessment type methods incorporate *desired* levels of service expectations rather than *adequate* levels, which are seldom less than perceptions and thus indicate significant service quality gaps which may be more apparent than real. Parasuraman et al. (1991b) do acknowledge that the wording 'should' in SERVQUAL may lead to unrealistically high expectation scores and they now offer a revised wording which focuses on what customers *would* expect from companies delivering excellent service, for example:

'excellent banks will have up-to-date equipment',
'when excellent banks promise to do something by a certain date they will do so'.

Even so, no measurement technique is perfect, the challenge is ongoing for both academics and practitioners to refine research tools and techniques.

CONCLUSIONS

To summarize the research and evidence to date it is clear that financial service providers are not only aware of the importance of service quality but are increasingly taking on board the key concerns relating to understanding the definitions of service quality, developing integrated service quality programmes to include both standards/specifications and personnel recruitment and development, monitoring progress in terms of consumer expectations and satisfactions with respect to routine service situations, and responding to consumer problems in non-routine service encounters, i.e. the service recovery process.

However, in the present constrained economic environment there is an enhanced requirement to be not only service-oriented but at the same time to be cost-effective. To achieve this, the service quality managers of the 1990s need a thorough understanding of and commitment to quality, an appropriate organizational culture, well constructed research among employees and customers, enlightened personnel policies, and effective systems and procedures.

Some particular research issues for the coming years pertain to service quality gaps, the influence of price, and links between service quality and customer loyalty. Research and practice to date has focused primarily on the gap between consumers' expectations and perceptions. Further attention needs to be paid to measurement of management's and employees' opinions and attitudes, and overall to minimize all the service quality gaps (Parasuraman et al., 1988; Zeithaml et al., 1988). Associated with this is the anticipation that measurement methods will be further refined.

A second issue concerns the relationship between price and consumer perceptions, i.e. the concept of value for money. Its relevance in retail financial services may be limited, but has more impact on business markets (see Smith, 1990b).

A third focus is the link between service quality, customer satisfaction and customer retention. Service providers realize that only a small proportion of dissatisfied customers complain (Goodman et al., 1986; Horowitz, 1990), but the service recovery process affords opportunity for organizations to redeem themselves when customers do draw problems to their attention. Hart et al. (1990) refer to the additional costs of replacing customers over those of trying to retain customers who may be dissatisfied. They also refer to evidence of customers who have complained and who have received a satisfactory response, subsequently being more loyal to a company and more likely to buy other services— demonstrating a relationship between customer retention and profitability and success.

In all, a number of benefits may accrue from well-designed and managed service quality initiatives:

- enhanced customer loyalty through satisfaction;
- attraction of new customers from positive word-of-mouth communication;
- increased opportunities for cross-selling and long-term relationships;
- employee job satisfaction, morale and commitment to the company;
- increased staff loyalty and reduced staff turnover;
- enhanced corporate image and possible insulation from price competition.

Overall, successful service quality leads to decreased cost and increased productivity and sales, market shares, profitability and business performance.

REFERENCES

Albrecht, K. and Zemke, R. (1985), *Service America: Doing Business in the New Economy*, Dow Jones-Irwin, Homewood, Illinois.

Babakus, E. and Boller, G. W. (1991), 'An Empirical Assessment of the SERVQUAL Scale', *Journal of Business Research*, Vol. 24, pp. 253–68.

Berry, L. L. (1980), 'Services Marketing is Different', *Business*, Vol. 30 No. 3, May/June, pp. 24–9.

Berry, L. L. (1981), 'The Employee as Customer', *Journal of Retail Banking*, Vol. 3 No. 1, pp. 33–40.

Berry, L. L. and Parasuraman, A. (1991), *Marketing Services: Competing through Quality*, The Free Press, New York.

Berry, L. L., Parasuraman, A. and Zeithaml, V. A. (1988), 'The Service-Quality Puzzle', *Business Horizons*, July–August, pp. 35–43.

Berry, L. L., Zeithaml, V. A. and Parasuraman, A. (1985), 'Quality Counts in Services Too', *Business Horizons*, Vol. 28 No. 3, pp. 44–52.

Buswell, D. (1983), 'Measuring the Quality of In-branch Customer Service', *International Journal of Bank Marketing*, Vol. 1 No. 1, pp. 26–41.

Carmen, J. M. (1990), 'Consumer Perceptions of Service Quality: An Assessment of the SERVQUAL Dimensions', *Journal of Retailing*, Vol. 66 No. 1, pp. 33–55.

Czepiel, J. A., Solomon, M. R. and Surprenant, C. F. (1985) (Eds), *The Service Encounter: Managing Employee/Customer Interaction in Service Businesses*, Lexington Books, Lexington, MA.

Goodman, J. A., Marra, T. and Brigham, L. (1986), 'Customer Service: Costly Nuisance or Low-Cost Profit Strategy?', *Journal of Retail Banking*, Vol 8 No. 3, pp. 7–16.

Grönroos, C. (1981), 'Internal Marketing—An Integral Part of Marketing Theory', in Donnelly, J. H. and George, W. R. (Eds), *Marketing of Services*, American Marketing Association, Chicago, pp. 236–8.
Grönroos, C. (1984), *Strategic Management and Marketing in the Service Sector*, Chartwell-Bratt, UK.
Grönroos, C. (1985), 'Internal Marketing: Theory and Practice', in Bloch, T. M., Upah, G. D. and Zeithaml, V. A. (Eds), *Services Marketing in a Changing Environment*, American Marketing Association, Chicago.
Grönroos, C. (1987), *Developing the Service Offering—A Source of Competitive Advantage*, Swedish School of Economics and Business Administration, Helsinki, Finland, September.
Grönroos, C. (1988), 'Service Quality: The Six Criteria of Good Perceived Service Quality', *Review of Business*, Vol. 9 No. 3, Winter, pp. 10–13.
Hart, C. W. L. (1988), 'The Power of Unconditional Service Guarantees', *Harvard Business Review*, July–August, pp. 54–62.
Hart, C. W. L., Heskett, J. L. and Sasser, W. E. (1990), 'The Profitable Art of Service Recovery', *Harvard Business Review*, Vol. 90 No. 4, July–August, pp. 148–56.
Horovitz, J. (1990), *Winning Ways: Achieving Zero Defect Service*, Productivity Press, Cambridge, MA.
Johnston, R., Silvestro, R., Fitzgerald, L. and Voss, C. (1990), 'Developing the Determinants of Service Quality', in Langeard, E. and Eiglier, P. (Eds), *Marketing, Operations and Humans Resources Insights into Services*, 1st International Research Seminar on Services Management, IAE, Aix-en-Provence, pp. 373–400.
Koula, S. (1992), *Service Quality and Internal Marketing in the Hellenic Bank in Cyprus*, MSc dissertation, Manchester School of Management.
LeBlanc, G. and Nguyen, N. (1988), 'Customers' Perceptions of Service Quality in Financial Institutions', *International Journal of Bank Marketing*, Vol. 6 No. 4, pp. 7–18.
Lehtinen, U. and Lehtinen, J. R. (1982), *Service Quality: A Study of Quality Dimensions*, Working Paper, Service Management Institute, Helsinki, Finland.
Lehtinen, U. and Lehtinen, J. R. (1991), 'Two Approaches to Service Quality Dimensions', *The Service Industries Journal*, Vol. 11 No. 3, pp. 287–303.
Lewis, B. R. (1989a), *Customer Care in the Service Sector: The Employees' Perspective*, FSRC, Manchester School of Management.
Lewis, B. R. (1989b), 'Quality in the Service Sector—A Review', *International Journal of Bank Marketing*, Vol. 7 No. 5, pp. 4–12.
Lewis, B. R. (1991), 'Service Quality: An International Comparison of Bank Customers' Expectations and Perceptions', *Journal of Marketing Management*, Vol. 7 No. 1, pp. 47–62.
Lewis, B. R. and Entwistle, T. W. (1990), 'Managing the Service Encounter: a Focus on the Employee', *International Journal of Service Industry Management*, Vol. 1 No. 3, pp. 41–52.
Lewis, B. R. and Mitchell, V-W. (1990), 'Defining and Measuring the Quality of Customer Service', *Marketing Intelligence & Planning*, Vol. 8 No. 6, pp. 11–17.
Lewis, B. R. and Smith, A. M. (1989), *Customer Care in the Service Sector: The Customers' Perspective*, FSRC, Manchester School of Management.
Orledge, J. (1991), *Service Quality: An Empirical Investigation of Two Measurement Techniques*, MSc dissertation, Manchester School of Management.
Parasuraman, A., Berry, L. L. and Zeithaml, V. A. (1991a), 'Understanding Customer Expectations of Service', *Sloan Management Review*, Vol. 32 No. 3, pp. 39–48.
Parasuraman, A., Berry, L. L. and Zeithaml, V. A. (1991b), 'Refinement and Reassessment of the SERVQUAL Scale', *Journal of Retailing*, Vol. 67 No. 4, Winter, pp. 420–50.
Parasuraman, A., Zeithaml, V. A. and Berry, L. L. (1985), 'A Conceptual Model of Service Quality in its Implications for Future Research', *Journal of Marketing*, Vol. 49, Fall, pp. 41–50.
Parasuraman, A., Zeithaml, V. A. and Berry, L. L. (1988), 'SERVQUAL: A Multiple-item Scale for Measuring Consumer Perceptions of Service Quality', *Journal of Retailing*, Vol. 64 No. 1, Spring, pp. 14–40.
Schelesinger, L. A. and Heskett, J. L. (1991), 'Breaking the Cycle of Failures in Service', *Sloan Management Review*, Vol. 32 No. 3, Spring, pp. 17–28.
Silvestro, R. and Johnston, R. (1990), *The Determinants of Service Quality—Hygiene and Enhancing Factors*, Warwick Business School, Warwick.

Smith, A. M. (1989), 'Service Quality: Relationships between Banks and Their Small Business Clients', *International Journal of Bank Marketing*, Vol. 7 No. 5, pp. 28–35.

Smith, A. M. (1990a), 'Quality Aspects of Services Marketing', *Marketing Intelligence & Planning*, Vol. 8 No. 6, pp. 25–32.

Smith, A. M. (1990b), *Quality Service and the Small Business–Bank Relationship*, MSc thesis, Manchester School of Management.

Smith, A. M. (1992), 'The Consumers' Evaluation of Service Quality: Some Methodological Issues', in Whitelock, J. (Ed), Marketing in the New Europe and Beyond, *MEG, Proceedings of the 1992 Annual Conference*, University of Salford, pp. 633–48.

Smith, A. M. and Lewis, B. R. (1988), *Customer Care in the Service Sector: The Supplier's Perspective*, FSRC, Manchester School of Management.

Smith, A. M. and Lewis, B. R. (1989), 'Customer Care in Financial Service Organisations', *International Journal of Bank Marketing*, Vol. 7 No. 5, pp. 13–22.

Turnbull, P. and Lewis, B. (1982) (Eds), 'The Marketing of Bank Services', *European Journal of Marketing*, Vol. 16 No. 3.

Zeithaml, V. A. (1988), 'Consumer Perceptions of Price, Quality and Value: A Means-End Model and Synthesis of Evidence', *Journal of Marketing*, Vol. 52, July, pp. 2–22.

Zeithaml, V. A., Berry, L. L. and Parasuraman, A. (1988), 'Communication and Control Processes in the Delivery of Service Quality', *Journal of Marketing*, Vol. 52, April, pp. 35–48.

Zeithaml, V. A., Parasuraman, A. and Berry, L. L. (1990), *Delivering Quality Service: Balancing Customer Perceptions and Expectations*, The Free Press, New York.

Part V

Communication and Pricing in Financial Services

CONTENTS

Introduction to Part V   211

15 Promoting Financial Services with Glittering Prizes   213
   S. PEATTIE and K. PEATTIE, *International Journal of Bank Marketing* (1994), **12** (6) 19–29.

16 Direct Marketing in the Financial Services Industry   229
   D. THWAITES and S. C. I. LEE, *Journal of Marketing Management* (1994), **10**, 377–390.

17 Mortgage-Pricing Determinants: A Comparative Investigation of National, Regional and Local Building Societies   242
   A. MEIDAN and A. C. CHIN, *International Journal of Bank Marketing* (1995), **13** (3), 3–11.

Introduction to Part V

This section deals with two rather different elements in the marketing mix: communication (or promotion) and pricing.

The changes that have taken place in financial services communication in the last 15 years or so, are dramatic, with annual TV advertising expenditure, for example, exceeding £500 million per annum.

Financial services communication experienced rapid growth, particularly in the advertising element of the communication mix, until early 1990s when a slight decrease in total annual expenditure occurred. Recently, however, the allocations to communications in financial services continue to increase, mainly because of three factors:

- Competition from other financial institutions, both from within the subsectors and from abroad, which requires more effort in communication, as elaborated below.
- The advent of computers and mass communications enables financial institutions to make better use of communication tools such as direct mail, that have resulted in the increase in the appropriation, and usage, of direct mail.
- With the increase in mergers and take-overs of other financial services organizations, the emerging 'new' financial services have come to realize the growing importance of mass communication and the economies of scale inherent in large communication budgets.

The use of various communication mix elements vary across the various financial services subsectors. For example, building societies make higher use of press advertising than banks whilst insurance companies use more direct mail. The need for communication in financial services is paramount because virtually all financial services offer largely abstract/intangible and fairly similar products and services.

Another interesting recent development in financial services communications is the increase in the use of sponsorships in order to increase the penetration and market share of selected financial organizations in certain segments of industry, commerce and markets. A variety of financial services sponsor sports and arts, theatre, exhibitions, agricultural shows, community projects, etc., achieving a good level of publicity, and improving the corporate image of the financial services firm.

There are two articles dealing with communications in this section; 'Promoting Financial Services with Glittering Prizes' looks at the use of competitions with financial services. It suggests that competitions are still in the early stages of innovation and diffusion in the banking sector, despite the efforts that various banks have recently made in this field. According to the authors, the competitions in financial services could be used in a more imaginative way, in order to create better integration between the tool (i.e. competitions) and the services being promoted. The advantage of this paper is that it highlights a promotional tool that has received scant attention in the marketing of financial services literature. It looks at the competitions within the frame work of sales promotions in relation to their tactical (short term) value as well as a part of strategic (long term) marketing planning for financial services.

In the second paper in this section, Des Thwaites and Sharon Lee investigate the roles and functions of direct marketing in financial services. The authors provide ample statistical information on the magnitude of budgets, methods, and segmentation methods employed by various subsectors in financial services. This could facilitate more focus and greater application of direct marketing methods in certain situations in the financial services subsectors.

Pricing has received relatively little attention in the published literature, despite its importance for marketing financial services. Pricing has several forms depending on the relevant financial services subsector: in banking it often means determining the fee structure, in insurance it mainly means rate making (or insurance premiums); setting mortgage interest rates are relevant to the building society sector, and deciding on transaction costs are relevant to stock brokers, and so on. There are a number of rather different basic approaches to pricing in financial services as follows: cost-based pricing and demand-oriented pricing for banking, rate making method in insurance, and building society pricing for mortgages. (For a more detailed discussion on Pricing in Financial Services see Ch. 6 in A. Meidan: *Marketing Financial Services*, Macmillan, 1996, pp. 142–164). It is clear, however, that the 'fragmentation' in the applicable pricing methods that are relevant to the various subsectors in the financial services is, in part, 'responsible' for the relative dearth of research and published literature on this subject. Another reason is perhaps the fact that financial institutions are 'shy' of providing a deeper insight into their pricing practices, as this could throw a light on their sources of revenue and profits.

The third paper presented in this sub-section, investigates the mortgage pricing determinants of 45 building societies, comparing institutions that are local, regional or national in their market focus. The paper identifies the primary pricing objective(s) of the various type(s) of building societies. The study suggests that mutuality has lost its attraction, as a factor in pricing, for about 90% of all the building societies investigated. The paper identifies the various factors that play a role in pricing mortgages, suggesting that these financial services organizations are more 'introvert' rather than 'extrovert' (external oriented). Most building societies are using pricing primarily as a *short-term* tool. It is clear that with an increase in deregulation and competition more innovative approaches to pricing, such as relationship pricing, pricing by segments, flexible pricing, etc., will have to be used.

15

Promoting Financial Services with Glittering Prizes

Sue Peattie and Ken Peattie

INTRODUCTION—THE GROWING USE OF SALES PROMOTIONS

If you pick up any financial services marketing text, the odds are fairly high that one important part of the marketing mix will be conspicuous by its absence—sales promotion. Yet, sales promotion is a major part of modern marketing activity. Growth in promotions was rapid during the 1980s and by the end of the decade it had equalled global expenditure on 'above-the-line' advertising according to WWP group figures (*Financial Times*, 1989). Sales promotion growth currently runs at 9 per cent compared with 6 per cent for advertising (Burnett, 1993), and for many large companies promotions already account for 70 per cent of the marketing communications budget. Promotions are often defined as marketing communications activities which do not include advertising, selling or public relations; or even more simply as 'special offers'. Although such simplistic definitions are somewhat flawed, they will suffice for the purposes of this article.

Several factors underlie the growth in promotions (Strang, 1976; Quelch, 1983; Shultz, 1987; Addison, 1988; Dickson and Sawyer, 1990).

- *Rising prices and advertising 'clutter'*: eroding mass media advertising's cost effectiveness as consumers become increasingly desensitized. The effectiveness of services advertising can also be hampered by their intangibility (Rathmell, 1966).
- *Growing sales promotions respectability*: through increasing use by market leaders and increasing professionalism among sales promotion agencies.
- *Shortening planning time horizons*: time pressure can make the fast sales uplift, that promotions are perceived to offer, attractive.
- *Micro-marketing approaches*: as a response to fragmenting markets, where sales promotions provide more tailored and targeted communication than do mass media.
- *A 'snowball' effect*: Lal (1990) suggests that firms in markets where promotions become common-place are almost obliged to follow suit, or risk losing market share.

Despite this expansion, and despite financial services taking a lead in bringing sales promotions out of their traditional stronghold of packaged foods and consumer goods (Addison, 1988), attitudes towards sales promotion within financial services have traditionally been somewhat ambivalent. This was perhaps most clearly demonstrated by the Halifax Building Society's advertising campaign which posed the question: 'Now there are Halifax estate agents, is this how other agents will sell their houses?' and presented a picture of two houses taped together under a 'two for the price of one' banner and another with a badly integrated extension labelled '25 per cent extra free' (Cummins, 1989).

This article aims to demonstrate the relevance and appropriateness of one sales promotion tool which represents a growing phenomenon within financial services, the promotional competition. The article is part of an ongoing project examining the use of competitions as a sales promotion tool, through studies of competitions themselves, their sponsors and the consumers that respond to them. The project began with a three-year national survey involving 2646 competitions. Within this total sample, there were 188 competitions run by service providers, of which 57 were related to financial services.

PROMOTING FINANCIAL SERVICES

Despite their growing importance, it is easy to see why sales promotions are overlooked in the financial services literature. Most 'below-the-line' activities rely on having a tangible product. It is not very practical to offer 10 per cent extra free, free samples or 'two for the price of one', when attempting to lend money.

Taking the economy as a whole, coupons and other forms of price manipulation are the dominant form of sales promotion. However, price-based promotions are difficult and possibly dangerous to use for financial services marketers for two reasons. First, setting prices for services is an already difficult process (Thomas, 1978); and second, consumers often use price as a surrogate measure of quality (Tellis and Gaeth, 1990).

Woods (quoted in Lovelock, 1984) suggests that promotional pricing within financial services has not proved worthwhile because of:

- relatively high customer loyalty;
- the danger of price wars, such as the 'disastrous' price wars waged in the USA over free checking in banks;
- discounting to stimulate trial being less effective than for goods;
- the often crucial role of pricing in overall positioning.

In search of added value

Price-based promotions manipulate the quantity/price equation to increase the perceived value of a product offering. As the Halifax advertisement implied, such 'value increasing' promotions generally cannot work for financial services by an increase in quantity, and therefore can only work through potentially dangerous margin and image eroding price reductions.

The other group of sales promotions, which are often overlooked, are the 'value adding' (sometimes referred to as 'packaged up') promotions. These leave the price and core product/service offering untouched, and offer the customer 'something extra' in the form of a free gift, a 'piggy-back' complementary product, or a competition.

It is these value-adding tools within the sales promotion tool-kit which financial services marketers have begun to exploit during the last ten years. The opportunity provided by such techniques was reflected in the title of the interview with Rodney Woods (as Group Marketing Officer at the United States Trust Co.) published in Lovelock (1984)—'Financial Service Marketers Must Learn Package Goods Selling Tools'.

The growth in competitions within financial services, particularly in America, was noted as early as 1987 in an Advertising Age feature entitled 'Banks Add Sweep-stakes to Financial Rewards'. In many cases these are simple 'open an account and win a prize' competitions, or they can be part of larger, more integrated marketing communications campaigns. To tie in with its 'Cititour' pro-bike race sponsorship, Citibank offered 500 'Citibikes' as competition prizes along with T-shirts and hat giveaways to those handing in a coupon from the competition brochure.

There are several aspects of competitions which made them particularly suitable for financial services marketing:

- *Differentiation opportunities.* Kotler (1988) identified creating competitive differentiation as a key challenge in service markets since innovations can be rapidly copied by competitors. Competitions offer a useful source of differentiation. Although they can also be replicated, 'me-too' competitions risk failure if early competitions have exhausted the current supply of available competition-minded consumers.
- *Link-up opportunities.* To above-the-line promotion or PR efforts. Abbey National ran a major national TV advertising campaign which featured its 'open an account and win a car' promotion.
- *Adding a tangible dimension to products.* Services cannot readily be displayed (Rathmell, 1966), but competition posters and leaflets provide opportunities for interesting, tangible and visible point-of-sale materials. Barclays have regularly used leaflets and posters highlighting competitions and their prizes.
- *Quality cue appeal.* The intangibility of services prompts customers to look for surrogate 'cues' to judge service quality. The pursuit of 'quality cues' among financial services competition sponsors is reflected in their choice of prizes. The cars offered were not the usual 1.1 Metro, but included the likes of a Vicarage Mk II Jaguar, an E-Type Jag and a Range Rover (all from Lloyds); while holiday destinations included the Caribbean (Barclaycard, Clydesdale Bank and Nationwide/Anglia), the Seychelles and Mauritius (Woolwich Building Society) and a trip on the Orient Express (Staffordshire Building Society).
- *Demand smoothing.* The perishability of services means that demand fluctuations are the 'most troublesome' services marketing problem (Zeithaml *et al.*, 1985). Competitions can encourage purchases during usually slack periods, or can support an attempt to bring forward seasonal purchases of products such as travellers cheques.
- *Consumer interaction.* Interactive marketing is vital for services (Kotler and Bloom, 1984), but difficult to create through advertising, which is generally a unidirectional means of communication, absorbed relatively passively by the potential consumer. One study found that under 25 per cent of TV viewers could recall an advertisement seen on the TV the previous day, and that under 10 per cent could name a brand they saw advertised on TV 30 seconds later when phoned by a market researcher (Bogart and Lehman, 1983). Competitions by contrast can create real interaction and involvement between the customer, the service and the service provider. This may involve the customer analysing the service to answer questions or devise a slogan, sending away for

information, or meeting the service provider (thereby creating new service encounter opportunities).
- *Cost certainty.* Barring accidents, competitions involve predictable costs and are most cost effective in maintaining perceived quality levels than 'giveaway' promotions. This is because giving customers attractive 'freebies' which project a quality image can be prohibitively expensive (particularly if demand is unexpectedly high, as Hoover discovered to their cost). Giveaways can still be effective where the target group of customers is relatively small, the long-term business potential is good, and the utility to the customer of a 'freebie' is high (children and students being good examples).
- *Price/quality stability.* A competition adds value by making use or awareness of a financial service a 'ticket' to enter the competition, without any need to alter the price or nature of the core service itself. This avoids any danger of sparking a price war, accidentally impairing perceived service quality, or lowering the customer's reference price.
- *Versatility.* Competitions are associated with producing short-term sales boosts, but they can contribute towards a range of communication and other marketing objectives (Peattie and Peattie, 1993a). Competitions can provide useful support for new product launches, for example during one month three different building societies used a competition to launch their new TESSAs. They can also help to change consumer behaviour; for example, in order to encourage consumers to purchase using their direct debit cards, the Barclays' Connections competitions required use of a Connect card for entry.

Promotions, competitions and consumer behaviour

Promotions have been shown to affect consumers directly in a variety of ways, leading to:

- retimed purchasing (Doyle and Saunders, 1985);
- brand switching (Vilcassim and Jain, 1991);
- increased volume of purchasing (Gupta, 1988; Neslin *et al.*, 1985);
- product-type substitutions (Cotton and Babb, 1978; Moriarty, 1985);
- store substitutions (Kumar and Leone, 1988; Walters, 1991).

For financial services competitions, it is mostly purchase retiming and brand switching that are relevant. Services' perishability mean that they are only consumed one at a time, so volume increasing competitions are rare (although not unknown; the Co-op Bank offered to match the competition winner's initial savings account deposit pound for pound as a prize). Product type substitutions may exist in terms of choice of investment target for example, but they are unlikely to be a major feature; and for practical purposes there will usually be no difference between the channel and the brand.

Ignoring confirmed non-users, we can define four types of consumer in relation to the service itself:

(1) *Potential users* who do not use the service, but who could be persuaded to do so through manipulation of the marketing mix. These are often the main target of promotions (Keon and Bayer, 1986).
(2) *Competitor loyals.* McAllister and Totten (1985) and Grover and Srinivasan (1992) show that successful promotions can attract substantial numbers of a competitor's otherwise loyal customers.

(3) *Brand switchers*. Grover and Srinivasan (1992) found distinct 'switcher' market segments whose consumers hop between competing brands. The importance and likelihood of switching in financial services will depend on the switching costs for different products. Frequently changing the location of a deposit account is unlikely to appeal to a consumer, even though they might purchase their travellers cheques from whichever provider had a particularly attractive offer.
(4) *Loyal customers*. Within own-loyal and competitor-loyal segments, we can distinguish between long-term, brand loyal consumers and those who tend to be 'last purchase loyal' (Kahn and Louie, 1990), who tend to be repeat purchasers until encouraged to realign their loyalties.

The consumer as a competitor

Consumers certainly like competitions. Surveys by Harris/Marketing Week (Cummins, 1989) and *Incentive Marketing* (1992), show that some 70 per cent of UK consumers participate in product- or service-related competitions.

We can intuitively divide up consumers into three types of 'competitive consumer' segments according to their attitude to competitions:

(1) *Non-competitors* who would consider competitions a waste of time, stamps or telephone units.
(2) *Passive competitors* who would enter competitions but would not change their normal purchasing behaviour just to enter a competition.
(3) *Active competitors* who would change their purchase behaviour (such as timing or brand choice) to enter an attractive competition.

It is important to note that this classification is for people in relation to a given product or service. They may well switch between categories in relation to the attractiveness of a given competition, which, according to Selby and Beranek (1981), is a function of five factors:

(1) the cost of entering;
(2) the monetary value of the prizes (or perhaps more accurately the utility of the prizes);
(3) the number of prizes and the perceived probability of winning;
(4) the pleasures of gambling (or perhaps more accurately of competing); and
(5) the desire to occupy leisure time.

They conclude that all five factors are important, but that the importance of the last two has been obscured by an overemphasis on rational-economic decision-making approaches based around the first three. This view is further backed up by survey data revealing that 60 per cent of competitors entered 'just for the fun of it' and 61 per cent of entrants into competitions were found to be 'unsure of what the prizes offered were' (*Premium Incentive Business*, 1986).

Cross-referencing the consumer's competitiveness against their brand involvement, produces a picture of the opportunities which using a sales promotion competition presents (Figure 1).

The implication of this model is that there are two key groups that a competition can be targeted at. New customers can be developed from among the potential users and some poached from competitors, and (providing that some are retained) this will provide long-term benefits of an increased customer base and an expanded market. Research

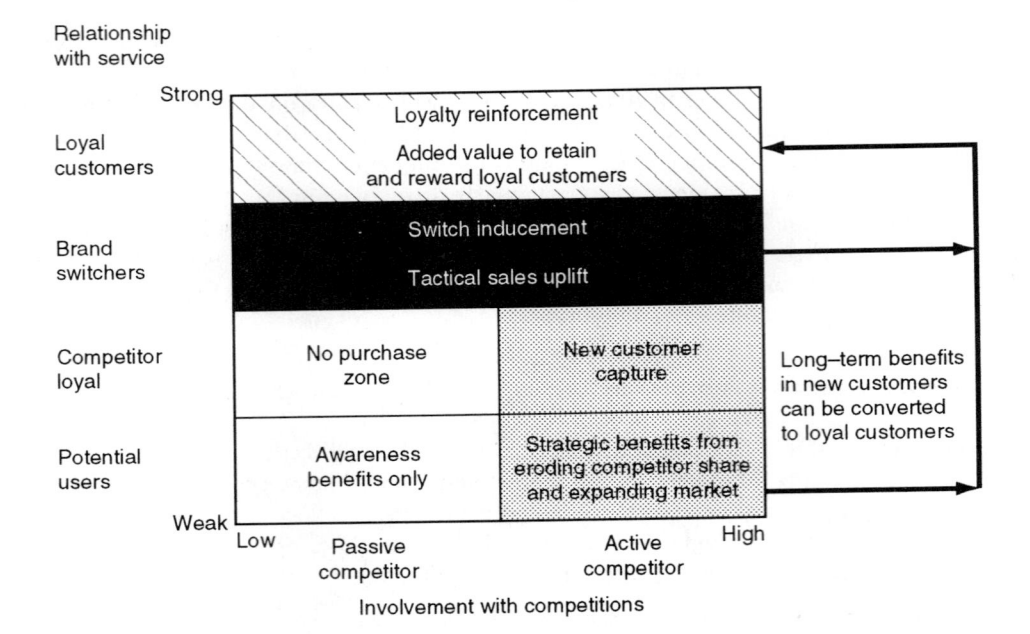

Figure 1. Promoting to the competitive consumer.

suggests that this is possible because consumers who try a promoted brand and are satisfied with it have an increased probability of a repeat purchase. This is particularly true of previous non-users (Cotton and Babb, 1978; Rothschild and Gaidis, 1981). The potential of competitions to create such changes in consumer behaviour is shown by the results of a Neilsen Promotion Services survey in Canada. This showed that 55 per cent of competition entrants will use a brand specifically to enter a competition, and 95 per cent of those will select the brand again following the competition.

Another benefit comes from increasing the usage among loyal or occasional purchasers. This will produce more of a short-term tactical sales uplift, of the type more traditionally associated with competitions and other promotions. A competition can reward loyal customers by adding value and perhaps adding some 'spice' to existing customer relationships. In financial services it is not uncommon to find competitions open to account holders only. Although such promotions may encourage the opening of new accounts, a key effect will be to reward and interest existing customers. This is important for bank marketers, for example, because a bank account is a service which is easy to take for granted until something goes wrong. The challenge for bank marketers is to draw attention to a service whose use could otherwise become so habitual that consumer involvement and brand loyalty will decline.

SALES PROMOTION COMPETITIONS FOR FINANCIAL SERVICES—THE SURVEY

The authors' own involvement in entering competitions as a hobby led them to appreciate what a widespread, growing, versatile and creative marketing tool promotional competitions are. It was a natural progression to use our experience of competitions, and the access to information on the competitions themselves which participation in the world of serious 'comping' brings, to study the use of competitions in marketing.

The authors gathered details on 2646 different UK sales promotion competitions over a three-year period by using a nationwide network of fellow 'compers' as information gatherers. Details from special packs, entry forms and competition rules were all studied to build up a picture of these competitions, which was encoded and then analysed using Minitab. The sample consisted only of competitions which were available on a national or regional basis (local ones were discounted) and which were associated with a product or service, as opposed to being all or part of the product or service itself (so the numerous competitions which are regular features of magazines were not included).

It is impossible to say how representative the sample is, since there are no reliable figures on the total number of promotional competitions being used. What can be stated confidently is that the many 'compers' from all over the country who contributed competition details are a dedicated group who will have missed relatively few widely available competitions.

The use of competitions as a tool in financial services marketing can be studied by analysing the 57 competitions which were included in a subset of 188 competitions sponsored by various service providers. The total sample provides opportunities to study how competitions are used by financial services, and to make comparisons with other types of services and to tangible goods. The results of the total sample are summarized in the Appendix to provide a context for the services and financial services subsets, and to allow the reader to draw comparisons between financial services and tangible goods (although a detailed comparison is beyond the scope of this article, for further details on the total sample see Peattie and Peattie, 1993b).

Extent of use

Table 1 puts the sample of competitions run by financial service providers in the context of the services subset. Services as a whole account for fractionally more than 7 per cent of all competitions in the total survey, which leaves them rather under-represented when one considers the importance of services within the total economy. Financial services are the largest service sector, confirming Addison's (1988) contention that financial services have been spearheading the acceptance of sales promotion among previous non-user markets.

Financial services involved

Table 2 shows the distribution of competition usage among financial service providers. It should be noted that there can be some blurring between the categories in terms of the service provider and the service provided. For example, a competition may be run by a travel services provider promoting a financial service such as travellers cheques or currency exchanges. The 54 financial services competitions originally classified in the analysis of all services in Table 1 are therefore supplemented by three competitions originally categorized as relating to other forms of service provider to give the total of 57

Table 1. Services survey results summary.

Services sponsor	Number of competitions	Average prize number	Average prize value (£'000s)	Market integration
Financial	54	10	8.4	Medium
Tourism and travel	47	10	5	Low
Food and drink	33	16	3	Medium
Leisure	23	21	6.75	Low
Communications	12	8	3.8	Low
Professional	6	4	0.35	Low
Photographic and miscellaneous retail	13	53	4.5	Medium

Notes
(1) Prize number and value are median averages for the total number and value of prizes awarded per competition
(2) Marketing integration is a modal average score between 1 (low) and 3 (high)—see text for details
(3) The financial category for this table excludes financially related competitions run by other types of service provider (e.g. travel agents)

which related to the provision of financial services. Table 3 presents an alternative presentation of results broken down by the financial service provided.

As might be expected, the banks and building societies; and mortgages, loans and foreign currency transactions dominated. These accounted for three-quarters of all competitions run in relation to providers and to services provided respectively.

Nature of competitions used

Financial services providers adopted a relatively conservative approach in devising the competitions that they used, with 84 per cent involving the answering of questions and 81 per cent involving a slogan. Only one of the competitions was jointly sponsored with another company. This was somewhat surprising given the opportunities that

Table 2. Financial services survey results summary by service provider.

Services sponsor	Number of competitions	Average prize number	Average prize value (£'000s)	Market integration
Banks	25	11	20	Low
Building societies	18	6	6.5	Medium
Credit services	6	18	4	Low
Specialist services	4	26	2.5	Medium/high
Secondary service providers	4	61	4.5	High

Notes
(1) Prize number and value are medium averages for the total number and value of prizes awarded per competition
(2) Marketing integration is a modal average score between 1 (low) and 3 (high)
(3) The 57 financial services competitions include three of those run by sponsors who are not primarily financial services providers, which were not originally classified as financial services in the analysis of the services sample presented in Table 1

Table 3. Financial services survey results summary by service provided.

Services sponsor	Number of competitions	Average prize number	Average prize value (£'000s)	Market integration
Mortgages and loans	28	9	10	Low
Foreign exchange	14	7	5.75	High
Card-based services	8	26	5.4	Medium
Pensions and insurance	4	8.5	7.5	Medium
Miscellaneous	3	26	2.25	Medium

Notes
(1) Prize number and value represent the average (median) number and total value of prizes awarded per competition
(2) Marketing integration is a modal average score between 1 (low) and 3 (high)

competitions provide, to link up with a consumer goods manufacturer and run a competition around a high-quality tangible product as a prize.

Prizes

For most competitive consumers, the prizes offered are clearly an important component of a competition. The *Premium Incentive Business/Better Homes & Gardens (PIBBHG*, 1989) survey of 500 US households found that for 45 per cent of entrants into competitions, the prize is the determining factor (compared with 36 per cent who are not interested in the prize itself).

We estimate that the 57 competitions linked to financial services involved offering 5821 prizes at a cost of around £1.1 million. Selby and Beranek (1981) note the problems of accurately estimating prize values, which worsen as prizes move away from easily valued products such as cars and holidays towards more unusual or experiential prizes such as lunch with Barbara Cartland or a part in a movie. Where there was any doubt about the value of the prize, a very conservative estimate was used. So the figure of £1.1 million will be an underestimate in one sense. However, this represents the approximate retail value of prizes (which is typically greater than the cost to the sponsor). The prize value figure is only a rough guide to the actual cost of prizes awarded. To this, the costs of planning, designing, delivering, administering and judging must be added, to estimate a cost for running competitions. The *New York Times* recently quoted the costs of competitions run by major service providers such as American Express as exceeding $5 million each. There are two key dimensions to the prizes, their value and their number. Since the attractiveness of a competition is partly related to the expected utility and the perceived probability of winning, sponsors could rely on high prize value or high prize numbers (or both) to make the maximum impact. Table 2 shows that among different financial services sponsors, the average values for the number and total value of prizes which typify their competitions vary by a factor of ten and eight respectively (the averages used are median figures, used because the arithmetic mean is skewed by a small number of prizes offering exceptionally valuable or numerous prizes). The sample, or subsets of it, can be divided up around the median values for the number of prizes offered and their value, to produce four categories of competition:

(1) *Jackpots* (few prizes/high value). A Lloyds Bank pensions competition offered an E-Type Jaguar and four MG Midgets as prizes.

(2) *Misers* (few prizes/low value). Birmingham Midshires Building Society offered a single weekend for two in Madrid in a travel money competition.
(3) *Everyone a winner* (many prizes/low value). A postal order competition run by the Post Office offered 101 relatively low value prizes linked to the TV programme *Coronation Street*.
(4) *Bonanzas* (many prizes/high value). Barclayloan's Beautiful Britain competition offered over 1300 prizes worth over £80 000.

The tendencies of different competition sponsors towards particular prize philosophies can be demonstrated by the creation of a prize philosophy matrix. Figure 2 presents such a matrix for the overall services subset which reveals that financial services and tourism back up their frequent use of competitions with considerable commitment in terms of number and particularly value of prizes. Breaking the financial services competitions down by both service provider and service provided (Figure 3) reveals that:

- The larger institutions, the banks and building societies, had a clear jackpot mentality, perhaps reflecting their ability to afford large prizes with the right quality cue effect.
- The money being invested in competitions by banks is quite astonishing, with a median value of £20 000 in prizes being offered. The nearest any other sponsor type gets to this figure in the total sample is the £10 400 for car companies.
- The smaller institutions and competitions run for card services tend to attract consumers by offering more prizes of relatively smaller value.
- The median average value of prizes offered in almost all forms of financial service competitions exceeds those for packaged foods, consumer goods, retailers, groceries and drinks—in other words, all the traditional strongholds of the promotional competition.

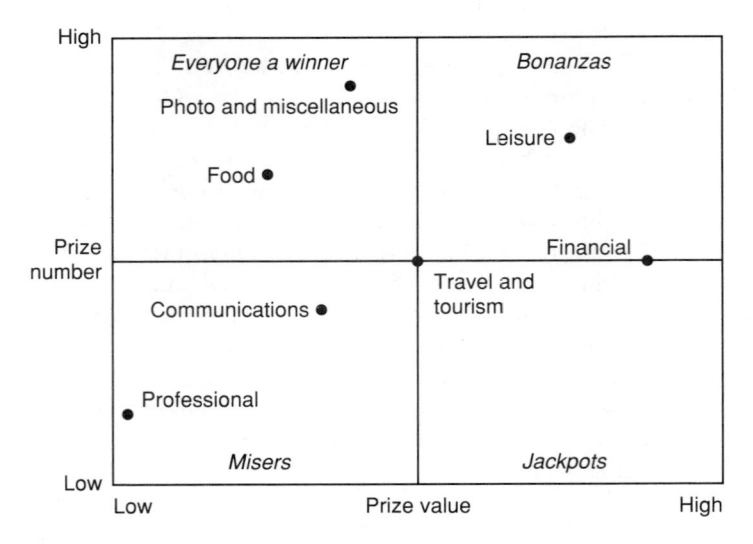

Figure 2. Services prize philosophy matrix.

Figure 3. Financial services prize philosophy matrix.

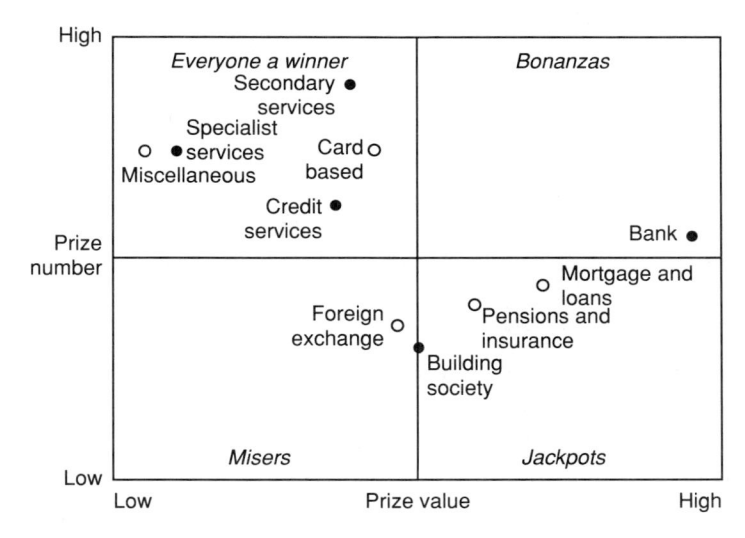

THE EFFECTIVENESS OF SALES PROMOTION COMPETITIONS

Measuring the effectiveness of competitions is not simple, and is almost impossible to do just by studying the competitions themselves. One obvious answer would seem to be to analyse sales patterns to determine the effectiveness of a promotion. However, this does not work for competitions where a purchase is not necessary, and ignores potential benefits of increased awareness or increased satisfaction among existing users. It is interesting to note the fact that the proportion of financial services competitions which required a purchase is much more in line with the total sample (which was dominated by tangible products) than with the rest of the services subset (see Table 4). This suggests that Rodney Woods' advice has been heeded, with financial services marketers looking to adopt competitions as a selling tool.

The evidence that exists on the effectiveness of the competitions run by financial institutions is patchy, but generally positive. The 'Quick Draw Sweepstakes' run by Fourth Financial Corp. (the biggest banking institution in Kansas) increased their credit card penetration by 3 per cent and their debit card penetration by 6 per cent (Friesen, 1989). More spectacularly, the Lippo Bank of Jakarta Indonesia is marketing strategy for 1989 relied on a major competition offering the potential of prizes for new customers. The

Table 4. Proportion of competitions requiring purchase.

	Total sample	Other services	Financial services
Percentage of competitions not requiring a purchase	25	66	25

result was a 164 per cent increase in loans, a 345 per cent increase in deposits and a 432 per cent increase in assets for the year (*Asian Business*, 1991).

Marketing integration

One measure the authors did devise to try and judge competition effectiveness, was the 'marketing integration' of the competitions. Competitions vary in terms of whether either the prize, or the mechanics of the competition, relates back to the product or service being promoted. We developed a very crude method of classifying a competition according to its marketing integration as follows:

- *Low*—no link between product and competition or prize.
- *Medium*—a link between competition or prize and product.
- *High*—product, prize and competition all related.

Table 1 shows the marketing integration scores associated with different service providers. Services overall score relatively poorly compared with goods, perhaps owing to the intangibility of services and a tendency to focus the mechanics of the competition (such as questions asked or slogans required) on the tangible prize, rather than the service itself. Financial service providers were generally no exception to this, with 80 per cent of their competitions being divided relatively evenly between low and moderate scores for marketing integration. However, there was some clear variation between the types of service offered, while most of the mortgage and loan related competitions featured low integration, most of the foreign exchange related competitions scored highly for integration (See Table 3).

The generally poor showing among financial services might relate to the lack of a tangible product to 'hang' the competition around. It might also relate to the lack of collaboration in the competitions, since all but one of them were solo efforts. In the total sample for all industry sectors, only 22 per cent of the competitions involving dual sponsorship were classified as low in marketing integration terms, compared to 48 per cent for the single sponsor competitions. This perhaps suggests that two marketing heads are often better than one.

GETTING THE MOST OUT OF COMPETITIONS

Like any element of the marketing mix, getting the benefits out of a competition require careful attention to planning and execution. Running competitions can be somewhat unpredictable, as one of the authors learned in conversation with a Canadian academic who had previously worked for one of Canada's largest trust companies. Their first foray into competitions drew such an unexpectedly massive response that in order to judge the competition in accordance with the rules, they had to load all the entries into a specially hired dumper truck and create a mountain of paper in the company car park. A local professor was then blindfolded and made to walk into the middle of the pile, after which he was pulled out by a rope clutching two fistfuls of lucky winners. This painted a delightfully zany picture of financial services marketing in action, but illustrates the need to plan a competition's implementation sooner rather than later.

Looking at over 2600 competitions has helped the authors to develop some insights into the art of developing sales promotions competitions. Other authors such as Toop (1991) and Keon and Bayer (1986) have put forward useful planning guidelines for marketers on the practicalities of running sales promotions. We have tried to add to this by developing the COMPETE checklist (Peattie and Peattie, 1993a), specifically to assist marketers in planning a successful sales promotion competition. The checklist prompts the consideration of seven key areas:

(1) *Co-sponsors* Will the competition be run by the company or shared with another service provider or manufacturer? If so, how will costs and responsibilities be divided?
(2) *Objectives*. What are the marketing objectives of the competition? What message will it send to customers and what effect should it produce? Is it only short-term sales uplifts, or are there more long-term objectives such as generating new users or raising product awareness?
(3) *Mechanics*. How will the competition be designed, delivered, entered and judged? How can the mechanics of the competition best support its objectives? What form of competition will most appeal to our target market? What could go wrong logistically and how could it be prevented?
(4) *Prizes*. What number and value of prizes will be required to make the competition attractive? Can the prizes be chosen to reinforce the product concept? What prizes will attract target customers?
(5) *Expenditure*. How much of the marketing budget and the time of marketing management should the competition consume? How can the judging be made as simple as possible?
(6) *Timing*. Should the competition be used to counteract seasonal lows, reinforce seasonal highs or 'spoil' rivals' promotions? Should the gap between launch and closing date be long to maximize the effect, or short to prevent loss of customer interest? How long should leaflets and posters be displayed for?
(7) *Evaluation* How will the effectiveness of the competition be measured in terms of achieving its objectives? Who should be responsible for evaluation, when and using what measures?

Although these points may appear to be very much a matter of common sense, even large and sophisticated companies, with a long track record of successful sales promotions, can be caught out if a promotion is not carefully planned, and if the fundamental questions are not asked. Hoover's experience pales by comparison with a bungled competition run by Pepsi-Cola in the Philippines which has cost the company over £8 million so far, has led to them facing over 22 000 lawsuits, and has provoked riots, death threats against company executives and grenade attacks on Pepsi lorries.

CONCLUSIONS

There are several conclusions which can be drawn about the use of competitions for financial services marketing from the survey:
- Despite their suitability as a promotional tool for financial services, competitions are still in the early stages of the innovation diffusion process.

- With over £1 million just in prizes being invested in the 57 promotions we sampled, financial services, and banks in particular, are obviously taking competitions very seriously.
- In view of the sums of money being invested in competitions, and the fact that the use of competitions as a promotional tool is now relatively commonplace, the neglect of such below-the-line techniques is becoming an increasing weakness in the conventional financial services marketing literature.
- There is considerable room for improvement among the competitions currently run by financial service providers in terms of breaking away from a very conservative, formula-based approach to competition design; and in terms of creating better integration between the competitions developed and the service being promoted.
- Opportunities exist for co-promoting competitions with manufacturers or other service providers, which are currently being neglected. Financial service providers have been involved successfully in other forms of joint promotions, such as the young savers offer run by Kelloggs and Barclays which encouraged children to open bank accounts through initial deposit tokens on packets of breakfast cereals. Jointly sponsored competitions could open up valuable new marketing communications possibilities in financial services.

For financial services marketers seeking to differentiate their service, entice new customers and reward existing customers in the search for competitive advantage, running a competition is a very attractive alternative. However, there are a number of caveats that a prospective competition sponsor should be aware of:

- Competitions, like any form of sales promotion, are only effective if not overused.
- Competitions that are developed with a short-term tactical outlook will only yield tactical and temporary benefits. Where possible a competition should form part of a strategically planned and integrated approach to marketing communications so that it complements and reinforces the company's brand image and advertising.
- Sales promotions tend to go wrong for one of two reasons. Either they do not receive the sort of thorough planning that is reserved for advertising campaigns, or the planning and evaluation is delegated too far down the marketing organization (Strang, 1976). To avoid disasters and capitalize on the potential to gain competitive advantage, promotions should be planned as carefully as any initiative of potential strategic importance.

Overall, competitions are a highly flexible and cost effective means of marketing communications which, when properly managed, can add value and distinctiveness into the market offerings of financial services providers. Their growing use in financial services will provide new opportunities for academic research, and will, it is hoped, provoke some rewriting of the marketing communications sections of financial services marketing texts.

REFERENCES

Addison, J. (1988), 'Promotional Rescue', *Director*, November, pp. 139–43.
Asian Business (1991), 'Lippo Bank: Small Is Beautiful', *Asian Business*, Vol. 27 No. 1, p. 102.

Bogart, L. and Lehman, C. (1983), 'The Case of the Thirty Second Commercial', *Journal of Advertising Research*, Vol. 23, February–March, pp. 11–18.
Burnett, J. J. (1993), *Promotion Management*, Houghton Mifflin, Boston, MA.
Cotton, B. C. and Babb, E. M. (1978), 'Consumer Response to Promotional Deals', *Journal of Marketing*, Vol. 42, July, pp. 109–13.
Cummins, J. (1989), *Sales Promotion*, Kogan Page, London.
Dickson, P. R. and Sawyer, A. G. (1990). 'The Price Knowledge and Search of Supermarket Shoppers', *Journal of Marketing*, Vol. 54, July, pp. 42–53.
Doyle, P. and Saunders, J. (1985), 'The Lead Effect of Marketing Decisions', *Journal of Market Research*, Vol. 22 No. 1, pp. 54–65.
Friesen, J. (1989), 'Product Knowledge Shoot Out Fires 'em Up in the Heartland', *Bank Marketing*, Vol. 21 No. 7, pp. 30–3.
Financial Times (1989), 'Worldwide Marketing Expenditure 1989', *Financial Times*, 30 November, p. 13.
Grover, R. and Srinivasan, V. (1992), 'Evaluating the Multiple Effects of Retail Promotions on Brand Loyal and Brand Switching Segments', *Journal of Marketing Research*, Vol. 29 No. 1, pp. 76–89.
Gupta, S. (1988), 'Impact of Sales Promotion on When, What and How Much to Buy', *Journal of Marketing Research*, Vol. 25 No. 4, pp. 342–55.
Incentive Marketing, (1992), 26 July, p. 5.
Kahn, B. E. and Louie, T. A. (1990), 'Effects of Retraction of Price Promotions on Brand Choice Behavior for Variety-Seeking and Last-Purchase-Loyal Consumers', *Journal of Marketing Research*, Vol. 27 No. 4, pp. 279–89.
Keon, J. W. and Bayer, J. (1986), 'An Expert Approach to Sales Promotion Management', *Journal of Advertising Research*, June–July, pp. 19–26.
Kotler, P. (1988), *Marketing Management: Analysis, Planning, Implementation and Control*, Prentice-Hall, Englewood Cliffs, NJ.
Kotler, P. and Bloom, P. N. (1984), *Marketing Professional Services*, Prentice-Hall, Englewood Cliffs, NJ.
Kumar, V. and Leone, R. P. (1988), 'Measuring the Effect of Retail Store Promotions on Brand and Store Substitution', *Journal of Marketing Research*, Vol. 25 No. 2, pp. 178–85.
Lal, R. (1990), 'Manufacturer Trade Deals and Retail Price Promotions', *Journal of Marketing Research*, Vol. 27 No. 6, pp. 428–44.
Lovelock, C. H. (1984), *Services Marketing*, Prentice-Hall, Englewood Cliffs, NJ.
McAllister, L. and Totten, J. (1985), 'Decomposing the Promotional Bump: Switching, Stockpiling and Consumption Increase', paper presented at ORSA/TIMS 1985 Joint Meeting, Chicago, IL.
Moriarty, M. M. (1985), 'Retail Promotional Effects on Intra- and Interbrand Sales Performance', *Journal of Retailing*, Vol. 61, Autumn, pp. 27–48.
Neslin, S. A., Henderson, C. and Quelch, J. (1985), 'Consumer Promotions and the Acceleration of Product Purchases', *Marketing Science*, Vol. 4, Spring, pp. 147–65.
Peattie, K. J. and Peattie, S. (1993a), 'Sales Promotion—Playing to Win', *Journal of Marketing Management*, Vol. 9 No. 3, pp. 255–70.
Peattie, S. and Peattie, K. J. (1993a), 'Sales Promotion Competitions—A Survey', *Journal of Marketing Management*, Vol. 9 No. 3, pp. 271–86.
PIBBHG (1989), 'Accounting for Consumer Behaviour: Why They Enter One Promo over Another', *Premium Incentive Business*, Vol. 48 No. 2, pp. 8–10.
Premium Incentive Business (1986), 'Prize Offering: Believability Affects Entrants' Response to Sweepstakes', *Premium Incentive Business*, Vol. 45 No. 3, p. 25.
Quelch, J. A. (1983), 'It's Time to Make Trade Promotion More Productive', *Harvard Business Review*, Vol. 61 No. 3, pp. 130–6.
Rathmell, J. M. (1966), 'What Is Meant by Services?', *Journal of Marketing*, Vol. 30, October, pp. 32–6.
Rothschild, M. L. and Gaidis, W. C. (1981), 'Behavioural Learning Theory: Its Relevance to Marketing and Promotions', *Journal of Marketing*, Vol. 45, Spring, pp. 70–8.
Selby, E. B. and Beranek, W. (1981), 'Sweepstakes Contests: Analysis, Strategies, and Survey', *The American Economic Review*, Vol. 17 No. 1, pp. 189–95.

Shultz, D. E. (1987), 'Above or Below the Line? Growth of Sales Promotion in the United States', *International Journal of Advertising*, Vol. 6, pp. 17–27.
Strang, R. A. (1976), 'Sales Promotion: Fast Growth, Faulty Management', *Harvard Business Review*, Vol. 54, pp. 115–24.
Tellis, G. J. and Gaeth, G. J. (1990), 'Best Value, Price Seeking and Price Aversion: The Impact of Information and Learning on Consumer Choices', *Journal of Marketing*, Vol. 54, April, pp. 34–45.
Thomas, D. R. E. (1978), 'Strategy is Different in Services Businesses', *Harvard Business Review*, Vol. 56, July–August, pp. 158–65.
Toop, A. (1991), *Crackingjack!: Sales Promotion Techniques and How to Use Them Successfully*, Mazecity, Sandhurst, Kent.
Vilcassim, N. J. and Jain, D. C. (1991), 'Modelling Purchase-Timing and Brand-switching Behaviour Incorporating Explanatory Variables and Unobserved Heterogeneity', *Journal of Marketing Research*, Vol. 28 No. 1, pp. 29–41.
Walters, R. G. (1991), 'Assessing the Impact of Retail Price Promotions on Product Substitution, Complementary Purchase, and Interstore Sales Displacement', *Journal of Marketing*, Vol. 55, April, pp. 17–28.
Ziethaml, V. A., Parasuraman, A. and Berry, L. L. (1985), 'Problems and Strategies in Services Marketing', *Journal of Marketing*, Vol. 49, Spring, pp. 33–46.

APPENDIX: COMPETITIONS SURVEY RESULTS SUMMARY

Sponsor	Number of competitions	Percentage of competitions	Average prize number	Average prize value (£000's)	Market integration
Retailer	1232	46.6	20	2.64	Medium
Packaged food	929	35.1	50	3.98	Medium
Consumer goods	517	19.5	11	3.5	Medium
Grocery items	344	13.0	14	3.0	Medium
Drink	319	12.1	11	3.0	Medium
Services	188	7.11	10	5.0	Low
Publications	118	4.5	7	2.0	Low
Tobacco	39	1.5	15	5.0	Low
White goods	32	1.2	20	5.9	High
Charities	25	1.0	15	1.0	Low
Generic	24	0.9	11	2.3	High
Cars	14	0.5	11	10.4	High

Notes:
(1) Groceries include all inedible consumables
(2) Prize number and value are median averages for the total number and value of prizes awarded per competition
(3) Marketing integration is a modal average score between 1 (low) and 3 (high)
(4) Jointly sponsored competitions are included in the figures for both sponsor types. Column totals for number and percentage of competition therefore exceed 2646 and 100 respectively

16

Direct Marketing in the Financial Services Industry

Des Thwaites and Sharon C. I. Lee

This article presents empirical research findings on the use of direct marketing by a representative sample of UK financial services institutions. A number of similarities and differences between banks, building societies and insurance companies are identified in relation to direct marketing programmes and the use of particular direct marketing techniques. While acknowledging some exceptions the research concludes that there is scope for a greater appreciation of the strategic value and workings of direct marketing. Institutions could usefully focus attention on achieving fuller integration of direct marketing with other marketing and communication activities and securing improvements in testing, database quality and timing.

INTRODUCTION

Most businesses operate in complex and competitive environments where demands are constantly changing and increasing levels of resources and management attention are focused on attracting and retaining customers. This situation promoted the marketing concept which Kotler (1988) describes as the determination, and subsequent satisfaction, of customer needs and wants more efficiently and effectively than one's competitors. Marketing represents the instrument through which this satisfaction has been delivered and has shown rapid growth over the past decade.

While marketing approaches based on mass communication, with general advertising and promotion directed to a mass market, have been in evidence, Bird (1989) considers that media fragmentation has reduced the effectiveness of this approach. As markets break down into heterogeneous segments a more precisely targeted marketing technique is required which creates a dialogue with smaller groups of customers, and addresses individual needs. This situation, coupled with changing demographics and lifestyles, decreasing data processing costs and escalating media and sales force costs, has contributed to the growth of direct marketing (Holder and Owen-Jones 1992). Employed alongside other advertising and promotion activities, direct marketing can create and reinforce brand awareness, maintain customer loyalty and sell goods and services directly. Consequently, it not only fulfils a promotion role within the mix but serves as a distributive function. It is this functional plurality which makes direct marketing an extremely potent marketing tool.

Despite the rapid growth of direct marketing the academic literature remains undeveloped and little empirical work has been undertaken. This paper seeks in part to redress this omission by responding to calls for research into the use and applications of direct marketing. The focus of the study is the financial services sector where direct marketing has grown significantly, particularly since 1986. Financial institutions now represent some of the major users of direct marketing techniques in the UK (Jefkins 1990).

DIRECT MARKETING

The US Direct Marketing Association describes direct marketing as 'an interactive system of marketing which uses one or more advertising media to affect a measurable response and/or transaction at any location'. Based on this definition Roberts and Berger (1989) highlight the key elements which contribute to the effectiveness of direct marketing and distinguish it from general marketing.

Firstly, direct marketing is interactive in that the company and prospective customer engage in two-way personalized communication. It represents a dialogue rather than a monologue. Responses, or even non-responses, provide valuable information and can be used to build a profile of the individual. For example, the company can determine the specific communication which generated a response (e.g. direct mail, TV direct response) and the channel through which the response was directed (e.g. mail coupon, freephone 0800 number). Conversely a non-response, while raising questions about the product offer, may also raise doubts about media, timing etc. This information is added to the company database, which aids planning and ensures more focused campaigns in the future. An effective database will trigger the right communication to the right target customer at the right time, through the right medium, thereby enhancing the customer's perceived value (Woodcock, 1992). Much of this activity is invisible to competitors, a trait less apparent in mass marketing.

A second feature of direct marketing is that the communication and response (transaction) can take place at any location, providing the prospect has access to the communication medium. It follows that direct marketing communications can transcend geographic boundaries and appeal to organizations seeking to expand into new locations.

A third positive aspect of direct marketing is that it is measurable and accountable. Measures of effectiveness, such as business generated and response rates, allow organizations to assess the return on their investment thereby influencing budgeting and future media selection. This contrasts with general marketing approaches which use less informative surrogates such as awareness or recall.

Direct Marketing also exhibits several other specific competencies the most striking of which is the capacity for precise targeting (Roberts and Berger 1989). In addition, it is highly controllable in terms of timing, message and creativity, thereby allowing complex customized messages to be transmitted. Furthermore, it can be the subject of exhaustive testing to establish which media, offer, price, incentive, creative, timing, etc. are most appropriate to a given target segment and campaign (Bird 1989).

Table 1 summarizes the key distinctions between general marketing and direct marketing.

While there are positive benefits to be derived from direct marketing the approach is not

Table 1. Key distinctions between general and direct marketing.

General Marketing	Direct Marketing
Reaches a mass audience through mass media	Communicates directly with the customer or prospect

Communications are impersonal	Can personalise communications
	    By name/title
	    Variable messages

Promotional programmes are highly visible	Promotional programmes (especially tests) relatively 'invisible'
Amount of promotion controlled by size of budget	Size of budget can be determined by success of promotion

Desired action either
    Unclear
    Delayed
	Specific action always required:
	    Inquiry
	    Purchase

Incomplete/sample data for decision-making purposes
    Sales call reports
    Marketing research
	Comprehensive database drives marketing programmes

Analysis conducted at the segment level	Analysis conducted at individual/firm level

Use surrogate variable to measure effectiveness
    Advertising awareness
    Intention to buy
	Measurable, and therefore highly controllable

Source: (Roberts and Berger 1989).

without its critics, for example, telemarketing has developed a poor image and can be seen as intrusive. However, the major complaints revolve around badly timed and imprecisely targeted direct mail, known colloquially as 'junk mail'. In an attempt to reduce costs many organizations take advantage of regular customer mailings to include other offers aimed at upselling or cross-selling. While this strategy reduces costs its effectiveness is open to question as the communication arrives at a time determined by the organization and is probably unrelated to the target customer's purchase cycle.

The use of out of date or inaccurate lists has exacerbated criticism of direct mail in particular and caused irritation to potential customers. Cobb (1992) highlights the difficulty and expense of maintaining accurate lists and suggests that changes in a customer list may run at approximately 9% per annum while business lists can reach 30% per annum. Identifying the most appropriate list is far from easy as, for example, some 26 lists of Marketing Directors are on offer. While there are potential problems with some direct marketing techniques managers must reduce these to a minimum as the alienation of potential or existing customers is clearly not in their interests. Managers require comprehensive lists that include several decision variables to develop an effective campaign. The aim is to provide the right product (**OFFER**) to the right person (**LIST**) at the right time (**TIMING**) in a manner which transforms attention into interest, desire, conviction and action (**CREATIVE**). Several authors have commented on the relative importance of these elements and there is general agreement that the list lies at the heart of direct marketing by virtue of its role in defining the target customer. As Bird (1989) suggests the most 'wonderful' mailing is unlikely to succeed if it goes to the wrong target, whereas the 'worst' mailing may succeed if it hits the right list. Timing and offer are similar in importance and rank second to the list but above creative (Bird 1989; Roberts and Berger 1989; Woodcock 1992).

Direct marketing activity and methods

Direct marketing expenditure in Europe during 1992 rose to £20.76bn. based on estimates by the European Direct Marketing Association reported in Mayes (1993). This represents an increase of 8% over 1990 figures. Spending in the UK also rose to £2.56bn; divided between direct advertising £1.42bn, mailings £1.04bn and tele-marketing/others £108m. The UK total represents 12% of European spending and places the UK third in the expenditure league behind Germany (37%) and France (19%). This trend in the growth of direct marketing in the UK seems set to continue based on a recent DunnHumby Associates (1993) survey which shows 67% of companies planning to increase spending with only 7% cutting back.

Table 5 highlights a range of media which are commonly used as the basis for direct marketing programmes. While the various media can be used independently, Roman (1988) strongly advocates integrated direct marketing. The logic of using multiple media is that different consumers respond in different ways to a given stimulus. By testing combinations of media the most productive and profitable blend can be established. Effectiveness is not, therefore, a function of the number of media used but of the coordination of those which are necessary.

DIRECT MARKETING IN THE FINANCIAL SERVICES INDUSTRY

The financial services sector has experienced significant demand and supply side changes over the last decade culminating in the removal of traditional lines of demarcation between institutions and greater competition across a wider product range. These developments are well documented in a growing body of literature (Lewis 1984; Thwaites 1989; Edgett and Thwaites 1990; Ennew et al. 1990; Thwaites 1991; McGoldrick and Greenland 1992). Specific attention has focused on the increasing role of marketing, both at a conceptual and process level (Easingwood and Arnott 1991; Thwaites and Lynch 1992), innovation (Moutinho and Meidan 1989; Thwaites 1992) and strategies for coping with a more hostile environment (Ennew et al. 1990; Thwaites and Glaister 1992).

In an attempt to remain competitive, new sources of distribution have been introduced (Howcroft 1992) and greater attention has been given to the quality of customer service (Lewis 1991). The growing use and value of information technology has also been recorded (Ennew et al. 1989; Scarborough and Lannon 1989; Stone and Clarkson 1989). Against this background direct marketing offers several applications which are particularly valuable to financial services suppliers (Martin 1991):

- lead generation for sales force;
- generation of retail traffic;
- keeping customers sold on product/service;
- cross-selling to existing customers;
- up-selling current and new products to existing customers;
- direct selling or new products.

Rapid technological developments in the financial services sector have provided time and place utility and reduced the need for customers to go into their branch to undertake transactions. Consequently sales opportunities have diminished. It is here that direct marketing can provide the communication medium through which meaningful long-term customer relationships can be developed. Direct marketing also offers scope for the removal of specific activities from the branch network to a central location and provides an effective market entry mechanism for non-traditional financial institutions. As financial services institutions seek to generate more profit per customer, while providing bespoke rather than standardized services, direct marketing may prove to be the most cost-effective way of developing and sustaining the relationship.

Previous research

Little attention has focused on direct marketing activities in the financial services sector during the past decade, although three studies do provide valuable insights. PA Management Consultants (1983) suggested that financial institutions (retail banks, building societies and insurance companies) could exploit direct marketing more fully. The techniques were very much in their infancy and would be enhanced through the development of more coherent strategies, and the acquisition of more information about customers and non-customers to improve targeting. Testing also required significantly greater attention. No doubt one of the contributory factors to poor targeting was the traditional approach to database development which focused on account numbers. Consequently it was difficult to establish a precise customer relationship. Eighty-eight per cent of the institutions surveyed had experience of direct marketing although 75% of these were making limited use of its full potential. Direct mail was the most popular media, followed by direct response coupons and inserts. The retail banks were the most sophisticated users of direct marketing although even this group had scope for much greater exploitation of the medium.

A more favourable picture emerged in 1986. Firth (1986) revealed that 89% of banks and 97% of building societies were using direct marketing compared to only 67% of insurance/life companies. This comparative shortfall appeared to stem from companies that were committed to operating through intermediaries and did not wish to damage this relationship. Direct marketing activities seemed better planned, but many institutions still faced problems, especially with costs, lead time and lists. The situation in 1989 (Firth and Lindsay 1989) did not show any major developments although more insurance/life companies had adopted directed marketing (78%). Of particular interest was the fact that almost 60% of institutions had established an in-house direct marketing department compared to less than 30% in 1986. Problems encountered varied across institutions but there was clear evidence of creative constraints as a direct implication of the Financial Services Act (1986). Nevertheless, the survey suggested high levels of growth across all sectors over the coming 5 years.

OBJECTIVES AND METHODOLOGY

Both anecdotal and empirical evidence suggests that direct marketing in the financial services sector escalated following legislative changes in 1986 when deregulation led to increasing competition. It is reasonable to postulate that the more hostile environment of the 1990s will facilitate its continued growth. However, it is recognized that the levels of usage may differ in terms of an institution's prime business activity, size, or experience of direct marketing. It is also suggested that more firms will come to realize the strategic potential of direct marketing as opposed to viewing it as merely a tactical marketing tool. More sophistication could be expected in relation to direct marketing campaigns with specific reference to the type of media used, segmentation and targeting techniques, evaluation methods and the organization of programmes—either by specialist agencies, general advertising companies or in-house departments. This study will, therefore, add to the developing literature on direct marketing by heightening our appreciation of the use and applications of these techniques by a range of financial services institutions.

Following a comprehensive review of the literature, a questionnaire was prepared, tested and subsequently mailed to the Chief Marketing Executive at 160 financial services institutions in early 1992. The sample of 15 banks comprised all the major clearing, savings and regional banks in England and Scotland listed in the City Directory, 1991. All building societies listed in the Building Societies Association Directory of Members, 1991 and still operating in 1992 were contacted ($n = 94$). The sample of 51 insurance companies was drawn by quota according to class of business (long-term or general). Martin (1991) indicates that approximately 25% of all insurance companies are in long term business, 64% in general business and the rest, composite. The sample is, therefore, a representative cross section of the major players in the insurance sector, based on the 1991 listing of the Association of British Insurers.

The nature of the sample of financial institutions closely resembles that of Firth and Lindsay (1989) although a greater number of smaller building societies are present. In certain cases similar questions have been included to facilitate more accurate assessment of trends and developments and provide consistency of measurement. The questionnaire contains a range of dichotomous, multiple choice and open questions and bipolar scales are employed to set simple quantitative measures to qualitative characteristics specifically to achieve aggregation and other quantitative manipulation. A range of statistical tests available in SPSS are used to analyze the data viz., chi-square, Kilmogorov-Smirnov, Mann–Whitney U, Kruskal–Wallis and the Spearman Rank Correlation Coefficient.

RESULTS

Inspection of the responses to the postal survey indicate that 75% of financial services institutions are involved in direct marketing activities (Table 2). Sixty-five per cent of these firms have only introduced direct marketing since 1986, which confirms the view that the techniques came of age following deregulation and increased competition in the mid 1980s.

Among those institutions not using direct marketing at the time of the study 29% suggest it will be introduced in the near future. The major reasons given for not using direct marketing are *not considered to be cost effective* (44%), *lack of requirement* (28%) and *no perceived benefit* (24%). This implies some degree of ignorance as to the workings and applications of direct marketing. No differences are revealed between the institutional groups on questions relating to whether direct marketing is used or when it was first introduced.

Table 2. Direct marketing activity.

	Responses	Percentage response rate	Number using direct marketing	Percentage using direct marketing
Banks	13	86.7	11	84.6
Building societies	53	56.4	38	71.7
Insurance companies	39	76.5	30	76.9
Total	105	65.6	79	75.2

Budget allocation

The research suggests the distribution of direct marketing spend differs between financial institutions ($P < 0.01$). Seventy-three per cent of banks spend in excess of £1 million compared to 43% of insurance companies and 16% of building societies (Table 3). This does not automatically indicate a reduced commitment to direct marketing by either building societies or insurance companies but is to some extent a function of size. Indeed a positive association between asset size and budget spend was identified ($r = 0.71$, $P < 0.01$). The supposition that institutions will begin to increase direct marketing budgets in line with greater experience and familiarity with the techniques is only weakly supported in that there is a low positive association between experience and spend ($r = 0.37, P < 0.01$).

Integration of direct marketing activities

Despite the strong support in the literature for the effective integration of direct marketing with other marketing and communication activities this study confirms earlier observations (Firth and Lindsay 1989) that financial services institutions still have some way to go in securing adequate levels of integration (Table 4). This may suggest that in some institutions direct marketing is considered as an independent tactical weapon to be utilized in response to particular situations, for example changes in interest rates, tax or pension laws.

A similar picture emerges in relation to the integration of different direct marketing media. Only 65% of institutions seek synergys from integration. The banks are, however,

Table 3. Direct marketing budget.

Budget (£ p.a.)	Banks ($n = 11$)	Building societies ($n = 37$)	Insurance companies ($n = 26$)	Total ($n = 74$)
Up to 250 000	1 (9)	24 (65)	10 (38)	35 (47)
>250 000–1 000 000	2 (18)	7 (19)	5 (19)	14 (19)
>1 000 000	2 (18)	2 (5)	4 (16)	8 (11)
>2 000 000	6 (55)	4 (11)	7 (27)	17 (23)

Figures in brackets represent the percentage of similar institutions in each budget category.
$P < 0.01$

Table 4. Integration of direct marketing activities.

Direct marketing integrated with	Banks ($n = 10$)	Building societies ($n = 36$)	Insurance companies ($n = 27$)
Above the line advertising	5.2	4.4	3.2
Sales promotion at point of sale	5.2	4.5	3.2
Public relations	2.7	4.1	2.5

Figures represent a mean score based on a seven-point scale.
1 = never integrated, 7 = fully integrated.
$P < 0.05$ in all cases.

much more effective in this regard with all but one of their number seeking integration. The extent to which institutions integrate aspects of their direct marketing appears to increase in line with the size of their budget ($P < 0.05$) which is itself related to the size of the organization, and the length of experience with the medium ($P < 0.01$).

Direct marketing methods

Table 5 identifies the different direct marketing methods used and highlights changes since the 1989 study conducted by Firth and Lindsay. The data clearly illustrate increased usage across the full range of methods.

Direct mail is extensively used and retains its position as the most popular method of direct marketing. The increasing use of leaflet inserts identified by Firth and Lindsay (1989) has continued and indeed escalated. This is largely due to tighter advertising regulations brought about by the Financial Services Act (1986) whereby more detailed information must be given in relation to financial products. The most dramatic growth is in telemarketing, which offers a range of benefits in terms of building and maintaining data bases, developing and updating lists, market measurement and testing, generating retail traffic, direct selling and customer care programmes. It provides a facility whereby elements of the direct marketing campaign can be integrated and indeed 81% of those institutions that claim they integrate aspects of their direct marketing cite telemarketing as

Table 5. Use of direct marketing methods.

Method	Percentage of institutions using the approach		
	1989 Firth and Lindsay ($n = 70$)	1992 This study ($n = 77$)	Percentage increase
Direct mail	97	97	0
Leaflet inserts	67	85	27
In-house piggybanks	60	78	30
Off-the-page press advertising	63	76	21
Two-stage press advertising	59	73	24
Door-to-door leaflets	41	52	27
Third-party piggybacks	33	47	42
TV direct response	23	35	52
Telephone marketing	21	57	171
Radio direct response	20	26	30

the major facilitating mechanism. The three institutional groups are relatively similar in their preference for particular methods of direct marketing. Only in the area of off-the-page advertising are real difference apparent. While 91% of banks and 89% of building societies adopt this approach only 52% of insurance companies find it of value ($P < 0.0001$). The complexity of many insurance and pension products, coupled with the disclosure necessary under the Financial Services Act (1986), may have encouraged a move to leaflet inserts. Off-the-page is now used mainly to generate leads, quality prospects, encourage requests for more information and to sell products which do not require long and complex explanations.

Segmentation and targeting

The data presented in Table 6 indicate that a majority of financial services institutions are heavily reliant on customer files, reflecting a high degree of cross and up-selling to existing customers. However, 59% of respondents admit that their files are still account-based rather than customer-based. This inevitably presents difficulties in the development of meaningful customer relationships.

Of the geodemographic systems Acorn and Mosaic are the most popular with 33% and 23% of institutions adopting them. It is interesting to note the apparent demise of socio-economic groupings in favour of more sophisticated techniques. Firth and Lindsay (1989) identified socio-economic as the second most popular approach with 43% of institutions using the technique. This study ranks it only fourth at 19%. Pinpoint and Superprofiles show limited usage which is somewhat surprising, particularly for Pinpoint, which through Finpin, offers a breakdown of financial awareness and activity.

Organization of direct marketing

The research reveals that 79% of institutions employ the services of specialist direct marketing agencies rather than relying on their advertising agency. This represents a significant change relative to the 53% revealed in Firth and Lindsay (1989). The banks (100%) and insurance companies (92%) invariably use specialist agencies although this trend is much weaker in building societies at only 59% ($P < 0.01$). The major benefits attributed to specialist agencies are their experience in the use of a variety of direct marketing methods and creative and copy writing skills. There is no evidence to suggest

Table 6. Use of segmentation and targeting methods.

Method	Institutions using the approach	
	Number	Percentage
Customer file	74	85
Acorn	26	33
Mosaic	18	23
Socio-economic	15	19
Pinpoint	7	9
Superprofiles	6	8

Note: Some institutions use a variety of methods.

that the use of direct marketing specialists is influenced by experience in the use of direct marketing although institutions with larger budgets are more inclined to use specialist agencies ($P < 0.0001$).

The trend to create in-house direct marketing departments identified in Firth and Lindsay (1989) is maintained and 67% of institutions confirm their existence. This development is particularly strong amongst insurance companies (83%). The presence of a relationship between budget spend and an in-house facility is also apparent ($P < 0.0001$). Ninety-two per cent of those institutions spending in excess of £100 000 have their own direct marketing department. Given the link between organization size and budget spend it is perhaps not surprising that the building societies are less inclined to create their own departments or use specialist direct marketing agencies.

Testing of direct marketing materials

As Bird (1989) emphasizes 'testing is the kernal of direct marketing'. Unfortunately many financial services institutions are slow in heeding the message with only 50% of respondents claiming to carry out this activity. No differences are evident between the three groups in the extent to which they test. Interestingly the institutions that claim better response rates are those that employ pretesting of direct marketing materials ($P < 0.001$). Personalization of materials does not produce evidence of improved responses.

Role of direct marketing

Respondents were asked to rank six roles of direct marketing commonly quoted in the literature (Table 7). Direct marketing's most valuable contribution is in relation to cross-selling, although trading-up and generating leads for the sales force also score highly. Looking at the different institutions, the banks place greater emphasis on direct marketing

Table 7. Most valuable role of direct marketing.

Role	Rank order of importance					
	1st	2nd	3rd	4th	5th	6th
Lead generation for sales force	21*	8	8	11	21	9
	(28)	(11)	(11)	(15)	(28)	(8)
Generation of retail traffic	6	7	4	11	15	35
	(8)	(10)	(6)	(15)	(21)	(41)
Keeping the customer sold on service	11	12	15	26	8	3
	(15)	(16)	(20)	(35)	(11)	(4)
Cross-selling	34	24	8	6	4	2
	(44)	(31)	(10)	(8)	(5)	(3)
Trading-up	19	15	26	9	7	2
	(24)	(19)	(33)	(12)	(10)	(3)
Selling to new prospects	10	10	7	15	19	17
	(13)	(13)	(9)	(19)	(24)	(22)

*To be read 21 institutions reported 'Lead generation for sales force' as the most valuable role of direct marketing. This represents 28% of the sample (rounded).
Some institutions ranked certain roles equally and consequently column totals do not equal 100%.

for cross-selling and encouraging existing customers to trade-up. They are less convinced of its ability to keep customers sold on services, selling to new prospects and lead generation.

The building societies also emphasize cross-selling and trading-up, but less strongly than the banks. They are by far the most emphatic in the assertion that direct marketing helps keep customers sold on services. The insurance companies are broadly similar to building societies with the exception that they are more supportive of direct marketing as a means of generating leads for the sales force and selling to new prospects.

Specific competencies of direct marketing

The benefits of direct marketing methods compared to other elements of the communication mix are assessed through an open question. Not surprisingly a broad range of views are expressed, although several features are cited by institutions on a regular basis; accountability and measurability (49%) and precise targeting (43%) are the most common responses. Control and flexibility (24%) and one-to-one communication (23%) also receive support, but regrettably testing benefits are only mentioned by 10% of respondents. The distinctions between institutions are in the areas of control and flexibility where the banks are more supportive of this benefit ($P < 0.05$). They also place greater credence on testability ($P < 0.001$).

Problem areas

Firth and Lindsay (1989) identified a number of areas which were a source of concern to direct marketers. Of particular relevance to banks was the ability to obtain accurate and up-to-date (clean) lists, although it was suggested that this problem may reduce in line with database improvements and investments in information technology. Lead time and creative were also highlighted although divergent trends were evident. Lead time was becoming more problematic while creative was becoming less so. Building societies expressed concern about analysis problems, primarily resulting from resource constraints, while insurance companies cited cost, despite assumed savings of commission through direct sales.

The current study reflects some changes with 69% of institutions reporting cost as a problem. Insurance companies are still more emphatic with 81% highlighting this feature. Lists are the second area of concern (46%) and as in 1989, banks express greater dissatisfaction than the other institutions (64%). Building societies and banks still experience problems with analysis (47% and 55%, respectively) although the insurance companies find this of much less concern (22%). Creative problems, identified as a major worry in 1989, are now less apparent. This, in part, suggests financial services institutions have accommodated the creative constraints and implications stemming from the Financial Services Act (1986).

SUMMARY AND CONCLUSIONS

The rapid growth of direct marketing in the latter half of the 1980s appears to have slowed somewhat during the 1990s. Nevertheless the financial services market remains highly competitive and the positive contribution made by direct marketing in relation to the acquisition and retention of customers is set to continue. However, this research highlights a variety of approaches, some of which are clearly sub-optimal. It is vital that there is fuller integration of direct marketing with other elements of promotion and distribution. Perhaps the growth of in-house direct marketing departments will contribute to an appreciation of the strategic value of the medium in developing and sustaining customer dialogue.

While there is some evidence of a systematic approach to the use of direct marketing the research suggests that in certain cases, not only is there a lack of comprehension of the strategic benefits, but also a lack of clarity about the workings of direct marketing. For example, greater consideration should be given to compiling effective databases and integrating information sources with a view to more sophisticated targeting. In addition, significantly more attention should be placed on testing, as this identifies which proposition and delivery mechanisms are appropriate, and on aspects of timing. The combined effect of these measures will be to improve cost effectiveness and reduce charges of 'junk mail'.

The evidence of greater use of several media within direct marketing programmes is a positive development as different campaigns demand different approaches based on particular objectives, products, target markets, etc. Experience with a range of techniques will lead to more effective integration and bring benefits through synergy, reinforcement and improved response rates.

Direct marketing has much to offer financial services institutions through leveraging their investments in more traditional elements of the communication mix and providing a distributive function. The evidence of this research is that for a number of institutions a greater appreciation of the role and applications of direct marketing will be necessary if the real benefits of this adaptive and valuable medium are to be gained.

REFERENCES

Bird, D. (1989), *Commonsense Direct Marketing*, London, Kogan Page.
Cobb, R. (1992), 'In Defence of the List', *Marketing*, 23 January, pp. 23–24.
DunnHumby Associates (1993), *Computers in Marketing*, Special Report, London. DunnHumby Associates.
Easingwood, C. and Arnott, D. (1991), 'Management of Financial Services Marketing: Issues and Perceptions', *International Journal of Bank Marketing*, Vol. 9, No. 6, pp. 3–12.
Edgett, S. and Thwaites, D. (1990), 'The Influence of Environmental Change on the Marketing Practices of Building Societies', *European Journal of Marketing*, Vol. 24, No. 12, pp. 35–47.
Ennew, C., Wright, M. and Watkins, T. (1989), 'Marketing Strategies in a Changing Competitive Environment. The Financial Services Sector in the UK'. In: *Marketing Audit of the 80s*, (Eds) Moutinho, L. *et al.* (Glasgow), Marketing Education Group, pp. 943–969.
Ennew, C., Watkins, T. and Wright, M. (1990), *Marketing Financial Services*, Oxford, Heinemann.
Ennew, C., Wright, M. and Watkins, T. (1990), 'New Competition in Financial Services', *Long Range Planning*, Vol. 23, No. 6, pp. 80–90.
Firth, L. P. (1986), *Direct Marketing in the UK Financial Services Industry 1986*, unpublished MBA Thesis, University of Bradford.
Firth, L. P. and Lindsay, D. (1989), *Direct Marketing in the UK Financial Services Industry*, Kingston Business School.
Holder, D. and Owen-Jones, C. (1992), 'Why Direct Marketing Works'. In: *The Absolute Essentials* (Teddington), The Direct Marketing Centre, p. 6.

Howcroft, B. (1992), 'Contemporary Issues in UK Bank Delivery Systems', *International Journal of Service Industry Management*, Vol. 3, No. 1, pp. 39–56.

Jefkins, F. (1990), *The Secret of Successful Direct Response Marketing*, Oxford, Heinemann.

Kotler, P. (1988), *Marketing Management: Analysis, Planning, Implementation and Control*, (6th Edn.), New Jersey, Prentice-Hall.

Lewis, B. (1984), 'Marketing Bank Services', *The Service Industries Journal*, Vol. 4, No. 3, pp. 61–76.

Lewis, B. (1991), 'Service Quality: An International Comparison of Bank Customers' Expectations and Perceptions', *Journal of Marketing Management*, Vol. 7, No. 1, pp. 47–62.

McGoldrick, P. H. and Greenland, S. J. (1992), 'Competition Between Banks and Building Societies in the Retailing of Financial Services', *British Journal of Management*, Vol. 3, pp. 160–179.

Martin, T. (1991), *Financial Services Direct Marketing*, Maidenhead, McGraw-Hill.

Mayes, R. (1993) 'Euro spend for DM Climbs to Top £20bn', *Precision Marketing*, 23 August, p. 6.

Moutinho, L. and Meidan, A. (1989), 'Bank Customers' Perceptions, Innovations and New Technology', *International Journal of Bank Marketing*, Vol. 7, No. 2, pp. 22–27.

P. A. Management Consultants Ltd. (1983), *Direct Marketing in Financial Institutions: A Preliminary Survey*, London, P.A.

Roberts, M. L. and Berger, P. O. (1989), *Direct Marketing Management*, New Jersey, Prentice-Hall.

Roman, E. (1988), *Integrated Direct Marketing: Techniques and Strategies for Success*, New York, McGraw-Hill.

Scarborough, H. and Lannon, R. (1989). 'The Management of Innovation in the Financial Services Sector', *Journal of Marketing Management*, Vol. 5, No. 1, pp. 51–62.

Stone, M. and Clarkson, A. (1989), 'MIS and the Strategic Development of Financial Institutions', *Marketing Intelligence and Planning*, Vol. 7, No. 12, pp. 22–30.

Thwaites, D. (1989), 'The Impact of Environmental Change on the Evolution of the UK Building Society Industry', *The Service Industries Journal*, Vol. 9, No. 1, pp. 40–60.

Thwaites, D. (1991), 'Forces at Work: The Market for Personal Financial Services', *International Journal of Bank Marketing*, Vol. 9, No. 6, pp. 30–36.

Thwaites, D. and Lynch, J. E. (1992), 'The Adoption of the Marketing Concept by UK Building Societies', *The Service Industries Journal*, Vol. 12, No. 4, pp. 437–462.

Thwaites, D. (1992), 'Organisational Influences on the New Product Development Process in Financial Services', *Journal of Product Innovation Management*, Vol. 9, No. 4, pp. 303–313.

Thwaites, D. and Glaister, K. W. (1992), 'Strategic Responses to Environmental Turbulence', *International Journal of Bank Marketing*, Vol. 10, No. 3, pp. 33–40.

Woodcock, N. (1992), 'How to Get the Best Out of Your Database'. In: *The Absolute Essentials* (Teddington), The Direct Marketing Centre, p. 3.

17

Mortgage-Pricing Determinants: a Comparative Investigation of National, Regional and Local Building Societies

Arthur Meidan and Alan C. Chin

INTRODUCTION

Recently, mortgage pricing has become an increasingly important issue for the building societies. The main reasons for this are the intense competition from retailing banks, new entrants into the market and other financial institutions, and the economic recession. Until the breakdown of the building society cartel in 1983, the issue of pricing was not given serious attention by individual building societies. Before 1983, interest rates and mortgage rates were fixed by the cartel and all members of the Building Societies Association acted as price-takers in the market. It is believed that much of the significant growth and constant high level of profitability of building societies during the 1970s and early 1980s was due to the firm foundation of interest rates fixed by the cartel. Comfortable margins provided a reasonable cushion to cover management expenses and provide an adequate profit for business growth.

In the early 1980s, banks sensed the lucrative markets that were traditionally dominated by building societies, namely retail (personal) savings and mortgage markets. The competition in the mortgage market intensified in the mid-1980s when many new players entered this market and managed to undercut a massive market share from building societies. Building societies started to realize that in order to compete with new lenders and banks they had to trim their margins. This action put pressure on the less efficient societies and this marked the official end of the cartel role of the Building Societies Association.

Pricing soon became an important marketing weapon to regain market share and to enhance the profitability of individual building societies. The pressure faced by building societies in the early 1980s also led to the review of the Building Societies Act of 1962 and the introduction of the new Building Societies Act followed in July 1986. The combined effect of the Building Societies Act of 1986 and the increased competition in the 1980s has caused building societies to be much more profit-conscious over a wider range of investments, including mortgage products.

Nowadays the building societies industry realizes that it is important to get the margins right and to keep costs under control. The fundamental role of pricing forces building societies to direct serious attention to pricing policies, in the light of their corporate objectives.

This study focuses on the pricing of mortgages—which are the major product on which most building societies concentrate. Mortgage pricing mentioned throughout this article is defined as the determination of standard mortgage rates that building societies in the UK offer to retail mortgage borrowers. More specifically the objectives of this study are to:

- compare and contrast the mortgage-pricing approaches between national, regional and local building societies; and
- identify the importance of various mortgage-pricing determinants which are to be taken into account when building societies determine their mortgage rates.

LITERATURE REVIEW

There is indeed very limited published research on pricing in building societies. Among the most important studies on pricing in financial services, we find Whittle and Handel (1987), who discuss the importance of conveying the perception of value of banks' prices. They suggest that this could be done through creating the right pricing environment through research, pricing committees and employee-training programmes. They also examine the variables influencing pricing in banks, such as operating costs, elasticity of demand and market segmentation.

Howcroft and Lavis (1989) recognized pricing as an essential component of retail banking. They stated that pricing in banking is implicit and overt because the true cost of customer service is often not truly reflected in the price charged. However, they stressed that, as retail banking becomes more competitive and price-driven, more accurate and explicit pricing becomes increasingly possible. More importantly, they brought up the issue of different customers' perceptions and requirements, which can be derived from different market segments.

Ford (1987) outlined five principal stages in the evolution of a bank's non-credit products and concluded that banks must price in order that they at least cover their costs and attain specific marketing and product strategic goals.

Research on pricing in banking is reflected in the work of other researchers. Pezzullo (1982), for instance, discussed the necessity of primary and secondary research, as an important basis on which pricing decisions for banks should be made. She also made a distinction between market demand and individual bank demand. Finally, she underlined the importance of government regulations as a determinant of banks' pricing. Channon (1986) introduced the concept of market penetration pricing for banks and also reiterated the idea that pricing strategies for banks are functions of demand, competitor prices and cost structure. Gwin (1986) raises the question of benefit pricing or pricing based on the value that customers place on services.

Llewellyn (1988) pointed out that factors such as competition from a wide range of financial institutions (clearing banks, insurance companies, foreign banks), as well as changes in Government regulations (e.g. allowing societies to develop optimum funding mix), have increased the menu of strategic options opened to building societies and their ability to use pricing as a possible competitive tool.

What is common among all the studies mentioned above is the recognition that pricing policies are influenced by determinants such as cost, competition, Government legislation, elasticity of demand and customers' perception of value. What has *not* been specifically investigated by previous studies is how these determinants influence the pricing decisions of building societies. It is this issue that this study attempts to investigate. Using the above pricing determinants as criteria, the present study compares the pricing approaches of national, regional and local building societies regarding the standard mortgage product. Literature review suggests that there are two basic approaches to pricing used by the building societies sector: *cost-based* and *market-driven*.

Cost-based

This approach is widely used in the general financial services sector. It involves calculating both direct and indirect costs for a particular service, say mortgage, and then a profit element is added to the total costs. The main advantage of this method is that, if cost structures are known, the pricing task becomes simplified. However, a cost-based pricing system takes no account of the competitive situation, nor the willingness of the customer to pay. In other words, it does not recognize any strategic objective(s) of a building society, except costs and profit; nor does it recognize that long-term goals can be met by sacrificing short-term goals (Day, 1987). In addition, cost calculations for services tend, generally, to be imprecise. Nevertheless, despite the imprecision of costs calculation, a cost-based pricing strategy is easier to carry out in a building society than in a bank, because the former derives its income mainly from mortgages, whereas the latter obtains revenue from a very wide range of services. The reason is simply that a bank faces the problem of disproportionate cost distribution over the various services it offers.

Market-driven

This approach to pricing is based on the *market price* for the service, which is the overriding factor (Lawrence, 1988). This type of pricing is generally used in highly-competitive environments where many players are offering similar services, e.g. mortgage lending. The advantage of this pricing approach is that not only is cost taken into account, but also the market considerations dominate pricing decisions. There are two methods in this category: competitive pricing and differential pricing. Competitive (or going-rate pricing) describes a situation in which the price is set according to what the market leader is charging. Differential pricing takes into account the ability and willingness of the market segments to pay. Usually, it is employed in order to try to maximize the profit margins of building societies.

THE MORTGAGE-PRICING DETERMINANTS

As the literature on mortgage pricing is indeed rather limited, unstructured interviews were conducted with chief executives, mortgage managers and product development managers of seven randomly selected building societies (three national, two regional and two local) in an attempt to identify the factors that affect mortgage-pricing policies in the building societies industry.

During the unstructured interviews, it became apparent that the mortgage-pricing policies of various building societies vary according to whether the society is national, regional or local (Meidan, 1986). Mortgage pricing is also influenced by the building societies' views on their main corporate strategies (regarding mortgage market(s)) and the importance attached to the six mortgage-pricing determinants:

(1) Costs
(2) Elasticity of demand
(3) Competitors' prices
(4) Customers' perception of value
(5) Government regulations
(6) Bank base rate.

The total number of building societies at the time of this study (1993) was 89. The distinction between national, regional and local building societies was based on two alternative criteria: total assets and the number of branches. Building societies with total assets of over £5000 million were classified as national; between £500 million–£5000 million assets were classified as regional and those with less than £500 million assets were classified as local building societies.

The alternative way of categorizing building societies is by the number of branches that each building society has. In this study, a national building society had more than 150 branches, a regional building society had between 30 and 150 branches and a local building society had fewer than 30 branches. Each method of categorization gave similar results: i.e. ten national, 19 regional and 60 local building societies were identified (see Table 1).

The six main pricing determinants mentioned above have received varied attention in literature and could be summarized (Figure 1) as follows.

Table 1. The national, regional and local building societies—total number of societies in each category and response rate to questionnaire.

Type of building society	Number of building societies	Response rate No.	Percentage
National (Assets: £5000m +; over 150 branches per society)	10	6	60
Regional (Assets: £500m to £5000m; 30 to 150 branches)	19	10	53
Local (Assets: less than £500m; under 30 branches per building society)	60	29	48
Total	89	45	50.6

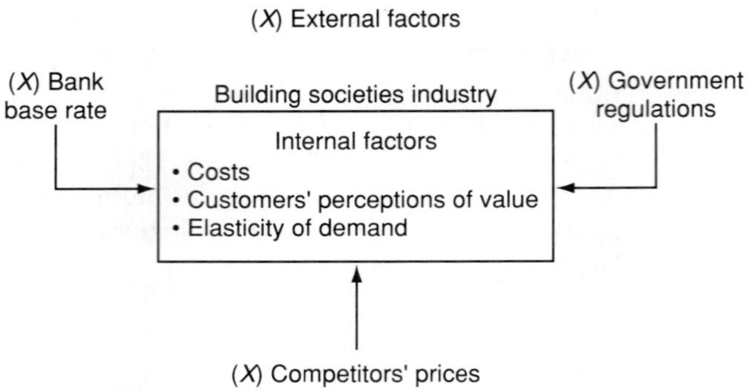

Figure 1. Internal and external factors affecting mortgage pricing in the building societies industry.

Costs

Pezzullo (1982) stated that, unless a firm makes the intentional decision to sell a product or service at a loss for reasons it considers appropriate, the cost of providing the product or service must serve as the floor under which the price must not go. The costs of a building society take three major forms:

(1) *Fixed costs.* Costs which remain fixed no matter how variable sales are. Fixed costs consist of two main components: direct, and general and administrative expenses (G & A). Direct costs relate to the principal resources the building society has in place to provide its services. These include: buildings, land, equipment, full-time staff and data-processing expenses. G & A costs are those that are incurred to support and administer the organization. Examples of these are: advertising, administrative salaries and expenses, insurance, etc.
(2) *Variable costs.* Costs which vary with the amount of sales (or accounts). These include postage, stamps, leaflets, part-time help and the like.
(3) *Total costs.* These consist of the sum of fixed and variable costs mentioned above. A building society must charge a price that will at least cover its total costs in the long run for the successful operation of the society.

The main cost component in the mortgage product is variable, i.e. the cost of capital (such as interest that the society pays on shares, deposits and loans). The fixed costs (overheads) are also a very substantial cost component because of the need to operate an extensive branch network, invest in technology, and pay staff's salaries and wages. As the costs of capital are comparable, building societies could reduce their mortgage price (rate) mainly by becoming more efficient in their management of fixed costs (overheads).

Elasticity of demand

Generally speaking, one of the major determinants of a pricing policy for a particular service—including mortgages—is the uncertainty about how the market will respond to a price change. When demand is inelastic, a price increase can actually increase total revenue, even though the number of mortgages has declined. When demand is elastic, a price increase can reduce total revenue because the decline in sales is significant. A building society, in trying to maximize its profits, should increase the price of inelastic services and reduce the price of elastic ones. In short, by knowing the elasticity of demand of each segment for each service/mortgage provided, differential pricing can be employed to achieve profit maximization.

Competitors' prices

A building society can use whatever knowledge it has of its competitors' mortgage prices as a guide in setting its own prices. Since financial products can be copied within a very short period of time, any competitive advantage will be essentially of short-term duration. In addition, customers have perfect information on prices offered by various building societies. As a result, according to our findings from interviews with building society managers, competitors' prices become an important guide for a building society. Societies will then price their services—including mortgages—in the light of projected profit and market share.

Customers' perception of value

This determinant of pricing has increased in importance since the 1970s. Gwin (1986) calls this factor 'benefit pricing', which basically means that pricing is carried out according to the benefits that customers perceive they can obtain from a particular service. If the benefits or the value of a service is high in a customer's eyes, he would be more willing to pay a higher price.

To illustrate this, a building society which has a prestigious reputation—say the Halifax or the Nationwide Anglia—and caters for diversified and huge market segments, can afford to price its services according to the perceptions of customers from different market segments. These building societies can cater for customers from the more affluent markets who perceive and expect greater value for their custom, as well as catering for the less wealthy market segments. In this way, a pricing policy which takes account of different perceptions from differentiated market segments is more likely to maximize profitability for the building society.

Government regulations

The most important Government regulation concerning building societies' pricing is related to the wholesale funding limit proportion (percentage) in relation to societies' total assets. Obviously, for larger building societies in particular, the access to corporate funding (in addition to retail deposits) as a potential source for funding retail mortgage demand is of some significance.

Bank base rate

Until 1983, building societies operated their price policies as a cartel. This is no longer the case and there are several explanations for the less regulated pricing policies in the mortgage lending market (Mansfield, 1990). As buyers have very good information on price-offers in the market, if a society charges higher mortgage rates, it will price itself out of the market, as customers can look for a cheaper price with other societies.

'Building societies have a rate called the mortgage base rate'

The bank base rate is the minimum bank lending rate that is fixed by the Bank of England. For mortgage lending, building societies have a rate called the mortgage base rate that fluctuates with the change of bank base rate. The mortgage base rate serves the minimum rate that a building society will offer on its mortgage products. However, unlike the bank base rate, the mortgage base rate is determined by individual societies rather than governing bodies.

Among the six determinants outlined previously, Government regulations, bank base rate and competitors' prices are the external factors that building societies cannot change as they wish. It is in the interest of building societies to manipulate the remaining three internal determinants (Figure 1) to adjust their price policies in the light of their objectives and strategies.

BUILDING SOCIETIES' STRATEGIES AND MORTGAGE-PRICING POLICY

The traditional marketing literature mentions the three main corporate strategies: focus, differentiation and cost leadership (Porter, 1980). These three corporate strategies are extremely well-known and have received a lot of attention in literature [see note 1]. This is—as far as we know—the first attempt to investigate these strategies in the context of building societies' strategies and pricing policies.

Focus

This strategy emphasizes a particular market segment only, as the target market. It involves offering a product/service which meets the needs of a specific group of customers. An organization which adopts the focus strategy will seek to serve the chosen segment particularly well. By doing so, a building society is more likely to achieve lower cost or differentiation—in that particular segment—compared with competitors who are not focusing on that market segment. Similar to the differentiation strategy, the focus strategy always creates some limitations on the overall achievable market share. It frequently involves a trade-off between profitability and sale volume. For example, the Clay Cross Building Society is a small local building society which concentrates on the local catchment areas in the small town of Clay Cross, near Chesterfield.

Differentiation

This strategy is based on offering a product or service that is unique to the market. Approaches to differentiation strategy can take many forms: design or brand image, technology, customer service, features, etc. This strategy increases the uniqueness of the product/service—as perceived by the customer—and hence reduces the price sensitivity of demand. It also reduces the risk of substitution. It should be stressed that the differentiation strategy does not allow the building society to ignore costs because it requires high levels of skill and creativity among staff and co-operation throughout the organization. These can include extensive research, product design and intensive customer support. The uniqueness of the product/service might, however, limit the market share gained by the company.

'The Skipton Building Society pursues the differentiation strategy'

The Skipton Building Society is one of the building societies that pursues the differentiation strategy. In its financial statement summary for 1991, it claimed that 'The Skipton Building Society will continue the policies of keeping the reputation, innovation and giving members a competitive product...' The Leeds Permanent Building Society, on the other hand, differentiated itself from competitors through introducing a free 'Home Arranger Service' which guides home buyers from start to finish throughout the process of house buying.

Cost leadership

This strategy is based on having the lowest costs, and hence the greatest profit margins. The cost leader will be in a better position than its competitors, because of its extra profit owing to a lower level of cost. Cost leadership requires aggressive construction of efficient-scale facilities, vigorous pursuit of cost reductions from experience, tight cost control and leanness of the organization. This strategy also requires heavy capital investment and aggressive pricing to build a high market share. High market share may in turn allow exploitation of any economies of scale and experience which lower costs even further. It appears that this strategy may only be possible for some of the larger building societies (Speed, 1990). Examples of building societies that could employ this strategy are the Halifax and the Nationwide Building Society.

Interestingly, it is seldom that a building society employs only one of the three generic strategies suggested above. Throughout the interviews of this study, it was found that the three generic strategies are not mutually exclusive. The building societies interviewed revealed that all three generic strategies are adopted by various societies simultaneously, in order to achieve a range of corporate objectives. Furthermore, a building society can, and always does, have more than one objective. For instance, Halifax Building Society wants to remain the 'No. 1' lender in the mortgage market, to achieve a certain level of profitability and to be differentiated from other competitors. At times, it also concentrates on certain market segments, for example, first time buyers. All three generic strategies are employed to achieve a range of objectives at the same time by an organization. Because of the range of mutually exclusive objectives, pricing decisions tend to be neither straightforward nor autonomous (Howcroft and Lavis, 1989).

METHODOLOGY

Following the preliminary interviews with building societies' executives mentioned above, seven-point Likert scale questionnaire was developed and pilot-tested with executives in five further building societies. The objectives of the questionnaire were to collect information on:

- The importance of each of the six price determinants (factors), that are taken into consideration when pricing mortgages and were previously identified following the literature review and interviews with building societies' mortgage managers. These were: costs, competitors' prices, customers' perception of value, elasticity of demand, Government regulations, and bank base rate.
- The importance of the three main strategies pursued by their respective building societies in the mortgage market (focus, differentiation, or cost leadership) and the importance of the three main pricing policy objectives for respective building societies (profit margins, market share, and mutuality).

Eighty-nine copies of the questionnaire, along with enclosed stamped self-addressed envelopes and covering letters, were mailed to the head office of all the 89 building societies listed in the *Directory of Members* in June 1993. In order to improve the response rate, five national and ten regional and local building societies' head offices were telephoned at random. The data collected were analysed by mean scores, rankings, and percentages.

There were two underlying assumptions throughout the analysis and the interpretation of the results of this study. These were as follows:

(1) If the difference between two means was greater than 10 per cent of the small mean, it was considered that these two means were significantly different from each other. (The scores have not been tested with t-tests, because the data collected—via Likert scale questions—were non-parametric; consequently, a non-parametric test has been used.)
(2) As the data collected represented a big proportion of the population (the response rate was 50.6 per cent or 45 building societies), it was logical to assume that a significant difference at the 10 per cent level between two means indeed represented a real difference within the building society industry.

As the investigation attempted to analyse comparatively the three categories of building societies (i.e. national, regional and local), it was necessary that the sample size in *each* category includes about (or more than) half of the population size in each subgroup. This has been achieved (see Table 1) and therefore the data analysis and results are realistic and meaningful.

STUDY FINDINGS

The importance of pricing determinants

As can be seen from Table 2, cost was the most important factor among all the six price determinants for all the three categories of building societies. National building societies stated that cost was an 'extremely important' determinant in mortgage pricing, while regional and local building societies ranked it as 'very important'. Since a national building society normally enjoys a bigger market share compared with a regional or local society and it inevitably has a larger distribution network and number of staff to handle the business, this distribution network plays a very important role in the cost structure and therefore this kind of building society must pay particular attention to cost savings.

Table 2. Importance of mortgage price determinants for national, regional and local building societies—mean scores and importance ranking order.

Price factors/determinants	National Order of importance	National Mean score[a]	Regional Order of importance	Regional Mean score[a]	Local Order of importance	Local Mean score[a]
Costs	1	1.17	1	2.00[b]	1	1.86
Competitors' price	2	1.83	2	2.00[b]	2	2.07
Bank base rate	3	2.50	4	2.60	4	2.66
Customers' perception of value	4	3.33	3	2.15	3	2.25
Elasticity of demand	5	3.50	6	3.70	6	3.21
Government regulations	6	5.33	5	3.50	5	3.14

[a] 1 being 'extremely important' and 7 'least important'.
[b] Although both cost and competitors' price have the same ranking mean, i.e. 2.00, the standard deviation (not presented here) for the 'costs' is smaller. Therefore it is ranked before the latter for regional building societies.

Competitors' price was the second most important regional pricing determinant for national building societies, but this factor was seen to be as important as costs by regional and—to some extent also—by local building societies. There is no significant difference between the ranking means of the three categories of building society and this supports the statement that competitors' price was a 'very important' pricing determinant throughout the building societies sector.

Customers' perception of value was considered almost equally important by regional and local building societies. However, again, national building societies indicated a rather different viewpoint towards this pricing determinant. A mean of 3.33 indicates that customers' perceptions of value is a 'fairly important' factor in mortgage pricing. Bearing in mind that the majority of national building societies normally cater for wider and more diversified markets than the other types of building societies, they are (relatively) less sensitive to a change in their customers' perception of value. National societies tend to give a lesser importance to this price determinant. Unlike national building societies, regional and local societies ranked this factor as a 'very important' pricing determinant. Being more close to their specific local and regional markets, customers' perception of value is more highly appreciated.

Elasticity of demand was ranked as rather less important by all three categories of building society. The possible reason could be that, since mortgage products provided by building societies are virtually identical and each building society only accounts for a very small proportion of the total market share in the industry (the characteristics of a perfectly competitive market), there is no point in pricing products particularly low in order to attract more business.

Mortgage rates, in general, fluctuate alongside the bank base rate fixed by the Bank of England, although the former is always higher than the latter. When the bank base rate is changed, it is usually the Halifax or the Nationwide Building Society that initiates the change in mortgage rate in the industry. Other building societies will then determine their own mortgage base rate according to these leaders. Hence, the bank base rate is regarded by all three categories as a fairly important index which building societies refer to when pricing their mortgages.

The most varied opinion concerning pricing determinants held by building societies was Government regulations. This determinant was regarded as 'unimportant' by national building societies. Local building societies, on the contrary, viewed this factor as 'important' in their mortgage pricing. Regional building societies ranked it less important. Although the same regulations apply throughout the industry, different opinions were observed. As far as mortgage pricing is concerned, there is no particular legislation imposed on the freedom of setting mortgage rates, yet local building societies are definitely more concerned about this factor as a possible mortgage price determinant, probably because of their limited access to corporate (wholesale) funds. As a result, local societies feel more vulnerable to Government legislation relating to funding sources and gearing ratios.

'Larger societies were proactive in their strategic marketing activities'

To sum up, it is apparent from Table 2 that cost and competitors' price are the two most important determinants in mortgage pricing in the building society industry. All three categories of building societies have ranked cost and competitors' prices as one and two, respectively. It is worth noting that both regional and local building societies have identical ranking, in comparison with national building societies which ranked the remaining determinants quite differently.

Main strategies employed by building societies

Table 3 indicates that the strategy most preferred by the majority (68 per cent) of all the building societies is the focus strategy. However, when closely examining the preferences of the societies investigated, it can be seen that about half of the national building societies prefer to adopt a differentiation strategy, with cost leadership in second place. Among the regional building societies both focus and cost leadership are equally preferred. Only for the local building societies is the focus strategy clearly the preferred one (26 out of 29 local building societies adopt this strategy), probably because they are too small to serve anything else except a particular segment (or a niche) of the mortgage market. Ennew et al. (1989), by comparison, suggested that 40 per cent of all building societies utilize a cost-focus strategy and about 29 per cent employ a cost-led strategy. Edgett and Thwaites (1990) have investigated the major differences in marketing strategies of large versus small building societies. Their study suggests that larger societies were proactive in their strategic marketing activities, while smaller societies were found to be reactive.

There are generally two types of corporate objectives pursued by building societies: profit and growth. A profit-oriented building society tends to emphasize short-term

Table 3. Main strategies employed by national, regional and local building societies (number of societies).

Main strategy employed	Category of building society			Total No. (percentage)
	National	Regional	Local	
Focus	1	4	26	31 (68)
Differentiation	3	2	2	7 (16)
Cost leadership	2	4	1	7 (16)
Total	6	10	29	45 (100)

profitability. The pricing objective for this building society would be to aim for profit maximization. On the other hand, a building society, the primary corporate objective of which is market share, would build its market share at the cost of short-term profit (Howcroft and Lavis, 1989). In this case, the pricing objective is to increase the customer base rather than the return on investment.

When investigating building societies' primary pricing objectives, three main objectives were identified: mutuality (i.e. equal benefits for the building society *and* the customers served), profit margins (which is a short-term objective) and market share (which is a strategic, long-term objective). The findings of the study (Table 4) suggest that about 80 per cent of all the building societies opt for profits margins as their primary corporate objective. Only six (13 per cent) of the building societies opt for market share, most of them local building societies that attempt to achieve a larger share of the local market in which they specialize. It is interesting to compare the present study results with Edgett and Thwaites' research (1990), which indicated that the primary objective of a majority (85 per cent) of all building societies in 1989 was sales growth.

CONCLUSIONS

This study suggests that larger building societies (i.e. national and regional) view profit margin rather than market share as their first priority. This can be explained as follows:

- Top management is frequently forced to pursue short-term returns (margins) which are shown on the annual profit and loss accounts on which their performance is assessed. Marketers who forgo short-term profitability to build a bigger market share, which is often believed to result in a bigger return in the long run, may be dismissed or penalized before the expected larger profit is realized. This pressure is termed as short-term pressure (STP) by Demirag and Tylecote (1992).
- It is usually easier to increase market share than profit margins, since mortgage products can always be priced more competitively to attract more custom—owing to the characteristics of a highly-competitive market environment. A reduction in price, however, normally cannot be offset by an increase in the volume sold in the financial services industry. The reason is that the production costs in the financial services industry are relatively low—compared with manufacturing industries—so they cannot be depressed much further. As a result, the profitability may be jeopardized. In other words, management usually have more difficulties in manipulating their profit margins than their market share.

Table 4. Primary pricing objectives of national, regional and local building societies compared.

Primary pricing objective	Category of building society			Total No. (percentage)
	National	Regional	Local	
Mutuality	—	1	2	3 (70)
Profit margins	6	8	22	36 (80)
Market share	—	1	5	6 (13)
Total	6	10	29	45 (100)

Overall, a large majority (80 per cent) of all the building societies indicated that their main mortgage-pricing objective is profit margins. Only some (17 per cent) of the local building societies have market share as their primary pricing objective. Mutuality (i.e. equal benefits for the building society *and* its customers), which was the main *reason* for the establishment and development of the building society movement, is now a primary pricing objective for just three (out of 45) of the building societies that took part in the study.

In order to facilitate the higher profit margins, building societies select strategies that match their size and market characteristics. For example, most (90 per cent) of the local building societies prefer to employ a focus strategy, probably owing to the fact that these societies are too small to serve wider markets or a larger number of market segments. National building societies, on the other hand, prefer to adopt mainly differentiation and cost leadership strategies, because of the variety of market segments and the larger national market in which they operate.

'Costs' and 'competitors' prices' were found to be the two most important mortgage-pricing determinants, each of these two factors being considered as a 'very important' pricing determinant throughout the building societies sector.

Customers' perception of value was considered 'very important' equally by both local and regional building societies. National societies—which cater for a wider, more segmented market—have ranked this determinant as only 'fairly important'. While all the three categories of building societies are fairly similar in the importance they attach to the elasticity of demand and bank base rate as pricing determinants, the societies differ on the importance attached to Government regulations; this despite the fact that these regulations apply equally throughout the industry. Local building societies are, overall, definitely more concerned about the roles of Government regulations and their effect on their pricing policies.

'This profit margin objective is achieved through a focus strategy'

In conclusion, this study seems to indicate that building societies' mortgage pricing is influenced primarily by internal industry determinants, such as costs and competitors' prices, and to a much lesser extent by market-related factors, e.g. customers' perception of value and/or elasticity of demand.

The high level of competition in the retail mortgage market has resulted in just very few societies (mainly local) using the pricing tool to achieve long-term strategic objective, such as market share. Four out of every five building societies are clearly short-term profit margin-oriented, and this applies to all the national building societies investigated.

This profit margin objective is achieved in the local building societies sector through the employment of a focus strategy. National and regional building societies aim at achieving their profit margins mainly by differentiation and cost leadership strategies.

As the retail mortgage markets become more price-competitive, building societies must reassess their price policies. The traditional pricing objectives, such as profit maximization and market share, are currently achieved through due attention to critical factors such as costs and competitors' prices. It is clear that, as deregulation and world market competition become even more prominent, pricing determinants such as value of service to special customers' segments, and/or the elasticity of demand of selected target market(s), may play a more important role in order to enhance customer loyalty and increase the usage of selected mortgage products.

NOTE

1. A very large number of papers on generic strategies have been published in the last 14 years or so; it is beyond the scope of this article—mainly because of length reasons—to review these publications, particularly as the focus of the study is on mortgage price policy as employed by local, regional and national building societies.

REFERENCES

Channon, D. F. (1986), *Bank Strategic Management and Marketing*, John Wiley & Sons, New York, NY, p. 135.
Day, A. (1987), 'Setting the right price', *International Journal of Bank Marketing*, Vol. 5 No. 5, pp. 20–6.
Demirag, I. and Tylecote, A. (1992), 'The effects of organizational, cultural and market expectations on technological innovation: a hypothesis', *British Journal of Management*, Vol. 3, pp. 7–20.
Edgett, S. and Thwaites, D. (1990), 'The influence of environmental change on the marketing practices of building societies', *European Journal of Marketing*, Vol. 24 No. 12, pp. 35–47.
Ennew, C., Wright, M. and Watkins, T. (1989), 'Marketing strategies in a changing competitive environment: the financial services in the UK', in Moutinho, L., Brownlie, D. and Livingstone, J. (Eds), *Marketing Audit of the '80s*, Marketing Education Group, Glasgow, pp. 943–69.
Ford, R. P. (1987), 'Pricing operating services', *The Bankers Magazine*, Vol. 170 No. 3, pp. 70–2.
Gwin, J. M. (1986), 'Pricing financial institution products: methods and strategies', in Winston, W. J. (Ed.), *Working for Financial Services*, The Howarth Press, London, pp. 182–201.
Howcroft, J. B. and Lavis, J. C. (1989), 'Pricing in retail banking', *International Journal of Bank Marketing*, Vol. 7 No. 1, pp. 3–7.
Lawrence, T. J. Jr (1988), 'Strategies for pricing core loans and deposits', *The Bankers Magazine*, November/December, pp. 47–52.
Llewellyn, D. (1988), 'The challenge from the building societies', *Banking World*, Vol. 6 No. 7, pp. 32–5.
Mansfield, E. (1990), *Managerial Economics: Theory Applications and Cases*, W. W. Morton and Company Inc., New York, NY, pp. 343–4.
Meidan, A. (1986), *Building Society Marketing and Development*, The Chartered Building Societies Institute, Ware, UK, pp. 75–7.
Pezzullo, M. A. (1982), *Marketing for Bankers*, American Bankers Association, Chicago, IL, pp. 126–38.
Porter, M. E. (1980), *Competitive Strategy: Generic Competitive Strategies, Techniques for Analysing Industries and Competitors*, The Free Press, New York, NY, pp. 34–40.
Speed, R. (1990), 'Building societies: new strategies for a competitive era', *The Services Industries Journal*, Vol. 10 No. 1, pp. 40–59.
Whittle, J. W. and Handel, W. M. (1987), 'Pricing strategies for competitive banks', *The Bankers Magazine*, Vol. 170 No. 5, pp. 45–50.

Part VI

Branch Management and Distribution

CONTENTS

Introduction to Part VI 259

18 Bank Branch Managers: Their Roles and Function in a Marketing Era 262
   S. DENG, L. MOUTINHO and A. MEIDEN, *International Journal of Bank Marketing* (1991), **9** (3), 32–38.
19 The Changing Lending Role of Managers in the Financial Services Sector 273
   M. HUGHES, *International Journal of Service Industry Management* (1992), **3** (4), 30–43.
20 Network Management and the Branch Distribution Channel 287
   S. J. GREENLAND, *International Journal of Bank Marketing* (1995), **13** (4), 12–18.
21 Branch Networks and Insurance Selling 299
   G. MORGAN, *International Journal of Bank Marketing* (1993), **11** (5), 27–32.

Introduction to Part VI

The distribution of financial services has rapidly evolved over the past decade. New methods of distribution have emerged and the old branch channel has been transformed from being transaction and processing driven to a highly customer-focused retail and selling setting.

The distribution of financial services is an extremely dynamic area that has been completely revolutionized in recent years. The principal motivating forces behind this stem from the ever growing need for enhanced efficiencies and the drive for accountability in bank functions. Greater industry competition and economic hardship have dictated that marketing activities must be more effective. Merger/acquisition activity has produced a confused corporate identity across some networks, as well as 'over-banking' in certain areas. Many outlets are out of fashion and require renovation to satisfy present day tastes. The dynamic found in many core retail areas resulted in many branches finding themselves in less than optimum locations. Financial consumers have become more sophisticated, with discerning needs that must be catered for, and frequently hold accounts with several institutions. The number of financial products and services on offer has grown substantially and outlets providing specialist services have been developed. Technological developments and miniaturization have increased efficiencies. Network management has become a focus of attention. The branch is now recognized as an important contributor to competitive advantage. Highly efficient telephone banking service delivery systems have been developed, refined and implemented by many institutions.

As the importance of financial services continues to grow throughout the world, pressures are building for a more effective and efficient marketing of the services offered to customers at the branch level. Financial services organizations need to rethink their strategies in the current environment and this applies also to branch level. Branch competition, always strong, is now fierce. Only those banks that can deliver what the customer wants in the most efficient way will be most successful. New advances in electronic funds transfers, such as automated teller machines, can be of tremendous help in meeting customer needs. Bank branch strategy is already changing in order to emphasize the need to communicate with and sell to customers. Branch management should concentrate on the key ingredients of customer orientation and competitive position by gathering and analysing customer information, understanding the direction and speed of competitive changes, relating these findings to the business capabilities, recommending a customer-orientated approach to service the market, developing strategic and tactical plans for implementation, and monitoring their progress. Bank branches that make the marketing orientation and integral part of their culture will find a sustainable competitive advantage. Implementing the marketing concept internally certainly would challenge many bank branches because it defies tradition. It would require numerous significant changes. The more marketing-oriented approach to financial services has been supported through changes in the branch networks, while the concept of large branch networks has been questioned in the light of rising costs.

Branch administration is an area of major concern for financial institutions, as any failure at branch level could affect the marketing success significantly and indeed the survival of the whole establishment. Branch managers are once again seen increasingly to be playing a distinctive and important role. The first article of this section by Deng, Moutinho and Meidan aims at presenting some of the new, versus the existing, functions of bank branch managers. It attempts to explore the nature and direction of the new functional roles of bank branch managers. Their findings reveal that the most important factors that help the bank branch managers to face new market trends are improving the quality of customer service, motivation of employees, developing effective relationships with customers, staff training and management training, and generation of new business.

The second article by Mark Hughes summarizes two studies of managerial work within the UK financial services sector. The focus here is on the managers' lending role, which has been identified as a major aspect of the role of the manager. Case studies of the mortgage lending role of managers in the building society and the small business lending role of managers in the bank are presented. The lending role of the managers studied did appear to be changing and it was possible to summarize these changes in terms of four aspects of the managers' lending role: the manager as line manager, salesperson, product expert and decision maker. In both organizations, managers in the branches underestimated future developments in terms of the scope of change. It is in this area of decision-making that future changes appeared most probable. Organizational change appeared to mirror cultural change taking place throughout the sector, with a move away from the traditional banking culture. The stereotypical branch manager appeared to be disappearing. It is unlikely that financial services organizations have been able to develop managers at the same pace as the expansion in the volume of their business. Parallel to this has been the need to develop skills within the managers to deal with the changing environment. The rationale for changes within managerial work in the financial services sector is a consequence of skilled and experienced managers becoming a scarce resource.

The third article in this section of the book is by Steven J. Greenland. It describes the continuing role of the branch in distribution strategies and outlines the key physical transformations that have occurred in the branch channel and the rationale behind them. The key issues discussed by the author relate to the scope of branch network management and the physical transformation of branch networks – branch members, ATM members, the importance of branch design, the evolution in branch design, the network hierarchy and the spatial arrangement of branch networks.

Following on the same theme, the final article by Glenn Morgan focuses on branch networks and insurance selling. The article presents evidence from three retail financial services institutions which are publicly considered to be successful examples of how to sell insurance products within branch networks. The author shows that each of the institutions organizes this process in different ways and each of them is consequently faced with a different range of problems. It is argued that these problems are endemic to the formation of an integrated insurance and deposit-taking operation. The article concludes by arguing that the operational problems are likely to be minimized where the process of integration is taken furthest.

18

Bank Branch Managers: Their Roles and Functions in a Marketing Era

Shengliang Deng, Luiz Moutinho and Arthur Meidan

Since the introduction of computers and electronic devices into the banking industry, the growth of traditional, full-service bank offices has slowed significantly. Indeed, many countries have experienced a steady decline in the number of bank branch offices. According to the Canadian Bankers' Association, Canada lost almost 400 branch offices, from 7414 in 1980 to 7007 in 1986. The phenomenon has prompted many industry analysts and banking experts to predict confidently that bank branch offices are 'doomed' in today's world, where financial information can be transferred in microseconds and where computers and ATM have invaded almost every family's life in North America. Today, however, to the surprise of many, a new reality is setting in. The old reliable, full-service branch office isn't dead. Rather, it is evolving—its role and image are changing (Berry, 1982; Rose, 1986).

As the importance of financial services continues to grow throughout the world, pressures are building for a more effective and efficient marketing of the services offered to customers at the branch level. Branch managers are assessed for their standards of written work, internal and external communication, appearance, customer service, and community relations, as well as for their staff efficiency and overall profitability. Hence, branch administration is an area of major concern for financial institutions, as any failure at branch level could affect the marketing success significantly and indeed the survival of the whole establishment.

The banking markets are changing rapidly and financial institutions have to adapt to these changes. Indeed, significant changes in the Eastern bloc, EC development towards one currency, and the global debt structure are likely to have an increasing effect on banks and financial markets in the 1990s. Financial services organisations need to rethink their strategies in the current environment and this applies to the branch level as well. Marketing is likely to become an even more important and fundamental driving force for Canadian banking strategy in the future (Canadian Bankers Association, 1985a).

Canadian banks operate in an environment that has compelled them relentlessly to improve their productivity. They function in a country with huge territorial space but a small bilingual population. They are full-service banks, serving governments, large corporations, small businesses, farmers, homeowners, and other financial institutions, at home and abroad. One significant trend has been the increasingly global nature of

Canadian banks. They have developed a formidable presence on the international scene to meet the needs of a nation that derives a large part of its income from global trade (Bradford, 1983). In many important spheres of activity, banks will have to emphasise more strongly their roles as information processing firms (Read, 1983). Canadian retail banking is only now entering its technology-driven phase. Other factors and developments affecting branch management are:

(1) Capital adequacy regulation affects the risk and return of a bank's portfolio of business, and this may constrain both the volume and kind of business opportunities that a bank may and will exploit.
(2) Polarisation of bank attitudes to risk, return on investment and market/industry concentration, promise to bring about the most fundamental upheaval ever seen in the selling of financial services (Hilton, 1987).
(3) Branch competition, always strong, is now fierce. Only those banks which can deliver what the customer wants in the most efficient way will be most successful. New advances in electronic funds transfers, such as automated teller machine, can be of tremendous help in meeting customer needs. Those banks that are forward looking enough to take advantage of the new technology, are those most certain to prevail in the competition (Rose, 1981; Diebold, 1983; Canadian Bankers Association, 1985b).
(4) Bank branch strategy is already changing in order to emphasise the need to communicate with and sell to customers. Traditional bank branches were not designed with these needs as a primary component of their strategy. Electronic-driven services to financial customers are likely to replace many traditional branches services (Berry, 1982; American Bankers Association, 1986; Gardener, 1987).

Three of the clearing banks in Britain (Midland, TSB and Barclays) have now decided to make their branch managers the salespeople for their own financial products. In North America, bankers want their branch managers to go a step beyond the sales culture to marketing management. This is an approach in which money centres and regional banks decentralise their marketing efforts. When branch managers and other employees, including front-line people, are involved in developing marketing strategies for their branch, the marketing efforts are more targeted and profitable. In this way branch managers will be able to provide their customers with 'best' and impartial services on a range of products most suited to meet their needs (American Bankers Association, 1990).

The present article aims at presenting some of the new—versus the existing—functions of bank branch managers. It attempts to explore the *nature and direction* of the new functional roles of bank branch managers. In doing so, this exploratory investigation throws some light on the criteria being used by branch managers to adapt to future trends in the financial service market.

THE FUNCTIONS OF BRANCH MANAGERS

Traditionally, the function of bank branch managers depended on branches' roles. These (Meidan, 1984) were to:

(1) Offer appropriate financial services to branch customers
(2) Attract customers to the branch

(3) Suggest financial services that should be developed
(4) Earn and contribute profits to the bank.

A number of characteristics and attributes helped the branch in becoming more efficient, and the branch manager could contribute in shaping these factors. They consist of (Gupta and Torkzadeh, 1988):

- *the facilities* and 'style' of the branch;
- *branch layout*, attempting to combine efficiency with personal service and pleasant atmosphere;
- *staffing*, i.e. the character, type of support required and training requirements;
- *automation*, i.e. the type of automatic and electronic facilities available inside and outside the branch;
- *merchandising*, or the marketing activities undertaken in the branch, including the display of promotional and/or audiovisual material.

In the last few years the branch managers have realised that in order to improve the branches' performance it is important to embark on the following activities:

(1) Assess branch strengths and weaknesses. This is normally done via analysis of customers' behaviour, opinions and attitudes.
(2) Analyse branches' personnel; their abilities, competence and efficiency in serving branch customers.
(3) Analyse branches' layout; physical impact and location.
(4) Study branch catchment area, in order to identify additional local opportunities.
(5) Develop marketing activity plans for each branch, for example trying to optimise the number of tellers in the branch—often employing too few tellers leads to long queues and 'upsetting' customers while, on the other hand, employing a too large number of staff in the branch leads to a significant increase in expenses.
(6) Joint responsibility with area managers in formulation of plans for and participation in publicity campaigns, including participation in sponsorship programmes, etc.

METHODOLOGY

Prior to the research a number of hypotheses were established. These included the following:

- *H1*—marketing activities would be important functional roles for branch managers in the future;
- *H2*—some underlying theoretical constructs would exist among the functional roles;
- *H3*—the demographic features of the branch managers would influence their perceived roles in the future.

The data for this study were drawn from a questionnaire mailed to a proportionate stratified sample across the ten provinces of Canada. The sample frame was based on the *1990 Bank Directory of Canadian Payment Association*. Of the replies, 98 were usable (an effective response rate of 40 per cent) and these were employed as the data set for empirical analysis: 21 function variables and six demographic variables were included in the study. The 21 function variables were identified on the basis of having undertaken 15 preliminary in-depth interviews with bank branch managers. The results of these interviews were used in the design of a questionnaire which was then used to collect attitudinal data on each of the 21 variables. The questionnaire was first pretested by obtaining several branch managers' evaluations of the extent to which the various items measured the constructs of interest, the clarity of each question asked and the effort required to answer. The sampling unit was defined as being the bank branch manager. Table 1 presents the demographic features of the respondents under study.

The data analysis used in the study involved a two-stage procedure. Stage one included the analysis of primary statistics, mainly mean scores and median value. Stage two was based on factor analysis and Pearson correlation analysis to identify the underlying functional constructs and the relationship between functional roles and demographic features.

STUDY FINDINGS

Table 2 summarises the descriptive findings. The analysis of the preliminary statistical values revealed that most important factors which help the bank branch managers to face new market trends, in descending order of importance are:

- Improving the quality of customer service;
- Motivation of employees;
- Developing effective relationships with customers;
- Staff training and management training;
- Generation of new business.

Table 1. Demographics of survey respondents/banks ($n = 98$).

Personal Age in years	%	Bank business experience	%
24 to 29	10.2	Less than 10 years	16.3
30 to 39	38.8	10 to 19 years	39.8
40 to 49	34.7	20 to 29 years	26.5
50 and older	16.3	More than 30 years	17.3
Education level		Sex	
High school graduate	46.9	Male	75.5
Attended college	30.6	Female	24.5
Bachelor degree	18.4		
Graduate degree/MBA	4.1		

Bank Bank branch customers		Bank employee number	
Fewer than 999	18.4	Fewer than 10 employees	44.9
Between 1000 and 2499	40.8	10 to 19 employees	23.5
Between 2500 and 4999	17.3	20 to 49 employees	18.4
Between 5000 and 9999	11.2	More than 50 employees	13.3
More than 10 000	12.2		

Table 2. Preliminary statistical values ($n = 98$).

Variables	Mean score	Standard deviation	Coefficients of variation	Median
Branch control	3.939	0.906	0.230	4.000
Marketing research	3.694	1.019	0.276	4.000
New business	4.367	0.888	0.204	5.000
Staff motivation	4.643	0.750	0.162	5.000
Staff training	4.582	0.798	0.174	5.000
Day-to-day management	3.939	0.906	0.230	4.000
Customer relationships	4.612	0.768	0.167	5.000
Analysis of competitors	3.694	0.913	0.247	4.000
Management training	4.367	0.866	0.198	5.000
Automation	3.673	0.982	0.267	4.000
Long-term plans for the branch	3.724	0.883	0.237	4.000
Involving in corporate goals and policy	3.469	1.057	0.305	4.000
Selling ability	4.337	0.824	0.190	5.000
Profitability of the branch	4.296	0.864	0.201	4.000
Local market share	4.327	0.847	0.215	4.000
Decision-making power	4.071	0.876	0.215	4.000
Quality of customer service	4.684	0.768	0.164	5.000
Branch layout and atmosphere	3.847	0.978	0.254	4.000
Promoting branch in local community	4.255	0.803	0.189	4.000
Minimisation of financial risks	3.888	0.994	0.256	4.000
Developing new product	3.439	0.909	0.264	3.000

These findings clearly indicate that bank branch managers are putting an emphasis on three critical areas to face future market development: human resource management and organisational behaviour in terms of the continuous motivation of branch employees as well as on the effective training programmes for staff and management; the implementation of an improved customer relationship management policy and the upgrading of the quality of customer service; and managers' desire to expand the business for the branch.

The second group of important factors to be taken into account when facing new market trends as perceived by bank branch managers can be described as:

- Selling ability of branch managers;
- Increasing the local market share of the branch;
- Increasing the profitability of the branch;
- Promoting the branch in local community;
- Increasing the branch managers' decision making power (i.e. authority);
- Day-to-day management and branch control;
- Minimisation of financial risks taken by the branch;
- Improve the branch layout and atmosphere;
- Developing long-term plan for the branch;
- Marketing research and analysis of competitors.

The importance attached by branch managers to the adoption of an improved marketing orientation is well demonstrated in these findings, through the rated mean scores allocated to the importance of branch managers' selling ability; increase in market share and profitability; promoting the branch within local community; improving the branch layout and atmosphere; marketing research and analysis of competitors. These findings confirmed our hypothesis *H1*.

Other factors of influence perceived as moderately important fall into effective management, including increase of branch managers' decision-making power, day-to-day management, branch control, developing a long-term plan for the branch, and minimisation of financial risks taken by the branch.

Two interesting points deserve attention here. First, despite the increasing utilisation of automation techniques in the banking industry, the factor 'Increasing the level of bank automation' was rated 19 out of the 21 factors. This might have three implications.

First, branch managers are concerned that the increasing level of automation will wipe out the existence of small branches soon (Hondros, 1978; Steeley, 1979) or branch managers believe that increasing automation can never replace human beings in the bank industry where human trust can hardly be placed in machines.

Second, a very low rating on 'being involved in setting corporate goals and policies' may indicate either that branch managers would like to have some strategic input at the corporate level, but head offices are too far from the field for them to do so, or that branch managers are reluctant to interact with top management. Keeping a distance from the top management may well give branch managers more freedom to control the branch, which was rated much higher among the variables.

Last, 'developing new financial products' was rated least important of the 21 functions in spite of their full recognition of the importance of marketing functions. This might indicate that financial product is very different from manufactured products in terms of R&D. In manufacturing sectors a low level manager is usually the initiator of a new product as he/she is closer to the production line and customers as well. In financial institutions, branch managers clearly regard this as headquarters' role.

Given the differences in the nature of functional items under study, and in order to confirm the grouping of these functions into different functional areas, factor analysis using varimax rotation was performed. These produced three factors, accounting for over 62 per cent of the variance (shown in Table 3). The first factor had high loadings on what was referred to as managerial ability, the second factor showed high loadings on decision-making power, and the third factor consisted of functional roles in the marketing area. The reliability estimates of these sub-scales were $\alpha = 0.938$, 0.816 and 0.814, respectively. The factor analysis confirms our hypothesis that some underlying constructs exist among the functional roles.

These findings show that marketing functions are becoming increasingly important and independent at the bank branch level and this may as well indicate the difference between traditional bankers and contemporary bankers. (Gupta and Torkzadeh, 1988).

In order to examine if the demographic features of the banks and the branch managers under study have any influence over the perceived functional roles in the future, Pearson correlation coefficients between the two sets of variables were computed. These are shown in Table 4.

Table 4 shows that the number of employees in a bank branch is significantly correlated with the function of marketing research, automation and involvement in corporate goals and policy. It seems understandable that the larger the branch, the more the branch managers want to see the full play of automation in management. Also it indicates a trend that the larger the branch, the more branch managers want to get involved in corporate goals and policy. On the other hand, number of customers of a bank branch is positively

Table 3. Factor analysis of functional roles ($n = 98$).

Functional roles	Factor 1 (managerial ability)	Factor 2 (decision-making power)	Factor 3 (marketing ability)
Branch control	0.41156	0.62396	0.09096
Marketing research	0.33679	0.15189	0.69962
New business	0.81339	0.03114	0.22605
Staff motivation	0.78576	0.24083	0.12089
Staff training	0.78105	0.34604	0.12548
Day-to-day management	0.36301	0.38105	0.47738
Customer relationships	0.71003	0.30474	0.18880
Analysis of competitors	0.29139	0.32078	0.66362
Management training	0.55579	0.52235	0.32412
Automation	0.18165	0.73759	0.23250
Long-term plans for the branch	0.29221	0.67171	0.26824
Involving in corporate goals and policy	0.01739	0.68181	0.37006
Selling ability	0.45031	0.29789	0.41652
Profitability of the branch	0.75422	0.09680	0.31250
Local market share	0.76656	0.23690	0.25177
Decision-making power	0.46342	0.57586	0.15456
Quality of customer service	0.78337	0.38957	0.07378
Branch layout and atmosphere	0.53324	0.36467	0.11149
Promoting branch in local community	0.61496	0.12664	0.40086
Minimisation of financial risks	0.46336	0.14884	0.57998
Developing new product	−0.00810	0.27986	0.76978
Percentage of variance explained	49.1	8.4	5.3
Cumulative percentage	49.1	57.5	62.7
Eigenvalue	10.3	1.8	1.1
Cronbach's α	0.938	0.816	0.814

associated with the function of marketing research, long-term plans for the branch and decision-making power. These findings indicate that a branch manager with more customers is very keen on understanding the customers through marketing research. Meanwhile more decision-making power at hand means better control over the business at branch level when more customers get involved. With the size of business increase at the branch level, a manager also tends to prefer to have a long term strategy.

At the personal level, a manager with longer business experience emphasised human resource management and branch profitability. Older managers also placed a strong emphasis on the above functional areas. Further, sex is associated significantly with customer relationships and selling ability. It seems that female managers show much more interest in marketing functions than the male managers. Last it is interesting to note that education level has no bearing at all on the perceived functional roles for branch managers in the future.

The above findings do confirm the hypothesis that the demographic features of the respondents affects their perceptions of the importance of different functional roles. This may give some indications to the bank headquarters about what type of branch managers they need to fit into their business objectives and environments.

Table 4. Relationship between functional roles and demographic features ($n = 98$).

Functional roles	Bank			Personal		
	Number of employees	Number of customers	Years of employment	Age	Sex	Education
Branch control	0.0492	0.0076	0.1650	0.2720*	0.0124	-0.1697
Marketing research	0.3286*	0.3165*	0.0355	0.0261	0.1017	0.1122
New business	0.0324	0.1149	0.0366	0.0252	0.1189	0.0421
Staff motivation	0.0591	0.1308	0.1126	0.1246	-0.0455	0.0811
Staff training	0.0961	0.1200	0.3005*	0.3191*	0.0012	-0.0755
Day-to-day management	0.0239	-0.0371	0.3038*	0.2261*	0.1703	-0.0012
Customer relationships	0.0349	0.1164	0.1170	0.1599	0.2958*	0.0281
Analysis of competitors	0.1266	0.1369	-0.0064	0.0264	0.1397	0.0895
Management training	0.1191	0.1646	0.3795**	0.4239**	0.0601	-0.1056
Automation	0.2944*	0.2467	0.1669	0.1766	-0.0283	-0.0431
Long-term plans for the branch	0.1382	0.3081*	0.1478	0.0852	0.0436	-0.1725
Involving in corporate goals and policy	0.3438**	0.1590	0.1700	0.1451	0.0391	-0.0882
Selling ability	0.0782	0.1346	0.0692	0.0663	0.3002*	-0.1315
Profitability of the branch	0.1098	0.1389	0.3225*	0.3587**	0.1628	-0.0968
Local market share	0.1169	0.1681	0.3385**	0.3529**	0.1736	-0.1304
Decision-making power	0.1339	0.3247*	0.1281	0.1383	-0.0467	-0.0835
Quality of customer service	0.0631	0.1642	0.0623	0.0688	0.0805	0.0043
Branch layout and atmosphere	0.0359	0.0994	0.1363	0.1533	0.0652	-0.0642
Promoting branch in local community	-0.0225	0.0947	-0.0415	-0.0316	0.1448	0.1573
Minimisation of financial risks	0.0236	-0.0262	0.0916	0.1353	0.1367	-0.0880
Developing new product	0.1430	0.1406	-0.0234	-0.0300	0.0386	0.0348
Managerial ability factor	0.0837	0.2665*	0.2663*	0.2891*	0.1345	-0.0431
Decision-making power factor	0.3046*	0.3229*	0.3056*	0.2897*	0.0063	-0.1438
Marketing ability factor	0.2456*	0.1150	0.0792	0.1009	0.2547*	0.0387

$p \leqslant$: * 0.05; ** 0.01.

DISCUSSION AND CONCLUSION

Though the findings of this study are derived from the Canadian sample, they do suggest several broad implications for theoretical development and practical banking strategies for bankers at large. The components of establishing a competitive advantage for the bank branch include:

- understanding the cost structure of the business;
- linking profit contributions to the resources deployed;
- identifying customer and prospective customer needs;
- monitoring market share and segment penetration;
- developing branch managers' marketing as well as sales skills.

Branch management should concentrate on the key ingredients of customer orientation and competitive position by gathering and analysing customer information, understanding the direction and speed of competitive changes, relating these findings to the business capabilities, recommending a customer-oriented approach to serve the market, developing a tactical plan for implementation, and monitoring its progress (Gupta and Torkzadel, 1988).

Bank branches that make the marketing orientation an integral part of their culture will find a sustainable competitive advantage. Branch managers should realise the benefits of market opportunities exploited, efficient organisation and market confidence. They should also track their customers' changing needs and focus on serving those needs (Reynolds and Well, 1978). The process is challenging, but the rewards of success are outstanding.

'Service may be perceived as qualitative by bank customers'

Quality service helps build customer loyalty and trust in banking, as in other businesses. Bankers may perceive service quantitatively, in terms of numbers of branches, automated teller machines, or kinds and numbers of accounts offered. Service may be perceived as qualitative by bank customers: measured in terms of attention and concern for their needs. Prompt and competent service helps ensure customer satisfaction (Gupta and Torkzadel, 1988). Good listening is the key to building customer trust. Active solicitation of customer opinion is another marketing tool (Cohen, 1987).

Recently bank branch managers have been requested to make more retailing efforts in their day-to-day management of bank branches, in particular, more participation in regional banking, building up relationships with customers, splitting up different types of retail customers and establishing relations with the community.

A recent study conducted by Donnelly et al. (1988) in the USA suggests that the quality of management at the branch level is the most important single factor that will separate high and low performance bank branches in the years ahead. Skills in management as well as skills in banking will be required, e.g. abilities to develop teamwork in the branch; develop a climate for service; communicate goals to branch employees; develop individual talent; get the bank strategy implemented, and challenge constantly the status quo in the branch.

Implementing the marketing concept internally certainly would challenge many bank branches since it defies tradition. It would require numerous significant changes. For example, staff have to be open and receptive to the needs of their customers; branch management needs to develop a 'quality at the source' philosophy: each branch unit would be responsible for its own quality assurance so no service would be provided to the customers that did not meet the customer's requirements; this would result in quality consciousness at all levels. The entire process must begin with the orientation of all internal units within the branch to the needs of the final customers, translated into requirements for each functional unit. This will assure consistency between each level's objectives and the requirements of the final customer. Branch managers have to monitor their customers' expectations and meet those expectations with strong employee and service performance. They need to learn how to retain customers, how to increase the amount of business done with existing customers and, in addition, how to attract new customers.

It is the on-going tracking of customer satisfaction levels that will allow branch managers to monitor their progress, spot developing weaknesses before they become major problems and provide a basis for rewarding consistently good performance.

FUTURE RESEARCH

This research is of an exploratory character and of limited scope. Further research on the new role and functions of bank branch managers should be undertaken because the results reported are limited in sample generalisability and situation generalisability. However, the findings provide a platform for future investigation and diagnosis.

Additional factors would be worth specifying and sample size could be increased. The investigation could examine disaggregately different types of geographic markets, as well as different types of financial institutions.

'Branch managers have to monitor their customers' expectations'

A comparative study across different cultures might be meaningful. It is the authors' belief that different cultural environments will certainly have bearings on the perceived role of bank branch managers in the future.

A priority for future empirical studies should be to examine the degree of fit between the role and new functions of branch managers and predicted psychographic/behaviouristic profiles of bank customers.

Future research should also explore the extent to which corporate strategy, as well as organisational structure and organisational behaviour issues, might have an impact on the design of new roles for bank branch managers.

ACKNOWLEDGEMENTS

This study was supported by a grant from College of Graduate Studies and Research, University of Saskatchewan. The authors thank Marc Mentzer and Jack Dart for their constructive comments on an earlier draft.

REFERENCES

American Bankers Association (1986), 'BancOne's Blueprint for Future Branches', *ABA Banking Journal*, April, pp. 134–5.
American Bankers Association (1990), 'Training Plan Puts Marketing in the Hands of Branches', *ABA Banking Journal*, February, p. 112.
Berry III, Alex B., (1982), 'Branch Strategies for the 80's' Journal of Retail Banking, Vol. 4 No. 2, June, pp. 37–44.
Bradford, W. E., (1983), 'Bank Productivity in Canada', *Canadian Banker & ICB Review*, Vol. 90 No. 2, April, pp. 60–2.
Canadian Bankers Association, (1985a), 'New Financial Service: Responses to a Dynamic Financial Marketplace', *Canadian Banker*, April, pp. 50–5.
Canadian Bankers Association, (1985b), 'Productivity in Banking', *Canadian Banker*, October, pp. 38–41.
Cohen, D., (1987), 'Listening Fosters Trustful Relationships (Customer Relationships in Banking)', *Bank Marketing*, Vol. 19, March, p. 50.
Diebold, J., (1983), 'Electronic Banking and the Changing Financial Marketplace', *Bank Magazine*, Vol. 166 No. 2, March/April, pp. 24–5.
Donnelly, J. H., Jr., Gibson, J. L. and Skinner, S. J., (1988), 'The Behavior of Effective Bank Managers', *Journal of Retail Banking*, Vol. X No. 4, pp. 29–38.
Gardener, E. P. M., (1987), 'Strategic Challenges for Banks in Europe', *European Management Journal*, Vol. 5 No. 4, Winter, pp. 268–75.
Gupta, Y. P. and Torkzadel, G., (1988), 'Re-designing Bank Service System for Effective Marketing', *Long Range Planning*, Vol. 21 No. 6, pp. 38–43.
Hilton, A., (1987), 'Banned: Your Faintly Biased Bank Manager', *Marketing*, 16 July, p. 9.
Hondros, P., (1978), 'Trust Automation Comes Out of the Back Room', *Trust & Estates*, June, pp. 364–66.
Meidan, A., (1986), *Building Society Marketing and Development*, CBSI, Ware, UK.
Read, C. N., (1983), 'Information Technology in Banking', *Long Range Planning*, Vol. 16 No. 4, pp. 21–30.
Reynolds, F. D. and Well, W. D., (1978), 'Life Style Analysis: A Dimension for Future-Oriented Bank Research', *Journal of Bank Research*, Autumn, pp. 181–5.
Rose, P. S., (1981), 'The Consumer in Banking: End of a Trend?', *Canadian Banker & ICB Review*, Vol. 88 No. 4, August, pp. 66–70.
Rose, P. S., (1986), 'The Bank Branch: Which Way to the Future?', *Canadian Banker*, Vol. 93 No. 6, December, pp. 42–50.
Steeley, J. E., Jr. (1979). 'When Management is Automated', *Datamation*, July, pp. 172–6.

19

The Changing Lending Role of Managers in the Financial Services Sector

Mark Hughes

INTRODUCTION

The article summarizes two studies of managerial work within the UK financial services sector. The work of the managers in this sector has received only limited attention from researchers[1]. The focus in this article is on the managers' lending role which has been identified as a major aspect of the role of the manager[2].

The literature relating to the financial services sector, management development and lending is reviewed, research data are presented in the form of two case studies, the changes in the lending role of the manager are summarized and conclusions drawn.

METHODOLOGY

In order to gain a better understanding of changes in the lending role of managers three major questions were addressed:

(1) What organizational/technological changes had taken place in the lending role of managers?
(2) Why had the changes taken place?
(3) What changes in the lending role of managers were anticipated in the future?

The host organizations were a major building society and a major clearing bank. The sample of managers interviewed comprised the following:

The Building Society
- 12 managers (branch)
- 8 managers (head office)

The Bank
- 12 managers (branch)
- 4 managers (head office)

The managers interviewed in the branches were those managers who would have been traditionally referred to as the 'branch manager', being the most senior managers working within a branch.

While the focus of the research was on lending within the branches, interviewing at both branch and head office level allowed a broader understanding of changes to be established. The changes in the lending role are illustrated through discussion about residential mortgages in the case of the building society and through small business lending in the case of the bank, as these were the principal areas of managerial involvement.

The interviews were conducted throughout 1989, the general interview guide approach[3] was adopted and the interviews lasted between one and one-and-a-half hours. Interviews allowed the preparation of detailed case studies of change in the lending role of managers in two specific organizations. Cronbach provides a strong rationale for such an approach.

Instead of making generalization the ruling consideration in our research, I suggest that we reverse our priorities. An observer collecting data in one particular situation is in a position to appraise a practice or proposition in that setting, observing effects in context[4].

The pilot study has been identified as being of particular importance, when carrying out case study based research[5]. A pilot case study in a regional building society was carried out, establishing that the methodology was appropriate and that the data being collected could be analysed.

The dissemination of the findings was through a report circulated to all participants on completion of the research. The report contained the full case study of the particular organization.

LITERATURE REVIEW

The financial services sector

Morison[6] identified four major factors influencing change in the financial services sector; legislation, market forces, volume of business and profitability. Discussion of these factors provides the context for the case studies.

Legislation seeking to deregulate financial services has presented opportunities for organizations, as well as placing constraints upon them. The most significant legislation has been the implementation of the Financial Services Act 1986 and the Building Societies Act 1986, which have given impetus to competition within the sector. There is increasing competition to offer financial services products both nationally and internationally. In this competitive environment, demands of customers are becoming more sophisticated.

The massive expansion in the volume of business has been addressed through the introduction of new technology. 'In the retail banking business, the enormous growth in the volume of transactions could not have been handled without computer back-up'[7].

Also, in recent years, there has been an increasing emphasis upon profitability within the sector. Specifically, organizations are concerned about comparisons of profits with competitors[6].

These forces have led to the banks and building societies taking a much more proactive stance to their financial markets, and developments are captured in the following quote:

Against this background of growing markets for financial services, increasing competition and an improving level of financial awareness and sophistication by the end users, both personal and corporate, the banks have had to develop their marketing skills to at least maintain their market share and profitability levels[8].

Marketing activities have been focused through the use of clearly defined sales targets. The achievement of such targets often form an important component of performance related pay schemes.

Also, the more marketing-oriented approach to financial services has been supported through changes in the branch networks, while the concept of large branch networks has been questioned in light of rising costs.

The banking culture reflects the institutional character and historical development of the banks, leading to the appearance of soundness, conservative respectability and orderly administration[9]. While building societies do not share the same historical background, they too have experienced cultural change. In the case of building society managers, Dixon views the change as a culture shock: 'Managers who went into societies thinking they were entering a sort of service will have to become more like entrepreneurs'[10].

Management development in the financial services sector

The branch manager has traditionally been the stereotypical pillar of the bank community; administrator of the branch; principal reference point for personal banking services; a salesman for an increasing range of non-banking services; and a specialist corporate banker[11].

In order to understand the role of managers in branches, it is necessary to explore their career paths. These usually involve upward progress through organizations and gaining an insight into the range of activities within their organizations.

In banks and building societies professional bodies oversee their professional examinations. Emphasis is placed upon staff, aspiring to management positions, gaining such qualifications. In order to aid this process financial and training support is often provided for staff. This is usually complemented by managers attending internal training courses at staff colleges.

As well as formal off-the-job training and development, emphasis is placed on on-the-job training experiences. This process is often aided through the presence of mentors, who may well be existing managers in branches. Job rotation plays a central role in the development of the manager, with placements in head office departments broadening the knowledge base of the manager. However, these career paths may change with increased mobility between financial services organizations and a reduced demand for generalist managers within branches as markets are more narrowly segmented. Cockerill[12] has identified how management development in the financial services sector needs to respond to the changing environment:

Dynamic environments in which organizational success is harder to achieve and resources are scarcer mean that we must use approaches to the selection and development of managers which have a demonstrable link to organisational performance.

The lending role of managers

The managers develop lending skills over time, through mechanisms described in the previous section. Also, managers take guidance from lending manuals, describing current lending policies within particular organizations. However, lending philosophies have changed as an entrepreneurial element has been introduced into the financial services sector; 'previously bankers had, at best, passive roles in which they waited for business to walk in the door'[13].

The foundation for sales is product knowledge, based upon the belief that managers cannot successfully sell lending products, unless they fully understand these products. The implication for the lending role of the manager has been that, as well as having knowledge of their own lending products, there is a need to be knowledgeable about the products of competitors.

In order to make lending decisions managers usually draw upon a number of information sources[14]. The lending decision making process may be understood as a bi-polar continuum. At one end is codified decision-making exemplified by credit scoring. Credit scoring involves characteristics of the applicant being allocated scores, if the cumulative score reaches a pre-determined level the application is successful.

At the other end of the continuum there is the loan application which is judged by managers based on their 'gut feeling' about the lending proposition[15]. However, these two positions may be viewed as extremes. Typically there is room for codification through lending policy and for the assessment of the customer by the manager. The position on the continuum depends very much upon the type of lending.

In the past decade, banks have switched from bank managers making personal loan decisions to credit scoring based decisions. Also, building societies are using credit scoring for personal loan decision making. The building societies have only been offering unsecured personal loans since the Building Societies Act 1986 and the availability of credit scoring eased entry into this market:

Credit-scoring systems, as they became available, have helped the banks, building societies and other finance companies to measure risk and set standards or disciplines which enable them to manage it. Credit-scoring has also replaced the need to have trained staff capable of assessing risk and making a judgement[18].

There has been considerable research interest in credit scoring business lending applications[16,17,18]. However, banks until recently appeared to resist such an option. Philip Langsdale (Director of Group Information Technology and Planning) describes the credit assessment system introduced into the corporate banking centres of Midland Bank:

It enables a manager to grant credit on the spot, where appropriate, gets rid of paperwork and other chores and allows him to get on with the real business of the bank, providing service to our customers. It's a powerful support system which enables managers to make quick, consistent and well founded decisions[19].

The potential of credit scoring for residential mortgage lending decision making has also been identified. Michael Tuke (Finance Director, Woolwich Equitable Building Society) was asked to look to the future in terms of technological developments in building societies:

... the advent of leading technologies such as knowledge-based systems may offer substantial benefits to the retail financial services sector. For example, a credit-scoring system that can learn from previous loan applications and their performance could assist the maintenance and improvement of the loan book quality[20].

In the following sections, case studies of the mortgage lending role of managers in the building society and the small business lending role of managers in the bank are presented.

CASE STUDY—MORTGAGE LENDING ROLE OF THE MANAGER

The building society was one of the largest building societies in the country, having grown through a succession of mergers. The building society was going through a transitional phase as a consequence of the latest and largest merger which had been between two major building societies.

The culture within the building society appeared to be a mix of task culture and role culture[21]. While there was a reliance upon rules and procedures, through a clearly defined hierarchy, there were also indications of task culture through a pre-occupation with 'getting the job done' and an emphasis upon the need for consequent organizational flexibility.

The main lending product of the building society was the residential mortgage, although the building society was placing increasing emphasis upon unsecured personal lending and commercial mortgages.

The discussion of technological and organizational change needs to be prefaced by an acknowledgement of the competitive environment for residential mortgages. One manager described the situation as follows: 'the greatest change in mortgage decision making was in terms of the changing market' (branch). Managers suggested that this had led to a need for swifter decision making and a more flexible approach on marginal decisions.

Organizational change

The residential mortgage application process traditionally began with the interview between the manager and the customer. However, in recent years the role of the interview had declined.

Less than 50 per cent of case are now interviewed, mainly because of the intermediary getting into the market. We find a lot of our business is intermediary introduced (head office).

Managers still regarded the interview as important, as it allowed them to explain the complexities of mortgages and offer the customer mortgage related products. The building society had expanded its range of mortgages to meet the increasingly sophisticated needs of customers. As a consequence managers were having to increase their product knowledge. A common concern among the managers in the branches was with the amount of 'paper work' on their desks, relating to changes in lending products.

The building society had responded to increasing volumes of work through a variety of mechanisms. Mandates representing the level up to which managers could lend without reference to Head Office were allocated to more staff. This was complemented by a title change, with assistant branch managers being retitled branch managers and branch managers being retitled district managers. The change from branch managers to district manager allowed these managers to take an overview of lending in their district. Districts tended to be no more than two or three branches. The district managers were able to offer some training and guidance to the less experienced branch managers. The district managers acted as an important communication channel, conveying views between the branches and Regional/Head Office, via monthly meetings with the regional manager.

The building society was looking to all its staff to possess a certain level of mortgage knowledge, in order that they could deal with routine enquiries 'we've always wanted to get even our basic counter staff to a level where they can answer questions over the counter of a fairly simple nature' (head office).

The promotion of lending products was encouraged through the introduction of targets. Although there had been quotas or targets as far back as the managers could remember, the quotas acted as an upper limit which the managers were not expected to exceed. The present targets were something which the managers were expected to aim for.

The situation in the market was different, you were not under pressure to lend money. Because you had a set quota which was very low in those days. Obviously, when you have three borrowers to every loan you can pick and choose which one you take (branch).

In terms of the involvement of head office in mortgage decision making, before the merger, two separate approaches were evident. In the one building society each branch was viewed as a miniature building society in terms of their autonomy to make lending decisions, while in the other building society the majority of work was dealt with at head office. In the merged building society, the policy was one of decentralized decision making, accompanied by an encouragement to view the mortgage lending guidelines as flexible.

Technological change

A technology audit revealed the following technology being used by the managers in connection with their mortgage lending work:

- *One per desk/Viewdata*—Two types of computer used for calculating repayments, quotations on insurance linked mortgages and access to market information.
- *Squarezone*—Sophisticated programmable calculator the size of a pocket calculator.
- *Computer based training*—An interactive computer-based learning package allowing staff to be trained without leaving their branch.
- *Wordprocessors*—Wordprocessing mortgage offers had been a recent innovation within the building society. Previously, information had to be taken from screens and typed.
- *Personal organizers*—Staff, including the manager, had personal organizers with details of the lending products. Amendments were issued whenever there was a change in the interest rates or lending policy.

Information handling is discussed in terms of the following capabilities of technology; information capture, information storage, information manipulation and information distribution[22].

The main information capture capability of the technology was processing mortgage applications. While this work was usually a clerical rather than managerial task, it was a major aspect of the mortgage application process, for which the manager was responsible.

The information storage capability was concerned with managing information generated in connection with the mortgage. This information needed to be efficiently managed, in order to free managerial time to deal with other aspects of lending. In connection with the management of information, managers suggested 'we are finding things are being made a lot simpler as time goes on' (branch).

In terms of information manipulation, technology was not being used in the mortgage decision-making process (discussed further in the following section). The potential existed for head office, 'drawing-off' performance information, rather than managers completing monthly returns. Unfortunately, information from all the branches was not compatible, consequently managers were having to complete monthly (paper based) reports.

Managers were able to use a computerized credit reference system for certain mortgage applications, where the mortgage was for above 95 per cent of the value of the property or the manager felt uneasy about the customer.

That is an important factor because if the screen indicates the customer has three CCJs (County Court Judgements) you are going to think twice about whether you do it or not. That is an important on-line tool (branch).

As well as concerns about access to references, managers required other information particularly when dealing with customers during interviews. The other aspect of information distribution was the display of information. In terms of the way the manager sold the product Viewdatas and one-per-desks (OPDs) were of major importance, because they displayed to the customer graphically what the manager was explaining.

Decision-making change

Despite the potential for using credit scoring in mortgage decision making this route had not been taken. There appeared to be two perspectives on the future of mortgage decision making in the branches. First, it had not changed in the past and was unlikely to change in the future.

The decision-making aspect hasn't really changed over 20 years and I can't see there being a requirement to change in the future (branch).

The second perspective was that there would be credit scoring in the future, but that the manager would be able to override a decision with an override facility, when appropriate.

The head office managers were exploring the possibility of credit scoring mortgage decisions, with a view to a more uniform mortgage consideration. Credit scoring was regarded as already being implicit within the guidelines issued to managers within the building society.

CASE STUDY—SMALL BUSINESS LENDING ROLE OF THE MANAGER

The bank was one of the largest clearing banks in the country with over 2500 branches employing in excess of 100 000. The culture could be described as a role culture[21] with a reliance upon rules and procedures and a clearly defined hierarchy, job titles did appear to be significant. However, there were indications that the bank was moving towards a task culture, particularly at head office where managers were emphasizing teamwork and organizational flexibility.

Organizational change

Managers maintained networks of contacts among local professionals. These contacts provided an important source of new business. Managers would take into account who had made the introduction, as part of their lending decision-making process.

There was an increasing expectation within the bank that managers visit their small-business customers' premises, rather than expecting the customer to visit the bank. Interviews at the customers' premises were felt to be more informal. An added advantage was that the customers were more likely to discuss their requirements where they could demonstrate a need, such as showing the manager an old piece of machinery they were seeking to replace.

Always managers would go out to customers, but there were those who would stay in their office and ask customers to come to them. By twisting arms gradually, by introducing targets to visit people, this has changed the philosophy and the thinking and changed attitudes (branch).

In order to provide time to carry out visits to premises, the bank introduced a number of changes. The use of credit scoring in the personal sector greatly reduced the amount of time required when making lending decisions. The managers were also able to delegate lending authority to other members of staff. However, managers were still responsible for this lending and consequently their role involved taking an overview of the personal sector within their branches.

In a similar manner more staff were able to make small-business lending decisions, one particular example was the small-business officers. Previously, the manager interviewed the new small-business customer; however, in the past year the bank had introduced officers who dealt with initial interviews where appropriate. This was an arrangement which many branches already operated and may be regarded as a formalization of an existing arrangement.

The officers were usually senior clerical level and dealing with small businesses was only one aspect of their role. They usually had delegated powers to lend to small businesses. The officers mainly fulfilled an information gathering role at interviews, recording information for use in subsequent lending interviews. The presence of the officers was felt to be a means of allowing managers to reallocate some of their time.

It is quite important because it now means that you have not got the situation where the start-up is completely cold coming in to see the branch manager. He should now be quite well prepared before he comes in to see somebody with a lot of paper work, to discuss his proposition in detail (head office).

The range of financial services products for small businesses had been greatly expanded. In particular, products related to lending such as insurance were being promoted. The managers were increasingly expected to meet targets for a whole range of financial services products while at the same time maintaining the quality of service. In the case of lending, there was a target to see a percentage growth in lending, which was part of the branch's contribution to the profits of the bank. The bank had recently introduced a personal reward package based on new products sold, and the contribution of the branch to the profitability of the bank were major aspects of this package.

As well as changes at the level of manager, there had been changes in the organization of the branch networks. The underlying philosophy is captured in the following quote.

We have changed the branches, so we are concentrating skills and ability within offices, appropriate to the type of customer they deal with. You used to have the situation where the small-branch manager would have to deal with at one moment, a lady whose mother had died and then the next interview was with a PLC (head office).

Two major changes had been the introduction of business centres and the linking of branches. The business centres were a cluster of offices rather than a single branch. They had a corporate business group at the core, with a chief manager and a team of account executives. The business centres dealt with the larger small businesses and mid-corporates. The chief manager chose which relationships were taken on, with a branch maintaining the account being kept fully informed about developments.

The 'branch linkings' involved the linking together of a number of branches in an area. One branch was designated lead branch at which the lead manager was based. The lead manager was responsible for the overall effective operation of the whole linking, administration and larger advances. The managers within the linking retained a degree of discretionary power depending upon their grade. The lead manager was not responsible for any advances within those discretionary powers. Any lending above the discretionary power when the branch was linked was transferred to the lead manager. The introduction of the 'branch linkings' were felt to speed up the decision-making process for larger borrowing and allowed easier access to managerial expertise. Access to managerial expertise was also assisted through the removal of the area offices, the advantages of this change being captured in the following quote:

To enable us to run our business more efficiently, by cutting out a layer of bureaucracy if you like. It goes beyond that because it improves the service to the customer (and) speed of decision making (head office).

Technological change

A technology audit revealed the following technology being used by managers in connection with their small-business lending work:

- *Branch processor system.* This was a desktop processor system, which was introduced gradually into branches. However, this pilot scheme had recently been abandoned.
- *Desktop visual display terminals (VDTs).* These were favoured over the branch processor system and were introduced initially into branches which did not have a branch processor. They did not provide extra information, but made access to existing information held on the mainframe easier.
- *Wordprocessor.* While these were not used by the managers, they indirectly proved very useful in dealing with increased volumes of correspondence and marketing.
- *Fax machines.* Used for communicating between branches and regional office and with business customers.
- *Dictation machines.* Used to provide the material for the audio-secretaries, as it was no longer practical to employ shorthand typists. Managers needed to keep detailed notes of small-business lending interviews; dictation machines aided this process.
- *Personal organizers.* Provided the managers with detailed and easily updated product information. They were very portable allowing them to be used on visits to customers' business premises.

Information capture took the form of processing information, typically small-business customer information files and lending applications. Information storage was a major priority for the bank, in the light of its size and its history as a paper-based organization. One manager referred to the desktop VDT as follows:

Without this sort of technical know-how now we'd never be able to handle the volume of accounts and transactions that we had to do in the past with manual posting to ledgers. The information is obviously quicker to recall, so one can make a quicker decision (branch).

Information manipulation took a number of forms in the Bank. The managers found technology aided the monitoring of their own customers' accounts and also the monitoring of the accounts handled by staff to whom they had delegated lending authority. Regional office were increasingly seeking performance information about individual branches. This served two functions; first to control the quality of lending and second to ensure targets were being achieved.

In terms of information distribution the priorities appeared to be access and display. The VDTs allowed far greater access to information and a much improved display of information. Managers needed information close at hand when dealing with customers, and technology assisted this process.

Technology helps with the increasing range of services being offered, i.e. insurance quotations. It helps you to make the sale, to close the sale quicker. Nothing (is) worse than getting details from a customer, then sending away for them and then sending them to the customer. It could go cold (branch).

The ease of access to information was felt by managers to impress customers, as it demonstrated the professionalism of the bank.

Decision-making change

Managers stressed the importance of the account profile in the small-business lending decision-making process, the VDTs were able to display account profiles, 'technology (is) not required to make decisions, but to speed-up decisions and information handling' (branch).

While the credit scoring of personal loans had been successfully introduced, managers in the branches were doubtful about credit scoring small-business loan applications. The quotes below were typical of the view of the managers in the branches.

I don't know of any specific scoring you could apply to small businesses. Each business in my knowledge has been different in context and style and the trade (branch).

To be valid I suppose credit scoring has to be objective. A business proposition is subjective, with new businesses and small businesses, decisions are made subjectively (branch).

Despite these reservations the introduction of credit scoring at the smaller end of the small-business market was under consideration. Head office managers suggested they were approaching such credit scoring with caution despite its successful introduction into the personal sector. Two advantages were identified; first, the risk to the bank could be reduced and second, time savings could be achieved.

That (credit scoring) has a lot of time savings. Particularly when you look at propositions which are fairly straightforward. If we knew what the customer wanted to do on paper, based on what we knew about him, based upon what he has told us, we could make a decision without troubling him to go through it all (head office).

SUMMARY OF CHANGES IN THE LENDING ROLE OF THE MANAGERS

The lending role of the managers studied did appear to be changing and it is possible to summarize these changes in terms of four aspects of the managers' lending role:

- The Manager as Line Manager
- The Manager as Salesperson
- The Manager as Product Expert
- The Manager as Decision Maker.

The manager as line manager

Whereas previously the managers were actively involved in most aspects of lending, in both organizations the lending behaviour of the managers was becoming much more narrowly focused. Organizations responded to an expansion in lending through a delegation of lending authority to more staff. The managers were often able to share their experience and skills with less senior staff and, in this sense, they took on an important local training role. Managers maintained overall responsibility for lending in their branches and consequently took an overview of the lending of their staff. In the case of the bank this overview had been considerably enhanced through the use of information technology.

Managers were often required to take on responsibility for more than one branch. These clusters were known as 'districts' in the building society and 'linkings' in the bank. The manager formed an important communication channel between branches and regional head office. This organizational form appeared to be concerned with responding to local needs, in a manner not dissimilar to matrix management. Performance information was required about the linkings and districts and information technology presented a means of data capture and distribution.

The manager as salesperson

In both organizations, increasing emphasis was being placed upon targets. These targets were given added relevance through their contribution to recently introduced performance related pay schemes. The role of the interview as an input into the lending decision making process was being played down. Instead, the interview presented an opportunity to gain an insight into the needs of the customer and to cross-sell related financial services products. Interviews were aided through the use of technology, allowing managers to display information to customers on screens during interviews.

The manager as product expert

Organizations were responding to the competitive environment through a diversified range of lending products. As a consequence of this diversification, managers found themselves constantly having to update their lending product knowledge. There had been two major responses to this need. First, technology offered a solution through the effective management of information. In both organizations, the personal organizer was regarded as a valuable aid, in maintaining an up-to-date record of product information. Second, managers were aided as more staff were being taught about lending products. This meant that the managers no longer needed to deal with the more routine enquiries. However, this development meant that more staff required access to information, and this was particularly the case with on-line information where the priority appeared to be more terminals on more desks.

The manager as decision-maker

A number of factors were identified which influenced the decision-making process, including the competitive environment, intermediaries and mandates/discretionary powers. Managers felt there had not been significant changes in their decision-making in the areas discussed to date.

The introduction of credit scoring into residential mortgage decision-making in the building society, was under consideration at the head office. Also, the introduction of credit scoring into small-business lending decision-making was being considered by managers at the bank head office.

In both organizations managers in the branches underestimated future developments in terms of the scope of change. It is in this area of decision-making that future changes appeared most probable.

CONCLUSIONS

The main changes in the lending role of the managers have been summarized in the previous section. Organizational change appeared to mirror cultural change taking place throughout the sector, with a move away from the traditional banking culture[11]. The technological changes also reflected broader organizational concerns about improved information handling[7]. In terms of lending decision-making, there were indications that both organizations were looking to further realize the benefits of credit scoring identified by commentators[8].

The stereotypical branch manager appeared to be disappearing[9]. Managerial activities were becoming more clearly focused with managers often taking an overview of the lending at branch level, rather than carrying out the lending. This was being facilitated through both technological and organizational change.

Morison identified legislation, market forces, volume of business and profitability as the four major factors influencing change within the financial services sector[6]. The influence of these factors was evident in both case study organizations. These factors appeared to be particularly significant to the lending role of the manager, where the manager was the interface between the bank and the customer. A more effective utilization of managerial time was being sought within both organizations as they responded to this changing environment.

The final conclusion is concerned with the need for further research in this area. It is unlikely that financial services organizations have been able to develop managers at the same pace as the expansion in the volume of their business. Parallel to this has been the need to develop skills within the managers to deal with the changing environment[12]. In this vein, it would be worth testing the following hypothesis. The rationale for changes within managerial work in the financial services sector is a consequence of skilled and experienced managers becoming a scarce resource.

ACKNOWLEDGEMENT

The author is very grateful for the constructive criticism and ideas offered by the editor and referees of this journal and Aidan Berry at the University of Brighton. Responsibility for the views expressed within the article remain with the author.

REFERENCES

1. Wield, D. V. and Smith, S. L., 'Banking on the New Technology—Choices and Constraints', *International Journal of Information Management*, No. 7. 1987, pp. 115–29.
2. Channon, D. F., *Bank Strategic Management and Marketing*, John Wiley and Sons, Chichester, 1986.
3. Patton, M. Q., *Qualitative Evaluation Methods*, Sage, Beverly Hills, 1980.
4. Cronbach, L. J., 'Beyond the Two Disciplines of Scientific Psychology', *American Psychologist*, Vol. 30 No. 2, pp. 110–27.
5. Dixon, B. R., Bonna, G. D. and Atkinson, G. B. J., *Handbook of Social Science Research*, Oxford University Press, Oxford, 1988.
6. Morison, I., 'The Cultural Revolution in Banking: A 20 Year Perspective', in Institute of Bankers (Ed.), *Jack of all Trades . . . Master of None*, Institute of Bankers. London, 1989.
7. Bladen, M. and Shreeve, G., 'Whose Hand on the Wheel?'. *The Banker*, Vol. 140 No. 767, January 1990, pp. 10–18.
8. Marsh, J., *Financial Services Marketing*, Pitman, London. 1988.
9. Child, J. and Tarbuck, M., 'The Introduction of New Technologies: Managerial Initiative and Union Response in British Banks', *Industrial Relations Journal*, Vol. 16 No. 3, 1985, pp. 19–33.
10. Dixon, H., 'Building Societies Branch Out', *Financial Times*, 2 January, 1987, p. 10.
11. Child, J., Loveridge, R., Harvey, J. and Spencer, A., 'Microelectronics and the Quality of Employment in Services', in Marstrand, P. (Ed.), *New Technology and the Future of Works and Skills*, Frances Pinter Ltd, London, 1984.
12. Cockerill, T., 'The Kind of Competence for Rapid Change', *Personnel Management*, Vol. 21 No. 9, September 1989, pp. 52–6.
13. Richardson, L., *Bankers in the Selling Role*, John Wiley and Sons, New York, 1981.
14. Berry, A., Citron, D. and Jarvis, R., *The Information Needs of Bankers Dealing with Large and Small Companies*, Certified Accountant Publications Limited, London, 1987.
15. Jankowicz, A. D. and Hisrich, R. D., 'Institution in Small Business Lending Decisions, *Journal of Small Business Management*, July 1987, pp. 45–52.
16. Duchessi, P., Shawky, H. and Seagle, J. P., 'A Knowledge-Engineered System for Commercial Loan Decisions', *Journal of the Financial Management Association*, Vol. 17 No. 3, Autumn 1988, pp. 57–65.
17. Shaw, M. J. and Gentry, J. A., 'Using an Expert System with Inductive Learning to Evaluate Business Loans', *Journal of the Financial Management Association*, Vol. 17 No. 3, Autumn 1988, pp. 45–56.
18. Hayes, R. S., 'Construction of an Expert System Simulation Model of the International Bank Loan Decision Process', paper presented to the European Accounting Association, Nice, France, 26 April 1988.

19. Andrews, B., 'The Growing Role of Computerised Expertise', *Financial Times*, 14 September 1989, p. 26.
20. Tuke, M., 'Success Will Go to Those Best Able to Manage Change', *Banking World*, Vol. 7 No. 12, December 1989.
21. Harrison, R., 'How to Describe your Organization', *Harvard Business Review*, September–October, 1972, pp. 119–28.
22. Buchanan, D. A. and Boddy, D., *Organizations in the Computer Age*, Gower, Aldershot, 1983.

20

Network Management and the Branch Distribution Channel

Steven J. Greenland

INTRODUCTION

The distribution of financial services in the UK has rapidly evolved over the past decade. New methods of distribution have emerged and the old branch channel has been transformed from being transaction and processing driven to highly customer focused retail and selling settings. This article describes the continuing role of the branch in distribution strategies and outlines the key physical transformations that have occurred in the branch channel and the rationale behind them.

THE REVOLUTION IN BANK DISTRIBUTION

The distribution of financial services is an extremely dynamic area that has been completely revolutionized over the past 10 years. The principal motivating forces behind this stem from the ever growing need for enhanced efficiencies and the drive for accountability in bank functions:

- Greater industry competition and economic hardship have dictated that marketing activities must be more effective.
- Since deregulation banks have had to compete more directly with building societies and their friendlier image.
- Merger/acquisition activity has produced a confused corporate identity across some networks, as well as 'over-banking' in certain areas.
- Many outlets dating from the 1960s/1970s are out of fashion and need renovating to satisfy present day tastes.
- The dynamism found in many core retail areas, especially with the spate of shopping centre developments in the 1980s and early 1990s, has resulted in many branches now finding themselves in less than optimum locations.
- Financial consumers have become more sophisticated, with discerning needs that must be catered for, and frequently hold accounts with several institutions.
- The number of financial products and services on offer has grown substantially and outlets providing specialist services have been developed.

- Technological developments and miniaturization have increased efficiencies and reduced the branch space required for duties such as administration. These have enabled processing and enquiry functions to be performed at highly efficient centralized locations. A significant proportion of cash withdrawals are via cost-effective automated teller machine (ATM) networks.
- The role that the branch can play in achieving numerous marketing objectives has been more fully realized and, accordingly, network management has become a focus of attention. The branch is now recognized as an important contributor to competitive advantage and has resulted in complete restructuring and rationalization of network activities.
- Highly efficient telephone banking service delivery systems have been developed, refined and implemented by many institutions.

Distribution strategies have been diversified and in the late 1980s some of the larger banks began experimenting with branchless telephone banking. Early market response to these was slower than anticipated. For example, Midland predicted a British telephone banking market of six million and launched First Direct in 1989. It took three years, however, to attract only 250 000 customers (Buchan, 1992). Since then all of the larger institutions, and several smaller ones, have also introduced some form of telephone banking service. Clearly, telephone banking has many advantages for the service provider as well as the customer. Provided a certain level of use is achieved the major advantages for the institutions are:

- *Low overheads*: telephone banking centres do not have to be in expensive city locations.
- *No branch specific costs*: such as expensive retail ground rents, refurbishment/design and branch maintenance costs, as well as costs associated with network management, etc.
- *Staff management*: opportunities for enhancing staff efficiencies, minimizing periods of non-activity associated with quiet branches.
- *Economies of scale*: associated with centralizing operations, are realized.

Advantages experienced by the telephone banking consumer include:

- *Improved access*. Banking facilities are available 24 hours a day, 365 days a year.
- *Fewer branch visits*. Branch visits are unnecessary unless to deposit cash.
- *Convenience*. Transactions and money management can be arranged and conducted over the phone at the consumer's convenience.

Many consumers, however, still prefer branch banking, seeing it as having distinct advantages over the 'impersonal' telephone service. The following responses selected from a series of group discussions conducted inside a working branch describe some of the benefits and demonstrate the continuing need for the branch and its personal service. These consumers perhaps represent late adopters of new technologies and fit into the 'traditionalist' and 'transition' market segment as described by Scovotti (1994).

For business you still need a bank branch, you still need advice and you still need to see somebody about some things.

If your statement's wrong you want to go in rather than just discuss it on the phone.

I prefer for the bank cashier to check that the money that I've given him is correct. For depositing the money I like the bank to stamp it, they tell me if any cheques haven't been signed.

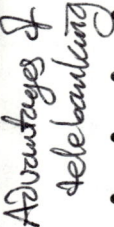

My only criticism I have of 'UK' banks is that everything is actually done over the telephone. Of course if you have a bank you can actually get a relationship going with the bank manager or the assistant manager, I think that it's a bit impersonal.

I find it easier if someone has been trained to talk about insurance and I can ask questions whereas you can't ask the machine questions, its either yes/no, yes/no which is off putting.

Undoubtedly there is a market segment to be catered for with non-branch services, especially among full-time workers. However, with lengthening branch opening hours the convenience attraction of telephone banking may be reduced and the promise of personal service and the opportunity for developing face to face financial relationships with institutions may be seen as being more valuable. It is, of course, in the institutions' interest that these personal relationships exist as they can be actively cultivated to promote image and stimulate cross selling. The high street branch is the key retail platform for selling services and an important medium for communicating with customers. It clearly has a valuable and continuing role to play in the distribution of financial services.

Branch and non-branch services complement one another; telephone banking has, in part, however, helped facilitate considerable reductions in branch numbers. Invariably, with continued rationalization of this sector, the cost benefits gained through telephone banking systems will fuel growth in this distribution channel. Accordingly, there will be further significant reductions in branch networks, perhaps in the region of another 20 per cent over the next five to ten years. The precise level of distribution assigned to each channel will depend on individual company strategies and the speed with which consumers adopt the non-branch telephone banking systems.

THE SCOPE OF BRANCH NETWORK MANAGEMENT

Activities comprising network management contribute to the 'marketing of place' within institutions marketing mix strategies. This element, neglected somewhat in the past, has moved to the forefront of competitive strategies. The activities involved occur on both a macro scale, concerning the entire network, and a micro scale, looking at site specific

Network–specific activities, i.e.

- Network strategy
- Rationalization/expansion programme development
- Researching/developing branch design/image concepts
- Location/site assessment procedures and concepts
- Developing strategies for coping with unfavourable town planning decisions

The development and implementation of "roll–out" programmes translating and incorporating the ideas and considerations from the "macro" network–specific activities into direct action at the front–end "micro" site–specific level

Site–specific activities, i.e.

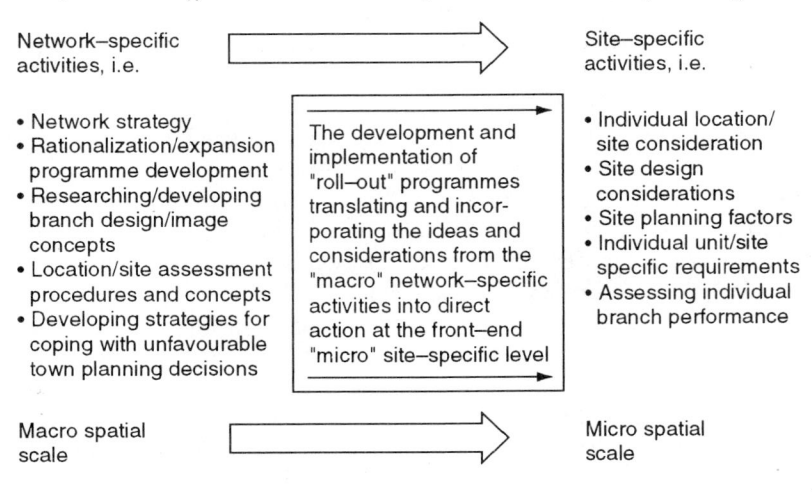

- Individual location/site consideration
- Site design considerations
- Site planning factors
- Individual unit/site specific requirements
- Assessing individual branch performance

Macro spatial scale → Micro spatial scale

Figure 1. The marketing of place in the financial services sector.

factors. Figure 1 illustrates these different scales and details the key activities. More specifically network functions have focused on rationalization and involved *inter alia*:

- The closure of non-profitable branches with markets that offer little promise for improvement.
- Downgrading service provision at certain outlets and upgrading at others, to lower costs and improve overall network efficiency.
- Relocating branches that are under-performing owing to their poor retail location and/or unsuitable premises to new sites.
- Opening new branches in geographical locations where the institution is under-represented.
- Refurbishing outlets according to systematically developed design concepts, to enhance their retail performance.
- Improving branch performance evaluation techniques to achieve the above more accurately and enable more effective network assessment.
- Assisting in the development of customer management strategies to minimize any dissatisfaction or disruption resulting from the restructuring and refurbishment process.
- Developing strategies for overturning unfavourable planning application decisions. (For more information, see Greenland, 1993.)

THE PHYSICAL TRANSFORMATION OF BRANCH NETWORKS

Management activities have physically transformed networks, greatly reducing branch numbers, increased the reliance on ATMs, drastically changing the appearance and function of branches, as well as re-organizing the overall geographic pattern of outlets.

Branch numbers

The trend in the UK financial service industry has been widespread branch closure. However, some building societies and certain banks, smaller in terms of branch numbers, such as Abbey National, and the Yorkshire Bank, have been expanding their branch and ATM networks, in certain regions, to be more geographically representative. The Yorkshire Bank is currently gaining approximately five branches per year in its effort to expand the network further south. The TSB suffers from a similar problem and is also reviewing its network, deleting branches at some locations while acquiring in others, strengthening its presence in the south.

The major institutions without exception have been rationalizing networks, reconsidering both their number and geographical spread of branches. Figure 2 displays the steady decline of the larger bank branch networks since 1981. These institutions have been actively reviewing their patterns of distribution in continuing efforts to optimize network potential. Additional benefit experience from this process has been the release of property investment capital. Proceeds from surplus premises have, however, deteriorated in a declining property market. Branch rationalization has been considerable and will continue until 'ideal' network size and pattern have been achieved and equilibrium with alternative service delivery systems has been reached.

The number of building society branches has, after dramatic increase in the 1970s and

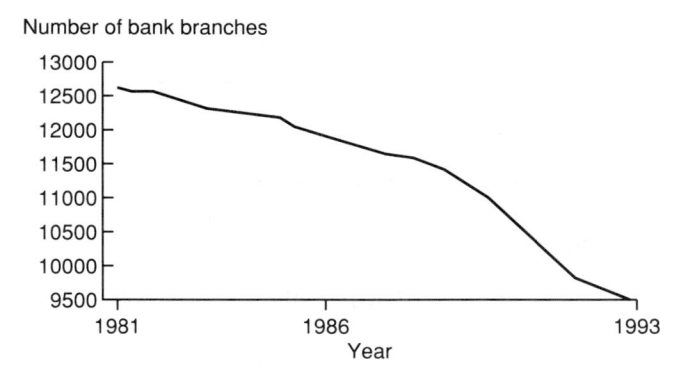

Figure 2. Changing branch numbers of the five UK banks with the largest networks. (Source, British Bankers' Association, 1994.)

early 1980s, also been in decline. The total number of building society outlets has fallen by almost 10 per cent over the past five years. This trend is largely the result of the closure or takeover of smaller institutions less able to survive in recession; the total number of societies has in fact more than halved in the past ten years (Building Societies Association, 1993).

ATM numbers

Rationalization has also been facilitated by the massive growth in automated banking which provides 24-hour access, seven days a week, to services. The increase in ATMs is, however, with a view to enhancing and complementing network efficiencies rather than eliminating the branch as the main customer/institution interface. Cash 'points' are a familiar feature of retail areas and machines have been developed which offer full 'touch screen' banking facilities and far more than simple cash withdrawal. Since 1981 the number of cash dispensers/automated teller machines has increased by approximately 10 000, to well over 15 000 in 1994. Their usage has increased enormously removing a considerable amount of counter service formerly required in branches (British Bankers' Association, 1994).

Many ATMs are associated with branch outlets but a recent growth area has been with isolated service machines that form the 'remote' ATM network, operating from transport centres, retail and service outlets and non-branch high street sites. These now represent almost 10 per cent of the network total. The availability of ATMs and sharing arrangements, giving card holders of one institution the ability to use the cash machines of several others, has reduced the customer demand for such extensive branch networks. The national ATM network is perhaps approaching saturation point and itself in need of appropriate rationalization.

The importance of branch design

The branch is a multi-functional facility providing an acceptable working atmosphere for staff, efficient service/product delivery for consumers, as well as an effective environment for communicating the required corporate message/image. The intangibility of financial service products means it has an even more significant role to play, when compared to the importance of outlet design in other retail settings. At the branch the only tangible points of reference a customer has to associate with an institution's products are the outlet's appearance, its functioning and layout, and the quality of service. Even service quality is, to an extent, a function of the environment, as staff satisfaction and performance levels are directly influenced by their work surroundings. It is difficult for financial service providers to differentiate themselves in terms of service range, price and interest rates etc., which to a large extent are determined by government economic policy. Neither can they differentiate by product, as new product developments are easily and swiftly duplicated by competitors. Image and its media portrayal has therefore proved the key weapon in differentiation and positioning strategies. The major players are establishing specific market niches for themselves, aiming to outperform competitors in terms of sophistication and effective/ appropriate service delivery to these segments. Within such positioning strategies the branch, the frontline physical presence on the high street, plays a crucial role and a great deal of resources have been channelled into improving the effectiveness of branch design.

The role of the designed environment in retail and service settings has been the focus for recent research activity (Baker, 1990; Grossbart *et al.*, 1990; Bitner, 1992; Greenland and McGoldrick, 1994). It is now appreciated that branch design and layout influence how cost-effective it is for:

- initially, visually attracting customers to the institution;
- communicating the desired corporate and product images, differentiating them from those of other institutions;
- creating the most effective balance between the various branch functions;
- selling, promoting and advertising products and services, as well as the institution;
- encouraging the customer to browse around and maximize the time spent in the branch;
- supporting and giving 'environmental substance' to media campaigns, e.g. National Westminster's advertising 'strapline', 'we're here to make life easier' has been incorporated into a branch design that aims to be straightforward and simple to use;
- providing an ergonomically sound environment and freeing more bank employees time for sales oriented activities;
- facilitating efficient and quality service delivery;
- developing customer/staff relationships;
- giving user satisfaction, both for staff and customers, aesthetically, emotionally and in terms of functionality;
- enabling the rapid implementation of any future environment alterations or refurbishments;
- providing an acceptable design life cycle;
- preventing robbery/fraud and giving staff and customers confidence in their safety and security.

As the branch role has been more fully realized, its design has been re-evaluated and transformed. Specific design concepts and strategies have been developed by the UK institutions and are currently being applied across their networks.

The evolution in branch design

Changes in branch function have released a considerable proportion of outlet space for alternative activities. Retail merchandising techniques are being incorporated in efforts to satisfy user requirements more fully, and maximize the selling opportunity and minimize operational and maintenance costs. Many institutions have developed specialist services, such as 'mortgage shops', estate agencies, business centres etc. to cope with this change, segmenting the market with highly focused product ranges.

With technological developments the major banks have been able to cut costs and gain economies of scale by removing processing and telephone enquiry functions from certain branches to centralized processing and enquiry locations. As a result a large proportion of the network's branch staff are no longer necessary, enabling considerable savings in employee costs to be made. Since 1989 the number of staff of the main high street banks has fallen by almost 15 per cent. Lloyds, a notable example, has reduced its staff numbers by almost 30 per cent and further reductions are likely.

Both the premises and remaining staff of such branches have been re-oriented from account based activities to more of a retail function, their goals being to attract, sell to and service customers. A recent survey suggests that the modern designs have been successful in achieving some of these goals (Greenland and McGoldrick, 1994). In many cases the traditional style bank sites do not provide the desired retail image or an effective cross-selling environment. Internally these are characterized by; a low customer area to staff area ratio, extensive use of bandit screens, small windows and a low adoption rate of retail merchandising techniques in the banking hall area. Any personal interviewing tends to be conducted at counter windows or in the branch manager's private offices. Since the late 1980s many of these unsuitable traditional style outlets have been deleted from networks, representing an important element of change in the urban landscape.

Modern branches are being designed more along the lines of stores; the services offered are considered the products and the staff, no longer bankers but retailers who require an environment in which they can apply their selling skills (McGoldrick and Greenland, 1992; Riley and Knott, 1992). The key areas in which modern design have developed are summarized below.

- New branch formats are heavily retail oriented.
- Standardized design formats are used to ensure consistent colour schemes, formats, and images are portrayed across the network.
- Exteriors consist of high profile, glass, shop window type frontages with automatic doors, eye-catching signs and effective displays.
- Up to 80 per cent of the branch interior is devoted to the customer and the sales area.
- Open planning and limited use of bandit screens is the norm.
- Prominent merchandising techniques/activities and staff reception/help desks occupy the sales area.
- Traffic flow concepts, such as 'hard' and 'soft' zones and walkways, are used to control the speed and direction of customer movement around the branch.
- Automated services grouped into lobby areas at the front of the branch, frequently with out-of-hours access, are increasingly incorporated and encourage the use of less expensive impersonal services.

- Ergonomically improved environments are provided for both staff and customers, ensuring efficient functioning and operation.
- Refurbishments frequently go hand-in-hand with staff training/re-orientation programmes to ease the pressures of change and help turn them from bankers into retailers.
- Post-refurbishment staff and customer comments are monitored, and performance indicators may be measured so that any design problems can be modified and branch formats 'tweaked' on an incremental basis.
- The average premises size required (e.g., 2000 sq. ft) is smaller than those of traditional outlets (e.g. 6000 sq. ft) and the costs of fittings per square foot significantly less.
- The fitting/refurbishment process itself has been reduced from about six months to about six or seven weeks.

The network hierarchy

The larger institutions have recognized that it is neither cost-effective nor necessary to offer uniform levels of service across their branch networks. The emergence of processing and enquiry centres has created possibilities for downgrading certain branches, especially in urban or suburban situations with other outlets nearby. Networks with hierarchical delivery systems have emerged, each hierarchy of branch providing different levels of service to the bank's customers (see Table 1). All major institutions in the UK's financial service industry exhibit at least some of these hierarchical levels, the actual number represented depending on individual network strategies. The amount of telephone enquiries and volume of processing performed at each branch level vary according to the degree to which these functions have been centralized. The geographical distribution of the different service delivery types and the proportion each contribute to the network as a whole also depends on the institution and is likely to change over time as efforts to enhance efficiency continue.

'Remote deposit boxes' and 'nominal or automated branches' at present form only a small part of networks but will become more important for some institutions. The Co-operative Bank for example, a smaller but highly innovative UK bank, has developed the 'bank point' kiosk concept. The kiosk is a portable, hexagonal unit, constructed of steel and glass, weighing 6 tonnes. It is a totally remote, un-staffed, automated facility, with a floor area of 120 square feet. Services such as ATMs, change machines, telephone interviewing links and interactive video screen interviewing facilities can be easily accommodated in the kiosk. It is portable, constructed off site and can therefore be installed very swiftly in new locations. For security purposes the kiosk is fixed to the ground and has bollards surrounding it to prevent ram raiding. Should a location prove inappropriate, it is a relatively straightforward procedure to move the entire unit to another site. The Co-op plans to install these at sites such as supermarkets, areas of work, education centres etc. Units such as this do not occupy existing premises and are, therefore, perhaps more able to gain planning permission from local authorities who do not favour giving up prime retail sites to financial service use, as they consider it to detract from a centre's overall retail appeal. The kiosk type unit may therefore enable institutions like the Co-op to expand its network swiftly and achieve that all-important distribution goal of gaining outlet locations at the most optimum sites. If the kiosk branch concept

Table 1. The UK's financial services industry network hierarchy.

Hierarchical level		Facilities provided
Level one	Remote ATM Remote deposit box	ATMs/deposit boxes detached from the branch, but usually serviced by a local parent or community branch
Level two	Nominal or automated branch	Predominantly 'remote' self-service outlet/kiosk projecting the corporate image; ATM's advanced touch screen banking machines, telephone links with community branches and maybe one or two sales assistants
Level three	Sub-branch	Small retail unit; ATM, cash counter, maybe an interview facility, limited service offering and perhaps limited opening hours. They frequency have no managerial presence but are visited by a 'nomadic' sales adviser from a parent/community branch
Level four	Parent branch	Retail/personal branch, typical town/suburban outlet, a more complete range of personal banking services in a retail oriented design
	Corporate branch	Outlet offering facilities for corporate/business customers only i.e., no tills/retail area. They frequently comprise management suites with parking areas operating from business park developments that have lower rents
Level five	Community branch	Financial supermarket; banking hall is broken into specific product areas, full service range including personal as well as business corporate services, tele-enquiry/tele-service/telesales support facility for lower level branches and frequently processing and administration assistance too. They tend to be large expensive city centre branches.
Level six	Regional headquarters	Administration/control centres for the regional network
Level seven	National headquarters	Administrative and management centres determining and implementing a national network policy via the regional headquarters

proves successful it could represent another significant element of change in networks, as well as the character of retail and employment centres.

The spatial arrangement of branch networks

Branches are organized into hub and spoke arrangements; the 'hub' branch provides higher levels of services and support functions to the smaller surrounding 'spoke' branches. Reorganizing and rationalizing the branch network in this manner, upgrading some outlets, downgrading others has also been a considerable cost cutting exercise, facilitating a further reduction in staff numbers and managerial presence, as well as increasing operational efficiencies. One leading UK bank, for example, which began its network review early in 1990, estimated the proposed implementation of some 300 closures and the downgrading of a similar number of outlets would bring revenue savings well in excess of £40m per year by the end of 1994.

The hierarchical nature and arrangement of branch networks is reminiscent of Christaller's central place theory (Christaller, 1966). This in part aims to predict the effective geographic distribution of different levels of product and service provision. The theory may help to explain some of the current network strategies. One of their primary objectives has been 'to ensure at least a minimum representation in all geographic areas in which the bank is located' (Council on Financial Competition, 1990). If a sub-branch is approached by a customer but does not offer the particular level of service required then that customer is referred or connected to another branch higher up in the hierarchy that does provide services of that order. Christaller's administrative principle is perhaps the most appropriate approach for predicting distribution patterns of financial service networks.

In Figure 3 each hexagon represents the administrative area for the higher order branch and encloses six lower order branches to which it provides higher level services too. It is much more effective to administer whole centres than parts of them. For instance if the lower order centres were spatially distributed equidistant from each higher order centre there would be confusion as to which parent branch each of the sub-branches should report to. This pattern of distribution actually maximizes the ratio of low-order to high-order branches and thus helps to minimize numbers of the more expensive, higher order centres across the network.

Central place theory does, however, operate under several idealistic assumptions and therefore represents a system that is not totally applicable to settings in the real world. What it does expose, though, are certain factors and concepts that might be considered when contemplating the ideal size, shape and structure of a branch network.

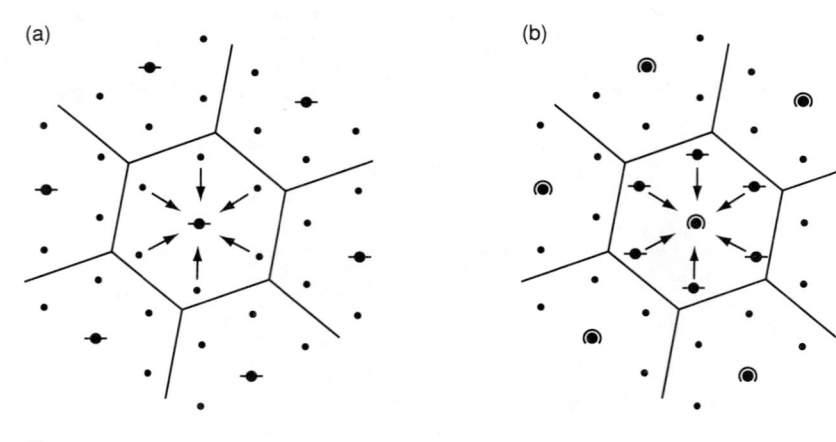

Key:

- • = Sub-branch
- -•- = Parent branch
- ◉ = Community branch
- → = Direction of administrative control

Figure 3. Christaller's administrative principal applied to the branch network: (a) lower service order pattern; (b) higher service order pattern.

CONCLUSION

The distribution of UK financial services has experienced dramatic changes over the past decade. The motivating factors behind these are numerous, being driven primarily by the need to cut costs and enhance efficiencies. Distribution strategies have been reconsidered and network management activities refined. The major industry players have continued expanding ATM networks and introduced telephone banking services helping facilitate considerable rationalization and re-structuring of the branch channel. Outlet and staff numbers have been significantly reduced and the branch function re-orientated to more of a retail and selling role. Despite declining numbers, the branch has become an even more prominent element in financial services marketing mix strategies, and although its role, design and format has been completely transformed, it remains the key distribution channel. The spatial arrangement of branches has also been a focus of activity and efficient branch hierarchies have evolved. In the future further rationalization is inevitable. As optimum network morphology constantly changes, with technological advancement and evolving delivery and distribution systems, the dynamism of the branch channel will continue.

ACKNOWLEDGEMENT

The research on which this article is based was funded by The Financial Services Research Centre, UMIST. It was conducted over a two-year period and has involved most of the leading players in the UK financial services industry. Further details on network management and the branch distribution channel can be found in McGoldrick and Greenland's book, *The Retailing of Financial Services*, on which parts of this article are based.

REFERENCES

Baker, J. (1990), 'A framework for examining the informational value of store environments', *Working Paper. Department of Marketing*, Texas A and M University, College Station, TX.

Bitner, M. J. (1992), 'Servicescapes: the impact of physical surroundings on customers and employees', *Journal of Creativity in Services Marketing*, American Marketing Association, Chicago, IL.

British Bankers' Association (1994) *Annual Abstract of Banking Statistics*, Vol. 11, May, Statistical Unit, British Bankers' Association, London.

Buchan, J. (1992), 'Called to account', *The Independent on Sunday*, 7 June, pp. 3–4.

Building Societies Association and Council of Mortgage Lenders (1993), *Building Societies Housing Finance*, No. 19, Section 6, BSA CML Publications, London, May.

Christaller, W. (1966), *Central Places in Southern Germany*, translated by C. W. Baskin, Prentice-Hall, Englewood Cliffs, NJ.

Council on Financial Competition (1990), *Branch Network Strategies in the United Kingdom*, Council on Financial Competition, August, Washington, DC.

Greenland, S. J. (1993) 'Change in the high street: banks that want planners to say yes', *Town and Country Planning*, Vol. 62 No. 2, June, pp. 152–3.

Greenland, S. J. and McGoldrick, P. J. (1994), 'Atmospherics, attitudes and behaviour: modelling the impact of designed space', *The International Review of Retail Distribution and Consumer Research*, 4 January, p. 1.

Grossbart, S., Hampton, R., Rammohan, B. and Lapidus, R. S. (1990), 'Environmental dispositions and customer response to store atmospherics', *Journal of Business Research*, Vol. 21 No. 3, pp. 225–41.

McGoldrick, P. J. and Greenland, S. J. (1992), 'Competition between banks and building societies in the retailing of financial services', *British Journal of Management*, Vol. 2 No. 3, Autumn.

McGoldrick, P. J. and Greenland, S. J. (Eds), 1994, *The Retailing of Financial Services*, McGraw-Hill, Maidenhead.

Riley, D. and Knott, P. A. (1992), 'Through the eyes of the customer: research into the new look and functioning of bank and building society branches', paper presented to the 155th ESOMAR Seminar on Banking and Insurance, January.

Scovotti, R. (1994), 'Telebanking: your electronic front door', Telephone Banking Track, Day 2, *European Self Service Banking Conference*, Edinburgh.

21

Branch Networks and Insurance Selling

Glenn Morgan

Over the last decade, the financial services industry has been characterized by the breakdown of old demarcations between deposit-taking institutions such as banks and building societies and insurance providers (Salomon Bros., 1990; Ennew *et al.*, 1991; Thwaites, 1991). It is increasingly the case that those institutions with extensive retail networks are using them to sell insurance and investment products (Burton, 1991; Howcroft, 1991; Stephenson and Kiely, 1991). This change is part of a wider process of change that has swept through the industry and created new and more intense forms of competition.

This article presents evidence from three retail financial services institutions which are publicly considered to be successful examples of how to sell insurance products within branch networks. The article shows that each of the institutions organizes this process in different ways and each of them is consequently faced with a different range of problems. It is argued that these problems are endemic to the formation of an integrated insurance and deposit-taking operation. The article concludes by arguing that the operational problems are likely to be minimized where the process of integration is taken furthest. However, since creating integration requires the most cultural and structural change, getting to full integration is likely to be a long and complex process. From the point of view of management, then, the most appropriate goal may be full integration but a series of short-term objectives *en route* to this goal are required to develop awareness in staff of the changes that are necessary.

THE RESEARCH

This article reports on research which has been carried out over the last two years in a number of financial services institutions. The main focus of the research has been on the process of selling life insurance and investment products; the research has considered in particular how the selling process is organized and managed both in branch environments and in direct sales force operations (Knights and Morgan, 1990; Morgan, 1990; Morgan and Knights, 1991; Morgan, 1992).

The case studies draw particularly from the research on financial institutions with retail branch networks. In each institution, a series of unstructured interviews with senior executives have been undertaken. These interviews focused on the sale and marketing of insurance and investment products, and how this fitted into the overall strategy of the organization. Documentary evidence was also examined and observation of sales practices took place. Sales and counter staff within particular branches were also interviewed. In addition, a series of one-off interviews with senior marketing executives in 10 banks and building societies took place, which enabled a broader view of developments in the industry to inform the analysis.

The research has examined the interface between tellers and insurance sellers in branch environments. The ideal of these institutions is to utilize customer information and contact in order to sell new insurance and investment products either within the branches themselves or outside. In the main, these institutions believe that selling insurance products is not a skill that can be simply tacked onto the other skills that are used in retail financial services. Instead, they believe that it requires certain special skills which need to be nurtured by an appropriate management and incentive scheme. However, too large a gulf between a specialist salesforce and the deposit institution's normal staff would undermine the potential advantages from bringing the two together. Thus it is characteristic of attempts to integrate insurance selling and the branches of deposit-takers that there is a system which ensures that potential sales opportunities are identified by a non-sales specialist (e.g. a teller or a person on an enquiry desk). This process of identification then allows the 'prospect' to be approached by the specialist seller either directly in the branch or at home. The key question for the management in these contexts is how to make sure this triangular set of relationships—customer, branch employee, specialist seller—works successfully. This requires creating structures, cultures, management controls and incentive systems that produce co-operation and cohesion rather than conflict and disorganization. In the case studies which follow different ways of managing these relationships are examined. For reasons of commercial confidentiality, the companies involved in the research were promised anonymity in any subsequent publications.

CASE 1: ShilCo

ShilCo is a major UK financial services retailer. It possesses a nationwide branch network and owns an insurance company (ShilInCo). ShilInCo products are sold almost entirely to ShilCo customers. Although some products are sold through direct marketing and IFAs, this is only a very small part of total business and ShilInCo's marketing and product development are increasingly co-ordinated with the needs of ShilCo itself. ShilCo branch staff are divided between ordinary cashiers and customer service representatives (CSRs). Any enquiries about insurance or investment products are referred to CSRs who establish in general terms the sorts of product which the customer needs. If these relate to general insurance products or mortgages, the CSR will conduct a full interview and, if possible, make the sale. If the customer's needs are related to FSA-regulated products, i.e. investments, then the customer will be referred on to a representative of the insurance company ShilInCo. The representative of ShilInCo will actually have a small office space in the branch and will keep a diary which will indicate when he/she will be in the branch. The ShilInCo representative will discuss the client's needs in the branch and may make a sale. More probably, however, an appointment will be made at the client's house and the sale will be made there. Other leads will be generated by the bank manager writing direct to clients with advice about the insurance and investment facilities offered by the company and either inviting them into the branch to see the ShilInCo representative or informing them that the ShilInCo representative will be visiting them at their home at a specified time.

Staff: targets and remuneration

All the ShilInCo staff are paid on a normal salary structure, with only a small commission element. Branches are targeted in a number of ways, including the amount of insurance premium income that is generated. Individual branch employees are also targeted in terms of the number of leads they are expected to generate for the ShilInCo sales representative. Career progression and favourable appraisal reports will be in part determined by the individual employee's ability to demonstrate a good working relationship with the ShilInCo person. The ShilInCo employee is paid by commission only. Although employed by ShilInCo, and provided with a car and various other benefits such as private health care, non-contributory pension and subsidized mortgage, the salesperson's salary is determined by the number, size and quality of sales made. As an employee of ShilInCo, the salesperson will be responsible to the ShilInCo management even though he/she will be working inside the branch alongside branch employees. The salesperson will be set targets for business by ShilInCo management on the basis of company targets and previous individual performance. Sales management apply strong pressure on the salesperson to meet targets. The ShilCo model is based on management's strong belief that insurance and investment selling involves different skills to normal money transmission and lending products allied to a determination to utilize the 'warm' lead generated in the branch to initiate the sales process. It is therefore not only committed to a dedicated salesforce and a specialist management system with different remuneration structures and target mechanisms from those appropriate to branch staff but also to these two groups working in the same physical location.

Management problems in ShilCo

ShilCo is often quoted as a fine example of how 'bancassurance' can work in the UK. Yet behind this image, there have been a number of clashes. These arise basically from the fact that there is a cultural clash between insurance and deposit-taking which is magnified by the actual physical proximity within a single branch of representatives of these distinct values. Branch staff at all levels have at various times resented the insurance sellers for a number of reasons, including their high earnings and their instrumental and at times high-handed attitude towards branch staff and customers. Furthermore, there was a perception within the ShilCo senior management that at a time when they were under intense pressure to cut costs both in branches and head office, the insurance company was still spending on ostentatious new buildings and presenting itself as highly profitable (since it was, in accounting terms, getting the use of the branch facilities for nothing).

These difficulties (together with changing market conditions) led at one period to a significant decline in productivity as, in certain branches, individual bank employees (at both management and clerical levels) informally withdrew co-operation from individual

ShilInCo representatives, thus making it far more difficult to generate 'warm leads'. At one point, it appeared possible that the two might become separate with ShilInCo seeking to cultivate a customer base distinct from that of the branch network and ShilCo employees selling the products of other insurers (though the regulatory system made that difficult). Instead, however, senior management of the two companies reached an agreement about how leads were to be handled and how the two groups of employees would be managed. This agreement stabilized the situation whilst ShilCo senior management set about bringing the insurance company under more direct control. ShilInCo underwent a series of major reorganizations during which many of the original senior management of the company left and were replaced by newcomers. These reorganizations removed any pretensions that ShilInCo might have had that it could go it alone, its independent marketing function was removed and combined with that of ShilCo, as was the main part of its business planning function. These served as both real and symbolic markers for the ShilInCo sales staff that they had to learn how to get on with branch staff. This in turn was reinforced by new forms of team building, targeting and monitoring that emphasized a positive relationship between the two groups of employees at branch level. Thus ShilCo is now much more clearly the more powerful entity with the insurer serving the needs of the branch network as defined by the ShilCo senior management. ShilCo is continuing to integrate branch and insurance staff both at head office (where there is now a single division of deposit-taking and insurance) and at branch level.

CASE 2: BulCo

BulCo is a major retail financial services institution with a nationwide branch network. It owns an insurance company (BulInCo) whose products it sells to its customer base through its branch network. As with ShilInCo, BulInCo products are sold primarily to BulCo's existing customers and therefore product development and marketing is increasingly co-ordinated between the two companies. Unlike ShilCo, however, BulCo attempts to keep its specialist insurance salesforce outside the branch environment. As with ShilCo, the initial contact is expected to be with cashier staff. These staff seek to screen out customers with the potential to buy investment and insurance products. Unlike ShilCo, however, in BulCo, customers can be referred either to specialist sellers within the branch (who are employed by BulCo) or to specialist sellers outside the branch (who are employed by BulInCo).

Salesforces: in-branch and out-of-branch

Within the branch, there is an in-house salesforce as well as a number of advisers who travel locally between branches. These specialist sellers within the branch will deal with loans and general insurance as well as certain FSA-regulated products. They receive a standard salary with a marginal commission element. In career terms, they learn selling as one of the elements of modern retail financial services practice and although they specialize, they may still find themselves doing routine cashiering tasks if necessary.

The out-of-branch salesforce is run by BulInCo. Unlike ShilInCo representatives, there is a basic salary but this is only small and commission earnings are expected to predominate. Recruitment, training and coaching is undertaken by specialist sales managers. A further distinction from ShilInCo reps is that BulInCo reps, although allocated to branches, are not expected physically to locate themselves there and wait for lead referrals and sales opportunities. Instead, the branch manager and the staff will seek to make appointments for the representative at the potential client's home. In theory, the representative may come into the branch to meet the manager and the staff but only to develop a friendly relationship, not directly to meet clients, though there is a temptation for them to spend time in the branch meeting customers as well as staff.

BulCo, then, have two potential sales channels—one is that of the specialist insurance company salesforce, the other is that of their own specialists within their branch. Branches are set targets for business under the various categories of product and managers have a certain autonomy as to how to distribute potential leads within the two salesforce categories. In general terms, it is expected that more complex products such as pensions and bonds will be sold by BulInCo reps, whilst more straightforward life insurance and investment products are sold in the branch. However, branch managers have a certain autonomy about how to manage this balance so long as they are achieving their overall targets.

In the case of BulCo, the branch environment is 'uncontaminated' by any outside influence. BulInCo still draw on branch leads but they work predominantly outside the branch. The interface between BulCo and BulInCo occurs through the lead generation process which can be via telephones and letters rather than as a direct face-to-face interaction. This is monitored within a matrix management system whereby the cross-cutting responsibilities of BulCo and BulInCo management are the subject of 'gate-keeping' by specially designated head office senior management in both companies whose role is to liaise and anticipate any problems or deal with them as they arise.

Management problems in BulCo

Problems in BulCo do not arise from the direct confrontation of different cultures, as is the case in ShilCo. Instead, the problems for BulCo revolve around its customer base. The organization is increasingly sales driven; employees in branches as well as in the insurance salesforce are targeted to sell. Every person the customer comes into contact with will be trying to sell. Customers may come to resent this and purposefully avoid the branch. From the employees' point of view, the pressure to sell means that there may be resistance to passing on leads. Until one's own targets have been met, why pass prospects to somebody else, even if that other person may be more experienced and skilled? BulCo's problems are to make sure that its customers are not experiencing over-selling but are, on the other hand, meeting with the appropriate type of salesperson from the range of possible sellers. As yet there still appears to be competition between the different sales channels and a degree of uncertainty amongst management as to how to manage this. On the one hand, this competition can be seen as a positive feature, contributing to the creation of a strongly sales-driven culture. On the other hand, it may be dragging down overall productivity because customers are not getting in front of the right type of salesperson for their particular needs. It may also be storing trouble up for the future in that customer resistance to over-selling may begin to grow. Senior management in BulCo are therefore seeking to develop a model of the selling process that will allow for a greater degree of discrimination between types of customers and the appropriate sales approach. In taking a more complex approach than ShilCo, BulCo appear to have avoided the worst of the clashes that have inhibited progress inside ShilCo; however, they have not yet been able to match the complexity of their conception with a working operational model. Once again, however, it is important to note that from the outside, BulCo is perceived to be a success in terms of its ability to integrate insurance and deposit-taking. From the inside, there remain many difficult issues to be resolved.

CASE 3: ColCo

ColCo operates a third distinctive model. It is a medium-sized provider of retail financial services; it owns an insurance company (ColInCo) whose products it sells through its branch network. In the past, ColInCo products have been sold by branch staff who have been given special training. These staff receive leads from cashiers and then try to sell insurance-based products to branch customers. In career terms, they are part of the normal grading structure within ColCo and receive no commission for their sales. Working in the selling function is seen as necessary to proceeding up the hierarchy of ColCo. In material terms, however, there is no immediate incentive for an individual staff member to take on the task. Sales are primarily conducted in the branch and there is little home visiting. The time, skills and incentives required to sell the more complex pension and investment products are not therefore provided.

ColCo's management feel that as a result they are not utilizing their bancassurance possibilities to the full. They have therefore decided to set up a specialist salesforce to sell insurance products to their customer base. This salesforce will receive leads from the branch staff which it will follow up through home visits. It will be physically located outside the branch network and will not therefore come into direct contact with the branch staff. It will be paid a basic salary (higher than BulInCo) with commission on top. Unlike BulInCo and ShilCo, however, the specialist salesforce will not be employed by the insurance company. On the contrary, they will be managed and controlled by ColCo. Although ColCo recognize that they will have to bring in specialist salesforce management skills, they nevertheless wish to keep ultimate control by integrating the salesforce within ColCo itself. Thus the insurance company remains effectively a manufacturer (of insurance products), whilst ColCo is the distributor and seller of the products.

Management problems in ColCo

The issues for ColCo revolve around two problems. First, does it produce sufficient business to make a specialist salesforce worthwhile? A specialist salesforce paid by salaries and commission is an expensive proposition; will it bring in enough new business to be a worthwhile investment? Second, can it be managed in such a way that it does not create a disruptive effect on the already existing branch selling system? ColCo employees have grown used to selling within the branch; now they will have to get used to passing leads on to salespeople they do not know. ColCo prides itself on the local knowledge of its branch staff and their care for customers as individuals. Under the new scheme, customers will be referred to salespeople with whom the branch staff may have only a passing acquaintance, yet whose actions may considerably affect customers' perceptions of ColCo as a whole. ColCo managers face a dilemma. If they want the salesforce to be economically viable, they will have to grow it quickly and achieve high targets; if they do this, however, they risk generating dissatisfaction amongst their branch employees. ColCo hope that by keeping the management of this process in the hands of one group of senior executives they can avoid the sort of intra-managerial conflicts which characterized ShilCo. Whilst this may be true, it is not yet clear that they can avoid a fall in morale amongst their branch employees.

SUMMARY

These three cases indicate the wide range of possibilities that are open to organizations seeking to integrate insurance selling with deposit taking (see Table 1). At one end (ShilCo), nearly all the selling of FSA-regulated insurance products is done by a salesforce from a separate company; at the other end, the salesforce is controlled by the branch network provider (ColCo); and, in the middle, there are effectively two salesforces, one controlled by the insurance company (BulInCo) and one controlled by the network provider (BulCo). It is worth noting that there is a further possibility which is embodied in the ColCo case, i.e. where there is no separate salesforce at all and the branch staff simply 'add on' selling to their other tasks.

Furthermore, each of these different models generates different sorts of problems for the companies in terms of management. In ShilCo, the problem was how to manage two types of employees operating in the same physical location; in BulCo, the problem was how to manage the complex range of selling practices without turning the customer off; in ColCo the problem was how to manage salesforce growth without undermining the morale of the branch staff.

CONCLUSIONS: MANAGEMENT IMPLICATIONS

In general terms, it is possible to distinguish two sorts of problems that are at issue here—operational problems and change problems.

Operational problems

From the case studies, it is clear that operational problems come primarily from trying to make the link between deposit-taking and insurance selling. They concern how to:

Table 1. Different models of bancassurance.

	Salesforce	
	Internally controlled	Externally controlled
First contact with salesperson		
In-branch	BulCo	ShilCo
Out-of-branch	ColCo	BulCo

- manage the lead generation process;
- ensure customers receive consistency of service;
- create a system whereby customer needs are properly addressed in order that they can be served by the appropriate person.

In theory, these operational problems are going to be most susceptible to resolution where insurance selling and the deposit taking functions are most integrated. In other words where:

- all the sellers and tellers are controlled by the same management;
- all receive the same core training and socialization into the company's mission statement;
- salary and career differentials are minimized;
- formal and informal contacts between the groups are maximized.

Unfortunately, however, achieving this sort of integration requires a protracted transformation in the culture and structure of financial services organizations to overcome the differences that currently exist. Thus they are linked to problems in the management of change.

Change problems

These can be summarized under a number of headings.

- changing a deposit-taking culture towards a more selling orientation;
- creating a salary and career structure which provides security of employment but within a framework which encourages motivation and performance;
- creating relationships within a branch environment that reorder status hierarchies and enable a team approach to the selling process.

The case studies indicate that companies find a number of different points of resistance to this change process, depending upon the strength of the existing culture and the approach to change that is used. In all three cases, there has been a move towards greater integration but this has not occurred without resistance and conflict.

Given these problems, managers need to recognize that the achievement of a successful bancassurance operation needs to be considered as part of an overall change programme. Bancassurance cannot be conceived as a quick way to increase the profitability of branch networks. If it is implemented without a full consideration of the consequences for existing staff and customers, it can lead to conflict and dissatisfaction, which can undermine rather than improve profitability.

Bancassurance and customer orientation

One way in which this can be avoided is by seeing bancassurance as part of an increase in customer orientation. What is it that the customer wants from the retail financial institution? Bancassurance operations which build from a view of customer wants and needs are less likely to create internal conflicts than those which see customers as passive recipients of products and services. In a customer-oriented bancassurance operation, insurance selling will be related to an overall portfolio of products and distribution channels that match the range of customer requirements as delineated through market research and the marketing plan.

The success of bancassurance operations is predicated upon the relationship between the customer and the bank or building society. It is that single relationship which has to be managed through the creation of multiple service ties (e.g. money transmission accounts, savings accounts, loans, insurance and investment services). By emphasizing coherent customer service and relationship management, the bancassurance operation can begin to develop a structure and culture that offers the potential for long-term success. A short-term orientation towards selling insurance into the client base can only undermine customer service.

Marketing has a central role to play in the bancassurance operation by virtue of its customer orientation. The range of products, distribution channels and promotion policies must be built on a clear view of what customers want. The temptation to emphasize short-term quantitative sales goals needs to be countered by an overall marketing vision of what customers want. A successful bancassurance operation will need to be market-driven if it is to survive the current intensive competitive situation.

Achieving this goal is a complex task. Greater integration at all levels of the organization can only be achieved gradually. It is necessary to identify in concrete terms both what the ultimate goal of integration would be and the marketing vision which lies behind that. Appropriate staging posts towards that goal also need to be identified. This is a complex management task; it should not be conceived that bancassurance is an easy solution to the profitability of deposit-taking institutions. On the contrary, it is a long and difficult road to travel as the cases examined here testify. The degree of structural and cultural change necessary is gradually becoming clear. The success of companies in achieving these levels of change will be a major determinant of their profitable survival in the future.

ACKNOWLEDGEMENT

The author wishes to acknowledge financial support from TSB plc and Huthwaite Research Group in conducting this research. Thanks are also due to former colleagues at the Financial Services Research Centre, Manchester School of Management, UMIST, for their comments, especially David Knights, Fergus Murray and Andrew Sturdy.

REFERENCES

Burton, D. (1991), 'Tellers into Sellers', *International Journal of Bank Marketing*, Vol. 9 No. 6, pp. 25–9.
Ennew, C., Watkins, T. and Wright, M. (1990), 'The New Competition in Financial Services', *Long Range Planning*, Vol. 23 No. 6, pp. 80–90.
Howcroft, B. (1991), 'Increased Marketing Orientation: UK Bank Branch Networks', *International Journal of Bank Marketing*, Vol. 9 No. 4, pp. 3–9.
Knights, D. and Morgan, G. (1990), 'Management Control in Sales Forces: A Case Study from the Labour Process of Life Insurance', *Work, Employment and Society*, Vol. 4 No. 3, pp. 369–89.
Morgan, G. (1990), 'The Management of Sales Forces', *Personnel Review*, Vol. 19 No. 3.

Morgan, G. (1992), *Strategic Issues in Personal Financial Services*, Datamonitor, London.

Morgan, G. and Knights, D. (1991), 'Gendering Jobs: Corporate Strategy, Managerial Control and the Dynamics of Job Segregation', *Work, Employment and Society*, Vol. 5 No. 2, pp. 181–200.

Salomon Bros. (1990), *Multinational Money Center Banking: The Evolution of a Single European Banking Market*, Salomon Bros, London.

Stephenson, B. and Kiely, J. (1991), 'Success in Selling—The Current Challenge in Banking', *International Journal of Bank Marketing*, Vol. 9 No. 2, pp. 30–8.

Thwaites, D. (1991), 'Forces at Work: The Market for Personal Financial Services', *International Journal of Bank Marketing*, Vol. 9 No. 6, pp. 30–5.

Part VII

Marketing Strategy

CONTENTS

Introduction to Part VII   311

22 Competition between Banks and Building Societies in the Retailing of Financial Services   313
   P. J. MCGOLDRICK and S. J. GREENLAND, *British Journal of Management* (1992), **3**, 169–179.

23 Customers, Strategy and Performance   327
   R. SPEED and G. SMITH, *International Journal of Bank Marketing* (1993), **11** (5), 3–11.

24 Strategic Marketing in Financial Services: Retrospect and Prospect   340
   C. T. ENNEW, M. WRIGHT and D. THWAITES, *International Journal of Bank Marketing* (1993), **11** (6), 12–18.

Introduction to Part VII

The literal meaning of the word strategy is 'the art of the army general' deriving from the Greek word for general 'strategos'. The implication of the term strategy is the long-term decision that will affect the whole organization, not just internally, but in its relations with the environment, customers, competition, etc. Examples of 'strategic' questions are:

- On which segments and target markets should the financial service organization concentrate its efforts?
- How should its resources be deployed?
- What should be the organizational mission(s) and goals?

In formulating and selecting a marketing strategy, the financial firm should first investigate its strengths, and weaknesses (which are mainly 'internal') and relate these to the opportunities and threats in the environment, which are mainly external factors. On the basis of this SWOT analysis, missions and goals are formulated and the marketing resources are allocated as appropriate.

There are a number of alternative marketing strategies for financial services, that could be generally grouped into two different sets: (1) 'offensive' strategies (including, geographical expansion, market penetration, new market, market leader and market challenger strategies) and (2) 'defensive' strategies (including: market followers, market-richer, diversification and rationalization strategies). For a more detailed description of strategies, see A. Meidan: *Marketing Financial Services*, Macmillan, 1996, Ch. 12. The selection of a marketing strategy starts, as mentioned, with SWOT analysis; however it eventually focuses on the target segment(s) that the financial organization sees it as 'its market'. In practice, the firm will take into consideration factors such as:

- Financial firm size and competitive position in selected markets
- Company's resources
- Competitors' marketing strategies
- The target market(s) buying behaviour and
- The environmental factors, particularly the state of the economy.

In this section we have included three papers: the first deals with the competition's impact on strategy, the second paper investigates the performance aspects of a strategy, and the final paper reviews the literature on strategic marketing in financial services.

McGoldrick and Greenland investigate the issue of competition and diversification in financial services. They suggest that the selection of a strategy is governed by the distinctive strengths that the various financial services sectors possess. Consequently, positioning and repositioning should be the result of buyer behaviour analysis and planning.

Speed and Smith relate the choice of a strategy to performance, the overall economic cycle and environmental factors. The authors present a range of factors/variables that are indicators of financial services performances. Their empirical study suggests that higher financial services performance is correlated with a wealthier customer base and higher levels of social class, i.e., customer-base related factors. Therefore, the study points towards a possible strategy of 'marketing relationships' as a way forward in acquiring and holding on to the 'best' (or chosen) customer segments. This strategy should be based on a selective use of marketing (and financial) tools.

The third paper in this section deals with 'Strategic Marketing in Financial Services'. Here, the authors review the literature on marketing strategy in general, and strategic financial services in particular. They look at the trends and prospects for strategic marketing, particularly in the light of the latest developments in Eastern Europe, European Union and world-wide deregulation and expansion.

As for the future, it is clear that a number of trends will continue to affect the development and implementation of marketing strategies in financial services organizations, as follows:

- Greater industry consolidation via mergers, acquisitions, and strategic alliances
- Changing distribution patterns, particularly as a result of continuing technological developments
- Better segmentation and expanded product offerings
- Continuing industry deregulation world-wide will affect and increase the competition.

22

Competition Between Banks and Building Societies in the Retailing of Financial Services

Peter J. McGoldrick and Steven J. Greenland

SUMMARY

Within the financial services sector there has been diversification on a vast scale, with varying degrees of success. Financial services are increasingly viewed as products, the various branch networks as channels of distribution. The competition between banks and building societies has become a major battleground in the war for consumers' financial services expenditure. Both types of organization have a strong presence in the high street and have become major users of media advertising and other marketing weaponry. Historically, they have both enjoyed strong but different forms of relationship with their customers; these differences are rapidly diminishing as each invades the other's trading territory. This paper presents results from a study of bank–building society competition, illustrating the attributes and dimensions upon which consumers tend to base their choices. Financial services retailers are urged to base their marketing strategies upon a clear understanding of consumer needs and motives, not upon 'me-too' responses to competitors' moves. As many product retailers have discovered to their cost, heavy marketing expenditure cannot be a substitute for a well founded retail marketing strategy.

INTRODUCTION

The 1980s were a time of unprecedented change within the personal financial services sector, with the removal of many barriers to competition. As financial and other institutions seek opportunities to diversify their activities, the traditional boundaries have been rapidly eroded. It is increasingly relevant to regard financial services outlets as a form of retailing, and the services themselves as their product ranges. While accepting the important differences between the retailing of goods and services, it is clear that many similar problems are faced in the formulation of retailing strategy, the utilization of the marketing mix and in the evaluation of marketing performance.

Financial institutions are keen to embrace retail marketing concepts yet generally have only developing experience of strategic and marketing planning. Many valuable lessons can be learnt from their counterparts in the consumer goods sector. For example, some of the less successful diversifications by some food stores in the later 1970s, selling high-risk, ego-intensive merchandise alongside basic groceries, bear a certain resemblance to plans for 'financial supermarkets'. Parallels can also be drawn with the positioning problems encountered by many product retailers. As banks and building societies become less differentiated in terms of their product offerings, branch environments, advertising messages and customer service levels, increasingly blurred images may be the result.

This paper first discusses the adoption of retailing concepts and techniques by banks, building societies and other financial services providers. The competitive context is then considered through a brief overview of channels of distribution for financial services. The focus then narrows to consider the especially important area of competition between banks and building societies. Empirical data are drawn from a study sponsored by TSB and conducted with the collaboration and support of CACI. A major element of this study has been the analysis of buyer behaviour in selecting between banks and building societies for the provision of major financial services. These results allow conclusions to be drawn as to the relative positioning of banks and building societies, providing a consumer-led perspective upon their diversification and marketing strategies.

FINANCIAL INSTITUTIONS AS RETAILERS

The term 'retail banking' has now become firmly established to distinguish 'small quantity' activities from the corporate side of the banking business. The concepts and techniques of retail marketing have been eagerly seized by most types of financial institution that have a direct interface with the consumer market. The propensity to refer to financial services as 'products' may be seen as further evidence of a desire to align with mainstream consumer goods marketing. As traditional retailers, such as Marks & Spencer, increasingly see themselves as offering products and related services, the distinctions between retail outlets and financial services outlets are eroded from both sides.

There are of course particular characteristics which distinguish product marketing from services marketing. Intangibility of the service and the inseparability of production from consumption are frequently cited (e.g. Cowell, 1984, p. 23). Yet it is easy to overstate even these important distinguishing characteristics. Many financial services do contain small but important tangible elements, such as the physical properties of the plastic card, the building society 'pass book' or the certificate of insurance. We must also ask whether production and consumption are truly simultaneous; when is an insurance policy or a savings account actually 'consumed'? These services typically provide long-term peace of mind and payments at some point in the future. Is this world so remote from the retailing of 'tangibles' such as lawn mowers or washing machines, which also are bought to provide longer-term services, namely, grass cutting and home laundry?

The adoption of retailing concepts is also extending to the use of space-related performance measures. According to one chief executive:

Banking products will in future be sold just like other consumer goods—hard, fast and at the lowest possible cost.... (The bank) may soon be assessing its branches on their profits per square-metre, much as retailers like Marks & Spencer look at their stores—and as go-ahead American retail banks such as Wells Fargo do already (*Economist*, 1989).

The elements of the marketing mix utilized by financial services retailers (e.g. Marsh, 1988; McIver and Naylor, 1986) have much in common with those used by product retailers, although the emphasis tends to be different. It is appropriate to look briefly at seven elements of the mix, noting some of the key marketing issues for banks and building societies:

(1) *Product range.* In spite of recent diversifications, it is notoriously difficult for financial institutions to differentiate their product ranges (Rothwell and Jowett, 1988, p. 23). Given the nature of their 'products', they are very easy to imitate if seen to be successful. The range also tends to be relatively small; accordingly, Watkins and Wright (1986, p. 119) expressed some doubts about the validity of the 'financial supermarket' analogy.

(2) *Pricing.* Consumers tend to have low awareness of and/or sensitivity towards credit cards APRs, largely because over half of consumers in the UK settle their accounts in full (King, 1988). Fundamental changes in pricing structure, such as the introduction of an annual fee by Barclaycard, can provoke a sharp response. Whereas product retailers have generally worked hard through the 1980s to shift consumer attention away from price (McGoldrick, 1990, p. 212), pricing is being given increased attention by financial services retailers. Most now offer interest-bearing cheque accounts, following a trend started in 1981 within the United States (Channon, 1986, p. 122).

(3) *Promotion.* Financial services retailers are now making intensive use of media advertising, which is regarded as a major weapon in their attempts to achieve distinctive positioning. The campaign by TSB to link its name to 'yes', and the 'innovator' theme by Barclays, represent major marketing expenditures. In contrast, many product retailers have recently scaled down their advertising expenditures in real terms (McGoldrick, 1990, p. 262). In line with a general trend in consumer goods marketing, some financial institutions have diverted funds from media advertising to publicity and sponsorships (Mintel, 1987).

(4) *Personal selling.* While selling is becoming almost a 'lost art' in many forms of retailing, its importance is largely undiminished within the financial services sector. The complexity of many services, plus high levels of perceived risk, necessitate a high level of personal selling. As financial institutions increase the pressure to 'cross-sell' services (Weinberg, 1987, p. 5) to existing customers, the need for well informed and well trained staff increases.

(5) *Service.* This broad area embraces many types of personal and electronic services, such as electronic funds transfer at the point of sale (EFTPoS), automatic teller machines (ATMs) and telebanking. As in the consumer goods sector, many retailers are giving great emphasis to service levels in their quest for competitive advantage. One problem is to identify the services' most relevant target customers; as Bateson (1985) found, some customers prefer to use ATMs, whereas others prefer personal service.

(6) *Environment.* From a situation where many branches were individually designed along very traditional lines, most financial institutions are placing far more emphasis upon the use of integrated designs. Kotler (1973) defined atmospherics as 'the conscious designing of space to create certain effects in buyers'. Branch design is now regarded as part of the selling/service function, playing a major role in helping to differentiate

the image of the organization. A major task for the banks has been to make their environments appear more 'user-friendly' (Corporate Intelligence Group, 1991).

(7) *Location.* Many managers and researchers have testified to the critical importance of location for product retailers. This is equally true for financial services retailers, especially in respect of transaction services, typically associated with regular branch contact. Large numbers of customers are gained and lost, primarily on the basis of branch locations. Given the high cost of maintaining a well located and extensive branch network, many institutions hope that developments such as ATMs and telebanking will help to overcome the constraints of existing locations.

This typology of the mix differs slightly from the frequently cited '7 Ps' of services marketing, namely, the traditional '4 Ps' of product, price, place and promotion, with the addition of people, physical evidence and process. As Cowell (1984) points out, the '4 Ps' were developed with reference primarily to manufacturing companies and are not sufficiently comprehensive for services marketing contexts. It should, however, be recalled that the original concept of the mix (Borden, 1965) comprised some 12 major elements; the much abridged '4 Ps' framework is generally attributed to McCarthy (e.g. 1978). Texts on the marketing of financial services have coped with the limitations of the mix framework in a number of different ways. For example, Marsh (1988) utilized an adaptation of the '4 Ps', whereas McIver and Naylor (1986) refer to seven 'active ingredients', viz. branch design pricing, selling, marketing communications, public relations, merchandising and internal communications.

There is clearly no universally adopted framework for the services marketing mix, although the '7 Ps' (Booms and Bitner, 1981; Cowell, 1984) have gained some popularity. Our typology uses this as a starting point but attempts to distinguish more clearly between the elements of most importance within the context of financial services retailing. The terms 'product range' and 'pricing' are considered preferable to 'product' and 'price', giving due emphasis to the multiproduct character of most forms of retailing. The term 'location' is used rather than 'place', which attempts to shift emphasis towards the accessibility and other key aspects of the branch locations.

At a more fundamental level, we are concerned by the assortment of attributes that tends to be included within the category of 'physical evidence'. As discussed earlier, it is felt that many of these are integral components of the 'products' within the range; our typology therefore identifies more specifically the 'environment' within the branch or other point of contact. There are also inevitably many areas of overlap between the 'people' and 'process' attributes. In adopting the alternative headings of 'personal selling' and 'services', we are attempting to focus rather more upon the two main functions to be achieved by the people and the processes that are employed. It must be accepted, however, that any such typology of the mix can only be a much simplified framework within which to consider a very wide range of marketing variables, many of which are closely inter-related.

CHANNELS OF DISTRIBUTION

The retailing of financial services includes a wide range of 'products' and 'channels of distribution'. These form an increasingly large and complex set of product-channel combinations, as financial institutions continue to diversify into new and related financial services. These diversifications are most likely to succeed when there is a 'common thread' with existing products. For example, Allied Dunbar achieved encouraging results when diversifying from their life assurance and pensions base into unit trusts, health insurance and mortgages; their move into personal banking, however, met a poor response (Weinberg, 1987). Traditional retailers are also expanding into other forms of financial services, having established a bridge-head through their store cards and other credit systems (Bliss, 1988). Other developments have included Debenhams Share Centres, Harrods Trust banking facilities and Harrods Estate Agency. Figure 1 depicts the major components of financial services retailing, plus the most salient elements of buyer behaviour which influence and constrain the development of new channels of distribution for the different types of financial services. The financial services are grouped within four main categories: (a) those providing the basic cash/cheque/credit/debit services; (b) house ownership and protection; (c) financial provisions for the future; and (d) financial investments. To an extent, these categories form a continuum, from the services which are basic and used by most of the market to those which represent more specialized services with an up-market bias. At the one end of the scale, the services involve little risk,

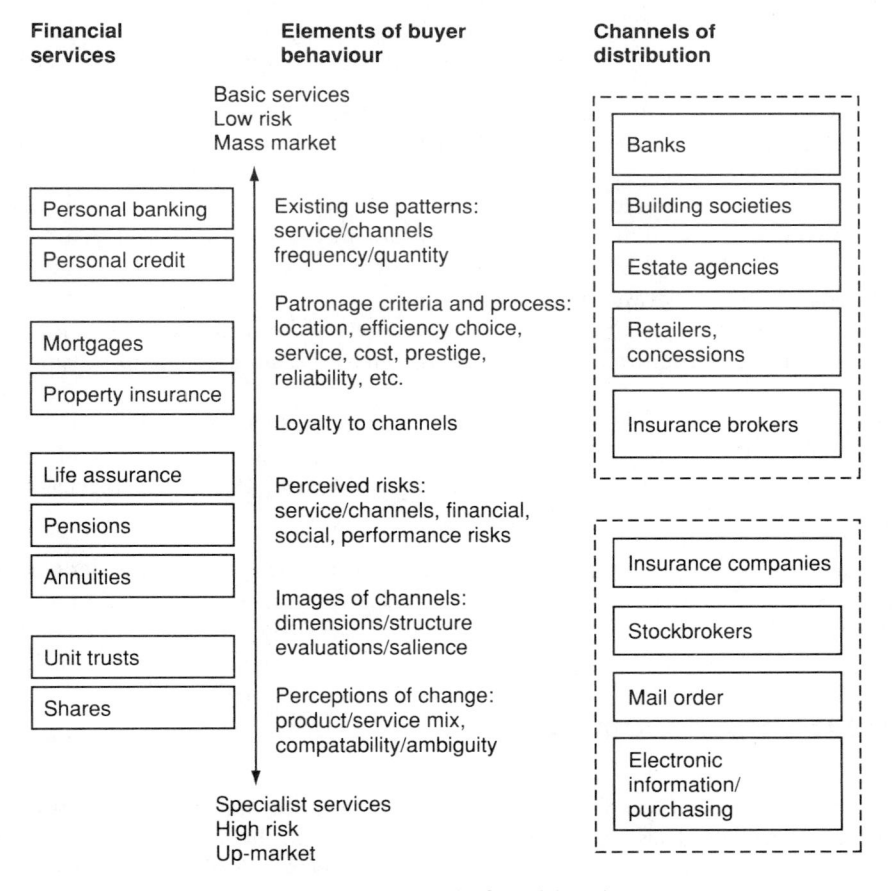

Financial services	Elements of buyer behaviour	Channels of distribution
	Basic services Low risk Mass market ↑	Banks
Personal banking	Existing use patterns: service/channels frequency/quantity	Building societies
Personal credit		Estate agencies
Mortgages	Patronage criteria and process: location, efficiency choice, service, cost, prestige, reliability, etc.	Retailers, concessions
Property insurance	Loyalty to channels	Insurance brokers
Life assurance	Perceived risks: service/channels, financial, social, performance risks	
Pensions		Insurance companies
Annuities	Images of channels: dimensions/structure evaluations/salience	Stockbrokers
Unit trusts		Mail order
Shares	Perceptions of change: product/service mix, compatability/ambiguity	Electronic information/ purchasing
	↓ Specialist services High risk Up-market	

Figure 1. Buyer behaviour and channels of distribution for financial services.

real or perceived; at the other end, the risks to the consumer are obviously greater and the decision process in selecting a supplier of these services is therefore more complex.

The existing channels of distribution are depicted within two main groups, the first typically involving personal contact with the consumer, usually through a 'High Street' branch. The second group comprises the channels which may either interact directly with the consumer, by non-personal means, or operate through various intermediaries. Although it is impossible to maintain rigid distinctions within either the services or the channels, it is felt that some form of classification is helpful in understanding the process of diversification within these channels.

There are at least two major perspectives that can be adopted in studying the changing linkages between the services and the channels. The changes may be regarded as strategy-led, with the focus upon researching the policies and strategies of the major service providers. Alternatively, the changes could be seen as market/demand-led, with the current strategies simply being responses, appropriate or otherwise, to organizations' interpretations of that demand. The latter perspective represents the greater research challenge but, in the longer term, offers the better prospect of achieving a fuller understanding of current processes and future opportunities.

The following elements of buyer behaviour represent key determinants of channel suitability for specific services; they suggest a research progression from the understanding of existing buyer behaviour through to the identification of future needs and preferences:

(1) *Existing use patterns*—depicting the current patterns of service-channel relationships, i.e. what proportions of each service are currently delivered by which channels, what are the change trends, etc.
(2) *Patronage decision*—developing an understanding of the reasons why specific channels are currently used and the nature of the consumer's decision process when alternatives are available. The extent of channel loyalty or inertia is also relevant, as is the extent of perceived risk in evaluating channel options.
(3) *Images*—monitoring the images held by consumers of the various channels, identifying the underlying structure of images and the elements most salient to specific choice situations.
(4) *Perceptions of change*—attitudes towards the diversification of financial services channels, feelings about the appropriateness of various combinations of products and services, perceived compatibility or ambiguity of various service-channel possibilities.

Each of these elements has strong theoretical underpinnings within the wider marketing literature and useful analogies can also be drawn with empirical studies within the field of retail marketing.

SCOPE AND METHODOLOGY

In order to avoid dissipating research resources over too vast an area of competition and buyer behaviour, the decision was made to focus much of the empirical work upon the intense competition between banks and building societies. The Building Societies Act 1986 provided the opportunity and stimulus for building societies to compete more directly with banks in many product fields (Drake, 1989). On the other hand, the building societies' share of mortgage advances for house purchases fell from 77 to 59 per cent between 1985 and 1988, although their share showed some recovery in 1989 (Key Note, 1990). The banks for their part have been understandably anxious to improve their balance between high value added financial services and the rather less profitable transaction services. This therefore offers a topical area for closer scrutiny as each party invades the other's traditional retailing territory.

The methodology of the empirical study comprised the following stages:

(1) *Corporate interviews*—managers and researchers within financial institutions were interviewed to help identify key issues and evaluate existing research material.
(2) *NOP/FRS database*—this large-scale, multiclient survey of consumers' financial services usage provides an authoritative view of patronage behaviour but does not extend to attitudes and motives. Permission was obtained to conduct further statistical analyses upon these data to test various hypotheses regarding channel usage. Strict conditions were applied to the publication of these reanalyses.
(3) *Group discussions*—the four groups comprised seven to eight participants and were divided using a male/female—AB/C1C2 social class split. In spite of the well documented problems with group discussions (e.g. Fahad, 1986), these provided a wealth of qualitative data and guidelines for the structured questionnaire.
(4) *Postal questionnaire survey*—the sample was based upon middle and upper class ACORN (a classification of residential neighbourhoods) groups; CACI produced a random sample from the households within each of the selected groups and provided the mailing labels. Over 500 usable questionnaires were obtained, sufficient to permit most forms of quantitative analysis. The questionnaire contained five main elements:
   (a) A battery of 22 factors which had emerged as especially salient in selecting *where* to obtain higher value financial services; nine-point scales were used to rate the banks and building societies on each factor, and to express the importance of each in choosing where to obtain a major loan, a mortgage, a life policy and a pension;
   (b) Indications of current/recent use of major product/channel combinations;
   (c) Intentions measures—asking which channel would be used if each type of product were obtained in the next 6 months;
   (d) Explanations of alternative channel use—completed by those with the more unusual product/channel combinations;
   (e) Basic classification data, to which were added ACORN and region codes.

SUMMARY OF RESPONSES

Extensive analyses have now been conducted on the data collected from the questionnaire survey. Within this paper it is possible to present only some of the 'top line' results indicating aspects of channel choice. More detailed analyses are available within working papers produced by the authors.

Comparative ratings—banks vs. building societies

From the group discussions it was apparent that there are still strongly held beliefs about the fundamental differences between banks and building societies. Differences between individual organizations within each category were recognized but these tended to be perceived as less distinct than the inter category differences. Table 1 summarizes the mean ratings awarded to each type of organization, based upon a nine-point scale, ranging from very bad to very good. Within each of the two categories, the mean ratings are ranked from 1 to 22, to assist comparisons of relative positioning. T-tests, applied on a paired basis, indicate whether the two means differ for each of the 22 factor ratings. It should be emphasized before interpreting this table that these mean ratings were obtained from the whole sample; significant sub-group differences emerged from subsequent analyses.

Of the aspects of financial services examined, 13 of the 22 proved to differ significantly between banks and building societies. Differences frequently occurred at levels greater than 0.1 per cent. Banks had significantly higher ratings than building societies on just two service factors, viz. 'offer a range of related services' and 'Convenience of branch location'. Building societies, on the other hand, rated significantly better than banks on 11 aspects of financial service. These are listed below with the factors that differed most significantly appearing first:

- Helpful, friendly staff.
- Clearly explain costs.
- Sympathetic understanding of problems.

Table 1. Banks and building societies compared.

Aspect of service	Banks' mean rating (rank)	Building societies' mean rating (rank)	Level of significance from t-tests (p)
Sympathetic/understanding	6.046 (16)	6.389 (14)	0.000
Helpful/friendly staff	6.495 (9)	6.978 (3)	0.000
Not too pushy	6.397 (12)	6.644 (8)	0.003
Time for decisions	6.734 (6)	6.865 (5)	0.028
Efficient staff	6.496 (8)	6.818 (7)	0.000
Range of related services	7.112 (4)	6.483 (11)	0.000
Convenient branch location	7.192 (3)	6.618 (9)	0.000
Modern, up-to-date attitude	6.704 (7)	6.885 (4)	0.017
Explains terms fully	6.398 (11)	6.600 (10)	0.003
Clearly explains costs	6.002 (17)	6.424 (13)	0.000
Confidentiality of details	7.834 (1)	7.778 (1)	NS
Branch manager availability	5.928 (18)	6.097 (18)	0.090
Branch manager personality	6.281 (13)	6.340 (15)	NS
Established/trusty institution	7.754 (2)	7.747 (2)	NS
Comfortable branch surroundings	6.239 (15)	6.222 (17)	NS
Expert advice	6.484 (10)	6.465 (12)	NS
Independent advice	5.609 (21)	5.500 (21)	NS
Flexibility to needs	5.924 (19)	5.952 (19)	NS
Flexible charges/conditions	4.967 (22)	5.265 (22)	0.001
Willingness to renegotiate	5.774 (20)	5.934 (20)	0.063
Ease of transfer	6.278 (14)	6.270 (16)	NS
Efficient/businesslike service	6.864 (5)	6.823 (6)	NS

NS = not significant.

- Efficient staff.
- Flexibility when imposing conditions or charges.
- Not too pushy.
- Explain terms fully and clearly.
- Modern up-to-date attitude.
- Allow customers to make decisions in their own time.
- Willingness to renegotiate payments and conditions.
- Availability of branch manager.

Importance of factors in selecting supplier of financial services

Respondents were asked to rate the importance of the same 22 aspects of service when selecting a supplier for a major loan, mortgage, life policy and pension. Again, nine-point scales were used, this time ranging from not important to extremely important. The four types of financial service were selected as being major areas of product development for most banks and building societies. It is accepted that the importance ratings are inevitably somewhat different from those that would apply to the choice of a supplier of transaction services.

Table 2 summarizes the ratings and the rank order of the ratings within each of the four categories. The sequence of the table is based upon the rank order for the first category, i.e. major loans. When interpreting these results it is important to recognize the limitations of self-reported importance ratings, notably:

Table 2. Importance of factors in selecting supplier.

Aspect of service	Major loan	Mortgage	Life policy	Pension
Clearly explain costs	7.5 (1)	7.7 (1)	7.3 (2)	7.4 (2)
Expert advice	7.3 (2)	7.1 (4)	7.1 (3)	7.4 (3)
Confidentiality of details	7.3 (3)	7.2 (3)	7.1 (4)	7.2 (5)
Explain terms fully	7.3 (4)	7.6 (2)	7.4 (1)	7.6 (1)
Established/trusty institution	6.7 (5)	7.1 (5)	7.1 (5)	7.3 (4)
Efficient staff	6.6 (6)	7.1 (6)	6.5 (6)	6.7 (6)
Time for decisions	6.4 (7)	6.7 (10)	6.5 (7)	6.7 (8)
Efficient/businesslike service	6.2 (8)	6.6 (11)	6.2 (10)	6.4 (10)
Flexibility to needs	6.2 (9)	6.8 (7)	6.3 (9)	6.6 (9)
Willingness to renegotiate	6.2 (10)	6.7 (8)	5.6 (17)	5.9 (17)
Flexible charges/conditions	6.2 (11)	6.5 (12)	5.8 (13)	6.0 (16)
Independent advice	5.9 (12)	6.4 (14)	6.5 (8)	6.7 (7)
Ease of transfer	5.8 (13)	6.4 (13)	5.8 (12)	6.1 (12)
Sympathetic/understanding	5.8 (14)	6.7 (9)	5.7 (15)	6.2 (11)
Modern, up-to-date attitude	5.6 (15)	6.1 (16)	5.8 (14)	6.1 (13)
Helpful/friendly staff	5.5 (16)	6.2 (15)	5.6 (16)	6.0 (15)
Branch manager availability	5.5 (17)	5.8 (18)	4.9 (18)	5.2 (18)
Not too pushy	5.4 (18)	5.8 (17)	5.9 (11)	6.0 (14)
Branch manager personality	4.7 (19)	4.9 (20)	4.4 (20)	4.6 (20)
Range of related services	4.6 (20)	5.3 (19)	4.7 (19)	5.0 (19)
Convenient branch location	4.1 (21)	4.4 (21)	3.7 (21)	3.8 (21)
Comfortable branch surroundings	3.3 (22)	3.5 (22)	3.3 (22)	3.4 (22)

(1) Respondents may have a wish to appear 'rational' in their actions and motivations (Oppenheim, 1986), which can lead to inflated ratings for the economic factors and suppress ratings for more emotional factors.
(2) The importance attributed to a factor may be a function of marketing emphasis, rather than *vice versa*; much price-based advertising may therefore influence the perceived importance of rates and costs.
(3) Importance ratings can be a function of a specific competitive context; if suppliers are fairly evenly matched on key factors, lesser issues are likely to assume far greater importance in that context (Meyer and Eagle, 1982).
(4) Some researchers (e.g. Howell, 1981) believe that importance ratings tend to understate the importance of a few major factors and overstate the importance attached to minor factors.
(5) Factors which exert indirect influences tend to receive low ratings; branch environment for example may indirectly influence behaviour by changing or reinforcing images of efficiency, trust, modernity, etc.

Having noted these important caveats, it must also be recognized that it is extraordinarily difficult to assess the relative importance of a large number of factors by alternative, experimental means. The ratings and rankings in Table 2 should therefore be treated as guidelines, rather than as universally applicable hierarchies of factors. Again, it should be remembered that these are based upon the whole sample; significant differences emerged when analysed by sub-group.

Choice of supplier for financial services

Respondents were also asked to indicate the most likely source of a number of major financial services, if these were to be obtained within the next 6 months. While accepting that a significant gulf can exist between expressed intentions and purchase outcomes, these questions were designed to assess the perceived viability/suitability of each channel for each product. Table 3 summarizes the responses for four of the products, taking the sample as a whole; again, there were important differences between the different segments within the sample. It is clear that the 'traditional' suppliers were still deemed to be the most likely option in very many cases, although some erosion of territorial boundaries is occurring. The banks have clearly established credibility in the retailing of mortgages, life policies and personal pensions. The building societies would also have some cause for satisfaction in that a third of respondents saw these as the likely source of a major loan (other than for a house purchase).

Table 3. Likely choice of supplier for financial services.

Likely source	Major loan (%)	Mortgage (%)	Life policy (%)	Personal pension (%)
Bank	62.6	18.0	13.5	20.7
Building society	33.0	77.2	10.6	9.6
Insurance company	0.6	1.0	46.4	32.1
Employer	–	0.2	0.2	1.8
Other	3.8	3.6	29.2	35.8

Particular attention was given to those respondents who had already obtained financial services through less traditional channels, and to the reasons for their choice. Some 8.7 per cent currently had a (non-house-related) major loan from a building society. The reasons most frequently given were that the societies offered the best deal, or that the existing mortgage collateral served as security. Some felt that the terms were easier, others expressed a preference for keeping all their financial services with one organization.

Of respondents, 12.5 per cent currently held a mortgage with a bank, the most significant reasons relating to the interest rates, the terms or the overall deal. Over 20 per cent of this subgroup saw the bank mortgage as a chance to combine this with other specific policies. A similar proportion again expressed the benefit of keeping all financial services with one supplier, as did many of those holding a current account with a building society. 17.9 per cent had used such an account within the last 3 years; most already had a savings account with the society before taking out the current account. The responses to this set of questions indicated some enthusiasm for the concept of 'one-stop shopping' for financial services. On the other hand, there are many who see a diversity of suppliers as a way of protecting the use or the confidentiality of each service.

MULTIVARIATE STRUCTURE

In constructing the battery of scales (Table 1) to rate images and choice criteria, it was necessary to combine some factors that had arisen within the group discussions. For example 'sympathetic' and 'understanding' proved to be very highly correlated in the pilot survey, as did 'established' and 'trustworthy'. In order to make the questionnaire more manageable for respondents, factors such as these were combined before the main survey.

To achieve a fuller understanding of buyer behaviour within a given market, it is desirable to look at factors at the most disaggregate level. Thus, much analysis has been conducted using all 22 factors. It is, however, also of interest to examine the multivariate structure within these sets of variables, and for some purposes to derive composite scores representing groupings of closely inter-related variables. The technique of principal component analysis (see, for example, Hair *et al.*, 1987) was therefore applied to each of the six batteries of scales.

Table 4 summarizes the outcome of one of these analyses, based upon the 22 rating scales for building societies. Some seven groups were derived, using the conventional criteria for determining the number of composite factors. The factor levels summarize the elements which link the variables within each grouping; only the more strongly weighted variables are listed in each case. Following this process, composite factor scores were produced and further analysed in relation to a number of segmentation variables, such as age, sex, marital status, employment and income.

Factor 1, combining ratings of flexibility, received significantly higher scores amongst the lower income groups and the older respondents, indicating that the building societies were better perceived in this respect by these groups. On factor 2, those not in full-time employment were far more likely to rate the building societies well on their helpful, efficient service! The quality of their advice (factor 3) was most favourably rated by the older and less affluent respondents. Trust and reliability were fairly evenly rated across the

Table 4. Factor analysis for building society ratings.

Factor 1: Flexible service	Flexibility in providing solutions to needs
	Flexibility when imposing conditions and charges
	Willingness to renegotiate payments and conditions
	Ease of transfer from one type of arrangement to another
Factor 2: Helpful efficient service	Sympathetic, understanding of problems
	Helpful friendly staff
	Efficient staff
	Efficient businesslike service
Factor 3: Clear expert impartial advice	Explain terms fully and clearly
	Clearly explain costs
	Expertise in giving advice
	Independence in giving advice
Factor 4: Trust and reliability	Keep personal and financial details confidential
	An established, trustworthy institution
Factor 5: Branch manager	Availability of branch manager
	Personality of branch manager
Factor 6: Branch convenience	Offer a range of related services
	Convenience of branch location
Factor 7: Lack of pressure	Not too pushy
	Allow customers to make decisions in their own time

groups. Factor 5, representing the qualities of the branch manager, was the only one to be significantly better rated by the more up-market respondents. These and similar analyses have shed considerable light upon the success of each type of institution in communicating key elements of their image to different segments within the market.

Given the availability of both image ratings and importance scores, it is also possible to apply a very different analytical approach to these data. Following the approach of Fishbein (1967), Bass and Talarzyk (1972) advocated the use of a 'multi-attribute attitude model', expressed in the terms:

$$Ajk \sum_{i=1}^{n} Wik\, Bijk$$

where:

Ajk = consumer k's attitude score for outlet j
Wik = importance weight assigned by consumer k to attribute i
$Bijk$ = consumer k's belief as to the amount of attribute i offered by outlet j
n = number of important attributes in the selection of a given type of outlet

Used in this context, n is equal to the 22 scaled variables, the B values are these summarized in aggregate form in Table 1, the W values are those summarized in Table 2. It was therefore possible to produce eight of these multi-attribute scores, expressing in single measures the composite attitudes towards banks and building societies in respect of each of the four financial 'products'.

This model clearly contains fundamental limitations, notably the assumption that consumers make almost simultaneous evaluations of many attributes when arriving at a choice of supplier (Fotheringham, 1987). It is, however, of interest to compare the scores by subgroup and to assess the extent to which these scores correspond with expressed intentions. For example, Table 5 compares those giving banks a higher multi-attribute

Table 5. Multi-attribute scores and source of major loan.

Multi-attribute scores of major loans	Likely source of major loan		
	Bank (%)	Building society (%)	Other (%)
Bank score higher	78.9	16.6	4.5
Building society score higher	48.3	47.3	4.4

Chi-squared value = 41.43 ($p = 0.000$).

score for major loans with those giving a higher score to the building societies; these two subgroups are tabulated according to their indications of the most likely source, if obtaining a major loan (not for house purchase) in the next 6 months. Those giving the building societies the higher multi-attribute scores are obviously more likely than the rest to use this source, although the table does illustrate the traditional and continuing power of the banks' image in this field.

CONCLUSIONS

Major changes have occurred within the channels of distribution for all forms of financial services, including personal banking and credit, mortgages and property insurance, life assurance, pensions, annuities, unit trusts and shares. Increases in consumer demand for financial services through the 1980s, coupled with the removal of many barriers to competition in the supply of these services, precipitated this dynamic phase. Innovations in electronic ordering, information and banking systems provided further stimulus for change, as did the revival of mail order and off-the-page selling. Traditional boundaries between banks, building societies, estate agents, insurance companies, stockbrokers and retailers are breaking down; more complex and aggressive channel structures are the result.

It is now increasingly relevant to draw analogies between financial services and 'products', and between high street branches and 'retailers'. No longer are transaction services the exclusive domain of banks, or mortgages and high interest savings accounts the exclusive domain of building societies. This rapid and partially enforced shift from specialization to diversification has led to some problems of positioning and to a blurring of images.

As the empirical research described within this paper has illustrated, these institutions still have distinctive areas of strength within their image structures. Repositioning should be the outcome of careful research and strategic planning not the by-product of a lemming-like rush towards one 'ideal' format. Many years ago, Pierre Martineau (1958) noted that: 'It is high time that we retailers recognize that we cannot be all things to all people. When we do that, we end up with no particular appeal to anybody'. Many retailers, to their cost, have since learnt just how right he was.

There is also a tendency for diversifications and changes to be implemented on the basis of competitive reaction and/or short-term profit projections, rather than being founded upon a thorough understanding of customer needs, motives and attitudes. This study has suggested some guidelines for investigating the buyer behaviour of the financial services consumer, specifically, the process of selecting a supplier of these services. Inevitably, the needs and requirements of a customer contemplating a high-cost, high-risk expenditure have proved very different to those associated with low-risk transaction services. It is clear that the financial services sector will offer a most worthwhile area of investigation by retail researchers in the 1990s.

REFERENCES

Bass, F. M. and W. W. Talarzyk (1972). 'An Attitude Model for the study of Brand Preference', *Journal of Marketing Research*, **9** (1), pp. 93–96.
Bateson, J. E. S. (1985). 'Self-service Consumer: An Exploratory Study', *Journal of Retailing*, **61** (3), pp. 47–76.
Bliss, M. (1988). 'The Impact of Retailers on Financial Services', *Long Range Planning*, **21** (1), pp. 55–58.
Booms, B. H. and M. J. Bitner (1981) 'Marketing Strategies and Organization Structures for Service Firms'. In: J. Donnelly and W. R. George (Eds), *Marketing of Services*, American Marketing Association. Chicago, pp. 47–51.
Borden, N. H. (1965). 'The Concept of the Marketing Mix'. In: G. Schwartz (Ed.), *Science in Marketing*. Wiley, New York, pp. 386–397.
Channon, D. F. (1986). *Bank Strategic Management and Marketing*. Wiley, Chichester.
Corporate Intelligence Group (1991). 'Banks', *The Retail Services Rankings*, January, pp. 4–13.
Cowell, D. (1984). *The Marketing of Services*. Heinemann, Oxford.
Drake, L. (1989). *The Building Society Industry in Transition*. Macmillan, Basingstoke.
Economist (1989). 'Why Saying Yes Isn't Enough', *Economist*, June 3, pp. 117–118.
Fahad, G. A. (1986). 'Group Discussions: A Misunderstood Technique', *Journal of Marketing Management*, **1** (3), pp. 315–327.
Fishbein, M. (1967). *Attitude Theory and Measurement*. Wiley, New York.
Fotheringham, A. S. (1987). 'Consumer Store Choice and Retail Competition'. In: *Fourth International Conference on Distribution*, CESCOM, Milan.
Hair, J. F., R. E. Anderson and R. L. Tatham (1987). *Multivariate Data Analysis*. Macmillan, New York.
Howell, R. (1981). 'Issues in Multi-attribute Modeling of Consumer Patronage'. In: R. F. Lusch and W. R. Darden (Eds), *Retail Patronage Theory*. University of Oklahoma, pp. 229–234.
Key Note (1990). *An Industry Sector Overview: Building Societies*. Key Note Publications, London.
King, D. (1988). 'Competition Hots Up for the Card of your Choice', *Times*, May 16, p. 34.
Kotler, P. (1973). 'Atmospherics as a Marketing Toiol', *Journal of Retailing*, **49** (4), pp. 48–64.
Marsh, J. (1988). *Managing Financial Services Marketing*. Pitman, London.
Martineau, P. (1958). 'The Personality of the Retail Store', *Harvard Business Review*, **36** (1), pp. 47–55.
McCarthy, E. J. (1978). *Basic Marketing: A Managerial Approach*. Richard D. Irwin, Homewood, IL.
McGoldrick, P. J. (1990). *Retail Marketing*. McGraw-Hill, London.
McIver, C. and G. Naylor (1986). *Marketing Financial Services*. Institute of Bankers, London.
Meyer, R. J. and T. C. Eagel (1982). 'Context-induced Parameter Instability in a Disaggregate-stochastic Model of Store Choice', *Journal of Marketing Research*, **19** (1), pp 62–71.
Mintel (1987). *Opportunities in Sponsorships*. Mintel, London.
Oppenheim, A. N. (1986). *Questionnaire Design and Attitude Measurement*. Gower, Farnborough.
Rothwell, M. and P. Jowett (1988). *Rivalry in Retail Financial Services*, Macmillan, Basingstoke.
Watkins, T. and M. Wright (1986). *Marketing Financial Services*. Butterworths, London.
Weinberg, M. (1987). 'Does Integration of Financial Services Work?', *Proceedings of the 6th Annual International Banking Conference*, Lafferty Conferences, London.

23

Customers, Strategy and Performance

Richard Speed and Gareth Smith

The correct relationship between marketing and traditional financial service skills has been subject to considerable debate as the performance of the UK financial sector has declined. This research seeks to examine this relationship, investigating how successful and unsuccessful financial service companies use marketing. The research presented here extends and builds on a previous study reported in this journal, which utilized peer assessment as a mechanism for measuring performance (Speed and Smith, 1991).

The justification for marketing activity is that it leads to superior business performance. The period which has seen the reregulation, environmental change and increasing competition in the UK financial services market has also seen a rise in marketing sophistication. One might expect the importance of marketing to rise with rising competition. Marketing and competition are intrinsically linked (see Saunders, 1987). Although marketing is traditionally considered to be about meeting customer needs, marketing success comes from doing this better than the competition. Marketing offers a mechanism to improve the ability of a firm to compete in the market place. As the level and sophistication of competition has increased, so the importance of marketing in financial services has risen. Marketing is a tool to deal with the problems of increasing competition and turbulence.

However, some commentators on the UK banking sector have suggested that the rise of marketing has had a detrimental effect on the industry (Skeel, 1991). These commentators suggest that the techniques of marketing have served merely to undermine the profitability of the banks' UK retail business, the traditional cash source. Marketing therefore has increased, rather than relieved, the problems of the industry. As competition increased better deals had to be offered to maintain the customer base. The greater competition and improving offers served to undermine the traditional customer loyalty found in the financial services industry, as customers took their business around the market in search of a better deal. The first effect of the dominance of marketing was to increase the costs, and therefore risks, of doing the same business with the same customers. Not only that, but any marketing innovation that was developed by a company was matched or bettered by competitors within weeks. To better an offering, a firm had to offer more, so further increasing the costs and risks. For instance, later entrants into the interest-bearing chequing account market found themselves having to offer higher rates, later entrants into credit cards offered lower rates. The cycle of competition led to ever-increasing product costs merely to maintain customers. The downturn in the UK economy converted many risks into certain failures, bad debts rose and the profitability of retail financial services declined drastically. It would appear from this analysis that the advent of marketing into financial services has merely served to increase the need to compete and simultaneously increased the costs of competing. Interpreting events in this light, therefore, it appears marketing is as much part of the problem as part of the solution.

Shortly before the downturn in performance of the UK financial services industry we carried out some empirical research examining the orientation of marketing strategy in the industry. These data therefore provide a valuable source of material through which to examine these competing claims about marketing and performance. In this article we seek to extend previous studies based on the data, and investigate the relative quality of performance measures that might be used by researchers.

The research sought to develop an understanding of what elements of marketing strategy were associated with differences in performance between financial service companies. In particular, it sought to examine the relevance of certain models of marketing activity to the UK financial services industry. An extensive review of literature identified three contrasting models of financial service marketing, based on customer selection, strategic orientation and internal operations respectively.

The relationship marketing model of financial services (Berry and Thompson, 1982) suggests that financial services marketing should not be directed at attaining profitability of individual transactions but rather at attaining profitability from establishing and maintaining a relationship with customers. Central to this model of financial services marketing is the idea of customer quality attracting and maintaining a customer base of sufficient wealth and sophistication to generate profitable relationships.

An alternative model of marketing strategy is based on the concept of generic strategy. This model of strategy is concerned with the activities of companies, rather than their customer targets, and several authors have argued the relevance of generic strategy concepts to the financial services industry (see for instance, Pollock, 1985; Varadarajan and Berry, 1983). In applying research, such as the PIMS project to financial services, researchers have emphasized the relationship between performance and variables such as higher pricing, innovation and profit orientation. In applying models such as Porter's generic strategies, authors have argued for a strategic orientation towards one of these generic types.

A final model for superior performance is based on what has been termed 'excellence' research, inspired by Peters and Waterman (1982). This strand of research places particular emphasis on managerial practice and the cultural aspects of an organization. This model of superior performance argues that managerial practices, such as encouraging entrepreneurial activity, encouraging loyalty, providing sympathetic career patterns, can all impact on company performance.

These three models of marketing deal with different dimensions of marketing strategy, and are not necessarily mutually exclusive. However, they do provide a broad range of issues over which the differences in marketing strategy associated with performance can be examined.

CREATING A DATABASE

In the first phase of the project a database on the marketing strategies, practices and organization of UK financial service companies was created. The data were collected using a semistructured questionnaire as the basis for interviews with marketing managers in a sample of 40 financial service companies. The areas covered by the questions are shown in Table 1. The questions were framed as statements and the interviewees asked to scale the accuracy of the statement as a description of their company. The scales were constructed to allow equal intervals to be assumed.

The sample was purposive in design, concentrating on the larger companies operating in the retail financial services market. This was done for two reasons. First, secondary sources suggested that companies amongst the larger financial service companies were leading attempts to adapt to the changed environment. Second, changes effected by larger companies would have the greater impact on customers. Because concentration in all sectors of the UK financial services industry is extremely high, a random sample would include a very high proportion of companies with low market share. Such a sample was undesirable because it would under-represent the companies who appeared to be leading the changes and whatever changes the smaller companies made would affect few customers. The most important aspect of the sample selection was therefore to gather companies whom secondary sources suggested were attempting to adapt to a changed environment. The sample was completed by identifying companies of similar size and type to those who had been so identified by secondary data.

A total of 26 companies participated in this section of the research (65 per cent success rate). Three of these interviews proved unsuitable for use in this analysis. The 23 remaining interviews were with nine insurance companies, six banks and eight building

Table 1. Variables in the database captured using Likert scales.

Competitive performance
v4   Relative performance
v5   Relative profitability
v6   Competitive advantage in capabilities
v7   Competitive advantage to customer
v15 Skill at marketing

Cross selection
v8   Recommendation by friends/family
v9   Reputation
v10 Friendliness
v11 Charges made/return paid
v12 Location
v13 Range of services offered
v14 Special services for segments

Segmentation/differentiation
v16 Use of segmentation
v17 Single segment target
v18 Differentiation
v19 Branding
v20 Wealth of customers
v21 Social class of
−26   customers

Profit orientation
v27 Importance of short-run profit

New product development
v28 First into a market
v29 Early into a market
v30 Entering established markets
v31 Late entry into a market
v32 Products new to the world
v33 Products introduced by others
v34 Products widely offered by others

Staff/culture
v35 Transfer of staff
v36 Attitude towards loyalty to the firm
v37 Attitude to career structure
v38 Attitude to job security
v39 Specialism of marketing staff
v40 Attitude to entrepreneurship
v41 Attitude to low level entrepreneurship

Corporate skills
v42 Cost reduction
v43 Discovering new segments
v44 Targeting new segments
v45 Increasing usage
v46 Meeting niche needs
v47 Creating uniqueness

societies. These companies included many of the major financial service companies in the UK.

MEASURES OF PERFORMANCE

An important element in this research was to consider alternative mechanisms for measuring the performance of financial service companies. To investigate the differences in marketing strategy and characteristics between the companies surveyed in constructing the database, it is necessary to construct some measure of performance. A wide variety of performance measurement techniques are available to the marketing strategy researcher, all of which display contrasting strengths and weaknesses (see Saunders *et al.*, 1991). This section briefly reviews the main methods with respect to applicability to the research situation encountered.

Financial measures of performance

Despite the popularity of financial data as a performance measure (see Buzzell and Gale, 1987) there are well-documented theoretical and practical problems with using financial data to measure performance (see Saunders *et al.*, 1991; and Speed and Smith, 1991, for discussions). These can be briefly restated here. Three major theoretical limitations with financial measures of performance can be identified. First, they assume that a single performance criterion can assess 'excellence'; second they focus only on outcomes to the exclusion of transformation processes within the firm; and finally they ignore the claims of other stakeholders beside the stockholder.

Practical problems also arise, including consistency of public data, because firms differ in their treatment of concepts such as depreciation, transfer pricing and the allocation of costs, so reported differences may in fact be spurious (see Fisher and McGowan, 1983). Comparability of data is a problem because the different traditions and regulations of the various sectors of the financial service industry are reflected in different reporting practices and the absence of disaggregated data for wholly owned subsidiaries. In the financial services industry the financial data available on all the companies in the database were sparse and unsystematic, and unsuitable as a basis for performance measurement. Alternative data-based measures, such as market shares, account openings or employee productivity, are subject to similar problems.

Opinion measures of performance

The alternatives to data-based measures are opinion-based measures. These can be based on self-assessment (Conant *et al.*, 1990), peer assessment (Barsoux and Saunders, 1989) and expert assessment (Varadarajan and Ramanujam, 1990). In the absence of suitable data sources, this study adopted a variety of opinion-based measures (see Speed and Smith, 1991, for a discussion of the use of peer assessment). This article concentrates on the use of expert assessment as an opinion-based measure of performance. This has the advantage that the assessors of performance are impartial with respect to the competitive situation. This is not the case with self-assessment or peer assessment which therefore have a potential source of bias (Chakravarti et al., 1981). The drawbacks are that it is time-consuming and costly. Expert assessment, unlike self-assessment for instance, involves the collection of data from an entirely separate sample. Experts must be identified and polled as to their perceptions of company performance. This research seeks to generate a comparative rating of companies in terms of performance, so any experts identified must be in a position to compare between companies on present activities. An average customer is not in a position to do this, having accurate information on the performance of one bank, one building society or one insurance company at any time. Hence the experts in the retail financial service industry can be defined as 'those with a professional knowledge of the industry', people who earn their living making the sort of comparisons necessary in this research.

A potential problem in selecting experts is that the number with expertise in all areas of the financial services market might be very small indeed, so even coverage across company types might be difficult. Second, experts' knowledge might be limited to specific areas, such as financial performance or product performance. One approach to eliminate such problems would be to gather experts together, to allow them to discuss the companies from the base of their own expertise, and achieve an agreed compromise between experts with different perceptions based on expert knowledge. However, there are drawbacks to such an approach. First, there is a cost problem; second, such a face-to-face meeting can be affected by group dynamics. For instance, there is a danger that such a meeting will produce a consensus judgement that overweights the opinions of the most vocal and underweights the opinions of the least.

A method to combat the problems of partial knowledge, the influence of personality and to overcome the costs of convening a face-to-face meeting is the Delphi method (Dankley and Helmer, 1963). The Delphi method is essentially a system of anonymous polling with feedback. There are several advantages that may be briefly stated. The group of experts are asked to give their opinions, justify them and, if necessary, revise them in the light of others' arguments, this process continuing until a consensus is reached. The effect of errors due to misunderstanding and misinterpretation would be reduced by introducing the feedback. Anonymity among the experts reduces the effects of reputation and opportunities for influence.

A Delphi survey of experts

Having defined experts as 'those with a professional knowledge of the retail financial services industry', the following groups were identified:

(1) Equities analysts/financial researchers
(2) Personal financial journalists
(3) City journalists
(4) Academics writing in the area.

The number of experts required to participate is not great. Studies with as few as five experts have been reported. A larger number might lead to logistical problems without leading to any great change in the consensus achieved.

The important thing is to have opinions from groups considering differing aspects of performance and circulate their comments. Financial analysts might tend to provide opinions centred on profitability of the business, whereas personal finance journalists have opinions based on product assessment.

THE STUDY

A total of 30 potential experts were contacted with a view to participation in this study. The list of areas from which experts might be drawn, and parameters for expert selection, were defined prior to selection of individuals. A list of all potential experts was created using a listing of banking and financial service market analysts supplied to the university by stockbrokers and fund management companies, examination of newspapers and academic publication abstracts and research registers. About 60 potential experts were identified. From this list of potential experts, a total of 30 were selected. All non-academic experts were asked for an interview with a view to increasing commitment to the study and response rates. A total of 21 experts finally participated in the study. The breakdown and participation rates of this group is given in Table 2. The overall participation rate was 70 per cent. The response from academics was low, but those who declined to participate generally felt themselves to be too poorly acquainted with the performance of companies to comment.

During the construction of the database, companies participating in the research were asked which other financial service companies they admired for their performance. Thirty-three companies were named by participating companies, and 14 of these companies were participants in the research (42 per cent), including five of the top six companies in terms of the number of companies which said they admired them. A further 10 companies amongst those admired by peers had been invited to participate but declined.

'All companies were judged by at least five experts'

The experts were shown a list of 30 companies. This list included the companies interviewed in construction of the database. The remaining companies were selected from the list of companies admired by those in the sample but not participating in the research. Some prominent firms which had not been listed as admired by peers were also included.

In addition, experts were asked to list any company that had been omitted from the list of 30 that they considered to have above average performance. These were included in

Table 2. Backgrounds of experts approached and participating.

	Number approached	Number participating	Percentage
City/banking journalists	5	4	80
Personal finance journalists	5	4	80
Equity analysts (stockbrokers)	11	9	82[a]
Equity analysts (fund managers)	2	0	0[a]
Academics	8	3	38

[a] Equity analysts' overall participation rate = 69 per cent.

later rounds of the study. Although few of the experts felt able to judge all the companies, all companies were judged by at least five experts from different backgrounds.

The experts rated each company using a seven-point Likert scale ranging from 'very much worse performance' to 'very much better performance'. The intervening points were labelled to allow equal intervals to be assumed.

In the second round, the experts were sent a document listing the companies, showing their score for each company, the average score for each company and a selection of the comments made by experts on each company. The comments were selected to the full range of reasons given by experts for the scores awarded. Experts were asked to change their scores, if they wished, and append any further comment they wished to make in the light of the feedback. A substantial group of experts revised at least one of their scores in the light of information sent to them in the second round.

The third round of the Delphi was carried out primarily for confirmation. Experts were sent a list of company scores in terms of the mean, median and mode scores for each company and their own second round score for each company. They were asked to confirm receipt and correct any errors they perceived in the information they were sent. No experts changed their assessment in the third round.

ANALYSIS AND FINDINGS

Comparison with alternative measures

One of the major factors in the decision to use more than one opinion-based measure of performance was the opportunity to compare the rating of companies resulting from each method of measurement. The measures were compared directly using Spearman rank correlation coefficients. It can be seen from the analysis presented in Table 3 that the expert assessment measure of performance compares well with the other measures based on self-assessment and peer assessment. The mean score awarded by experts correlates with all alternative measures at a level of at least 5 per cent. Complete results of the studies using self-assessment and peer assessment as performance measures are available elsewhere (Speed, 1991; Speed and Smith, 1991).

The correlation between the self-assessed measure of performance and the expert-assessed measure confirms the perception of the researcher that managers were being realistic in their assessment of their own company's performance. As has been pointed out, bias due to competitive sentiment or experimental effects was a potential problem with peer assessment

Table 3. Spearman's Rank Correlation Coefficients for alternative indicators of company performance.

	EXPRANK	PEERRANK
SELFRANK	0.3762[b]	0.5085[a]
PEERRANK	0.4532[b]	

Significance level = [a]1 per cent; [b]5 per cent.
SELFRANK = companies' own assessment of their performance relative to their competitors; PEERRANK = assessment of companies' performance by peers; EXPRANK = mean score awarded by experts ranking companies' performance.

and self-assessment, respectively. The correlation observed between the various performance measures constructed by different means suggest that bias was not a problem. The findings suggest, therefore, that not only are managerial assessments of own company performance consistent with peer assessments of competitor's performance, both are consistent with assessments made by external experts. In this respect the research supports and extends the findings of Dess and Robinson (1984) and Venkatraman and Ramanujam (1986) who reported managerial assessments to be consistent with the firm's internal performance measures and externally published data respectively. Given the cost of carrying out expert surveys, this finding should be welcomed by researchers into financial services.

Methods

Three techniques were used to analyse the data gathered from the Delphi poll of experts. First, the ratings of companies' performance gathered from the experts by the Delphi study were analysed using t-tests to test the hypothesis that each company had average performance (represented by a rating of four). Of the 30 companies experts were asked to rate, 13 were shown by t-test to have mean ratings significantly greater than average and three were shown to have mean ratings significantly below average. The remaining 14 companies did not have mean ratings significantly different from a rating of four, representing average performance. There was no significant difference between the ratings of companies with the type of company, i.e. the proportion of banks, building societies and insurance companies rated as above average as compared to below average were not significantly different.

Spearman's rank correlation coefficients were calculated between the mean score of companies in terms of expert rating and their scores on descriptive variables in the database. To identify those variables which best distinguish between those companies sampled in constructing the database considered by experts to have above average performance and those with average or below average performance, discriminant analysis was used. The small sample involved presents problems in using multivariate techniques, and the approach adopted to overcome these is briefly summarized here (a fuller explanation appears in Speed and Smith, 1991). Those associated with discriminant analysis are well documented (Franks et al., 1965). The first problem is that the traditional hold-out technique for validation cannot be used, since the sample is too small to allow splitting. To allow effective validation of the derived function, two refinements on the basic technique of discriminant analysis were therefore used: jackknife analysis (Tukey, 1958) and the U-method (Lachenbruch and Mickey, 1968). Both of these techniques reuse the sample, by drawing subsets of cases and cross comparing the findings. The use of these techniques presents an additional problem. These validation techniques and the discriminant analysis technique *itself* are sensitive to the ratio of cases to variables, with a minimum ratio deemed necessary for discriminant analysis, 5:1 (Klecka, 1980) and for jackknife 5:1 (Huberty et al., 1987). It is necessary therefore to reduce the number of variables utilized to improve this ratio. Stepwise selection methods cannot be used since the jackknife requires simultaneous entry of a preselected set of variables. The standard technique of applying factor analysis cannot be utilized with small samples, since it too is sensitive to case:variable ratios (Hair et al., 1992).

Variable selection was therefore determined by a two-stage process. Stepwise discriminant analysis was carried out on all variables using both the full set of cases and the subsets of cases generated for jackknife analysis. The results of this process were examined to determine the frequency with which variables were included at an early stage in the analysis of sets of cases. On this basis a set of variables which appeared most frequently early in the stepwise analysis for the various sets of cases were established. The possible combinations of these variables were examined using jackknifed discriminant analysis to determine the optimum discriminant function in terms of discriminatory power and coefficient stability.

Eight of the companies in the sample used to construct the database had above average performance, 15 had average or below average performance.

Findings

Examining Table 4, showing the correlation between the mean score awarded by experts in the Delphi study and the descriptive variables collected in the database, a clear finding

Table 4. Spearman Correlation Coefficients between mean Delphi ratings and database descriptive variables.

Variable	Rank correlation coefficient
v6	0.3714^b
v8	-0.6646^a
v20	0.4458^b
v21	0.4914^a
v22	0.4810^a
v23	0.4306^b
v25	-0.3695^b
v26	-0.5728^a
v27	0.4269^b
v29	0.3475^b
v42	0.4747^b

Significance level = [a] 1 per cent; [b] 5 per cent.
v6 = Capabilities and offerings of the company.
v8 = Importance of recommendation by family or friends to customers selecting the company as a financial service provider.
v20 = Wealth of customers, compared with those of competitors.
v21 = Proportion of customers from social class A, compared with competitors.
v22 = Proportion of customers from social class B, compared with competitors.
v23 = Proportion of customers from social class C1, compared with competitors.
v25 = Proportion of customers from social class D, compared with competitors.
v26 = Proportion of customers from social class E, compared with competitors.
v27 = Importance of a good current profit performance to company.
v29 = Accuracy of 'early to enter the market with a new product' as a description of the company.
v42 = Skill at reducing the costs associated wtih supplying existing services, compared to competitors.

from the data analysis is that the majority of differences between companies with different levels of performance are related to customers. The analysis of correlations suggest that higher performance is associated with a wealthier customer base, higher levels of social class and differences in selection criteria. The better performing companies perceive their customers to be less influenced by family and friends in making their choice of supplier.

However, some variables devised on the basis of the generic strategy model are correlated with performance. Better performing companies reported a greater current profit orientation and superior skills in relation to cost control, as well as tending to be early into a market with a new product.

The discriminant analysis carried out on the sample, which had been divided into 'above average' and 'average and below' performing companies resulted in the discriminant function shown below (standard errors for the jackknife estimate of the coefficients are shown in parentheses):

$$Ds = 0.813 + 0.725 \text{ v8} - 0.879 \text{ v20} \qquad (1)$$
$$(2.207)(0.229)a \qquad (0.470)b$$
$$a = t > 2.508(t0.01); \qquad b = t > 1.717(t0.05).$$

v8 = Importance of recommendation by family or friends to customers selecting the company as a financial service provider.
v20 = Wealth of customers, compared with those of competitors.

The two coefficients were both shown to be stable by t-tests on the confidence interval which were significant at the 5 per cent level. The resulting function discriminates well between the two groups with the resulting validation confusion matrix being significant at 5 per cent level (Table 5).

'Superior performance is related to customer base'

It should be noted that when using the jackknife, the final discriminant function is not generated directly, rather the jackknife function is generated from a set of functions based on subsamples. As a result, any diagnostics derived are appropriate to the subsample functions rather than the jackknife function.

The discriminant analysis resulted in companies classified as admired by experts having negative discriminant scores and those not admired, positive. Hence the signs attached to the coefficients suggest that the companies admired by experts had high scores on the

Table 5. Confusion matrix: classification accuracy using U-method.

	Predicted group	
	Average or below performance	Above average performance
Actual group		
Average or below performance	10 66.7%	5 33.3%
Above average performance	1 12.5%	7 87.5%

Overall classification accuracy = 72.7 per cent.
Fisher Exact Test $p = 0.027$.

variable reporting relative wealth of customers and low scores on the variable reporting the importance of family/friends recommendation as a means of recruiting customers. It appears, therefore, that the companies admired by experts are those attracting wealthy customers who do not select their financial service provider on the basis of an existing relationship with family or friends.

DISCUSSION AND MANAGERIAL IMPLICATIONS

First, it should be noted that the discriminant function identified is similar to that found using peer assessment, confirming the reliability of the measures (see Speed and Smith, 1991): both highlighted customer wealth as an important discriminating variable. These results clearly suggest that superior performance in the UK financial service industry is related to customer base. Both correlation and discriminant analysis using expert assessment indicate that superior performing companies are distinguished by wealthier customers, customers who are less influenced by family and friends in their selection of a provider.

The findings suggest that not only are better performing companies' customers recruiting and retaining a wealthier customer base, they are doing it in a different way. Much has been written about the value of wealthier customers in financial services (see, for example, Mason and Mayer, 1974; Stanley et al., 1979). Wealthier customers are more likely to have greater sums on deposit and engage in larger transactions. Since the administration costs of financial service products vary little with transaction size, these customers are more profitable. They are also more profitable because they are more sophisticated in their use of personal financial services. They are more willing and likely to use ancillary products, where profit margins are higher, for instance in banking, credit cards, foreign exchange and personal loans. This sophistication arises in part from the fact that they are more likely to be professionally advised on their financial service needs and also from the proliferation of personal finance advice in the press, particularly the quality papers.

In recruiting these customers, the better performing companies are less reliant on the recommendation of family and friends in choosing the company to supply financial services. Research has suggested that an existing family or employer connection has been particularly important in recruiting customers for banks and protection insurance business. The admired companies appear therefore to have broken this traditional link. The two variables therefore indicate two aspects of a particular strategy that admired companies pursue. The admired companies attract and retain a more wealthy customer base and do not rely on recruitment from those with relationships with existing customers.

'The better companies balance market- and finance-oriented activity'

Although there is no direct evidence from this research, the ability to attract and retain wealthy customers is likely to be heavily dependent on product quality and service standards since, as pointed out, wealthy customers are more likely to be advised or have access to information and be more confident in their financial dealings. The findings therefore provide some support for the relationship banking model. They suggest that superior performance is based on forming relationships with the right sort of customers. However, it should also be noted that the findings also indicate that companies with superior performance place a stronger emphasis on cost control and current profitability. These findings suggest that there is selectivity in what the better performing companies are prepared to offer to their customers, and considerable effort is made to ensure that existing products do not become major cost burdens. This approach, balancing market-oriented and finance-oriented activity has been proposed by Doyle (1987) as a model for achieving success and the findings appear to support such a view.

The findings counter the argument that the poor performance of the UK financial services sector has been the result of moving away from the traditional way of doing things, with too great an emphasis on aggressive competition and too little on traditional prudence. However, this research suggests that this has not been the case. The better performing financial service companies are characterized by a greater emphasis on control of costs and profitability and by greater selectivity in targeting their customers. For the better performing companies, the argument that financial service companies are engaging in irresponsibly aggressive competition can be dismissed. However this does not imply that the better performing companies are concentrating on the traditional virtues of financial services. Selectivity and profit orientation are keystones of the marketing concept. Thus the research suggests that it is through successful application of the marketing concept that the better performing companies have achieved their position.

The key lesson for success in retail financial services to arise from this research is the relationship between selectivity and profit orientation, on the one hand, and company performance on the other.

REFERENCES

Barsoux, J-L. and Saunders, J. A. (1989), *Britain's Most Admired Companies*, Economist Publications, London.
Berry, L. L. and Thompson, T. W. (1982), 'Relationship Banking—The Art of Turning Customers into Clients', *Journal of Retail Banking*, 4 June, pp. 64–73.
Buzzell, R. D. and Gale, B. T. (1987), *The PIMS Principles*, Free Press, New York, NY.
Chakravarti, D., Mitchell, A. and Staelin, R. (1981), 'Judgement Based Marketing Decision Models: Problems and Possible Solutions', *Journal of Marketing*, Vol. 45, pp. 13–23.
Conant, J. S., Mokwa, M. P. and Varadarajan, P. R. (1990), 'Strategic Types, Distinctive Marketing Competencies and Organizational Performance: A Multiple Measures-Based Study', *Strategic Management Journal*, Vol. 11, pp. 365–83.
Dankley, N. and Helmer, O. (1963), 'An Experimental Application of Delphi to the Use of Experts', *Management Science*, Vol. 9 No. 3.
Dess and Robinson (1984).
Doyle, P. (1987), 'Marketing and The British Chief Executive', *Journal of Marketing Management*, Vol. 3 No. 2, pp. 121–32.
Fisher, F. M. and McGowan, J. J. (1983), 'On the Issue of Accounting Rates of Return to Infer Monopoly Profits', *American Economic Review*, March, pp. 82–97.
Franks, R. E., Massy, W. F. and Morrison, D. G. (1965), 'Bias in Multiple Discriminant Analysis', *Journal of Marketing Research*, Vol. II, pp. 250–8.
Hair, J. F., Anderson, R. E., Tatham, R. L. and Black, W. C. (1992), *Multivariate Data Analysis*, 3rd edn., Maxwell Macmillan, New York, NY.
Huberty, C. J., Wisenbaker, J. W. and Smith, J. C. (1987), 'Assessing Predictive Accuracy in Discriminant Analysis', *Multivariate Behavioral Research*, Vol. 22, pp. 307–29.
Klecka, W. R. (1980), 'Discriminant Analysis', Sage University Paper series on Quantitative Applications in the Social Sciences No. 07-019, Sage Publications, Beverly Hills and London.

Lachenbruch, P. A. and Mickey, M. R. (1968), 'Estimation of Error Rates in Discriminant Analysis', *Technometrics*, Vol. 10, pp. 1–11.
Mason, J. B. and Mayer, M. L. (1974), 'Differences between High and Low Income Savings and Chequing Account Customers', *Bank Administration*, Vol. 50, June, pp. 48–64.
Peters and Waterman (1982).
Pollock, A. J. (1985), 'Banking: Time to Unbundle the Services?', *Long Range Planning*, Vol. 18 No. 1, pp. 36–41.
Saunders, J. A. (1987), 'Marketing and Competitive Success', in Baker, M. J. (Ed.), *The Marketing Book*, Heinemann, London, pp. 10–28.
Saunders, Prawn and Laverick (1991).
Skeel, S. (1991), 'Banks Bloodied and Bowed', *Management Today*, March, pp. 49–52.
Speed, R. (1991), 'Marketing, Strategy and Performance in the UK Retail Financial Services Industry', unpublished doctoral thesis, Loughborough University of Technology.
Speed, R. and Smith, I. G. (1991), 'Marketing Strategy and Company Performance: A Discriminant Analysis in the Retail Financial Services Industry', *International Journal of Bank Marketing*, Vol. 9 No. 3, pp. 25–31.
Stanley, T. J., Berry, L. L. and Danko, W. D. (1979), 'Personal Service versus Convenience; Perceptions of High Income Customers', *Journal of Retail Banking*, June, pp. 54–61.
Tukey, J. W. (1958), 'Bias and Confidence in Not-quite Large Samples', *Annals of Mathematical Statistics*, Vol. 29, p. 614.
Varadarajan, P. and Berry, L. L. (1983), 'Strategies for Growth in Banking: An Exposition', *International Journal of Bank Marketing*, Vol. 1 No. 1.
Varadarajan, P. and Ramanujam, V. (1990), 'The Corporate Performance Conundrum: A Synthesis of Contemporary Views and an Extension', *Journal of Management Studies*, Vol. 22 No. 5, pp. 463–83.

24

Strategic Marketing in Financial Services: Retrospect and Prospect

Christine T. Ennew, Mike Wright and Des Thwaites

INTRODUCTION

The concept of marketing as an integrated management function probably only gained acceptance within the financial services sector during the course of the 1980s. Prior to that time, marketing was concerned primarily with advertising and selling existing product ranges. In the same period, the marketing of financial services came of age academically with the launch of the *International Journal of Bank Marketing* in 1983 and the appearance of a growing number of texts on the subject (see for example, Donnelly *et al.*, 1985; Watkins and Wright, 1986; McIver and Naylor, 1987; Marsh, 1988; Ennew *et al.*, 1990). As Michael Baker argues in this issue, there is considerable progress to be made before the truly marketing-led provider of financial services appears. Nevertheless, the evidence of the past decade suggests that the extent to which financial services organizations can be considered to be marketing oriented has increased.

This article examines the development of marketing in financial services, with a particular focus on marketing strategies and strategic marketing. The first section provides an overview of the move towards marketing in the financial services sector and particularly the switch in emphasis from a tactical to a strategic perspective. Current trends and issues are discussed in the second section, while prospects for the future are presented in the next section. A brief conclusion is presented in the final section.

THE DEVELOPMENT OF MARKETING IN FINANCIAL SERVICES

Traditionally, marketing in most Financial Services Organizations (FSOs) was synonymous with selling, advertising and public relations, and it was not until the 1970s that marketing departments were formed on any scale (Newman, 1984). A period of rapid environmental change in the 1970s and 1980s led to the development of marketing as a more integrated function within financial services organizations, with a strategic as well as a tactical role to play in business development. This pattern of change is well documented. Newman (1984), presents a comprehensive analysis of the development of the marketing function within financial services during the 1960s, 1970s and early 1980s which emphasizes the move from marketing as a passive, tactical activity towards a more integrated strategic activity. This trend is supported by evidence from later surveys which document the change in strategic emphasis as FSOs moved away from a finance/operations orientation towards a marketing orientation (Hooley and Mann, 1988). However, the same study notes the relatively low level of awareness of strategic marketing planning tools among marketing executives in FSOs and the tendency for marketing to be regarded as a relatively low status activity. Similarly, Morgan and Piercy (1990) argue that marketing is still a relatively new management function within financial services.

Although arguably there are few FSOs that could be cited as exemplars of marketing excellence, the past decade had seen a clear move towards marketing as a more integrated management function in financial services. There is considerable evidence for this trend in the UK (Ennew et al., 1989; Thwaites and Lynch, 1992) and the USA (Brooks, 1987) as might be expected, but similar patterns across a variety of markets including Hong Kong (Yee-Kwong, 1992), Australia (Adler, 1991), Kuwait (Yavas et al., 1990) and Malaysia (Shanmugam, 1989).

While the tactical importance of marketing appears to be well established, the notion that marketing has a strategic dimension is comparatively new in the financial services sector and has developed primarily as a consequence of a period of rapid environmental change in the 1970s and 1980s (Clarke et al., 1988; Thwaites, 1989). The financial marketplace has become increasingly global, technology has developed to improve the speed and variety of service provision and a trend towards deregulation has widened the potential product range for the majority of suppliers (Wright, 1990).

The twin processes of deregulation and technical change have lowered the barriers which had traditionally existed between different institutional or strategic groups. The natural consequence of lowering these barriers has been a redefinition of the marketplace (financial services rather than banking or insurance) and an increase in the intensity of competition (Ballarin, 1986; Ennew et al., 1990). While the latter has represented a significant threat to many providers of financial services, the former has created the opportunity for others to offer their consumers a more integrated range of financial services (Thwaites, 1991). Regulatory developments have also had a marked impact on the distribution of financial services (Ennew et al., 1989; Shelton, 1990). In particular, the polarization requirements of the Financial Services Act in the UK forced providers of savings and investment products to address the strategic issues relating to tied or independent status and, where the former was chosen, raised the additional issue of choice of partner. Developments on the demand side, including rising incomes, and a higher degree of consumer sophistication and financial awareness in many segments of the market (Watkins, 1990) reinforced the effects of supply side changes and created additional opportunities in the form of increased demand. Increased threats have arisen in the form of a growing level of consumerism, increased competition and the need to rebuild balance sheets which were severely damaged by poor lending decisions (Farrance, 1993).

The financial services sector is presented with a further set of threats and opportunities as a consequence of the process of liberalizing financial markets within the European Community (Wright and Ennew, 1990). In principle, the Single Market Programme will affect all financial services, both personal and corporate, but in practice, it seems likely that the impact will initially be greatest in the corporate sector. While this is widely recognized by firms in the industry, a survey conducted by the Bank of England (Bank of England, 1989) suggested that in the UK at least, the opportunities were perceived to be much greater than the threats. Across Europe, many FSOs are re-examining their operating environment and considering whether it is appropriate to move into non-domestic markets, how to enter these markets and the positions to adopt in them. Greenfield entry is generally viewed as impractical, particularly in relation to personal markets because of the high costs associated with establishing a physical presence. Clearly these costs do not automatically preclude the use of this method of market entry, as the Halifax have recently announced their intention to apply for a licence to establish a subsidiary in Spain to provide savings and mortgages products to the personal market. However, such an approach to new market entry may well be the exception rather than the rule and acquisition and joint ventures seem likely to remain the preferred strategies. The extent of cross-border merger and acquisition activity appeared to increase during the late 1980s and appears likely to continue into the 1990s, at least among insurance companies (Whitmore, 1993). However, such an approach is costly and presents problems of integration. Similarly, there is evidence of growing interest in joint ventures and other forms of collaboration, although these approaches also present problems (Glaister and Thwaites, 1992), including control, management of the venture and strength of commitment. At the same time as looking for opportunities to exploit new markets, these same organizations have to prepare strategies to deal with the threat of increased competition from non-domestic suppliers. Already, Deutsche Bank and Crédit Lyonnais have indicated their interest in gaining membership of the UK Clearing House Automated Payments System (CHAPS).

As the environment facing suppliers of financial services has become increasingly competitive and turbulent (Thwaites, 1989), the importance of marketing in guiding business development has increased (Ennew et al., 1989). Deregulation removed the traditional restrictions on the types of product which particular institutions could supply, and thus created the opportunity for expansion into new markets. It also presented the threat of an increase in the number and variety of competitors in a specific market. In this situation, tactical marketing was no longer appropriate; no financial services organizations could afford simply to continue supplying the same products to the same markets without some consideration of their possible reactions to the changing opportunities and threats which now confronted them. Rather, the aim of FSOs should be to select a mode of strategic behaviour which is appropriate to the levels of environmental turbulence and configure the organization in a manner which is consistent with the chosen mode. Research by Thwaites and Glaister (1992) suggests that a number of UK building societies have failed to achieve the minimum levels of aggression necessary to compete in the more turbulent financial services marketplace of the 1990s. Others have chosen an appropriate level of aggression but have not secured a resource match consistent with these strategies and as such have failed to achieve the line of balanced behaviour necessary for success.

Although differentiation is widely recognized as a route to increasing competitive effectiveness, the fundamental problem facing providers of financial services was that of identifying a basis for differentiation. Services cannot be patented so product types and features can generally be copied with ease (Davison et al., 1990) and consequently do not provide a clear basis for building a competitive position. Accordingly, the search for competitive advantage has tended to focus on the process of service delivery rather than the service itself. Two particular areas present themselves as providing a basis for service differentiation, namely technology and service quality, although branding has also been identified as a significant contributor to the process of differentiation, as argued by Saunders and Watters in this issue. Howcroft and Lavis (1987) suggest that the organizational image is perhaps one of the most important forms of branding available in financial services because of the significance of consumer trust in the service provider. However, as Stewart (1991) notes, any corporate identity and image must reflect an organizational reality otherwise the effect will be negative. Clearly, there is still some progress to be made in this area and recent work suggests that although some FSOs have managed to create a distinct visual image they have been less successful in relation to the creation of a genuine corporate identity (Balmer and Wilkinson, 1991).

The application of technology to service production and delivery provides a means of reducing costs or increasing the value associated with a particular service. Developments in artificial intelligence as described by Curry and Moutinho later in this issue can be applied to the management process itself as well as enabling some of the more complex elements of financial services to be mechanized (loan applications, financial advice), thus reducing the costs associated with a particular service. Similarly, the general trend towards customer-based rather than account-based information systems provides the foundation for more efficient target marketing and the potential to offer additional product benefits as is the case with TSB's Family Bonus Scheme. The application of IT in service delivery has the potential to provide at least a short-term competitive advantage. For example, First Direct appear to have built a strong competitive position in a particular target market on the basis of a unique delivery system. That delivery system does not involve leading edge technology and can be copied by the competition but, because of the complexity of the system, any copying is likely to take time and in the interim, First Direct can benefit from significant first-mover advantages.

Service quality, as discussed by Lewis in this issue, has been widely identified as a much more realistic basis for establishing a competitive position. Where an FSO can develop and implement effective programmes for service quality, such programmes can provide a real competitive advantage because of the difficulties associated with copying. Consequently service quality and customer care are seen as increasingly important as a basis for differentiation in the financial services marketplace (Lewis, 1989a, 1989b). Precise definitions of these terms are elusive, although it is important to note that there are significant differences between the two concepts (Gibbs, 1993; Lewis and Smith, 1989). Customer care tends to be the broader concept and one which relates to the overall attitude and philosophy of the organization, while service quality focuses more specifically on the process of service delivery. Within the concept of service quality, further distinctions are relevant. Of particular importance is the distinction between technical and functional quality (Richardson and Robinson, 1985). The former deals with specific dimensions of the service product and the performance of that product while the latter is more concerned with the delivery of the service. Similar distinctions are proposed by Grönroos (1984) and Lehtinen and Lehtinen (1991) with the suggestion that a third dimension may be appropriate, namely corporate quality. Irrespective of the precise framework chosen, an important point to note is the distinction between process and outcome and it is generally thought that the process component is of most significance in consumer assessments (Zeithaml, 1981).

TRENDS IN MARKETING STRATEGIES

In the buoyant marketplace of the mid- to late 1980s, the initial response was bullish with many organizations seeking to take full advantage of the opportunity to offer new products to new markets. In most instances, the products themselves were not new to the marketplace although they were new to the organization. Increasingly, differentiation strategies directed at the market as a whole or at specific sectors replaced traditional cost-based strategies in which specific institutional types focused on traditional product ranges (Ennew et al., 1989; Edgett and Thwaites, 1990). However, more recent evidence suggests that this rapid differentiation and diversification may be causing problems for many FSOs because it has resulted in a blurring of images and a lack of clear positioning (McGoldrick and Greenland, 1992). Indeed, as will be argued later, such developments may perhaps be best viewed as a process of experimentation with product/market withdrawals being necessary in cases in which the experiment has failed (Ennew and Wright, 1990).

In most FSOs face-to-face encounters are the primary mechanism for service delivery and the customer's relationship with the personnel providing the service may be stronger than with the organization itself. As the complexity of the service increases, the greater is the need for trust and confidence in the service provider (Eiglier and Langeard, 1977; Bowen and Schneider, 1988; Grönroos, 1990). This confidence element is particularly important when the service involves very specific skills (e.g. investment or money management) or where the risks associated with the service may be high (e.g. managing money). As a consequence, attracting and retaining the appropriate personnel becomes central to the success of the service business, since these personnel will be the key to attracting and retaining profitable business. The skills acquired by these individuals are frequently highly specific to the firm and the markets within which it operates. Consequently, the production and delivery of financial services has traditionally been highly integrated. Banks and building societies are heavily reliant on branch networks and many insurance companies have a high level of dependence on their own tied salesforces. Even in cases where external arrangements for service provision (broker networks, independent agents, etc.) are chosen, these typically involve close links with the ultimate service provider. The extensive changes in the marketing environment for financial services which occurred in the second half of the 1980s, presented a significant range of opportunities to FSOs for expansion, diversification and differentiation. To exploit such opportunities required new skills to manage an increasingly varied range of products. Firms looking to move into new markets or new market segments have found these skills difficult to create internally and rather easier to gain by acquisition, as was illustrated by building society and insurance company decisions to move into estate agency by purchasing existing networks in the mid- to late 1980s. For example, of 14 building societies entering estate agency in the late 1980s, only three chose to enter via cold starts (Yorkshire, Woolwich, and Abbey National) and these three were all subsequently involved in more extensive entry via acquisition, joint venture, or franchising.

However, when the skills of individual employees are a key to the success of a business, acquisition is also a risky strategy because of the possibility that specialist personnel will not remain with the acquired firm (Thomas, 1978). Again, estate agency business provides a clear example of the pitfalls which providers of services may encounter. In cases in which the original founder of the business chose not to remain with the business following acquisition, this represented a significant loss of managerial skill and knowledge which the acquiring company often had difficulty in replacing. Furthermore, even in cases in which the previous owner remained with the business, the new owner faced significant problems in relation to motivating and remunerating these individuals.

Marketing strategies in the late 1980s were characterized by the tendency among established financial institutions to move into areas from which they had often been precluded. Firms not previously offering financial products, such as retailers, also began to enter the new market. Many financial institutions took advantage of the opportunities presented by legislative and other changes through a major programme of strategic change involving new product development, diversification, experimentation with new organizational structures, and an increase in mergers and acquisitions (Ennew et al., 1990). For example, a survey conducted in 1987, the year following a number of the important legislative changes, found that although almost two-thirds of financial institutions at this time were focused on narrow market segments, 54 per cent of respondents were planning to become leaders across a wide variety of new markets (Ennew et al., 1989). Evidence of similar trends in relation to building societies is presented by Edgett and Thwaites (1990). The precise form of strategic change varied across organizations and was dependent to some extent on the nature of existing strategies and the resources available. Hence smaller building societies, which were legally constrained in their diversification, did not plan to diversify as much as larger societies. For those societies not restricted, other organizational or financial constraints may operate (Wriglesworth, 1989). Mergers provided a rapid means of achieving diversification. Some smaller FSOs even indicated a willingness to be acquired, either to provide a viable base for limited increased range of services or to make it worthwhile for another type of institution (e.g. an insurance company or finance house) to consider a joint venture arrangement.

The problem of managing new acquisitions, as seen earlier, raises the general issue as to whether an activity or product should be provided within the firm itself or through some form of market or joint arrangement with another firm. The latter approach may be effected through such mechanisms as joint ventures, minority shareholdings, franchising, etc. Glaister and Thwaites (1992) highlight the importance of joint ventures in providing a cost-effective method of entry into international markets. Similarly, in domestic markets, collaborative arrangements also offer a cost-effective means of expanding the product range. For example, the Building Societies Act 1986 enables societies to offer unsecured loans for the first time. The vast majority of societies choosing to offer unsecured loans do so through links either with one of the Scottish clearing banks or the Co-op Bank or (more common) with a finance company. These links may provide benefits to both societies and finance houses. They enable smaller societies, in particular, to enter the market, and provide ready access to the necessary expertise. For finance houses, the advantages relate to access to a wider branch network and reduction in vulnerability to losing customers if societies supplied the product on their own. Indications are that greater attention could have been paid to more flexible links than has actually occurred. These outcomes suggest that acquisition may not be the most effective means of gaining and sustaining a market presence and that some early movers may subsequently need to unwind their acquisitions.

At the start of the 1990s, the expansion, diversification and differentiation that characterized the late 1980s began to be reassessed. Farrance (1993) suggests that such reassessments may reflect the concept of FSOs as being 'strategically tired'. The industry as a whole has begun to question whether some aspects of the regulatory framework, such as those relating to the FSA, are inappropriate, too cumbersome, or still do not go far enough, such as the provisions of the Building Societies Act. Individual financial institutions are also consolidating and re-evaluating the ways in which they have responded to these developments. As it is becoming increasingly apparent that the scope for diversification in the financial services sector is rapidly reaching its saturation level, denoted by evidence of a decline in the rate of movement towards differentiation (Edgett and Thwaites, 1990), it is highly likely that divestments could be equally important in this process of re-evaluation and subsequent exit in the same way as mergers and acquisition activity had been in the initial strategic responses. Indeed, there has already been evidence of significant divestment activity among the banks and other FSOs (Ennew *et al.*, 1992), many of whom have disposed of businesses which were acquired or developed in the wake of the stock exchange liberalization (Gardner, 1990).

Besides entry and subsequent exit, a certain amount of divestment activity has been directly related to firms' strategies in the light of the legislative changes recently implemented. For example, the polarization provisions of the FSA saw institutions opting for independent status or investment intermediaries divesting tied activities. In addition, a number of groups sold insurance broking activities to become tied parts of other groups. All the above factors suggest that a considerable amount of reassessment of diversification undertaken in the late 1980s is taking place.

PROSPECTS

The prospects for strategic marketing for the remainder of the decade will be conditional on the outcomes of the process of reassessing the expansion and diversification of the 1980s. Some FSOs are looking to refocus onto their core activities, having found that attempting to be 'all things to all men' is both extremely difficult and very costly. Whether this is a short-term response to the recession, or a longer-term change in strategic direction, is unclear. What is clear is that future competition is likely to be much more global in orientation and there will be a limit to the number of FSOs which can genuinely seek to be market leaders in such circumstances. The growing importance of *Allfinanz* or *Bancassurance* is one indicator of the strength of commitment on the part of the banks to maintaining a strong position in the financial services marketplace, although such developments are not without problems (Knights *et al.*, 1993). Indeed, as noted earlier, cross-border acquisitions to develop these activities may be expected to continue at high levels (Whitmore, 1993). For the majority of players though, the preferred route may well be some form of product or market specialization in recognition of the difficulties associated with competing head-on with the major players. However, a potential consequence may be that the problems of diversification, noted earlier in relation to the UK market, may be repeated in the context of cross-border activities. Irrespective of whether FSOs engage in extensive narrowing of product ranges, there will remain a need to continue to reinforce the integration of activities and to place emphasis on internal marketing in order to obtain optimum benefits from offering the chosen range of products.

'Quality of service and customer care will remain key components'

Quality of service and customer care will inevitably remain as key components in the overall service offer, but subject to the constraints of controlling cost ratios and remaining price-competitive. Indeed, the whole issue of pricing is set to return to the agenda in the form of the debate over current account charges. In an era when the popularity of the banks with business and personal customers is close to an all-time low, the issue of how to reintroduce a system of charging on current accounts will present a major strategic challenge to the main players in this market.

Two further issues, which are at present less pressing but may offer significant opportunities or pose significant threats, relate to Eastern Europe and environmentalism. Increasingly, major players in the financial services sector will have to consider how to respond to the pressures created by the transformation of Central and Eastern Europe. Early evidence of the possible strategic responses is provided by Haiss (1992) in the context of the Austrian market. Similarly, the pressure to 'go green' is currently of limited significance in the strategic marketing activities of most FSOs, although there is evidence of some notable tactical responses (McKechnie and Ennew, 1993) and one bank, the Co-operative, has attempted to build its market position on the strength of an ethical and environmental orientation. Although the full extent of the impact of these issues on strategic marketing in financial services is uncertain, both Eastern Europe and environmentalism are areas which are likely to require close monitoring in the immediate future.

CONCLUSION

The growing recognition of the importance of marketing in the financial services sector is generally attributed to the competitive pressures created by a period of rapid environmental change during the mid-1980s. FSOs were keen to exploit the strategic opportunities offered by deregulation and an expanding market, particularly in relation to retail financial services. Accordingly, both corporate and marketing strategies placed considerable emphasis on diversification (often through acquisition), market segmentation and product differentiation. This was arguably a period of experimentation; given the new opportunities that had been created, the trend seemed to be one of attempting to exploit the opportunity before it disappeared. However, in many cases, such strategic responses were to prove inappropriate and unsuccessful, and the 1990s has witnessed a gradual reversal of many of the trends of the 1980s. This reversal is in part attributable to changing economic fortunes and the onset of recession which curtailed the expansion of the marketplace. Equally important may be the recognition by management that their organization had grown too diverse and needed to refocus on core competences.

REFERENCES

Adler, B. (1991), *Marketing Financial Services in Australia*, Macmillan, Melbourne.
Ballarin, E. (1986), *Commercial Banks amid the Financial Revolution*, Ballinger, Cambridge, MA.
Balmer, J. M. T. and Wilkinson, A. (1991), 'Building Societies: Change, Strategy and Corporate Identity', *Journal of General Management*, Vol. 17 No. 2, pp. 20–33.

Bowen, D. E. and Schneider, B. (1988), 'Services Marketing and Management: Implications for Organizational Behaviour', *Research in Organizational Behaviour*, Vol. 10, pp. 43–80.
Brooks, N. A. L. (1987), 'Strategic Issues for Financial Services Marketing', *International Journal of Bank Marketing*, Vol. 5 No. 2, pp. 5–19.
Clarke, P. D., Edward, P. M., Gardner, P. F. and Molyneux, P. (1988), 'The Genesis of Strategic Marketing Control in British Retail Banking', *International Journal of Bank Marketing*, Vol. 6 No. 2, pp. 5–19.
Davison, H., Watkins, T. and Wright, M. (1989), 'Developing New Personal Financial Products— Some Evidence of the Role of Market Research', *International Journal of Bank Marketing*, Vol. 7 No. 1, pp. 8–15.
Donnelly, J. H., Berry, L. L. and Thompson, T. W. (1985), *Marketing Financial Services*, Dow Jones-Irwin, Illinois.
Edgett, S. and Thwaites, D. (1990), 'The Influence of Environmental Change on the Marketing Practices of Building Societies', *European Journal of Marketing*, Vol. 24 No. 12, pp. 35–47.
Eiglier, P. and Langeard, E. (1977), 'A New Approach to Service Marketing', in Eiglier, P., Langeard, E., Lovelock, C. H., Bateson, J. E. G. and Young, R. F. (Eds), *Marketing Consumer Services: New Insights*, Marketing Science Institute Report No. 77-115.
Ennew, C. T. and Wright, D. M. (1990), 'Retail Banks and Organisational Change', *International Journal of Bank Marketing*, Vol. 8 No. 1, pp. 4–9.
Ennew, C. T., Watkins, T. and Wright, M. (Eds) (1991), *Marketing Financial Services*, Heineman, Oxford.
Ennew, C. T., Wong, P. and Wright, M. (1992), 'Organizational Structures and the Boundaries of the Firm: Acquisition and Divestment in Financial Services', *Service Industries Journal*, Vol. 12 No. 4, pp. 478–97.
Ennew, C. T., Wright, M. and Watkins, T. (1989), 'Personal Financial Services: Marketing Strategy Determination', *International Journal of Bank Marketing*, Vol. 7 No. 6, pp. 3–9.
Ennew, C. T., Wright, M. and Watkins, T. (1990), 'The New Competition in Financial Services', *Long Range Planning*, Vol. 23 No. 6, pp. 80–90.
Farrance, C. (1993), 'Can Banks Succeed in the Current Market Place?', *International Journal of Bank Marketing*, Vol. 11 No. 2, pp. 3–9.
Gardner, E. (1990), 'A Strategic Perspective of Bank Financial Conglomerates in London after the Crash', *Journal of Management Studies*, Vol. 27 No. 1, pp. 61–73.
Gibbs, P. T. (1993), 'Customer Care and Service: A Case for Business Ethics', *International Journal of Bank Marketing*, Vol. 11 No. 1, pp. 26–33.
Glaister, K. W. and Thwaites, D. (1992), 'International Collaborative Agreements in the Financial Services Sector', in Whitelock *et al.* (Eds) 'Marketing in the New Europe and Beyond', *Proceedings of the 1992 Marketing Education Group Conference*.
Grönroos, C. (1990), 'Relationship Approach to Marketing in Service Contexts: The Marketing and Organizational Behaviour Interface', *Journal of Business Research*, Vol. 20, pp. 3–11.
Haiss, P. R. (1992), 'The Twin Challenges to Austrian Banking: The Environment and the East', *Long Range Planning*, Vol. 25 No. 4, pp. 47–53.
Hooley, G. J. and Mann, S. J. (1988), 'The Adoption of Marketing by Financial Institutions in the UK', *Service Industries Journal*, Vol. 8 No. 4, pp. 488–500.
Knights, D., Morgan, G. and Sturdy, A. (1993), 'Bancassurance and Consumer Protection in the UK: Problems and Prospects', Report prepared for the Centre de Recherche sur L'Epargne, Paris.
Lehntinen, U. and Lehntinen, J. R. (1991), 'Two Approaches to Service Quality Dimensions', *Services Industries Journal*, Vol. 11 No. 3, pp. 287–303.
Lewis, B. (1989a), 'Quality in the Service Sector: A Review', *International Journal of Bank Marketing*, Vol. 7 No. 5, pp. 4–12.
Lewis, B. (1989b), 'Customer Care in Service Organizations', *Marketing Intelligence & Planning*, Vol. 7 Nos 5/6, pp. 18–22.
McGoldrick, P. J. and Greenland, S. J. (1992), 'Competition between Banks and Building Societies in the Retailing of Financial Services', *British Journal of Management*, Vol. 3, pp. 169–79.
McKechnie, S. A. and Ennew, C. T. (1993), 'Environmentalism and the Banks: A Stakeholder Perspective', Paper presented to the 2nd SIMRU Conference, Cardiff, March.

McIver, C. and Naylor, G. (1986), *Marketing Financial Services*, Chartered Institute of Bankers, London.
Marsh, J. R. (1988), *Managing Financial Services Marketing*, Pitman, London.
Morgan, N. and Piercy, N. (1990), 'Marketing in Financial Services Organizations: Policy and Practice', in Teare, R., Moutinho, L. and Morgan, N. (Eds), *Managing and Marketing Services in the 1990s*, Cassell, London.
Newman, K. (1984), *Financial and Marketing Communications*, Holt, Rinehart and Winston, London.
Richardson, B. A. and Robinson, C. G. (1985), 'The Impact of Internal Marketing on Customer Service in a Retail Bank', *International Journal of Bank Marketing*, Vol. 4 No. 5, pp. 3–29.
Shanmugam, B. (1989), 'Marketing of Financial Services in a Developing Country: The Malaysian Experience', *International Journal of Bank Marketing*, Vol. 7 No. 4, pp. 33–8.
Shelton, D. (1990), 'Impact of Financial Services Act on Investment Products', *International Journal of Bank Marketing*, Vol. 8 No. 2, pp. 12–16.
Stewart, K. (1991), 'Corporate Identity: A Strategic Marketing Issue', *International Journal of Bank Marketing*, Vol. 9 No. 1, pp. 32–9.
Thwaites, D. (1989), 'The Impact of Environmental Change on the Evolution of the UK Building Society Industry', *Service Industries Journal*, Vol. 9 No. 1, pp. 40–60.
Thwaites, D. (1991), 'Forces at Work: The Market for Personal Financial Services', *International Journal of Bank Marketing*, Vol. 9 No. 6, pp. 30–36.
Thwaites, D. and Glaister, K. (1992), 'Strategic Responses to Environmental Turbulence', *International Journal of Bank Marketing*, Vol. 10 No. 3, pp. 33–44.
Thwaites, D. and Lynch, J. E. (1992), 'Adoption of the Marketing Concept by UK Building Societies', *Service Industries Journal*, Vol. 12 No. 4, pp. 437–62.
Watkins, T. (1990), 'The Demand for Financial Services', in Ennew, C. T., Watkins, T. and Wright, M. (Eds), *Marketing Financial Services*, Heinemann, Oxford.
Whitmore, J. (1993), 'Insurance: Putting a Premium on Market Share', *Acquisition Monthly*, June, pp. 59–61.
Wriglesworth, J. (1989), *Building Societies Research*, UBS Philips & Drew.
Wright, M. (1990), 'The Changing Environment of Financial Services', in Ennew, C. T., Watkins, T. and Wright, M. (Eds), *Marketing Financial Services*, Heinemann, Oxford.
Yavas, U., Yasin, M., Wafa, M. and Al-Qudsi, S. (1990), 'Kuwaiti Commercial Banks: Challenges and Strategic Responses', *International Journal of Bank Marketing*, Vol. 8 No. 1, pp. 25–30.
Yee-Kwong, R. C. (1992), 'Strategic Marketing Practices: A Comparative Study of the Hong Kong Banking Industry', *International Journal of Bank Marketing*, Vol. 10 No. 6, pp. 11–18.
Zeithmal, V. (1981), 'How Consumer Evaluation Processes Differ between Goods and Services', in Donnelly, J. H. and George, W. R. (Eds), *The Marketing of Services*, AMA Proceedings, Chicago, pp. 186–90.

Index

Emboldened pages indicate chapters. Most references are to United Kingdom, except where otherwise stated.

a priori segmentation 79, 80, 81-2, 84, 107
Aaker, D.A. 87-8
Abbey National Bank (formerly Building Society) 13, 50, 215, 290, 344
access
  accessibility of segmentation analysis 79
  and service quality 171, 175, 179
  and telephone banking 288
Access (credit card) 87
accountability 4, 239
accuracy 192
ACORN (a classification of residential neighbourhoods) 86, 237, 319
acquisitions *see* mergers and acquisitions
action and decision-making 67
actionability of segmentation 79
active competitors 217, 218
added value *see* -added *under* value
Addison, J. 213, 219
address lists and direct mail 231, 239
adequate and desired expectations, difference between 203, 205
Adler, B. 341
advertising
  competition between banks and building societies 315, 322
  competitions 213, 214, 215
  costs 211, 232
  direct marketing 229, 232, 236-7
  ineffective 13
  insurance product development 149
  management of financial services 33, 39-41
  network management and branch distribution channel 292
  segmentation 86
  service quality 183, 184, 200
  success factors for new services 129, 131
  targeting 20
  youth market 96, 99, 104

advice, clear and impartial 323-4
affective stage in decision-making 67
age, segmentation by 80, 81, 84; *see also* youth market
AI (artificial intelligence) 143
AIB Group (formerly Allied Irish Banks) 6, 10-12, 15
AIDA (awareness, interest, desire, action) 67
Albrecht, K. 199
Allfinanz *see* bancassurance
Allied Dunbar 47, 317
Allied Irish Banks *see* AIB
Alwin, D.F. 172
American Bankers' Association 263
American Express 221
Ames, B. Charles 9, 10, 12
Anderson, W.I. 82
Ansoff, H.I. 85
apathetic minimalists 112, 113-14, 116
applications as positioning strategy 87
Arbeit, S. 81
Arnott, David 74, 232
  management of financial services 28-44
Arora, R. 69, 82, 143
artificial intelligence (AI) 143
Asia 71, 224-5, 341
Asian Business 224
Assent credit card (Barclays) 131
assurance *see* insurance
assurance of quality 199
AT & T 14
ATMs (automated teller machines) 4-5, 121, 258
  bank branch managers 262, 263
  competition between banks and building societies 315, 316
  consumers/customers perceptions of innovations and new technology 137, 138-9, 140-4, 145

351

management of financial services 30, 34
network management and branch
  distribution channel 288, 290, 291,
  294-5, 297
numbers of 291
segmentation 82
youth market 91, 96, 97, 101, 104
attitudes 81-2, 83, 152; *see also* perceptions
  under consumers/customers
attribute as positioning strategy 87
augmented offerings 199
Australia
  IJBM articles from 198
  retrospect and prospect 341
  see also measurement *under* service quality
Austria 347
automated teller machines *see* ATMs
automation *see* technology
Automobile Association 129
Avkiran, Necmi Kemal: on quality
  measurement 167, 169-82
awareness 11, 67
Awh, R.Y. 82

Babakus, E. 170, 204, 205
Babb, E.M. 216, 218
Baker, J. 292
Baker, K. 86, 107
Baker, Michael J. 7, 67, 340
  bank marketing as myth or reality 6-15
Ballarin, E. 341
Balmer, J.M.T. 343
bancassurance 306-7, 346
  integration and differentiation in
    management of 4, 5, **45-57**
  core activities 50-1
  future 54-6
  nature of 46-50
  in operation 50-4
  see also selling and branch networks *under*
    insurance
bank *see* banks
Bank Directory of Canadian Payment Association
  264
Bank of England
  bancassurance 50
  bank base rate 248, 251
  survey by 342
Bank Marketing 14
'bank point' concept 294-5
Bank of Scotland 13
Banking Acts 50
Banking Technology 125
Banking World 125
bankruptcies and Bankruptcy Association 13

banks
  base rate and mortgage-pricing 245, 246,
    247-8, 251
  branch managers: roles and functions 259,
    262-72
    changing lending role 273-4, 279-82
    discussion 270-1
    findings 265-9
    future research 271
    methodology 264-5
  and building societies *see* between banks
    and building societies *under*
    competition
  central *see* Bank of England
  charges 13, 101
  consumers and rhetoric and 'reality' of
    marketing financial services 16, 18
  image 12-14
  insurance *see* bancassurance; selling and
    branch networks *under* insurance
  major *see* Co-operative; Lloyds; Midland;
    National Westminster; TSB
  marketing as myth or reality 5, **6-15**
    evolution of 6-8
    normative theory, applying 8-10
    practice of banking 12-14
    transferability of marketing concept 8-10
  promotion *see* competitions
  small business clients *see* small business
    under service quality
  strategies *see* strategy and performance
    under consumers/customers
  see also branches; perceptions of
    innovations *under* consumers/
    customers; retail financial services
    under segmentation; service quality;
    small business clients *under* service
    quality; youth market
Bannock, G. 184
Barclaycard 87, 215, 315
Barclayloan 222
Barclays Bank
  Assent credit card 131
  bancassurance 49
  bank branch managers 263
  charges criticised 13
  competition between banks and building
    societies 315
  competitions 215, 216, 222, 226
  'Money Doctor' 145
Barclays Life 150
Barsoux, J.-L. 330
Bartlett's test 177
base rate *see under* banks
Bass, F.M. 324
Bateson, J.E.G. 64, 65

Bateson, J.E.S. 315
Bayer, J. 216, 225
Beane, T.P. 108
Beckman, M.D. 80
behaviour stage in decision-making 67 *see also under* consumers/customers
Bellenger, D.N. 83
'benefit' pricing 247
Beranek, W. 217, 221
Berger, P.O. 230, 231, 232
Bergiel, B.J. 81
Berry, Leonard 14, 199, 200, 202, 262, 263, 328
'best price' 34, 41
Better Homes and Gardens 221
'better-of-the-same' customers 141, 142, 143
Bingham, Graham H. 68
  youth market 62-3, 91-105
Bird, D. 229, 230, 231-2, 238
Birmingham Midshires Building Society 222
Bitner, M.J. 28, 292, 316
Blackwell, R.D. 67
Blis, M. 317
Blois, K.J. 73
Bloom, P.N. 215
Bogart, L. 215
Boller, G.W. 170, 204, 205
bonanzas 222-3
Booms, B.H. 73, 316
bootstrap validation and segmentation 84
Booz, Allen and Hamilton 155, 156
Borden, N.H. 316
borrowing *see* loans
boundaries of product eroded 20
'boundary-spanning role' of staff 65, 73
Bourke, Kevin J. 6, 10, 11
Bowen, D.E. 65, 73, 344
Bradburn, N. 172
Bradford and Bingley Building Society 49
Bradford, W.E. 263
branch processor system 281
branches 3-4, 344
  bancassurance 46, 47, 50, 54
  closures 290-1, 295
  consumers/customers perceptions of innovations and new technology 145
  design *see* premises
  distribution channel *see* network management
  management 71, 258-60, 305-7; *see also* branch managers *under* bank; changing lending role of managers; network management and branch distribution channel; selling *under* insurance
  mortgage-pricing 245
  numbers 262, 290-1
  segmentation 87-8
  service *see* measurement *under* service quality
Brand, G.T. 72
brand/branding 343
  bank marketing as myth or reality 7, 14, 18
  competitions 217-18
  involvement 217-18
  lack of awareness of 70
  management of financial services 33, 34, 39-41
  segmentation 79
  see also switching
Brent Walker 47
Bretani, U. de 33, 124, 125, 133, 151, 156
Brien, R.H. 12
Britannia Building Society 49
British Bankers' Association 291
Brockmann-Smith, M.B. 101-2, 103
brokers and intermediaries, insurance 148, 153, 233, 317
Brooks, A.L.N. 106, 341
Brown, M. 80
Brown, T.J. 170
Bruicker, F.S. de 148
BSA *see* Building Societies Association
Buchan, J. 288
Buerger, J.E. 183
building societies
  bancassurance 48, 49-50
  and banks, competition between *see under* competition
  changing lending role of managers 273-4, 277-9
  consumers and rhetoric and 'reality' of marketing financial services 16, 18
  diversification 48
  image 4, 100-1
  insurance *see* selling and branch networks *under* insurance
  management of financial services 34
  promotion
    see also competitions
  seen as friendlier than banks 4, 100-1
  segmentation 80
  strategies *see* strategy and performance *under* consumers/customers
  switching to 23
  see also competition between banks and building societies; service quality; youth market
Building Societies Act (1962) 242
Building Societies Act (1986)
  bancassurance 48
  changing lending role of managers 274, 276

competition between banks and building
    societies 318
mortgage-pricing 242
retrospect and prospect in financial
    services marketing 345, 346
segmentation mapping 106
youth market 91
Building Societies Association 242, 291
Directory of Members 234, 250
Building Society Commissioner 50
buildings *see* premises
BulCo case study 52-3, 302-4, 305
Burnett, J.J. 81, 82, 84, 213
Burton, D. 50, 299
Business 125
business centres 281
Business Development Loans 145
businesses *see* corporations
Buswell, D. 198, 200
Buy Grid model and buy phases 67
buyers *see* consumers/customers
buying centre concept 72
Buzzell, R.D. 330

cable 136
CACI 314, 319
Calantone, R. 82
Campaign 125
Canada
    competitions 218, 224
    consumer buying behaviour 68, 69, 71
    IJBM articles from 198
    segmentation 83
    service quality 200-1
    see also branch managers *under* bank
Canadian Bankers' Association 262, 263
canonical correlation analysis 82
capital accumulators 112, 115-16
car insurance 23, 98
card-based services 82
    competitions 215, 221, 222, 223
    debit cards 137, 223
    see also credit cards; smart card
Carlson, C.L. 172
Carmen, J.M. 170, 172, 204
cash reserves and risk management 109-10,
    111
cashcard account and youth market 94-5, 96,
    97, 104
cashpoints *see* ATMs
cautious investors 112, 114-15, 116
CCL Assurance 150
Central and Eastern Europe 202, 262, 347
central place theory 296
Chakravarti, D. 331

Chan, A.K.K. 71
change 19, 156
    ease of 31, 32, 36, 40
    management role *see* changing lending role
    organizational 158-9, 277-8, 280-1
    problems and insurance selling 306
    sensitivity to 31, 32, 35-6, 40
changing lending role of managers 259, **273-
    86**
    case study
        mortgage 277-9
        small business 279-82
    decision-making 284
    leading 276-7
    line manager 283
    literature 274-7
    methodology of research 273-4
    product expert 283-4
    salesperson 263, 283
channels of distribution *see* distribution
Channon, D. 47, 243, 315
CHAPS (Clearing House Automated
    Payments System) 342
Charcol, John (brokers) 131
charge-cards 82
charges
    bank 13, 101
    credit card 315
    service quality 184, 188, 191
    small business clients and 190
Chase Home Loans 129
cheques/chequing
    cashing by young people 95
    cheque guarantee card 95, 97
    chequebooks 95, 96, 97
    discredited 188
    see also current account
chi-square 141, 234
children 95; *see also* youth market
Chin, Alan C.: on mortgage-pricing 242-55
Chiplin, B. 66
Chi-squared test 81, 82
choice
    competition between banks and building
        societies 322-3
    criteria 67, 69, 81-2
    selective perception and 67
Chonko, L.B. 82
Christaller, W. 296
Churchill, G.A., Jr. 170, 171, 173, 178
Clancey, K.J. 82, 84, 86
Clarke, P.D. 18, 341
Clarkson, A. 232
Clay Cross Building Society 248
Clearing House Automated Payments System
    (CHAPS) 342

Clerical and Medical insurance company 49, 150
closures 290-1, 295
cluster-based segmentation analysis (*post-hoc*) mapping 107
   retail financial services 79, 80, 81, 82-3, 84-5, 107
   success factors for new services 128, 133-4
Clydesdale Bank 215
Cobb, R. 231
Cockerill, T. 275
Codes of Practice 122, 204
cognitive stage in decision-making 67
Cohen, D. 270
ColCo case study 53-4, 304-5
collaboration *see* co-operation
collateral 184, 323
Colonial Mutual Life 150
Commercial Union 49, 149
commission 301
   'tainted advice' from intermediaries 48-9
communication
   internal and external and management of financial services 29, 33, 34
   pricing 211-12; *see also* competitions; direct marketing; pricing *under* mortgage
   service quality 171, 175, 177, 179
   strategy and success factors for new services 126, 129-30, 133, 134
   success factors for new services 128, 131, 132
   see also promotion
companies *see* corporations
comparative ratings in study of competition between banks and building societies 320-1
COMPETE checklist 225
competition 3
   bank branch managers 263, 270
   between banks and building societies 311-12, **313-26**
      distribution channels 316-17
      financial institutions as retailers and marketing mix 314-16
      methodology 318-19
      multivariate structure 323-5
      responses 320-3
   competitors' loyals tempted away by competitions 216, 218
   consumers and rhetoric and 'reality' of marketing financial services 17, 18, 20
   consumers, strategy and performance 327-8, 329
   direct marketing invisible to 230
   insurance product development 147, 153, 161
   as major *IJBM* topic 30
   mortgage-pricing 242-4, 246, 247, 248, 251, 252, 253, 254
   network management and branch distribution channel 287
   as positioning strategy 87
   prices and mortgage-pricing 245, 247
   promotion 211
   retrospect and prospect 341, 342
   service quality 184, 203-4
   success factors for new services 132
competitions 211-12, **213-28**
   added value 214-16
   consumer behaviour 216-17
   effectiveness 223-4
   financial services involved 219-20
   growing use of 213-14
   integration with marketing 224
   nature of 221-3
   see also prizes
complaints, rarity of 206
complete linkage cluster analysis 83
complexity of financial services 23
computers *see* electronic; information technology; technology
Comrey, A.L. 172
Conant, J.S. 330
concept testing 33, 34, 39-41, 68
conceptual segment profitability 116-17
Confederation Life 150
confidence *see* trust
confirmatory factor analysis 139-40
Connect card 216
Connections (Barclays) 216
consistency 129
consumers/customers
   behaviour 61-3, 92, 318
      competitions 216-17
      as major *IJBM* topic 30
      see also buying behaviour *below, and also* mapping segmentation; retail *under* segmentation; youth market
   buying behaviour in financial services 61-3, **64-77**
      characteristics of services 64-6
      future 73-4
      understanding 66-9
      see also segmentation; youth market
   care *see* service quality
   databases, out of date 86
   expectations *see* expectations
   inertia 17
   management of financial services 35-8, 42
   needs *see* needs, consumer
   new 206
   orientation and bancassurance 306-7

perceptions 341
  of change 318
  expectations 200-1, 203, 205-6
    measured *see* SERVQUAL
  of innovations and new technology 122-3, **136-46**
    building on past results 143
    findings 140-3
    implications 143-5
    list of innovations 136-8
    methodology 138-40
  of value and mortgage-pricing 244, 245, 246, 247, 251, 253
  see also service quality
rhetoric and 'reality' of marketing financial services 5, **16-27**
  limitations in responding to consumer needs 20-4
  marketing orientation in UK 17-20
service *see* service quality
'sovereignty' 19
staff relationship with *see* model *under* interaction
strategy and performance 312, **327-39**
  database creation 328-30
  findings 333-7
  managerial implications 337-8
  measures of performance 330-2
  methodology 332-3
  types and competitions 216-18
  see also needs; retail financial services *under* segmentation; segmentation; youth market
consumption and production separate 65, 70, 314
convenience 23
  consumer buying behaviour 70
  of telephone banking 288
  youth market 96, 101
Cooil, B. 84
Cooper, R.G. 124, 125, 133, 151, 155, 156
co-operation
  bancassurance 55-6
  bank branch managers 264
  management of financial services 29, 33-4, 39-41
  in promotion 225
    lack of 224, 226
  retrospect and prospect 342, 344, 345
Co-operative Bank 87, 121, 216, 294, 345, 347
Coopers & Lybrand 13
core offering 124, 199
Cornhill 150
Cornish, P. 108
corporations/corporate
  capability and strategies for future

  research 85-6
  consumer buying behaviour 71, 72
  Corporate Intelligence Group 316
  identity programme 11
  quality 343
  skills concept 329
  strategy in management of financial services 33, 39-41
  see also banks; building societies; insurance companies; organization; small businesses
correlation analysis 82, 125
costs 3, 7
  advertising 211
  -based mortgage-pricing 244
  competition between banks and building societies 320
  competitions 216, 217; *see also* value *under* prizes
  consumers perceptions of innovations and new technology 141, 142
  rhetoric and 'reality' of marketing financial services 17, 21
  strategy and performance 327-8, 331, 338
  determinant of mortgage-pricing 245, 246
  direct marketing 232, 235
  insurance product development 153, 160-1
  leadership strategy and mortgage-pricing 249, 252
  low *see* profitability
  mortgage-pricing 243, 244, 246, 249, 250-1, 252, 253
  network management and branch distribution channel 288, 295-6
  retrospect and prospect 343
  see also risk; value
Cotton, B.C. 216, 218
Council on Financial Competition 296
country analysis as major *IJBM* topic 30; *see also* international/global financial services marketing
Coutts 87
Cowell, D. 314, 316
Cox, E.P. 82
Crawford, C.M. 155
creative problems and direct marketing 239
credibility/credence
  qualities, financial services low in 65, 70
  service quality 175, 176, 179
credit
  reference system 279
  scoring 19, 276, 282
  see also credit cards
credit cards 69, 121, 327
  charges 315

competitions *see under* card-based services
consumers/customers perceptions of innovations and new technology 137, 139, 142, 144
   interest rates 315
   segmentation 81, 84, 86, 87
   success factors for new services 131
   youth market 97-8
   see also smart cards
Crédit Lyonnais 342
Cronbach, L.J. 274
cross-selling 92, 166, 206, 329
   competition between banks and building societies 315
   consumers and rhetoric and 'reality' of marketing financial services 18, 22, 23
   direct marketing 232, 237, 238, 239
Crouch, S. 172
Crown Life 150
cues to quality 215
Cummins, J. 214, 217
currency 98, 131, 262
   mortgage 131
current account
   interest-bearing 47, 96, 97, 103, 315, 327
   youth market 94-5, 96, 97, 103
   see also cheques/chequing
current effect on performance scale 31, 32
Curry L.B. 343
customers *see* consumers/customers
customized messages in direct marketing 230
Czepiel, J.A. 199

Dangar Research Group 171
Dankley, N. 331
Data Processing (DP) department 33, 34, 39-41
Davison, H. 18, 124, 160, 342
Day, A. 244
Dean, Helen 24-5
Debenhams Share Centres 317
debit cards 137, 223
decision-making
   bank branch managers 266, 267, 268-9
   change and changing lending role of managers 279, 282, 284
   changing lending role of managers 284
   consumer buying behaviour 66-7, 72
   insurance product development 151
   service quality 188
   small business clients and 191
'defensive' strategies 311
delivery
   easy-to-duplicate 124
   hierarchy of system 294-5, 296
   retrospect and prospect 342-3
   service quality 166, 204
   unique system *see* First Direct
Delphi methods and customers, strategy and performance 331, 332-3, 335
demand 19, 341
   elasticity 244, 245, 247, 251
   smoothing 215
Demirag, I. 253
demographic data and segmentation 83
   bank managers 265, 267
   a priori 79, 80, 81-2, 84, 107
   youth market 91, 92
Deng, Shengliang: on bank branch managers 259, 262-72
Denny, M. 108
Denzin, N.K. 172
Department of Trade and Industry 13, 50
dependability and consumer buying behaviour 70
depersonalization trend 144
deposit accounts *see* savings
depth of product line and management of financial services 35-8, 42-3
deregulation 3; *see also* legislation and regulation
Derrick, F.W. 108
desensitization to promotion 213
design
   branch *see* premises
   product 16
   service quality 201
desired and adequate expectations, difference between 203, 205
Dess L.M. 334
determinant attribute analysis 82, 83
Deutsche Bank 342
development of product *see* innovation/new product
Dickson, P.R. 213
dictation machines 281
Diebold, J. 263
differentiation 7, 315, 329
   competitions 215
   integration *see* bancassurance
   lack of 144
   mortgage-pricing 254
   retrospect and prospect 342-3, 344, 345-6
   strategy and mortgage-pricing 248-9, 252
   success factors for new services 127, 128, 131, 132-3, 134
   see also segmentation
direct costs 244
Direct Line 121, 149-50
direct mail 211, 231-2, 233, 236, 240
   segmentation 86, 87

success factors for new services 126, 128, 129, 131, 133, 134
direct marketing 212, **229-41**
  activity and methods 232
  costs 232, 235
  defined 230
  in financial services 232-3
  insurance product development 148, 154
  integration of activities 235-6
  methods 236-7
  objectives and methodology 233-4
  organization 237-8
  problem areas 239
  role 238-9
  segmentation and targeting 237, 239
  specific competencies 239
  telemarketing 231, 232, 236-7
  testing 238
  see also advertising; direct mail
Direct Marketing Association, US 230
direct response marketing 236
Director 125
Directory of Members (BSA) 234, 250
disclosure of commission 48-9
discounting 214
discretion see trust
discriminant analysis 82, 84, 107, 334-7
dissatisfaction, customer 92, 101-3, 104, 206
  small business clients 187-92
dissonance, post-purchase 67
distribution of banks, revolution in 287-9
distribution channels
  competition between banks and building societies 316-17
  short 65
  see also network management
diversification
  building societies 48
  competition between banks and building societies 313, 317, 325
  consumers/customers perceptions of innovations and new technology 145
  retrospect and prospect 345-6
divestment 346
Dixon, B.R. 275
Donaldson, B. 73
Donnelly, J.H. 155
Donnelly, J.H., Jr. 270
Douglas, T. 86
Doyle, P. 80, 216, 338
DP (Data Processing) department 33, 34, 39-41
Drake, L. 319
Drayton, J.L. 93
dual-threshold factors and service quality 199
Dumaine, B. 155

Dun and Bradstreet 186
Dunkelberg, W.C. 183
DunnHumby Associates 232

Eagle, T.C. 322
Eagle Star 150
ease of change 31, 32, 36, 40
Easingwood, Christopher J. 74, 232
  insurance product development 151, 159, 161
  management of financial services 28-44
  success factors for new services 122, 124-35
Eastern and Central Europe 202, 262, 347
EC see European Union/European Community
economic model of management of financial services 33, 34, 39-41
economies of scale 7, 288, 293
Edgett, S. 156, 232, 252, 344, 345, 346
effectiveness
  competitions 223-4
  marketing 11
effects, hierarchy of 67
efficiency and service quality 4, 184, 186, 187, 201
EFT (electronic funds transfer) systems 142, 258, 263
  EFTPoS 91, 137, 143-5, 315
  see also ATMs
Eiglier, P. 64, 344
elasticity of demand as determinant of mortgage-pricing 244, 245, 247, 251
electronic
  funds transfer see EFT
  letter of credit 136, 144
  see also technology
emergence of marketing 19-20
empathy and service quality 170, 199
empirical studies and consumer buying behaviour 70-3
  tabulated 68-9, 70
employees see staff
endowment mortgage 48, 55
Engel, J.F.: Engel-Kollat-Blackwell model 67
enhancing factors and service quality 199
Ennew, Christine 47, 48, 232, 252, 299
  retrospect and prospect of strategic financial services marketing 340-9
Ennis, D.M. 108
Entwistle, T.W. 202
environment of outlet see premises
environmentalism 347
Equitable Life 150
errors 13, 101, 188, 189; see also failure

established customers 81; *see also* perceptions *under* consumers/customers
estate agencies 317, 344-5
ethnicity 68, 83
EU *see* European Union/European Community
Europe 347
　bancassurance 45, 55
　consumers/customers perceptions of innovations and new technology 137
　direct marketing 232
　Eastern *see* Central and Eastern Europe
　IJBM articles from 198-9
　retrospect and prospect in financial services marketing 341-2
　service quality 199, 202
　see also European Union/European Community
European Bankers' Small Business Seminar 184
European Direct Marketing Association 232
European Journal of Marketing 198
European Union/European Community
　Economic and Monetary Union 4
　insurance product development 147, 160
　one currency developments 262
　Single Market 3-4, 30, 55, 160, 341-2
　see also Europe
evaluation *see* screening and evaluation
Evans, R.H. 80
everyone a winner competitions 222-3
excellence research 328
existing customers 14, 218 'farmed' *see* cross-selling
expectations of consumers/customers 165
　insurance product 145
　perceptions 200-1, 203, 205-6
　　measured *see* SERVQUAL
　service quality 203
　small business clients and 192-3
expenditure *see* costs
experience qualities, financial services low in 65, 70
expert assessment 330-8

factor analysis bank branch managers 267
　consumers/customers perceptions of innovations and new technology 139-42
　marketing activity 35-43
　quality measurement 172-9
　segmentation 82, 83
　success factors for new services 125, 128
Fahad, G.A. 319
failure of marketing 9, 216, 226, 328; *see also* errors

Family Bonus Scheme (TSB) 343
Far East, *IJBM* articles from 198
Farrance, C. 345-6
fax machines 281
fee income 145
Ferrari 79
Fidell, L.S. 177
fiduciary responsibility of services 65-6
File, K.M. 71
finance
　companies 81
　management of financial services 33, 39-41
　see also costs; financial services; profitability
Financial Advisor 125, 128
financial maturity scale 111-12
Financial Services Act (FSA, 1986)
　bancassurance 48-9, 50, 51, 54
　changing lending role of managers 274
　consumer and rhetoric and 'reality' 16, 22
　direct marketing 233, 236-7, 239
　insurance selling and branch networks 302
　management of financial services 30, 34
　retrospect and prospect 341, 346
　youth market 91
financial services marketing 3-5
　development of 340-4
　see also bancassurance; branches; communication; consumers/customers; innovation; insurance; management; marketing; mortgage; pricing; product; promotion; segmentation; service quality; strategies
Financial Services Organizations *see* FSOs
Financial Times 14, 213
Financial Weekly 125
financially confused customers 112-13, 116
FinPin 86, 237
First Direct (Midland) 88, 121, 288, 343
First International Research Seminar in Services Management 35
'first to market' 34
first-mover advantages *see* First Direct
Firth, L.P. 233, 234, 235-8, 239
Fishbein, M. 324
Fisher, F.M. 330
fishing analogy 92, 104-5
Fitts, R.L. 82
five-point scale 172
fixed costs 246
Fletcher, R. 107
FlexAccount (Nationwide Anglia) 87, 130, 131
flexibility
　competition between banks and building societies 323-4

direct marketing 239
  service quality 186, 187, 188
  small business clients and 189-90
focus strategy and mortgage-pricing 248, 252, 254
Ford, D. 69, 243
foreign exchange and currency 98, 131, 221
formal organization structures 151
Forum of Private Business 183-4
Foster, R.N. 157
Fotheringham, A.S. 324
foundation products and segmentation mapping 109-10, 111
Fourth Financial Corp. 223
Foxall, G.R. 67, 70, 73
France 45, 137, 232, 342
franchising 344
Franks, R.E. 334
free banking 47, 96, 97, 103
free gifts 95, 96, 97, 103
free overdrafts 96, 97, 103
frequency data 81-2
Freud, Sigmund 67
friendly image of building societies 4, 100-1
Friends Provident 50
Friesen, J. 223
Fry J.N. 82
FSA see Financial Services Act
FSOs (Financial Services Organizations) 340-7; see also retrospect and prospect
Fulcher, D.G. 82
functional dimension of marketing 12
functional quality 343
Furlong, C.B. 68
fusion, data 86
future
  bancassurance 54-6
  consumers/customers 92
    buying behaviour in financial services 73-4
    perceptions of innovations and new technology 144
    see also youth market
  financial services marketing 346-7
  profitability 184
  research into bank branch managers: roles and functions 271

G.A. Direct Line 87
Gaeth, G.J. 214
Gaidis, W.C. 218
Gale, B.T. 330
gambling 217
gap model of service quality 199-200, 203-5
Gardener, E.P.M. 263

Gardner, D.M. 190
Gavaghan, K. 79
Gee, N. 80
general marketing distinct from direct marketing 231
generation of retail traffic in direct marketing 232, 238
generic strategy concept 328, 336
geographic segmentation and youth market 92
Germany 45, 137, 232, 342
GFI (goodness-of-fit index) 140, 141
Gibbs, M.L. 71, 72, 74
Gibbs, P.T. 343
Girobank 83, 87, 130
Glaister, K.W. 232, 342, 345
global see international
Gluck, F.W. 157
goals of bank branch managers 266, 267, 268-9
Goodfellow, J.H. 80
Goodman, J.A. 206
goodness-of-fit index (GFI) 140, 141
goods distinct from services 65, 314
government see legislation and regulation
Gower, Jim 48
G.R.E. Choices 87
Green, P.E. 79
Greenland, Steven J. 232, 344
  competition between banks and building societies 311-12, 313-26
  network management 259, 287-98
Grönroos, C. 44
  bancassurance 65, 70, 73
  retrospect and prospect 343, 344
  service quality, recent developments in 199, 202, 204
Grossbart, S. 292
group discussions 319
Group Information Technology and Planning 276
Grover, R. 216-17
Guardian Royal Exchange 55
Gubar, G. 113-14
Gummesson, E. 64
Gupta, S. 216, 264, 267, 270
Gutmann, J. 184
Gwin, J.M. 80, 107, 243, 247

Hair, J.F. 323, 334
Haiss, P.R. 347
Hakansson, H. 69
Halifax Building Society
  bancassurance 50
  competitions 214

mortgage-pricing 247, 249, 251
retrospect and prospect in financial services marketing 342
Halifax Card Cash 87
Handel, W.M. 243
Hanna, S. 108
Harris/Marketing Week surveys 217
Harrison, Tina S.: mapping segmentation 63, 106-18
Harrods Trust and Estate Agency 317
Hart, C.W.L. 203-4, 206
Harvard Business Review 9
Hayes, A. 81
Helmer, O. 331
help lines 130, 204
Hesketh, J.L. 204
heterogeneity of services 65
'hi-tech value/cost-oriented' customers 141, 142
hierarchy
    delivery system 294-5, 296
    effects 67
    needs 67, 109-10
    network 294-5
Hilton, A. 263
HOBS 121
Holder, D. 229
holding companies 46, 54
hold-out method 84
holistic approach needed 108
home banking 88, 91, 98, 136, 144; *see also* banking *under* telephone
Hondros, P. 267
Hong Kong 71, 341
Hood, J. 81
Hooley, G.J. 341
Hoover 216, 225
Hopper, M. 144
Horowitz, J. 206
housing crisis 19
Howard and Harris algorithm 82
Howard, J.A. 67
Howard-Sheth model 67
Howcroft, J.B. 47, 299, 343
    consumers/customers perceptions of innovations and new technology 143, 145
    mortgage-pricing 243, 249, 253
Howell, R.D. 170, 322
hub and spoke arrangement of networks 295
Huberty, C.J. 334
Hughes, Christopher 13
Hughes, Mark: changing lending role of managers 259, 273-86
human resources management 167; *see also* staff

hygiene factors and service quality 199
hypothetical banks survey of youth market 96-7

idea exploration as key activity 156-7
identification card, smart card as 137
identity *see* image
ideological changes 19
IJMB *see International Journal of Bank Marketing*
image
    banks 12-14
    competition between banks and building societies 318, 324
    consumer buying behaviour 68
    as major *IJBM* topic 30
    retrospect and prospect 343, 344
    segmentation 81, 83
    service quality 166, 206
    youth market 92, 100-1
IMP (Industrial/International Marketing and Purchasing) 67, 69, 72, 73
impersonal nature of telephone banking 288
importance rating 321-2
improvement *see under* product
Incentive Marketing 217
incentives *see* competitions
income 81
    low disposable *see* youth market
    raised 19, 341
    wealth 84, 337
incremental product development *see* improvement *under* product
independent advisers 48, 49
indirect costs 244
Indonesia 223-4
Industrial Marketing and Purchasing *see* IMP
ineffectiveness 13
inefficiency and service quality 187-9
inertia 17
information
    capture 278, 281
    changing lending role of managers 276, 278-9, 281-2
    distribution 282
    handling 278
    insufficient, small business clients and 191
    lack of 101
    manipulation 279, 282
    out of date 86
    processing 69
    service quality, inadequate 184, 188, 192
    storage 278-9, 281-2
    two-way and consumer buying behaviour 65, 66
information technology 343

consumers and rhetoric and 'reality' of
    marketing financial services 16, 18, 19
direct marketing 232
management of financial services 34
see also electronic; technology
Ingham, H. 48
innovation/new product 121-3
  bank branch managers 266, 267, 268-9
  consumers, strategy and performance 329
  development
    consumers and rhetoric and 'reality' of
      marketing financial services 19
    as major *IJBM* topic 30
    management of financial services 29, 33,
      35-8, 39-41, 42, 43, 44
  direct marketing 232, 238
  insurance product development 147, 149
  lack of 156
  see also factors *under* success; launch;
    perceptions of innovations *under*
    consumers/customers; product
    development *under* insurance;
    technology (mainly new)
inseparability in services 65, 70, 314
insolvency 13
Institute of Bankers (Scotland) 6-7
insurance
  competitions 221
  lack of interest in 23
  life *see under* life
  motor 23, 98
  product development 122, 123, **147-62**
    findings 152-60
    focus of study 151
    formal organizational arrangements
      158-9
    key activities in development process
      155-8
    marketing adopted in insurance
      companies 149-50
    marketing specialists 159
    sample of companies 150-1
    successful 147-8
    top management and 160
    types of development 153-5
  selling and branch networks 259-60, **299-308**
    case studies 299, 300-5
    management implications 305-7
    research 299-300
  youth market 98
  see also bancassurance; insurance
    companies
Insurance Acts 50
Insurance Age 125, 128, 129
insurance companies 317, 344

bancassurance 45, 47-8, 49
consumers and rhetoric and 'reality' of
  marketing financial services 16, 22
innovation *see* product development *under*
  insurance
management of financial services 34
marketing adopted in 149-50
strategies
  see also strategy and performance *under*
    consumers/customers
youth market 98
see also insurance
Insurance Directory & Year Book 150
intangibility of services 65, 70, 314; *see also*
  tangibility
integrationdifferentiation *see* bancassurance
marketing 220, 224
service quality 203-4
interaction/interactive 206, 239-bases
  approach *see* perceptions of
    innovations *under* consumers/
    customers
  direct marketing 230
  marketing, competitions as 215-16
  model of relationship between buyer and
    seller 65, 67, 69, 70, 71, 72-4, 328
interdepartmental relationships in
  management of financial services 29,
  33-4, 39-41
interest rates 67, 131, 141
  credit card 315
  fixed by cartel 242, 247
  mortgage 242, 246, 247-8, 251, 323
  service quality 184
  see also under current account
interface with customers *see* interaction; staff
intermediaries
  insurance *see* brokers
  success factors for new services 127, 128,
    130, 132, 133, 134
  'tainted advice' from 48-9
International Journal of Bank Marketing (IJBM)
  bank marketing as myth or reality 14-15
  management of financial services 28, 30-1,
    43
  retrospect and prospect in financial
    services marketing 340
  see also recent developments *under* service
    quality
International Marketing and Purchasing *see*
  IMP
international/global financial services
  marketing 14, 202, 341, 342, 346
  banks 262-3
  cash management 137, 144
  co-operation 342, 346

comparisons 68, 201; *see also* Canada; Europe; United States
corporations 137
financial services 71, 72
product fit and success factors for new services 126-7, 128, 130, 132-3, 134
inter-organisational integration and bancassurance 54-5
interviews
  with managers 277, 280
  research
    changing lending role of managers 274
    competition between banks and building societies 319
    consumers, strategy and performance 332
    consumers/customers perceptions of innovations 140
    insurance product development 150, 152
    mortgage-pricing 244-5
    service quality 169, 184, 186
    youth market 93
intra-organisational integration *see* co-operation
Investor's Chronicle 125
Iron Trades 150
irresponisbility of advertising to young 99
IT *see* information technology

jackknife analysis 84, 334, 336
jackpots 221-3
Jacoby, J. 190
Jain, D.C. 216
Jain, A.K. 68, 82
Jefkins, F. 230
job rotation 275
Johne, Axel: insurance product development 122, 123, 147-62
Johnson, E.M. 155
Johnson, R. 81, 122, 199
Johnson, S.C. 155
Johnson-Laird, P.N. 170
joint ventures *see* co-operation
Jones, S. 156
Joseph, L. 84
Jowett, P. 315
Joy, A. 68, 70

Kahn, B.E. 217
Kaiser, H.F. 177
  Kaiser normalisation 128
  Kaiser-Meyer-Ohlin measure 128, 177
Kamakura, W.A. 109, 110, 111-12
Kamal, P. 174

Katona, G. 110
Kaynak, E 69
Keirl, C. 170
Kelloggs 226
Keon, J.W. 225
Key Note 319
Kiely, J. 47, 74, 299
Kilmogorov-Smirnov test 234
King, D. 315
Kinnaird, D. 82
kiosk concept 294-5
Kitching, D.W.C. 106
Klecka, W.R. 334
Kleinschmidt, E.J. 124, 125, 133, 156
k-means clustering 82, 83
KMO (Kaiser-Meyer-Ohlin measure) 128n, 177
Knights, David 48, 50, 299, 346
  consumer and rhetoric and 'reality' of marketing financial services 16-27
Knott, P.A. 293
Kollat D.T. 67
Kotler, P. 67, 79, 86-7, 149, 215, 229, 315
Koula, S. 202
Krosnick, J.A. 172
Kruskal-Wallis test 173, 234
Kumar, V. 216
Kuwait 341

Labaw, P. 173
Lachenbruch, P.A. 334
Lal, R. 213
Lamont, Norman 14
Langeard, E. 64, 124, 125, 344
Langrehr, F.W. 81
Langsdale, Philip 276
Lannon, R. 232
Laroche, M. 68, 69, 70, 83, 143
'last purchase loyal' 217
late adopters 288
launch
  competitions 216
  first management of financial services 33, 39-41
  as key activity 156, 157
Laurent R.L. 83
Lavis, J. 143, 145, 243, 249, 253, 343
law *see* legislation and regulation
Lawrence, T.J.Jr. 244
Lawson, R. 143
Leach, C. 108
lead
  generation in direct marketing 232, 238
  time and direct marketing 239
leadership

cost 249, 252
leading role of manager 276-7
leaflets 236, 237
LeBlanc, G. 169, 174, 186, 198, 200
Lee, Sharon C.I.: direct marketing 212, 229-41
Leeds Permanent Building Society 248
Legal & General 150
legislation and regulation
  bancassurance 46, 48-9, 50, 51, 54
  bank branch managers 263
  changing lending role of managers 274, 276, 284
  competition between banks and building societies 318
  consumers and rhetoric and 'reality' 16, 19, 22
  direct marketing 233, 236-7, 239
  insurance product development 147
  insurance selling and branch networks 302
  as major *IJBM* topic 30
  management of financial services 30, 33, 34
  monopoly 7
  mortgage-pricing 242, 243, 244, 245, 246, 247, 248, 251, 252
  retrospect and prospect 341, 342, 345, 346
  segmentation mapping 106
  service quality 165
  youth market 91, 103
Lehfeld, A.K. 108
Lehman, C. 215
Lehtinen, J.R. and U. 199, 343
leisure and competitions 217
Leonard, M. 68
Leone, R.P. 216
Lesser, J.A. 174
letter of credit, electronic 136, 144
Levitt, Ted 7
Lewis B., Barbara R. 81, 170, 232, 343
  consumer buying behaviour 66, 68
  service quality, recent developments in 168, 198-208
  youth market 62-3, 91-105
life
  assurance/insurance bancassurance 49-50
    competition between banks and building societies 322
    management of financial services 23, 32-3
    product development 150, 152, 153, 156, 157, 158
    see also selling *under* unsurance
  cycle approach 92, 107, 108, 110
lifestyles 18, 92
Likert and Likert-type scales 329, 333
  service quality 170, 172, 200, 205, 249

Likert, R. 170
limitations in responding to consumer needs 20-4
Lindgren, J.H. 80, 107
Lindsay, D. 233, 234, 235-8, 239
line function, marketing as 14
line manager role of manager 283
link-up opportunities and competitions 215; *see also* co-operation
Lippo Bank of Jakarta 223-4
LISREL 123, 140-2
Llewellyn, D. 243-4
Lloyds Bank
  bancassurance 49
  Business Development Loan 145
  charges criticised 13
  competitions 215, 221
  network management and branch distribution channel 293
loans/borrowing attitude of youth market 98-9
  availability and consumer buying behaviour 70
  banks' negative image 13, 14
  competition between banks and building societies 322-3, 324-5
  competitions 221, 224
  managers *see* changing lending role of managers
  segmentation 81
  service quality 183-4, 190
  Third World 47
  youth market 97-9, 104, 109-16
  see also changing lending role of managers
location
  competition between banks and building societies 316, 324
  consumer buying behaviour 70
  direct marketing transcending 230
  problems 4, 258, 287, 290
London & Edinburgh 150
Long Range Planning 6
long-term
  relationship *see* model *under* interaction
  savings 66
  studies of segmentation needed 85
Louie, T.A. 217
Lovelock, C.H. 64, 65, 214, 215
loyalty
  competitions 217, 218
  consumers, strategy and performance 327
  consumers/customers perceptions of innovations 139
  segmentation 81
  service quality 165-6, 206
  youth market 92, 95, 105

see also satisfaction
Lupton, T. 29-31, 44
Lynch, J.E. 18, 232, 341

Ma, V.S.M. 71
McAllister, L. 216
McCarthy, E.J. 316
McClure, J.W. 184
McGoldrick, Peter 232, 292, 293, 344
  competition between banks and building societies 311-12, 313-26
McGowan, J.J. 330
McIver, C. 315, 316, 340
McKechnie, Sally 108, 347
  consumer buying behaviour 62, 64-77
McKenna, R. 147
McKibbin, G. 184
McQueen, John 13
Mahajan, V. 133, 161
mail order 317
mail shots *see* direct mail
Malaysia 341
management
  branch *see under* branches competition between banks and building societies 324
  customers, strategy and performance 337-8
  insurance product development 151, 154, 157, 158, 160
  issues and perceptions 5, **28-44**
    areas of marketing activity prioritized 28, 32-5, 37-8
    marketing activity factors 35-43
    methodology and list of main areas of activity 28, 29-32
  mortgage-pricing 253
  phases in implementation 11
  problems and insurance selling and branch networks 301-2, 303-5
  role *see* changing lending role of managers
  service quality 167
    perspective of 201
    recent developments in 199, 202
    small business clients 184-5, 186-7, 188, 191, 192-3
  small business clients 190-1
Management Today 131
Manchester and Stockport *see* mapping segmentation; small business clients *under* service quality; youth market
Mann, S.J. 341
Mann-Whitney *U*-test 178, 234
Manning, T. 69, 70
MANOVA 81
Mansfield, E. 247

Manufacturers Life 150
mapping segmentation for personal financial services 63, **106-18**
  methodology and findings 109-16
  research problem 108
  understanding consumer 107-8
market-based approach 148-9-driven mortgage-pricing 244
  share 253
  see also market research; marketing
market research
  bank branch managers 266, 268-9
  bank marketing as myth or reality 12-13
  consumers and rhetoric and 'reality' of marketing financial services 18
  insurance product development 159
  lacking 18, 23
  management of financial services 33, 34, 39-41
  success factors for new services 127, 129, 131, 133, 134
Marketing 125, 129-30
marketing
  mix 87, 314-16
    see also in particular location; premises; pricing; product; promotion; service
  concept 7, 16
    transferability of 8-10
  department and management of financial services 35-8, 42
  plan 8
  research *see* market research
  see also financial services marketing
Marketing Week 125, 130, 131
marketplace phase in implementation 11
Marks and Spencer 4, 129, 314
Marrs, C.H. 80
Marsh, J. 315, 316, 340
Marshall, Alfred 67
Martenson, R. 68, 81
Martin, T. 232, 234
Martineau, Pierre 325
Maslow, A.H. 110
Mason, J.B. 81, 82, 3367
'mass marketing to units of one' 23, 24
materialism of youth 92
Mathews, H.L. 107
Mathur, S.S. 148
Matthews, B. 83, 143
maturity, financial, scale of 111-12
Maxwell, Robert 47
Mayer, M.L. 81, 337
Mayes, R. 232
measurement
  direct marketing 230, 239
  measurability of segmentation 79, 80, 83

performance 330-2, 333-4
service quality 166, 199-200, 204-5
media
  fragmentation 229
  range of 232, 236, 240
  youth market 92
  see also advertising
Meidan, Arthur
  bank branch managers 259, 262-72
  branch management 258-60
  communication and pricing 211-12
  consumers
    buying behaviour 61-3, 68
    perceptions of innovations and new
      technology 122-3, 136-46
  direct marketing 232
  financial services marketing 3-5
  mortgage-pricing 212, 242-55
  product innovation 121-3
  quality 165-8
  segmentation 83, 107
  strategy, marketing 311-12
Mercedes 78
mergers and acquisitions 4, 258, 287
  retrospect and prospect 342, 344, 345, 346
  see also AIB
Meridian (Midland) 87, 121
Meyer, R.J. 322
  Kaiser-Meyer-Ohlin measure 128n, 177
Mickey, M.R. 334
micro-marketing 213
Middle East, *IJBM* articles from 198
Midland Bank
  bancassurance 49
  bank branch managers 263
  changing lending role of managers 276
  charges criticised 13
  consumers/customers perceptions of
    innovations and new technology 137
  Exchequer Accounts 87
  First Direct 88, 121, 288, 343
  Meridian 87, 121
  network management and branch
    distribution channel 288
  Orchard 121
  segmentation 79
  success factors for new services 130
  Vector 87, 121, 130
Midshires Building Society 222
Miller, V.E. 133
mind set *see* psychographic segmentation
MINITAB 93, 219
Minster 150
Mintel Report 315
misers 222-3
mission statement 10

mistakes *see* errors; failure
Mitchell, P. 170
Mitchell, V.-W. 204, 205
Moak, D.L. 125
modelling, econometric 33, 34, 39-41
'Money Doctor' (Barclays) 145
Money Management 125, 128
Money Marketing 125, 128
monitoring
  bank branch managers 270
  insurance product development 156
  results of marketing 8
  service quality 204-5
  see also screening and evaluation
monopoly legislation 7
Monte Carlo method 84
Moreno, Roland 137
Morgan, F.W. 83
Morgan, Glenn
  bancassurance 45-57
  consumer and rhetoric and 'reality' of
    marketing financial services 16-27
  insurance selling and branch networks 259-
    60, 299-308
Morgan, N. 341
Moriarty, M.M. 216
Morison, I. 274, 284
mortgage
  hanging lending role of managers 276, 277-9
  competition between banks and building
    societies 319, 322-3
  competitions 221
  currency 131
  endowment 48, 55
  interest rates 242, 246, 247-8, 251, 323
  low rate 129
  pricing and building societies 212, **242-55**
    determinants 244-8, 250-1
    findings 250-3
    literature 243-4
    methodology 249-50
    strategies 248-9, 252-3
  youth market 97-8
MOSAIC 86, 237
motor insurance 23, 98
Moutinho, Luiz 68, 83, 232, 343
  bank branch managers 259, 262-72
  consumer perceptions of innovations and
    new technology 122-3, 136-46
multi-attribute attitude model 324-5
multi-dimensional scaling 83
multiple regression analysis 82
multivariate techniques 81, 323-5
Murray, K.B. 66
mutuality and mortgage-pricing 253, 254

Nadler, D.A. 160
National and Provincial Building Society 49
National Westminster/NatWest
  bancassurance 49-50
  branch distribution channel 292
  Business Development Loan 145
  charges criticised 13
  customer perceptions of innovations and new technology 137
Nationwide Building Society/Nationwide Anglia
  bancassurance 55
  competitions 215
  FlexAccount 87, 130, 131
  mortgage-pricing 247, 249, 251
Naylor, G. 315, 316, 340
needs, consumer
  bank branch managers 270
  branch distribution channel 287
  concept, scepticism about 17, 20-1
  direct marketing 229
  hierarchy of 67, 109-10
  identification 8, 16-18
  limitations in responding to 20-4
  new 19
  service quality 199, 203
negative items and statements 170, 204
neo-liberalism 19
Neslin, S.A. 216
network management and branch distribution channel 259, **287-98**
  physical transformation 290-6
  revolution in bank distribution 287-9
  scope 289-90
network-specific activities 289
new branches 290
new product
  managers in insurance 158; *see also* innovation/new product
new technology *see* technology
New York Times 221
Newbould, G. 80
Newman, K. 340-1
Nguyen, N. 169, 174, 186, 198, 200
Nicosia, F.N. 67
Nielsen Promotion Services 218
'nominal or automated branches' 294-5
Nonaka, I. 155
non-comparability of financial services 23
non-competitors 217
non-profitable products 32-3
NOP/FRS database 319
normative approach 8-10, 80
Norusis, M.J. 177
Norwich Union 150
NOW account 81

NPD (new product development) *see* innovation/new product
Nunnally, J.C. 173
Nyquist, J.L. 73

objectives and competitions 225
'offensive' strategies 311
offering concept 148
office banking 136, 144
Office of Fair Trading 48, 145
Office of Population Census and Surveys 93
OFT *see* Office of Fair Trading
Ohlin: Kaiser-Meyer-Ohlin measure 128n, 177
oligopoly 184
one-per-desk computers (OPDs) 278
'one-stop shopping' 323
'on-the-move' custo 140, 141, 142, 143
opening account 95-7
opening hours 101
operational problems and insurance selling 305-6
Oppenheim, A.N. 322
optimal segmentation 86
Orchard (Midland Bank) 121
organization
  change
    changing lending role of managers 277-8, 280-1
    insurance product development 158-9
  direct marketing 237-8
  formal structures 151
  as major *IJBM* topic 30
  see also corporations; FSOs
Orledge, J. 205
outcome *see* process and outcome
output quality 199
overdrafts 83
  free 96, 97, 103
  youth market 96, 97, 98, 103, 104
overheads low for telephone banking 288
Owen-Jones, C. 229

PA Managment Consultants 233
'package' of products 109
PAF *see* Principal Axis Factoring
Papasavvas J. 51
ParaBank 170
Parasuraman, A. 186
  quality measurement 169, 170-1, 177
  service quality, recent developments in 199, 200, 203, 204, 205, 206
parents and youth market 95-6
Parmee, D. 51
passive competitors 217, 218

Pavlov, Ivan Petrovich 67
Payne, R. 170
Pearson correlation analysis 265, 267
Peattie, Sue and Ken: competitions 213-28
peer assessment 330-1, 333
Peircy, N. 44
pensions 322
Pepsi-Cola 225
perceptions *see under* consumers/customers
Percival, J. 134
performance
  current effect on 31, 32
  gap and service quality 199-200
  measurement
    customers, strategy and performance 330-2, 333-4
    see also strategy and performance *under* consumers/customers
perishability of services 65, 215, 216
Personal Identification Number 137
personal organizers 278, 281
personal selling 315; *see also* cross-selling; staff
personality 92
personalization of promotional materials 236
personnel *see* staff
Peter, J.P. 173
Peters, T. 147, 328
Peterson R. 184
Pezzullo, M.A. 243, 246
Philippines 225
philosophical dimension of marketing 12
physical development as key activity 156, 157
physical transformation of branch networks 290-6
PIBBHG see Premium Incentive Business
Piercy, N. 341
pilot studies 171-2, 173-7, 274
PIMS project 328
PIN (Personal Identification Number) 137
Pinpoint 237
Pitts, R.E. 92
place *see* location
planning
  bank branch managers 266, 267, 268-9
  competitions 213, 225, 226
  marketing analysis 149, 150
  product changes as key activity 156
point-of-sale *see* PoS
'polarisation' principle 48
Pollock, A.J. 328
'pond and stream' analogy 92, 104-5
Pool, A.A. 82
poor bank service *see* dissatisfaction
Porsche 79
Porter, M. 13, 133, 247
PoS (point-of-sale) 236

EFTPos 91, 137, 143-5, 315
positioning 3, 7, 149, 214
  defined 86-7
  management of financial services 33, 34, 39-41
  strategies for future research 85-6
  unclear 344
Post Office 95, 222
post-hoc segmentation *see* cluster-based segmentation analysis
post-purchase dissonance 67
potential users 216, 218
Precision Marketing 125, 129, 130-1
premises and branch design 4
  branch distribution channel 287, 290, 291-3
  branch managers 264, 266, 268-9
  competition between banks and building societies 315-16
  service quality and small business clients 192
  spatial arrangement 295-6
Premium Incentive Business 217, 221
pretesting 171
pricing
  bad risks out of market 22
  communication 211-12; *see also* competitions; direct marketing; pricing *under* mortgage
  competition between banks and building societies 315, 316
  competitions 213, 214, 216
  of competitors and mortgage-pricing 245, 247
  low as success factor for new services 127, 128, 131, 133, 134
  management of financial services 29, 33, 34, 39-41
  policy and management of financial services 35-6, 38, 42
  as positioning strategy 87
  'price-sensitive' customers 141, 142
  service quality 183, 184, 206
  success factors for new services 127, 131, 133, 134
  surrogate measure of quality 214
  wars 214
  see also under mortgage
Prince, R.A. 71
Principal Axis Factoring 174-7
principal components factor analysis 82, 83
prizes, competition 221-3
  value of 217, 220, 221-3, 225, 226
proactive marketing 252
probability of winning competitions 217
process and outcome, difference between 199, 343

product
  boundaries eroded 20
  class, as positioning strategy 87
  competition between banks and building societies 315, 316
  deletions and management of financial services 33, 39-41
  design 16
  development *see* innovation/new product; product development *under* insurance
  expert role of manager 283-4
  extensions and management of financial services 33, 39-41
  fit
    internal marketing and success factors for new services 126-7, 130, 132-3, 134
    success factors for new services 126-7, 128, 130, 132-3, 134
  improvement 151, 153, 154-5, 184
    scope for 31, 32, 35-6, 39-40, 41
  knowledge 276
  led 17
  line
  management of financial services 33, 39-41
  width and depth 35-8, 42-3
  management of financial services 29, 32, 33
  new *see* innovation/new product
  'package' 109
  positioning *see* positioning
  proliferation 33, 39-41, 106, 287
  range and service quality 201
  tailored 8
  see also differentiation; innovation
production and consumption separate 65, 70, 314
professionalism, improvement in 184
profitability 3-4
  bank branch managers 266, 268-9, 270
  changing lending role of managers 274, 284
  conceptual segment 116-17
  consumers and rhetoric and 'reality' of marketing financial services 17, 24
  consumers, strategy and performance 327, 328, 329, 338
  future 184
  mortgage-pricing 242, 244, 249, 253-4
  pre-eminence of 21-4
proliferation, product 33, 39-41, 106, 287
promotion 7, 211-12, **213-28**
  added value 214-16
  bank branch managers 266, 268-9
  benefits of 224-5
  competition between banks and building societies 315
  consumers
    behaviour 216-17

  perceptions of innovations and new technology 145
  effectiveness 223-4
  extent of use 219, 220
  financial services involved 219-20
  growing use of 213-14
  insurance product development 149
  management of financial services 33, 39-41
  marketing integration 224
  nature of 220-1
  prizes 221-3
  service quality 184, 199
  youth market 96-7
  see also advertising; communication; competitions
Provincial Insurance 150
Prudential 150
psychographic segmentation 81-2, 92, 108
publicity and public relations 149, 236, 264; *see also* advertising; promotion
Punj, G. 84

Quadrant Research Services 169
quality 3
  competitions 215, 216
  cues to 215
  as positioning strategy 87
  of service *see* service quality
  success factors for new services 126, 128, 129, 131, 132-3, 134
quantitative segmentation analysis 80, 84
Quelch, J.A. 213
questionnaires
  bank branch managers 264-5
  competition between banks and building societies 319
  consumers, strategy and performance 329
  direct marketing 234
  management of financial services 31-2
  mortgage-pricing 249-50
  service quality 170, 172
  success factors for new services 125, 128
  youth market 93
queuing
  bank branch managers 264
  consumers/customers perceptions of innovations and new technology 140
  service quality 188, 192
  small business clients and 191-2
  youth market 100, 101
Quinn, J.B. 148, 161

Rados, D.L. 84
Ramanujam, V. 330, 334

Rathmell, J.M. 213, 215
rationality 67, 322
rationalization *see* closures
reactive marketing 252
reactive product development 154
Read, C.N. 263
recession 19
recovery, service 204
Reese, R.M. 83
regression analysis and segmentation 81, 82, 83, 84
regulation *see* legislation and regulation
Reidenbach, R.E. 92, 125
Reinertson, D.G. 155
relationship
  between buyer and seller 265-6
    see also model *under* interaction
  marketing 22
reliability and service quality 171, 192, 199
remote deposit boxes 294
repackaging *see* improvement *under* product
repeat analysis 84
research, marketing *see* market research
residential neighbourhoods classification *see* ACORN
respectability of promotion 213
responsiveness and service quality 170, 175, 199
'retail banking' concept 314; *see also* banks
retail stores and financial services marketing 4, 37, 129, 314, 345
retrospect and prospect of strategic marketing in financial services 312, **340-9**
  development of financial services marketing 340-4
  future 346-7
  strategies, trends in 344-6
returns on capital 160, 263
Reuters 136
rewards 218; *see also* free gifts; prizes
Reynolds, F.D. 81, 270
Richardson, B.A. 343
Riggall, J. 81
Riley, D. 293
risk
  consumers, strategy and performance 327-8
  high 22, 184
  low, insurance product development and 151, 153-4
  management and cash reserves 109-10, 111
  minimisation and bank branch managers 263, 266, 267, 268-9
    see also costs
Ritchie, J.R.B. 68
Roberts, M.L. 82, 84, 86, 230, 231, 232

Robertson, D.H. 83
Robinson, C.G. 343
Robinson, P.J. 67, 72, 334
roles 69
  bank manager *see* branch managers *under* bank; changing lending role of managers
Rolls Royce 79
Roman, E. 232
Rose, P.S. 262, 263
Rothman, K. 86
Rothschild, M.L. 218
Rothwell, M. 315
Royal Bank of Scotland 13, 50
  subsidiary *see* Direct Line
Royal Insurance 150
Royal Scottish Assurance 50
ruthlessness of banks 13

safety *see* security
sales promotion *see* promotion
salespersons
  insurance 302-3
  management 30, 33, 39-41, 263, 283
    see also staff
Salomon Bros. 45, 299
satisfaction, customer 22
  small business clients 186-7
  youth market 92, 101-3, 104
    see also loyalty
saturation 19, 346
Saunders, J. 80, 216, 327, 330
savings and deposit accounts 242
  banks as strong places for 12-13
  frequent savers 81
  long-term 66
  youth market 94-5, 97, 109-16
Sawyer, A.G. 81, 82, 213
scale *see* economies of scale
Scandinavia 68, 71, 198, 199, 202
Scanlon, Gerald 10
Scarborough, H. 232
Schelesinger, L.A. 204
Scheuing, E.E. 122
Schiele, G.W. 92, 104
Schneider, B. 65, 73, 344
scope for improvement
  management 35-6, 39-40, 41
  scale 31, 32
Scotland 6-7, 234, 345
  banks 13, 50, 121, 149-50, 215
Scott, J.A. 183
Scottish Equitable 50
Scottish Mutual insurance company 50
Scovotti, R. 288-9

screening and evaluation 156, 157, 225; *see also* monitoring
search qualities, financial services low in 65, 66
security of organization 23
segmentation 8, 329
   bank branch managers 270
   consumers and rhetoric and 'reality' of marketing financial services 18, 19, 22
   direct marketing 237
   as major *IJBM* topic 30
   management of financial services 33, 34, 39-41
   mortgage-pricing 248
   retail financial services 62, **78-90**
      model for firms 84-5
      strategies for future research 78, 85-8
      typology and evaluation of research 79-84, 88
   service quality 184
   success factors for new services 124
   youth market 92
   see also differentiation; mapping segmentation
Selby, E.B. 217, 221
selective perception and buyer choice 67
self-assessment 148, 330-1, 333
self-service bank 137, 144
sensitivity to change 31, 32, 35-6, 40
service quality 14, 165-8, 315
   bank branch managers 265-6, 268-9, 270
   competition between banks and building societies 323-4
   consumers, strategy and performance 337
   as major *IJBM* topic 30-1
   measurement in branch banking 167, **169-82**
      conceptual framework 169-71
      research design 171-3
      results 173-9
   recent developments 168, **198-208**
      concerns in 1990s 203-5
      customer perspective 200-1
      definitions and measurement 199-200
      employee perspective 201
      integrated approach 203-4
      management perspective 201
service quality
   measurement 199-200, 204-5
   monitoring 204-5
   needs and expectations, changing 203
   research 200-2
   retrospect and prospect 343, 346-7
   small business clients 167-8, **183-97**, 201
      banks' view 184-5
      findings 186-93

      list of topics and findings 195-7
      previous research 183-4
      research study 185-6
   'Ten Commandments' of 14
   youth market 101, 102-3
   youth perceptions of 99
   see also staff
services distinct from goods 65, 314; *see also* financial services
SERVQUAL 166, 167, 170-1, 200, 204-5
Shanmugam, B. 341
Shansby, J.G. 87-8
Shelton, D. 341
Sheth, J.N. 67
ShilCo case study 51-2, 301-2, 305
short-term pressure 253
Shostack, G.L. 65
Shulman S. 184
Shultz, D.E. 213
significance, tests of 125
Silvestro, R. 199
Singapore 30
'single-life cycle' 92
site-specific activities 289
size of institution
   consumer buying behaviour 70
Skeel, S. 327
Skipton Building Society 248
Slocum, J.W.Jr. 107
small businesses
   changing lending role of managers 279-82
   consumer buying behaviour 71
   defined 185, 192
   see also under service quality
smart cards 121, 137, 139, 142, 144
smiling and friendly atmosphere stage 149
Smirnov *see* Kilmogorov-Smirnov test
Smith, Anne 201, 204, 206, 343
   service quality to small business clients 167-8, 183-97
Smith, Gareth 18, 106, 107
   customers, strategy and performance 312, 327-39
   segmentation, retail financial services 62, 78-90
Smith, P.G. 155
Snelson, P. 147, 151, 155, 156
'snowball' effect 213
social class 92
socio-economic data 19, 81-2, 237
South Africa 71
Spain 342
spatial arrangement *see* premises
Spearman Rank Correlation Coefficient 178, 234, 333-5
specialization/specialists, marketing 346

consumers/customers perceptions of innovations and new technology 144
direct marketing 237
insurance products 151, 152, 154, 159
service quality small business clients 185, 191
Speed, Richard 18, 106, 107, 249
   customers, strategy and performance 312, 327-39
   segmentation, retail financial services 62, 78-90
speed valued *see under* time
Spencer, A. 68
split banking 95, 104
sponsorship 211
SPSS 174-5, 178, 234
Squarezone 278
Srinivasan, V. 216-17
staff 14
   bank branch managers 263, 265-6, 268-9
   branch distribution channel 288, 293, 295
   changing lending role of managers 275, 280
   competition between banks and building societies 320-1, 323-4
   conduct and service quality 170, 175, 177, 179
   consumers/customers
      buying behaviour 65, 68, 70, 73
      perceptions of innovations and new technology 139, 141
      relationship with *see* model *under* interaction
      strategy and performance 329
   implementation 11
   insurance selling and branch networks 300, 303
   management of financial services 33, 39-41
   morale and service quality 165, 166, 167
   professionalism and consumer buying behaviour 70
   reduced numbers 293, 295
   service quality 183-4, 185, 186, 187, 188, 201, 206
   success factors for new services 132
   targets and remuneration and insurance selling 301
   training 33, 39-41, 265-6, 275, 278, 304
   youth market 99, 104
   see also service quality
Stafford, J.E. 12
Staffordshire Building Society 215
stages
   in adoption of marketing 149-50
   in decision-making 66-7, 72
   in insurance product development 155-8

in quality measurement study
   main 172, 173-7
   pilot 171-2, 173-7
'stand alone' products 144
Standard Life 50, 87
standards *see* Codes of Practice; quality
Stanley, T.J. 81, 337
Stanley, T.O. 107
Stanton, W.W. 83
Steeley, J.E.Jr. 267
Stephenson, B. 47, 74, 299
stepwise discriminant analysis 334-5
Stewart, D.W. 84
Stewart, K. 343
Stockport *see* Manchester and Stockport
Stone, M. 232
Storey, Chris: success factors for new services 122, 124-35
STP (short-term pressure) 253
Strang, R.A. 213, 226
strategies 311-12
   bank branch managers 263
   defined 311
   integrated in bancassurance 46
   management of financial services 33, 39-41
   mortgage-pricing 248-9, 252-3, 254
   segmentation 78, 85-8
   success factors for new services 133-4
   trends in 344-6
   see also between banks and building societies *under* competition; differentiation; positioning; retrospect and prospect; strategy and performance *under* consumers/customers
Straub, D.W. 172
strengths, analysis of 264, 311
Strong, E.K. 67
students 81; *see also* youth market
Sturdy, Andrew: consumer and rhetoric and 'reality' of marketing financial services 16-27
substantiality and segmentation 79, 80, 83, 86
substantive nature of marketing 9-10
substitution 216
success
   factors for new services 122, **124-35**
      communication strategy 126, 129-30, 133, 134
      determinants of 132-3
      differentiated product 127, 131, 132-3, 134
      direct mail targeting 126, 129, 133, 134
      intermediary support 127, 130, 133, 134
      low price 127, 131, 133, 134
      market research 127, 131, 133, 134

methodology 125-8
  overall quality 126, 129, 132-3, 134
  product fit and internal marketing 126-7, 130, 132-3, 134
  strategies 133-4
  technology, use of 127, 130, 132-3, 134
  insurance product development 147-8
Sudman, S. 172
Sullivan, A.C. 81
Summe, G.L. 148
Sun Alliance 150
Sunday Express 13, 14
Sunday Times 13, 14
Superprofiles 237
supply
  -based approach 17, 149
  excess 7
support
  by bank and small business clients 189-90
  services and insurance product development 148, 154
Sweden 68, 71
switching
  competitions 216, 217, 218
    consumers/customers perceptions of innovations and new technology 139, 141
  lack of 23
  youth market 92, 100, 101-3, 104
SWOT analysis (strengths and weaknesses) 264, 311
sympathetic understanding 320

Tabachnick, B.G. 177
'tainted advice' from intermediaries 48-9
takeovers *see* mergers and acquisitions
Takeuchi, H. 155
Talarzyk, W.W. 324
tangibility 14, 199, 215, 314; *see also* intangibility
Tanner, I. 29-31, 44
targeting 7, 16
  advertising 20
  direct marketing 233, 237, 239
  see also direct mail; direct marketing; focus
tax relief cancelled 33
Taylor, R.D. 81
Taylor, T. 83
teamwork and insurance product development 156, 157, 158
Teas, R.K. 70, 71, 72
technical quality 343
technology (mainly new) 3, 4, 258
  bank branch managers 263, 266, 267, 268-9

branch distribution channel 288-9, 293, 294-5
change and changing lending role of managers 278-9, 281-2
changing lending role of managers 284
consumers/customers perceptions of innovations and new technology 139-40, 141, 142
direct marketing 232, 233
insurance product development 147
as major *IJBM* topic 31
management of financial services 29, 33, 34, 39-41
retrospect and prospect 341, 343
service quality 166, 201
success factors for new services 128
use of and success factors for new services 127, 130, 132-3, 134
youth market 91
see also electronic; information technology; perceptions of innovations *under* consumers/customers
telecommunications, international 137; *see also* telephone
telephone
  banking 4-5, 88, 130, 258, 288-9, 315
    see also home banking
  help lines 130, 204
  interviews 150, 152, 169
  marketing (telemarketing) 231, 232, 236-7
Tellis, G.J. 214
'Ten Commandments of Services Marketing' (Barry's) 14
TESSAS 216
Thatcher, Margaret 48
Third World 47
Thomas, D.R.E. 214, 344
Thompson, S. 48, 328
Thwaites, Des 18, 47, 299
  direct marketing 212, 229-41
  mortgage-pricing 252, 253
  retrospect and prospect of strategic financial services marketing 340-9
time
  competitions 225
  planning, horizons shortened 213
  retimed purchasing 216
  speed valued 192, 201
  wasted 188, 189, 191; *see also* queuing
tolerance, zones of 203, 205
Toop, A. 225
Torkzadeh, G. 264, 267, 270
total costs 246
total systems approach 137
Totten, J. 216
Trade and Industry, Department of 13

training, staff 33, 39-41, 265-6, 275, 278, 304
transfer of money delayed 189
transferability of marketing concept 8-10
travel agents 98
travellers' cheques 98
trust, confidentiality and discretion 324, 344
   consumer buying behaviour 66, 74
   service quality 191, 192, 193
TSB
   bancassurance 47, 49
   bank branch managers 263
   charges 13
   competition between banks and building societies 314, 315
   Family Bonus Scheme 343
   network management and branch distribution channel 290
t-tests 81, 320-1, 334
Tuck, M. 67, 70
Tuke, Michael 276
Turnbull, P.W. 198
   consumer buying behaviour 67, 69, 71, 72, 74
Tushman, M.L. 160
two-way information and services 65, 66
Tylecote, A. 253
Tynan, A.C. 93

Ulrich, T.A. 183
U-method 334, 336
Unconditional Service Guarantees 203
underwriters 157, 159
unemployed 91, 93
Unilever 87
unique delivery system *see* First Direct
unique product 248
unique service 124
United Kingdom
   bank branch managers 263
   competitions 214, 215-16, 219, 222
   consumers/customers
      buying behaviour 68, 71
      perceptions of innovations and new technology 137
   IJBM articles from 198
   retrospect and prospect in financial services marketing 341, 342, 346
   segmentation 79, 80, 81, 83
   service quality, recent developments in 199, 200, 201, 203-4
   see also preliminary note (2) to index; Scotland
United States
   banks 314, 315
      branch managers 263, 270
      performance 14
      slow learning of marketing 149
   competitions 215, 221, 223
   consumers
      buying behaviour 68, 69, 71, 72
      and rhetoric and 'reality' 24
   direct marketing 230
   foreign banks in 30
   IJBM articles from 198-9
   price wars 214
   retrospect and prospect in f[m[341
   segmentation 79, 80, 81-2, 83
   service quality 199, 201
United States Trust Co. 215
unprofitable products 32-3
up-selling 232, 237, 238, 239; *see also* cross-selling
usage data in segmentation analysis 80, 81-2

validation of segmentation 84-5
value
   -adding 214-16, 218, 343consumers/customers perceptions of innovations and new technology 141, 142
   perceptions and mortgage-pricing 245, 247
   of prizes *see under* prizes
   see also costs
Varadarajan, P. 328, 330
variable costs 246
Varimax 128n, 174-7, 267
VDTs (visual display terminals) 281, 282
Veblen, T. 67
Vector (Midland Bank) 87, 121, 130
Venkatraman N. 334
Verbraucherbank 137
versatility of competitions 216
videotex 137
View Data/Viewdata 136, 278, 279
Vilcassim, N.J. 216
visual display terminals 281, 282
Vollering, J.B. 143
volume of business and changing lending role of managers 274, 284
Volvo 79

Wagner, J. 108
Wall, T.D. 170
Wallis *see* Kruskal-Wallis test
Walters, C.G. 81
Walters, R.G. 216
Ward's method clustering 83, 133-4
warm leads, selling to 86
Wason, P.C. 170

Waterman R.H. 328
Waters, D. 82
Watkins, T. 23, 133, 143, 315, 340, 341
Watson, I. 73
Watt, A.W. 143
weaknesses, analysis of 264, 311
wealth 84, 337
Webster, F.E.Jr. 67, 72
Weinberg, M. 315, 316
Wells, W.D. 113-14, 270
Wells, W.P. 81
Wells Fargo 314
West, A. 83
Whitmore, J. 342, 346
Whitney *see* Mann-Whitney
Whittle, J.W. 243
width of product line and management of financial services 35-8, 42, 43
Wilcoxon test 173, 178
Wilkes, R.E. 81, 84
Wilkinson, A. 343
Wills, G. 80, 108
Wind, Y. 107
  consumer buying behaviour 67, 72
  segmentation 79-80, 84, 85
Winer, R.S. 84
Wishart, D. 85
women and segmentation 80, 81
Woodcock, N. 230, 232
Woods, Rodney 214, 215, 223
Woolwich Building Society 49, 215, 276, 344
wordprocessors 278, 281
Wrigglesworth, J. 345

Wright, Mike: retrospect and prospect of strategic financial services marketing 315, 340-9
WWP group 213

Yavas, U. 341
Yee-Kwong, R.C. 341
Yorke, D.A. 71, 72, 80, 84
Yorkshire Bank 290
Yorkshire Building Society 49, 344
youth market for financial services 8, 62-3, 68, **91-105**
  environment 92
  image, perception of 92, 100-1
  opening account 95-7
  present account ownership 94-5
  research methods and sample 93-4
  satisfaction and dissatisfaction 92, 101-3, 104
  segmentation 92
  staff and service, perceptions of 99, 104
YTS (Youth Training Scheme) 93, 94, 96, 97
Yucelt, U. 69

Zeithaml, V.A. 28, 215, 343
  service quality, recent developments in 199, 200, 202, 206
  youth market 65, 66, 70
Zemke, R. 199
Ziff, R. 199
Zikmund, W.G. 170
zones of tolerance 203, 205